DELIVERING SOCI
Governance and ser
in the U

Derek Birrell and Ann Marie Gray

First published in Great Britain in 2017 by

Policy Press
University of Bristol
1-9 Old Park Hill
Bristol BS2 8BB
UK
t: +44 (0)117 954 5940
e: pp-info@bristol.ac.uk
www.policypress.co.uk

North American office:
Policy Press
c/o The University of Chicago Press
1427 East 60th Street
Chicago, IL 60637, USA
t: +1 773 702 7700
f: +1 773-702-9756
e:sales@press.uchicago.edu
www.press.uchicago.edu

British Library Cataloguing in Publication Data
A catalogue record for this book is available from the British Library.

Library of Congress Cataloging-in-Publication Data
A catalog record for this book has been requested.

ISBN 978-1-4473-1917-7 hardcover
ISBN 978-1-4473-1918-4 paperback
ISBN 978-1-4473-1919-1 ePub
ISBN 978-1-4473-1920-7 Mobi
ISBN 978-1-4473-1921-4 ePdf

Cover design by Lyn Davies
Front cover: image kindly supplied by Getty
Printed and bound in Great Britain by CMP, Poole
Policy Press uses environmentally responsible print partners

Woodland
CARBON
www.woodlandcarbon.co.uk
CMP (UK) LTD
Printed on Carbon Captured paper

Derek Birrell:
To my granddaughter Keeley

Ann Marie Gray:
To David

Contents

List of tables and boxes

List of tables and boxes

List of abbreviations

ADASS	Association of Directors of Adult Social Services
ALB	arm's length body
ALMO	arm's-length management organisation
BIC	British Irish Council
BMA	British Medical Association
CAF	Common Assessment Framework
CCG	Clinical Commissioning Group
CHP	Community Health Partnerships
CQC	Care Quality Commission
CRCs	Community Rehabilitation Companies
DBIS	Department for Business, Innovation and Skills
DCLG	Department for Communities and Local Government
DETR	Department for Environment, Transport and the Regions
DHSSPS	Department of Health, Social Services and Public Safety (NI)
DoE	Department for Education
DoH	Department of Health
DSD	Department for Social Development
DUP	Democratic Unionist Party
DWP	Department for Work and Pensions
EFA	Education Funding Agency
ETI	Education and Training Inspectorate
HEFC	Higher Education Funding Council
HMRC	Her Majesty's Revenue and Customs
HRA	Housing Revenue Account
ICPs	Integrated Care Partnerships
LGA	Local Government Association
LGO	Local Government Ombudsman
LHBs	Local Health Boards
LSP	local strategic partnership
NAO	National Audit Office
NDPB	non-departmental public body
NHE	National Health Executive
NHS	National Health Service
NICE	National Institute for Health and Clinical Excellence
NIE	Northern Ireland Executive
NIHCE	National Institute for Health and Clinical Excellence
NIHE	Northern Ireland Housing Executive
NIAO	Northern Ireland Audit Office
NOMS	National Offender Management Service
OECD	Organisation for Economic Co-operation and Development

OFCOM	Office of Communications
Ofqual	Office of Qualifications and Examination Regulations
Ofsted	Office for Standards in Education, Children's Services and Skills
PAC	Public Accounts Committee
PCT	Primary Care Trust
PESA	Public expenditure statistical analysis
PFI	Private Finance Initiative
PHSO	Parliamentary and Health Services Ombudsman
PPP	public/private partnership
PSA	public service agreement
quango	Quasi-autonomous non-governmental organisation
RSG	Revenue Support Grant
SCF	Scottish Funding Council
SCIE	Social Care Institute for Excellence
SDLP	Social Democratic and Labour Party
SEN	special educational needs
SNP	Scottish National Party
SSAC	Social Security Advisory Committee
TMOs	Tenant Management Organisations
TUC	Trades Union Congress

Acknowledgements

We would like to thank a number of people for their encouragement and support in the successful completion of this book. We have received enormous help from Liz McNeill and Amanda Higgins in producing the text. Our colleagues, especially Cathy Gormley Heenan, Goretti Horgan and Ruth Fee have provided support and encouragement. Thanks to Michael Hill for his advice and constructive comments. A huge thanks to the team at Policy Press for their excellent support and helpful comments, especially Laura Vickers, Emily Watt and Jo Morton.

ONE

Introduction: the changing landscape of welfare governance and delivery

Social policy and governance

There have been significant changes in the nature of social policy and governance in the UK since the 1990s. Major developments in social policy have applied both to overall principles and the details of delivery and provision, with a shift from universalism to welfare pluralism, neo-liberalism, selectivity and residualisation, and with an emphasis on markets, privatisation, less statutory provision, consumerism, participation, personalisation, the use of performance indicators and the pursuit of efficiency (Bochel et al, 2009; Hill and Irving, 2009; Taylor Gooby, 2013). The exact balance and mix of change has varied under the direction of successive UK governments, from the Conservatives (Thatcher and Major) 1979–97, to Labour (Blair and Brown) 1997–2010, the Conservative–Liberal Democrat Coalition 2010–15 (Cameron and Clegg), the Conservatives (Cameron), and since 2015 (May). The same period has also seen significant developments in the overall system of governance. This could be seen conceptually as a shift from public administration, new public management and network governance to new public governance and in developments such as outsourcing, internal markets, partnership working, arm's length delegation, devolution, localism, decentralisation, performance management, regulation and participation (Osborne, 2010; Pollitt and Bouckaert, 2011; Flynn, 2012; Burnham and Horton, 2013). There is a close relationship between the changes in social policy and the changes in governance arrangements, and both categories of change have implications for the format in which welfare services are delivered to users. Newman (2006) notes that the social policy accounts of the modernisation or transformation of welfare states intersect with the narratives of change in governance as both are seen as deriving from new realities. The view can be expressed that many of the changes in governance impacted upon social policy (Bochel, 2011), that governance is highly salient for social policy implementation and inevitably consideration must be given to the means of implementation before establishing policies and services (Bochel and Bochel, 2004). The nature of the relationship can be seen as highly interdependent. Thus, Jessop (1999) suggested that there are three interrelated issues: the changing definitions of welfare; the changing institutions responsible for its delivery; and the practices in and through which welfare is delivered. Daly (2003) described the importance of the close relationship between policymaking and implementation and the identity of the actors and institutional setting for the delivery of services. Hill (2013) argues that in the UK, there has been a strong tendency to see organisational reform as the key to securing more efficient policy delivery. The role of the state and the relationship between the different levels and form of governance are therefore important across a range of activities – commissioning, planning, funding, purchasing, designing, regulating and evaluation – in determining the nature of the welfare services delivered.

The scope of social welfare services

The scope and definition of social welfare services has been somewhat contested. The traditional understanding has been to refer to the five services that historically dominated with the establishment of the welfare state and that can still be identified as making up the core of service provision: health; social care (formerly referred to as personal social services); housing; education; and social security or welfare benefits. Historically, the definition of welfare services in the UK has been closely linked with state provision and also the area of the academic study of social policy (Alcock, 2003, p 2). The administration and delivery of welfare was to readily extend to informal provision, third sector provision and increasingly private sector provision (Hill and Irving, 2009, p 4). The boundaries and nature of welfare services was to expand into other areas, some closely related, such as aspects of employment services, youth services, addictions, community development, urban and rural regeneration, and equality and social inclusion. Other services embraced had less connection with traditional core areas of social policy and included aspects of criminal justice and probation, services for immigrants and asylum seekers, and support related to fuel poverty. While the concept of social policy is quite strongly rooted and widely acknowledged and used, some issues have emerged over the usage of the term 'welfare' and what aspects of service delivery fall within it. This has arisen more as a contemporary issue through the practice of using the term 'welfare' in a restricted sense to refer to social security or benefits. This has happened largely because of ideological or political influences on the debate but may cause confusion as, for example, much of the legislation still refers to 'social security'. As the term 'social services' has no agreed meaning, the term 'welfare services' is used in this book in its broadest sense to cover what are now considered to be the main core services.

Trends in delivery and governance

The traditional model that underpinned the delivery of welfare services has been described as the public administration model of welfare delivery (Butcher, 1995, p 2). The public administration model referred largely to a near-monopoly of state provision of welfare or where the central focus of welfare delivery was on the role of the state and statutory provision at every level of delivery (Daly, 2003, p 123). The core features of the system were therefore: public organisations; government departments; quasi-autonomous non-governmental organisations (quangos); and public bodies, National Health Service (NHS) bodies and local government. These bodies are staffed by civil servants, public officials and professionals, operating through hierarchical decision-making structures and accountable to elected representatives. This model, with a dominant role for state bureaucracies, was under challenge and did not align with developments in welfare pluralism even before Mrs Thatcher's government came to office. The Conservative government's social policies meant greater use of contracting out and markets and consequently a shift from the public sector to private, voluntary and informal providers of welfare. This period was also marked by the replacement of the established public administration model by the new public management model. The latter set of concepts or doctrines emphasised the use of markets, internal competition in the public sector, the adoption of private sector practices and performance management and cost-cutting. New public management resulted in a rethinking of the relationship between welfare delivery and the state, leading to distinctions between 'enabling not providing', 'commissioning not providing' and 'steering not rowing' (Burnham and Horton, 2013, p 29) and advocating a managerialist concept of government to achieve welfarist goals (Minogue et al, 1998). Interpretations of new public management were to influence new thinking on the disaggregation and greater flexibilities within the public sector, demonstrated in structural changes affecting service delivery through executive agencies, quangos, e-government and regulatory and improvement bodies (Bochel, 2011, p 252). The Conservatives' ideological position on change in welfare policies and public management was replaced by the 'third way' position of the Labour government first elected in 1997.

Labour's 'third way' applied to both social policy and governance. The social policies adopted moved further down the direction of a pluralist rather than a statist or enabling welfare state (Powell and Hewitt, 2002). This saw a rejection of a residual welfare state and a move towards a model of welfare based on the promotion of equality of opportunity and social inclusion rather than dependence on the welfare state (Newman, 2001). An increasing feature towards the end of Labour's second term in office was a move to a model of competition between public and private suppliers (Lund, 2008). Developing a 'third way' to governance and delivery was to have a particularly strong influence on the nature of welfare policies. This led to adaptations of the new public management model but also some radical new approaches. A degree of privatisation, internal markets and the purchaser–provider split, especially in health care, were accepted and provider diversity, competition and choice continued (Powell, 2012). At the same time, Labour evolved a set of propositions that could be seen as amounting to a new governance style. This promoted partnership working rather than competition, the involvement of stakeholders, emphasising the value of social inclusion, the use of evidence, attention to what works and more evaluation and decentralisation. A key contemporary tenet has been expressed as 'it is the delivery that matters, not the means, state, market or civil society' (Newman, 2006, p 13). These modernisation agendas were to be applied with varying degrees of success to areas of welfare, for example, mental health services (Perri 6 and Peck, 2004). One of the most significant changes in UK public governance and welfare delivery in recent times was to be completed successfully by Mr Blair as part of this modernisation process – the establishment of devolution for Scotland, Wales and Northern Ireland.

The Conservative–Liberal Democratic Coalition government had to contend with the obstacle of achieving two-party agreement. An operating consensus was heavily focused on the fiscal deficit by reducing expenditure on social policies and also on reforming welfare with the aim of reforming welfare benefits to reduce both expenditure and welfare dependency. A major idea produced by the Coalition was the Big Society (Bochel, 2011). Underpinning this was the thinking that welfare and other services should be delivered at the most local level possible, where feasible, by private and community organisations and by unpaid individuals through informal welfare. This commitment was, in part, interpreted as meaning an enhanced role for the voluntary sector but such a development never really prospered in the face of public expenditure cuts and the domination of public sector-outsourced contracts by a small number of large national private companies. The general idea was to have some influence on changes in the delivery of aspects of education and health and social care. Examples included giving more governance powers direct to schools, the creation of GP commissioning groups, the development of the personalisation agenda primarily in adult social care and local government referenda. The Big Society agenda had close linkages to a new localism agenda so that decentralisation and democratic engagement were related to giving not just powers to communities, neighbourhoods and individuals, but also some new powers to local councils (such as public health), even if this appeared contradictory (Smith and Wistrich, 2014, p 81). The ideas reflected in the Big Society concept can be related to changing ideas about the role of the state and, as Bochel and Powell (2016, p 14) point out, the direction implied by the massive cuts in Big Society narratives was 'clearly towards a much smaller state, with no real clarity over what, if anything, would replace it'. The continuing changes in the central UK state as a direct provider of services, particularly welfare services, and the introduction of market mechanisms at various stages led to a more fragmented and dispersed pattern of service delivery and regulation (Newman, 2001, p 13). This has been termed a 'differentiated polity' by Rhodes (1997), with different forms of public, private and independent bodies all involved in relationships and networks and under new forms of funding regulation and control. These new forms of governance could be seen as 'government plus', through an extension of government powers, and 'network governance', with complex interactions and interdependencies. Network governance was defined by Rhodes (2007) as having two faces: first, public sector change, fragmentation and joined-up governance; and, second, a shift from strong executive governance to networks, representing a hollowing out of the state. This has been seen as arising from diverse actions and practices rather than by an identifiable structural process determining the form of network governance (Bevir and Rhodes, 2013).

The Conservative government elected in 2015 with a small majority was able to pursue goals that had an impact upon welfare policies and delivery systems. Planned reductions in public expenditure and the implementation of radical welfare reform had major consequences on aspects of social security, health and social care, education, and housing, and involved changes in delivery processes. This was to become particularly salient through decisions on the role and functions of local government. The increasingly complex, plural and fragmented nature of policy implementation and service delivery continued and this resulted in the identification of an alternative model to new public management, called 'new public governance'. This has been seen as different from traditional public administration and has been described as a conceptual tool to respond to the challenges of service delivery in the 21st century (Osborne, 2010). The new public governance thesis drew heavily upon network governance and organisational partnerships but included contract governance with strong statutory regulation and oversight. The perspective does have a strong emphasis on service delivery and on questions concerning the most effective organisational architecture and appropriate values underpinning delivery (Osborne, 2010, p 11). This makes it of particular interest to principles and processes underlying the delivery of welfare services and welfare pluralism. The more radical approaches and interventions of recent governments have led to new considerations of a process of rolling back the state and removing government functions. Newman (2013) suggested that austerity government in the UK was characterised by the 'divestment' of services and governance functions away from the state and the proliferation of new hybrid organisations. The term 'governance' has come to mean a move away from traditional forms of government and state activity but it is important to note that despite these developments, government remains as one of the important and necessary constituent elements of governance (Pollitt and Bouckaert, 2011). These changes have had major implications for social policy, including the rolling back of the welfare state and the impact of austerity on the scale and nature of service delivery (Taylor Gooby, 2013).

Focus of the book

The focus of the study is on the delivery of welfare services, relating governance to social policies. The analysis is based on the major providers of welfare services in the UK, identified as: government departments and executive agencies; non-departmental public bodies and other quangos; local government; the devolved institutions; private and third sector bodies; and inter-organisational partnerships. It is necessary in the analysis to identify and assess changes and the current role of these institutions in delivering services compared to a role in commissioning services or the regulation of services. Such developments have prompted attention being paid to bodies with a regulatory role over delivery. The analysis then considers the delivery configuration for each of the major areas of welfare services; health, social care, education, housing, welfare benefits, and other related services.

Contemporary principles and agendas influencing delivery

A number of principles and agendas have come to dominate narratives by government and other bodies, and to influence policies that have determined the delivery of welfare services. These can be listed as: devolution; contracting out; the austerity agenda and responses to austerity; rolling back the state; partnership working; localism; participation; regulation and inspection; and e-government. It is now possible to argue that changes to welfare governance and delivery have fundamentally altered the nature of the welfare state. The configuration of welfare pluralism has seen a reducing role for statutory services, with much greater responsibility passed to the private and voluntary sectors. However, strong central policy direction and government control via regulation, guidance, performance targets and inspection have seen central government retain considerable power over welfare services.

Devolution

Since 1999, the establishment of devolved institutions of government has had a major impact on the delivery of welfare services. The majority of welfare services fall into the category of devolved matters, and legislative and administrative responsibility rests with the devolved administrations in Scotland, Wales and Northern Ireland. Devolution adds an additional layer to the configuration of public governance, creating four-country governance. Almost all of the major areas of social policy are devolved and this has led to assessments that devolution in Scotland was largely concerned with social policy (Mooney et al, 2006), that the National Assembly for Wales was a social policy assembly (Chaney and Drakeford, 2004) and that Northern Ireland also has major social policy responsibilities (Birrell, 2009). As devolution has developed, questions have arisen as to whether there are now four systems of welfare provision in the UK. Comparison of the devolved institutions does indicate some differences in powers. In health, social care, housing and education, the devolved powers were the same. Social security was devolved to Northern Ireland but not to Scotland and Wales, though, in practice, a policy of parity with the rest of the UK was pursued. Employment policy and the civil service were also devolved to Northern Ireland. The Scotland and Northern Ireland administrations have responsibility for policing and justice, whereas Wales does not. In terms of the focus of devolved social policies, the Scottish and Welsh governments have pursued strong value commitments to principles of social justice and reducing inequalities. This has produced a policy context different from Northern Ireland and England. The delivery of devolved services has operated through the main statutory administrative structures, devolved government departments, quangos and local government, and attention has been paid to more connected and joined-up governance. Parry (2012) has written of the development of a devolved model of public governance that is more joined-up, more participative and more localist. Devolution has continued to evolve, with an enhancement of devolved powers in all three countries and, in particular, a discussion of greater fiscal devolution. Following the Scottish referendum, the UK government has acted to introduce more fiscal devolution for Scotland in addition to the devolution of more welfare powers (Smith Commission, 2014), and new enabling legislation will pave the way for more powers to be devolved to the Welsh government.

Contracting out

Contracting out of public sector services has been increasing since the 1990s. This has normally meant contracting out of provision to private sector organisations, although contracting out to the third sector also falls within the concept. This development is not restricted to the UK, but has been widespread, and the trend is seen as likely to continue for the foreseeable future as an important part of governance processes (Cohen and Eimicke, 2003). Contracting out, or outsourcing, of public services is a form of procurement or commissioning. However, some government–business financial arrangements do involve collaborative interactions, such as the public–private partnerships in the UK used to build schools and hospitals (Hodge and Greve, 2010). Contracting out can also be seen as distinctive from privatisation, where the state ceases to have any involvement, including funding, despite some overlap in the popular usage of the terms. Contracting out brings a series of governance issues, including the degree of specialisation of the public agencies necessary for carrying out procurement or commissioning, as with the development of clinical commissioning groups in England. The availability of private providers has raised issues concerning the domination of the market by a few very large providers and has caused difficulty for participation by smaller voluntary groups. The adding of public value to procurement has also been the subject of legislative action by the UK government and issues also remain concerning processes and levels of monitoring and inspection of the delivery of services by the private sector carried out by government bodies. In most areas, contracting out is highly regulated but further complications can arise, for example, through subcontracting arrangements Contracting out is of particular importance in social care, aspects of health provision, public health, housing support services, youth services, the treatment of offenders and early years and childcare. The complexity of the process has been increased by some notable failures in contracting out related to welfare reform, social care and prisons. It is also the case that the devolved administrations have not been so committed to contracting out.

Austerity impact

Austerity policies since 2010 have focused on reducing and eliminating the budget deficit through cuts in public expenditure. This has led to changes in welfare service provision and the restructuring of delivery. There has been a government emphasis on savings through efficiencies in delivery. Restructuring has included the removal of services or the transfer in whole or in part from the public sector, the expansion of the contracting out of services, the sale of public assets, and reductions in the numbers of civil servants. The impact of austerity has been different between services. Social security benefits have been subject to the most radical changes and expenditure cuts, with changes leading to a growth in the contracting out of assessments of entitlement to benefits and the return to work programmes. Expenditure on education and health has been given some protection, but by 2016, there were real-terms cuts in school budgets. The NHS was required to make £22 billion savings by 2016 and the Department for Education plans £215 million savings by 2020. Local councils are to be given more fundraising powers but the delivery of adult social care still faces major challenges, and planned cuts to the education services grant will see the role of local authorities further diminished.

Public sector bodies have responded to the UK government's austerity measures either directly or indirectly. A major objective has been for local councils, quangos and the devolved administrations to achieve mitigation of the impact on services for local populations or more vulnerable groups. Thus, adjustments have been made to delivery modes, through contracting out, partnerships or sharing services with neighbouring bodies. Such decisions may be taken outside UK departments by quangos or local government, or organised by the devolved administrations. Many public bodies have discretion as to how they produce efficiencies in methods of delivery, through new ways of working, sharing backroom services, the use of e-government or restructuring the organisation and costs of contracted-out services. Other responses have been more innovative, including investment to promote prevention measures that will reduce costs in the long term, for example, to tackle homelessness or entry into residential care. The devolved administrations' budgets have increased in cash terms but fallen in real terms, and the Scottish and Welsh governments in particular have been committed to using their devolved powers to protect their populations from the UK government's austerity measures, with largely similar party positions in Northern Ireland. In Scotland, this has meant using devolved powers, for example, over social care to compensate for cuts in social security benefits.

Rolling back the state

Changes in the format of the central UK government have resulted in much consideration of the role of the state and this has implications for the delivery of welfare services. Three aspects contribute to the changing framework of analysis as it impacts upon service delivery in the main areas of social policy. First, the perspective of 'rolling back the state' has been translated as one of the main objectives of recent UK governments. Assessing the evidence for such a process or its scale requires a consideration of: a reduction in the functions of state bodies, including quangos and local government, plus the impact of devolution;

the decrease in civil servants and other public sector employees; levels of public sector expenditure; and the growth of private provision and providers. The second perspective is that of replacing government by governance or networks and partnerships. These changes have been called profound but it has been argued that government still plays a role in governance (Peters and Pierre, 2006). Issues arising have included: the private–public boundary and partnerships; the operation of organisations outside core ministerial departments; and the scale of delegated governance to quangos and single commissioner bodies (Flinders, 2006). The shift from direct provision still leaves the state with considerable power, including through commissioning and regulation. The third perspective is that of multi-level governance. This approach moves from the traditional central and local government tiers in the British system to including the devolved or regional dimension, as well as the European Union (EU) dimension (Bache and Flinders, 2004). European agencies are involved in funding and regulating rather than direct provision. This perspective also draws attention to elements of global or international governance. With the bedding in and future enhancement of devolution in the UK, the multi-level governance perspective has more salience, and a consideration of Northern Ireland points to a further level of cross-border governance in Ireland (Birrell and Gormley-Heenan, 2015).

Partnerships

The development of welfare pluralism has been marked by a growth in partnership working between the different components of the public sector and the private and voluntary sectors. The burgeoning of partnerships has also been promoted by specific party policies, such as the Labour governments' policies on stakeholder involvement and the 'third way' between state and market (Clarke and Glendinning, 2002), Liberal Democrat views on public participation and Conservative Party adoption of the Big Society policy, and devolved administrations' support for partnership approaches. Another influence has come from EU programmes as many required local and regional partnership arrangements based on the involvement of civil society and decentralised delivery mechanisms. The focus on partnerships has been seen as a new interplay between the state, business and civil society (Schuppert, 2013). The growth of partnership working can also be seen as covering more joined-up working within the component parts of the public sector, for example, between quangos and local government. Partnerships have developed in almost all areas of social welfare provision. Health, social care, public health, early years and education all display examples of partnership working, mainly with the voluntary sector, but the most important development relates to the integrated agenda bringing together NHS bodies and local council social care services through the joint commissioning of services and, in some cases, structural integration. Housing and social support, urban regeneration, youth services, addiction services, the treatment of offenders, and early years provision all demonstrate partnership working. Partnership working may be directed at the coordination of a range of services either because of their connection in pursuing integrated approaches or on a locality or area basis, for example, area partnerships or community planning led by local government. In recent years, area-based partnerships have been developed along thematic lines to address issues seen as particularly complex, such as the Total Place initiative piloted by the Labour government or the Whole Place Community Budgets introduced by the Coalition government. The scale of partnership development has led to different organisational forms and modes of delivery and to much evaluation of what makes successful partnerships and the significance of equity in partnerships, the nature of relationships and the sharing of resources.

Localism

For a considerable period of time, localism has been an idea regularly endorsed by the major political parties, being referred to in, for example, a government White Paper, *Open Public Services* (HM Government, 2011), as including the principle that public services should be decentralised to the lowest appropriate level. While localism might suggest a strategy of increasing the functions of local government, with implications for welfare service delivery, in practice, strategies related to localism have been rather more restricted. Thus, the Localism Act introduced in 2011 was concerned mainly with empowering local communities to do things and dispersing power more widely, increasing local community control of finance, strengthening accountability, and diversifying the supply of public services. New strategies have seen what is called devolution to local government, with proposals to give large cities in England, as combinations of local authorities, powers over economic development, transport and also health and social care (Sandford, 2015a). More generally, local authorities in England have seen a reduction in delivery powers, with the exception of the acquisition of public health. Commitments to localism also differ in the devolved administrations, with strong support in Scotland, fairly strong support in Wales but a history of little support for localism in Northern Ireland. Localism can also be interpreted as the advocacy of localist approaches to service delivery in terms of assessing need, accessibility, boundaries, localised decision-making and responsiveness. Localism and decentralisation remains an issue for all public bodies involved in service delivery, including departments, executive agencies and non-departmental public bodies (quangos) but has become more contested in the context of austerity and greater central direction.

Participation, personalisation and co-production

Principles of public and service user participation have attracted lip service and support from most bodies involved in delivering welfare services. The Labour governments in particular had driven an agenda to use participation to improve standards rather than depend on managers (Lund, 2008). Other parties have been largely supportive, although sometimes more focused on consumerist approaches. User participation can be aimed at various aspects of service delivery, from needs assessment to the formulation of policy, to participation in the actual delivery of services, and to involvement in research and the evaluation of outcomes. A traditional and common form of participation has been consultation involving users, organisations of users, lobbyists or the public but more recent expressions of participation have embraced the idea of co-production, which focuses on the service user as an active and resourceful participant, and no longer a passive recipient of services (Bochel et al, 2008).

Personalisation refers to an approach to service delivery based on the understanding that the individual is best placed to understand their needs and how services should be tailored to best to meet those needs. The idea that services delivered should be person-centred is not so radical, but this was further developed with the policies of successive governments proposing that citizens should take greater responsibility for their own lives. Person-centred support has been seen as representing a shift from service users adapting to the services they use to services adapting to the needs of their service users (Beresford et al, 2011). Personalisation shares values with co-production in relation to valuing the expertise of the service user. The personalisation agenda has become closely associated with a move to direct payments in social care and individual budgets in health care. A personal budget means that an individual can decide how council or statutory funding is spent to meet their needs, as well as control the purchase of services or employment of provider (Carr, 2010), thereby giving more choice, control and independence. The practicalities of implementing personal budgets in social care can present challenges for local councils (Baxter et al, 2013). While individual budgets in health have been judged successful in meeting needs, there are doubts as to whether it can be rolled out successfully to all (Slasberg et al, 2014). Other initiatives have also been subsumed under the personalisation heading, for example, self-directed social care, and also in other services, including personalised learning for school children, personalised support in housing and personalised conditionality for moving people into work, raising the possibility of personalising the welfare state (Needham, 2010). Personalisation has been criticised as promoting a form of outsourcing to independent providers (Ferguson, 2007), but the personalisation agenda has created the possibility of new front-line relationships in public services (Needham, 2010).

Co-production has been identified as a transformative way of thinking and is being increasingly applied to new types of public service delivery (Needham, 2012). The idea can be broken down into co-design, co-decision-making, co-delivery and co-evaluation (SCIE, 2013) and implies an equity in relationships different from traditional participation. Co-production has made the most impact on the delivery of adult social care and has been facilitated by the development of user organisations. The idea has been applied to health, particularly by the Scottish government (2009b), and has led to discussion on its applicability to other services.

Performance and scrutiny

Assessing performance has emerged as a dominant theme across public services. Underpinning this has been a concern to increase efficiency in public service funding and delivery, to address concerns about the quality and transparency of services, and to facilitate greater accountability to central government and to users. A number of methods have been adopted in the pursuit of performance management, including: targets, for example, waiting lists; public service agreements; performance indicators; league tables; the 'traffic light' system; and, more recently, outcome-focused indicators whether user based or desired outcomes. Generally, performance management has been about establishing formal, regular and rigorous data collection to indicate trends.

This has been complemented by the development of inspection regimes, especially in education and health and social care, systems of audit with a focus on value for money, and forms of parliamentary scrutiny. While these may have direct consequences for policy, they are often highly relevant to service delivery and pressures to change delivery patterns. Increasingly, inspection has been accompanied by sanctions and penalties for underperformance, such as the introduction of 'special measures' for schools judged to be 'failing' and the removal of services, such as children's services, from underperforming local authorities. Concerns about quality and risk have on occasion led to high-profile public inquiries, such as the Francis Inquiry (The Stationery Office, 2013) and the Jay Inquiry (Jay, 2014), which have attracted considerable media and public attention.

E-government

An emerging theme has been the use of e-government, with accompanying debate about the impact, advantages and disadvantages. Benchmarks tend to be set concerning: accessibility to intended users; affordability to users; awareness of intended users of the service or of innovations; and appropriateness, particularly for older people. The management of e-services and assistance to users are largely practical issues and e-government has developed in other ways to provide information and advice to the public. Some areas of controversy remain relating to total dependence by government on e-services, for example, for the new universal credit benefit. Government actions in other areas may present obstacles to promoting the use of e-government in delivering services, for example, library closures.

Key sources for the book

As a major focus of the book is on contemporary changes in the governance and delivery of welfare services, a major source of material has been papers, reports and publications of statutory bodies. These are sourced from government bodies, the UK government (with largely England-only documentation) and the governments of Scotland, Wales and Northern Ireland. The range includes departments, executive agencies, non-departmental public bodies, other quangos and single commissioner bodies, and also local government bodies. Particular attention was paid to reports and papers reviewing the operation of aspects of governance and delivery that had produced assessments leading to changes and restructuring recommendations for change. Significant reviews of devolution and local government in particular have been under way, and reviews of quangos have recently been completed. Representative bodies were also a valuable source of reports, particularly in the local government area, through the Local Government Association covering England and its counterparts in Scotland, Wales and Northern Ireland, as well as local government bodies representing staff, such as the Association of Directors of Adult Social Care (ADASS) and the British Medical Association (BMA). A significant number of specialist think-tanks and research institutes produce relevant work, including the Institute for Governance, the New Local Government Network, the Local Government Information Unit and the Public Policy and Management Association, and there is also work carried out on governance and delivery by the larger national institutes, for example, The King's Fund, The Nuffield Trust and The Joseph Rowntree Foundation, and contributions from voluntary organisations, such as Shelter. The work of parliamentary committees in the House of Commons is useful for contemporary analysis arising from inquiries and scrutiny, particularly the findings of the Public Accounts Committee. These relate closely to comprehensive reports from the National Audit Office. The briefing reports and research reports of the House of Commons Library have become a major and thorough source of the analysis of contemporary developments. Parliamentary sources are replicated within the Scottish Parliament and the Assemblies in Wales and Northern Ireland, through committees, audit offices and research information offices. Books and academic journal articles are extensively used and quoted, covering particularly the theoretical, political, evaluative and comparative dimensions.

The structure of the book

The majority of chapters and the core of the book are organised around the main forms of delivery and the main methods used to deliver welfare services. After an introduction, the next chapter looks at devolution in the UK and governance and the delivery of welfare in the devolved administrations. Three chapters are devoted to the main forms of government that exist in the UK, government departments, local government and delegated governance. The chapters focus on the main role of each sector, recent changes and their functions in delivering the main welfare services. Two further chapters are devoted to other major mechanisms for service delivery: the independent sector, comprising the private and voluntary sectors; and the role of partnerships. Two themes that have become particularly salient in the delivery of welfare services are examined in two of the remaining chapters – user and public participation, and regulation and performance – again describing general developments before dealing with each service separately. Governance and delivery in the UK now very much involve distinct systems for each of the four countries, and as well as treatment in a separate chapter, some aspects, such as the role of local government, are analysed in the chapter dealing with that mode of delivery. This facilitates coherence and also comparisons. Some categories of bodies that have a more limited role in delivery, particularly EU institutions and activity and global influences, are dealt with as appropriate throughout the chapters.

The introductory chapter sets out the focus of the book on governance and delivery and sets out the parameters of social welfare services used in the book. The main trends in government and governance in relation to the delivery of welfare services are explained as they have developed within recent UK government administrations, including the emergence of some relevant policy themes. Chapter Two relates to the role of the devolved administrations, continuing with government departments but in the setting of devolution. The focus of devolution on the major areas of social policy is explained and the degree of convergence and divergence within the UK is discussed. A comparison is made between the origins, structure and functions of the devolved systems of central administration and their access to resources. Their effectiveness is discussed in the context of reforms and evaluations of the operation of devolved governance. Responsibilities for the delivery of the major welfare services, including health, social care, education and housing, are mapped against the organisation of central administration. Attention is drawn to any significant divergence from each other and from England and also the increasingly complex arrangement for delivering welfare benefits within the UK.

Chapter Three considers the structure and working of UK government departments, including Whitehall ministerial departments, executive agencies and non-ministerial departments. The general dimensions of the separation of policy and delivery functions, territorial coverage, and the configuration of services into departments are identified. An account is given of major policy and public sector reforms that have shaped the central administrative structure and the current functions of the system are explained. The major welfare services are mapped against departments and executive agencies and a comparison is made between the services in relation to responsibilities for the delivery of welfare services and related functions.

Chapters Four and Five turn to local government throughout the UK, traditionally the major delivery mechanism for the majority of welfare services. A short account is given of the development of the structure, functions and funding of local government in the more recent period and variations within the UK noted, as well as the degree of diversity in the structures in England. The main focus of the chapters is on the major changes in the responsibilities of local government for delivering welfare services. This includes the loss of responsibilities for direct provision in housing, education and social care, the change to a commissioning role, and the growth of partnership working. An area of new responsibilities, including public health, is also noted. Local–central relations remain an important dimension and contemporary trends in localism and centralism are explained. Attention is also paid to the impact of austerity on local government services, changes in the financing of local government and the response of local councils. Current proposals and actions related to local government reforms, including the city devolution agenda for England, are analysed in terms of their impact on welfare services.

Chapter Six deals with the large area of delegated governance and the operation of all quangos and arm's length bodies, and includes quangos in the devolved administrations. The chapter identifies the different types of quangos, explains the reasons for the expansion of this sector of governance and also analyses recent attempts throughout to reduce the number of quangos and introduce reforms related to their composition and accountability. Quangos now play a major role in the delivery and also the regulation of major areas of social welfare services. The chapter has a focus on identifying the key quangos in each area of social welfare provision, and their particular importance within the NHS. Consideration is also given to their complex relationship at times with government departments, as well as making an assessment of their effectiveness as a key provider of social welfare services.

Chapter Seven explores the role of partnerships in the delivery and governance of welfare. It identifies the terminology used to describe partnerships and the different types of partnerships. There is discussion of the factors accounting for the proliferation of partnerships in the governance and delivery of welfare. The chapter examines the factors identified to be important to the successful working of partnerships and the evidence about the outcomes of partnership working for users, particularly with regard to health and social care and to the area-based partnerships set up at local authority level. Some attention is also given to the governance of partnerships and to their cost-effectiveness.

The following chapter continues the theme of the provision of welfare by agencies other than the state by looking at the outsourcing and privatisation of welfare services. The meaning of privatisation and quasi-markets and the use of outsourcing, contracting out, commissioning and procurement are explained. The nature of the independent sector and the range of providers in the private and voluntary sectors are considered and there is discussion of the background of the government promotion of private sector provision. A focus of the chapter is to review recent developments, to examine the extent of outsourcing and the scope and degree of privatisation in the areas of employment services, social care, health, children and youth services, education, and housing, and to assess the issues arising from this. Attention is also given to the growth of the personalisation agenda and the use of individual budgets and direct payments in health and social care.

As a concept, public and user participation is now firmly embedded in welfare policy and legislation across the UK. Chapter Nine examines key developments with regard to user and public participation. The terms and definitions are outlined and there is discussion of the rationale for user and public participation from the perspective of government, users and the public. There is consideration of policy and legislative developments and the structures and initiatives put in place to encourage participation. Much of the debate has focused on the degree and extent of involvement and on the effectiveness of the models of engagement being used. Questions have been raised about whether these are sufficient to enable user and public participation to be transformative and these issues are discussed in regard to user and public involvement across a range of welfare areas.

Chapter Ten covers what has become an increasingly important and dominant theme in welfare delivery and governance – the regulation, scrutiny and inspection of services. The chapter looks at the influences underpinning this focus, including concerns about cost-efficiency and cost-effectiveness, value for money, and demand for greater transparency. Consideration is also given to the increasing emphasis on measuring and monitoring quality and the complexity of doing so. The chapter includes an assessment of the methods adopted in the pursuit of performance management and in order to regulate services.

The final chapter provides an assessment of the principles underpinning changes in the delivery and governance of welfare. It looks at the modernisation agenda and examines trends and changes in the governance and delivery of welfare under a number of headings, including: the reformulation and restructuring of welfare services as a result of neo-liberal influences; the impact of devolution on changes in governance and delivery; and reformulation and restructuring in response to modernisation influences, such as privatisation before partnerships, personalisation, user participation and co-production.

Terminology

Throughout the book, 'the UK' refers to England, Scotland, Wales and Northern Ireland and 'Great Britain' refers to England, Scotland and Wales. The term 'UK government' is used to refer only to government in London. England, Scotland, Wales and Northern Ireland are referred to as 'countries' rather than other possible terms such as 'territory', 'region', 'nation', 'jurisdiction', 'sub-state' or 'sub-national unit'. The term 'social welfare services' is used to refer to all the main services related to social policies and is not used to mean only welfare benefits or social security. The term 'devolution' refers to the system of government set up for Scotland, Wales and Northern Ireland but, unless specified, not to what is sometimes called city devolution in England.

TWO

The devolved administrations and welfare delivery

The establishment of devolution in Scotland, Wales and Northern Ireland in 1999 brought a largely but not entirely new dimension to the delivery of social services in the UK and also to descriptions and accounts of the system. This chapter considers how a significant feature of devolution was that the majority of social welfare services were devolved for each country by the 1998 legislation and in subsequent additional legislation. It looks at the context of and nature of devolved powers across the UK, the resourcing of devolved services, and the structures for service delivery within each jurisdiction with regard to the main areas of welfare provision. Consideration is also given to changes to devolved powers, particularly in the wake of the referendum on Scottish independence.

The devolution of social welfare services

From 1999, Scotland has had full legislative, executive and administrative powers over devolved matters, which included the core areas of health, social care, children's services, education, housing, planning and justice and policing. The main social service exclusions were social security and employment matters. Northern Ireland had a similar core set of devolved subjects, which covered health, social care, children's services, education, housing and planning, but also included social security, employment and equality matters. Policing and justice were originally not devolved but became devolved matters following political agreement in 2007. The method used to devolve powers to Scotland and Northern Ireland means that the UK law lists non-devolved matters and everything else is a devolved matter. The original scope of devolved matters was greater for Northern Ireland than for Scotland and also included the controversial subjects of homosexuality and abortion. Initially, control over abortion was reserved to Westminster but responsibility was transferred to the Northern Ireland Assembly with the devolution of policing and justice in 2008. The allocation of devolved powers to Wales in the 1998 legislation was different and more limited than in Scotland and Northern Ireland. A list of devolved competences was contained in the Government of Wales Act 1998 under what is known as a conferral system and all other matters were not devolved, although, in practice, the 18 subjects identified as matters of competence were not dissimilar to devolved matters in Scotland and Northern Ireland, including core social service areas, health, social care, children's services, education, housing and planning. However, the most significant difference with the Welsh form of devolution was that the Welsh Assembly Government (WAG) could take executive action but did not have primary legislative powers, only subordinate legislative powers. This more limited form of devolution was later amended to enhance Welsh legislative powers. The Government of Wales Act 2006 ensured that the Assembly had the powers to make laws known as measures, but with the involvement of the Westminster Parliament in an unwieldy process. The 2006 Act did make provision for a referendum in Wales and the ensuing passage of a commencement order to give the Welsh Assembly primary legislative powers over 20 areas of competence. The Welsh Assembly Government took on their new powers on 11 May 2011, largely bringing Wales into line with Scotland and Northern Ireland, with similar devolved systems (Birrell, 2012). Table 2.1 sets out the social welfare functions that have been devolved in each country and clearly shows that the majority of social welfare services fall into the devolved category. This is reflected in the description of the Scottish Parliament as largely concerned with social policy (Mooney et al, 2006), while Chaney and Drakeford (2004) called the Welsh Assembly a social policy assembly.

The introduction of the administrative system for devolution in 1999 did not in practice mean a radical upheaval for the new devolved levels of government. Prior to political devolution, all three countries had a form of administrative devolution and, significantly, this had related to most areas of social policy. A Scottish Office in Edinburgh developed with responsibilities for delivering education, health services, planning and housing functions, even though political control rested in London. The scope of service delivery increased with the growth of the welfare state, and before devolution, St Andrews House was in charge of most social services administration, with the exception of social security and taxation (Keating, 2005). Wales developed a similar structure, although established much later, in 1964. The Welsh Office had responsibility for education, health, housing and local government, and continued to acquire functions as a multifunctional

Table 2.1: Devolved social services

Scotland	Northern Ireland	Wales
Health	Health	Health
Social Care	Social Care	Social Care
Education	Education	Education
Higher Education	Higher Education	Higher Education
Housing	Housing	Housing
Children and Young People	Children and Young People	Children and Young People
Planning and Regeneration	Planning and Regeneration	Planning and Regeneration
Justice and Policing	Justice and Policing	Local Government
Local Government	Local Government	Welsh Language
	Social Security	
	Employment	
	Equal Opportunities	

Source: Adapted from Birrell (2012).

office with planning and local development functions, thus covering most areas of social policy (Mitchell, 2009). Historically, Northern Ireland had the most developed system of administrative devolution, originally under the old Stormont system of political devolution from 1922 to 1972. In practice, during the period of Direct Rule by Westminster from 1972 until 1999, the old Stormont structure of government departments continued, as did the separate Northern Ireland Civil Service. They operated under the control of the Northern Ireland Office, created in 1972. This meant that almost all areas of social policy were administered through the Northern Ireland departments, including social security (Birrell, 2009).

The development of devolved services

Devolved responsibilities developed after 1999 in a flexible and low-key manner introduced by order-in-council and with cross-party agreement, for example, to promote energy efficiency and to give the Scottish government new powers to recoup charges for National Health Service (NHS) treatment. The St. Andrews Act 2006 imposed new duties on the Northern Ireland Executive in relation to poverty and social inclusion and permitted financial assistance to energy projects. Major extensions to devolved powers have been limited but became the subject of much discussion, inquiries and reports in Scotland both before and after the referendum on independence. A more limited process of investigation and debate took place in Wales but relatively little debate occurred in Northern Ireland. Decisions on the actual devolution of new powers have been few or are still pending. Following recommendations by the Scottish National Party (SNP) (Scottish Executive, 2007) and by other parties (Commission on Scottish Devolution, 2009), the reaction of the UK government was to suggest a modest package of changes that was picked up by the incoming new Coalition government (Scotland Office, 2010). The Scotland Act 2011 focused on new powers to devolve setting tax rates (see later) but other powers devolved were limited to covering air weapons, speed limits and drink–drive limits. Following the SNP electoral victory in 2011, the Scotland Bill was amended to devolve further powers in relation to the misuse of drugs, the administration of elections, BBC appointments and the role of the Lord Advocate (Seely, 2014). This legislation had not been fully implemented when the result in the Scottish referendum on independence on 18 September 2014 opened up the whole question of a greater devolution of powers to Scotland. A commitment to take action was made by the UK prime minister, supported by all three main UK parties. Lord Smith was appointed to lead a commission working with the five parties in the Scottish Parliament to agree on further powers to strengthen the devolution settlement and enable the delivery of better outcomes for Scotland (Smith Commission, 2014). There were three pillars to the proposals: one covering constitutional and intergovernmental matters, transport, and broadcasting; a pillar strengthening financial responsibility; and a third pillar related almost exclusively to social policy that, most significantly, proposed a division of welfare benefits between reserved and devolved responsibilities. Some major benefits, pensions and universal credit, and child benefit remained reserved to the Department for Work and Pensions but the Scottish Parliament would be able to make administrative adjustments to the frequency and aspects of payments. Powers over other benefits would be devolved, including: benefits for disabled people, carers and those who are ill; discretionary housing payments and the Social Fund; and powers to top up reserved benefits and create new benefits. Also proposed for devolution were core employment support services for unemployed people, consumer advocacy and advice, and aspects of energy efficiency and fuel poverty.

The response of the Coalition government in a command paper, *Scotland in the United Kingdom: An Enduring Settlement,* had the intent to implement the Smith Commission Agreement into law at the beginning of the new Parliament and transfer powers to Scotland (HM Government, 2015b). The most significant proposals for the delivery of social policy were the social security proposals, which provide powers to create new benefits or payments in devolved areas of welfare responsibility, to make discretionary payments and also to give the Scottish Parliament control over employment programmes that support those at risk of long-term unemployment. The benefits to be devolved fell into three categories: disability and carers benefits; benefits comprising the regulated Social Fund; and discretionary housing payments. In all, these benefits accounted for only 14.7% of all identifiable welfare spend in Scotland (Kennedy, 2015), although the Scottish Parliament would have powers to make additional discretionary payments at its expense in any area of welfare.

In addition, the Scottish Parliament will have legislative competence to pass laws to help disabled people into work (HM Government, 2015b, para 4.1.5). This gives the Scottish government the flexibility to structure part of the welfare system to suit Scottish circumstances. In relation to civil protections, the Scottish Parliament will be able to legislate on equalities in respect of public bodies in Scotland, legislate on socio-economic rights in devolved areas and has the power to operate certain tribunals and consumer advocacy and advice services (HM Government, 2015b, para 6.1.3). Following the Smith recommendations, a number of issues were recommended for further consideration around health, immigration, student visas, asylum, human trafficking, food and health and safety. The draft clauses received general support from the Scottish Affairs Committee, which regarded the proposals as faithfully fulfilling the vow of the three main Westminster parties to devolve further substantial powers, in particular, the powers to shape the welfare system in Scotland (Scottish Affairs Committee, 2015). The views of the House of Commons Political and Constitutional Reform Committee were less supportive, in not wishing such a major transfer of powers (Political and Constitutional Reform Committee, 2015). The attitude of the SNP to the draft bill proposals was very critical, with the Smith Commission's recommendations described as underwhelming and then watered down further by the UK government's paper (Scottish National Party, 2015).

In Wales, there was also discussion and official reports on increasing powers, again mostly dominated by the subject of greater fiscal devolution. A new commission on devolution in Wales (The Silk Commission) was set up to look at the case for devolved fiscal powers and also review the powers of the National Assembly for Wales in general. The Silk Commission reported in two parts: Part 1 on fiscal duties; and Part 2 on the devolution of other powers (Commission on Devolution in Wales, 2014). The implementation of Silk was to be pursued through the Wales Act 2015, but the Silk 2 recommendations were not progressed so rapidly. These recommendations for the devolution of greater powers covered: the devolution of policing (but not criminal justice), community safety and crime prevention; planning powers related to aspects of energy, water and sewerage; further powers relating to the rail franchise, bus and taxi regulation; and drink driving and speeding. On wider aspects of devolution, there were recommendations on a change from the conferred model to the reserved model of the allocation of powers. The reception of the Silk proposals was low-key, with limited enthusiasm for the recommended powers and the focus on constitutional change. The UK Coalition government was more positive but the implementation of Silk 2 became a matter for the new UK Conservative government and Parliament, and would not be attached to an existing Wales Bill going through with the Silk 1 recommendations. Discussions between the Secretary of State and the four main parties in Wales led to an area of agreement on powers and a move to a reserved powers model but there was no agreement on the devolution of policing and criminal justice. A command paper, *Powers for a Purpose: Towards a Lasting Devolution Settlement for Wales* (Wales Office, 2015), was published. Known as the St David's Day Agreement, this introduced the reserved powers model to Wales; similar to Scotland and Northern Ireland, everything not reserved is devolved, with a funding floor of protection for Wales to assist with devolving tax powers. The proposed list of powers are somewhat marginal to social policy, covering aspects of energy, port development, air passenger tax, Office of Communications (OFCOM) appointments, voting age and elections.

Since the major devolution of policing and justice powers to Northern Ireland in 2008, there has been little demand or debate on the further devolution of powers to a system that already has more devolved powers than Scotland or Wales. There has been no general demand for more fiscal powers, with one major exception: the devolution of the setting of corporation tax. This has been pursued not as a revenue–raising measure, but as a mechanism to boost the weak private sector by attracting inward investment and by competing with the lower rate of corporation tax in the Republic of Ireland. The Treasury and Secretary of State have been involved in discussions and consultations (HM Treasury, 2011) and agreed in 2015 to the conditional passage of legislation devolving corporation tax as part of the Stormont House Agreement (Northern Ireland Office, 2014). The introduction of this measure would have consequences in leading to a reduction in the Northern Ireland block grant of around £250 million per year, which, in turn, may put further pressure on expenditure on social services. The Stormont

House Agreement was necessitated by a number of political impasses in the Assembly and Executive, with a major difficulty concerning welfare reform. The anomaly of the largely devolved status of social security but with total specific funding by the Treasury led to conflict over the passage of a Northern Ireland Welfare Reform Act. Sinn Fein and the Social Democratic and Labour Party (SDLP) acted to block the legislation and the Treasury began to 'fine' Northern Ireland with reductions in its block grant for the extra costs incurred. In the Stormont House Agreement, the UK government agreed to a package of financial flexibilities, borrowing and asset sales to help fund the costs of a different welfare regime. Continuing disagreements over the interpretation of the scope of this arrangement delayed implementation. A compromise agreement was reached in November 2015 (Northern Ireland Executive, 2015), with the UK government providing further financial support and the Executive being able to top up the UK welfare reform arrangements that would be introduced in Northern Ireland. The 'bedroom tax' would not apply. Overall, there was no change in devolved delivery responsibilities in this 'Fresh Start' agreement. Other, more radical, alternatives, such as making benefits a reserved matter, were not much debated. A number of changes in the status of powers took place in 2014, in that the Northern Ireland Act 2014 prepared the way for the devolution of the Human Rights Commission, the Civil Service Commissioners and the Parades Commission by changing their status from excepted to reserved matters. This means that only an order in council is needed at Westminster to implement the devolution of these matters.

Resources for devolved government

From 1999 until 2016, the devolved administrations largely relied on funding from the UK Treasury, determined by the application of the Barnett Formula. This had been introduced in Scotland and Wales in 1978 and in Northern Ireland from 1980 and continued after devolution on a non–statutory basis. The core of the formula is a baseline plus increments, and is set out in Box 2.1.

Box 2.1: Barnett Formula

Baseline of previous year's allocation × Population proportion
× Comparability devolved percentage × Changes to UK departments

Source: HM Treasury (2010)

Essentially, it provides a rough equitable distribution not based on a calculation of need or a negotiation, and it has been seen as a robust mechanism. The use of this mechanism meant that, originally, very limited revenue-raising powers were devolved, mainly local government taxation. Scotland was given the power to vary the basic rate of income tax by three pence in the pound, but this option was never used and was allowed to lapse in 2007. The total costs of reserved services, such as social security, in Scotland and Wales were met by the Treasury, as they were in Northern Ireland under special agreements. The control of revenue flows by the Treasury contrasted with the control of the allocation of this revenue as expenditure, which was wholly at the discretion of the devolved administrations. The actual outcome of the Barnett Formula and other revenue created a difference in identifiable expenditure per head between England, Scotland, Wales and Northern Ireland.

Such figures have given rise to claims of unfair treatment, in particular, that Wales does not receive an allocation that reflects its level of need (House of Lords, 2009). The Treasury has been a strong advocate for maintaining the Barnett Formula (Bell and Christie, 2007) for reasons of simplicity, stability, robustness and equity, underpinned by the sharing of risks across the UK.

As devolution developed, there was growing pressure on the need not to amend the Barnett Formula, but to reform the devolved financial arrangements through creating greater fiscal devolution. In Scotland, the debate was framed by the Calman Commission in 2009 and its key consideration of how to improve the financial accountability of the Scottish Parliament (Commission on Scottish Devolution, 2009). The UK income tax rate could be reduced by 10 pence in the pound, with a reduction in the block grant, and the Scottish government could choose to harmonise the rate or set a different rate, which Scotland would fund from its block grant. Also proposed was the devolution of other minor taxes: landfill tax, air passenger duty, stamp duty, land tax and aggregates tax. At the time, the Scottish government did not support Calman's recommendations and did not see them as offering real and effective fiscal and economic levers. Both the then UK government and the incoming Coalition government endorsed the Calman recommendations despite the criticism that they would impact on only 20% of Scottish government income. The Scotland Act 2012 was passed, reducing the rate of income tax by 10% in each tax band along with a reduction in the block grant.

The Scotland Act 2012 had devolved three powers: setting its own rates of income tax from 2016; introducing taxes on land transactions and waste disposal from landfill; and introducing other potential new taxes in Scotland (Seely and Keep, 2015). The Smith Commission set up after the referendum had as one of its

Table 2.2: Identifiable expenditure by country (£ per head)

	2010–11	2011–12	2012–13	2013–14	2014–15
Scotland	10,212	9,965	10,275	10,275	10,374
Wales	9,829	9,720	9,671	9,924	9,904
Northern Ireland	10,706	10,673	10,859	10,961	11,106
England	8,588	8,376	8,468	8,678	8,638

Source: HM Treasury PESA (2016).

three objectives the strengthening of the financial responsibilities of the Scottish Parliament. The report largely confirmed the legislative proposals and Scotland's powers to set income tax rates and thresholds of income tax on non-savings and non-dividend income. It was proposed that the Barnett Formula would continue and the principle was adopted of no detriment to either government as the result of the decisions to devolve further powers. Also suggested was that Scotland's fiscal framework should provide sufficient additional borrowing powers to ensure budget stability and smooth Scottish public spending.

The UK government published a command paper setting out new powers to build on the income tax and borrowing powers already devolved through the Scotland Act 2012. A new Scottish Bill implementing the Smith recommendations would ensure that over 50% of the money spent by the Scottish Parliament would be funded by revenues raised in Scotland. The main UK political parties were committed to taking forward the new Scottish Bill after the election of May 2015. So, in terms of revenue and spending powers, this was interpreted by the Scottish Affairs Committee as representing a significant transfer of power (Scottish Affairs Committee, 2015). Agreement was reached between the Scottish and UK governments in February 2016 on the block grant adjustments for taxation and welfare, with full devolution of income tax rates in 2017 (Scottish Government, 2016).

Following the 2007 election, the Welsh government set up an independent commission to review the existing Barnett Formula and possible alternative funding mechanisms. Apart from suggesting a needs-based system to replace Barnett, the Holtham Commission endorsed the Calman Proposal that devolved administrations should have some responsibilities for raising their own revenue (Holtham, 2010). These proposals were received in Wales with caution and the UK government suggested a further inquiry in the changed context of full legislative devolution for Wales. Part 1 of the Silk Commission reported on the further devolution of fiscal powers to improve financial accountability. A major principle was the recommendation that responsibility for income tax should be shared between Cardiff Bay and Westminster, with the Welsh government being able to vary income tax rates within the UK income tax structure. Alongside the legislative arrangements, it was agreed to implement the full devolution of business rates from April 2015. This legislation will mean that the Assembly will be responsible for 10% of all taxes collected in Wales (HM Government, 2015a).

Northern Ireland demonstrated different perspectives on increasing devolved revenue-raising powers. There was little support for a review of the Barnett Formula or increasing devolved fiscal powers over income tax. Specific action was taken to devolve long-haul air passenger tax. The issue of further devolved financial powers was dominated by a campaign for the devolution of corporation tax. This would not contribute directly to Northern Ireland revenues, but was seen as promoting inward investment through the setting of a low level of corporation tax. As part of the Stormont House Agreement, the UK government would introduce legislation to enable the devolution of corporation tax, pending agreement, and this was achieved for 2018 at a rate of 12.5%. Over the time of devolution, ad hoc measures of funding had also been delivered by the UK government, for example, for reform and investment or special loans, while the European Union (EU) and international funds had been available to boost expenditure on peace and reconciliation projects, usually delivered on a partnership basis.

The role of devolved government departments

The organisation of devolved government was based on the previous territorial office structure. There was no move to create a separate civil service in Scotland or Wales and a single Permanent Secretary from the Home Civil Service headed up each administration. The structure of departments was largely based on existing territorial structures but with a corporate unit for the devolved core executive and other units for support functions. In Scotland, the Scottish Executive operated with seven departments, including departments responsible for health, education, development and justice, and enterprise and lifelong learning (Lynch, 2001, p 43). The functions of the Welsh Assembly Government were essentially originally those of the Welsh Office and were readily adopted with the transfers of further powers from Whitehall (Shortridge, 2010). Thus, a devolved central administration was established without the need for major restructuring (Prosser et al, 2006). Wales has now moved to six ministerial portfolios, five of which relate mainly to Social Policy: Finance and Local Government; Health, Well-being and Sport; Communities and Children; Economy and Infrastructure; and Education. The civil service is now organized in four groups: the office of the First Minister and Cabinet Office; the Health and Social Services Group; the Economy, Skills and Natural Resources Group and the Education and Public Services Group. More substantial change was needed in Northern Ireland, but mainly to meet the political demands of the power-sharing arrangements of the Executive. The six Northern Ireland departments that had retained their separate statutory identity during Direct Rule became 11 devolved separate departments. These covered the main social policy areas of health and social care, education, social security, employment and learning, housing development and planning, and departments including higher education and rural development. While Northern Ireland departments were based on the Whitehall model of the ministerial department, Scotland and Wales moved away from this model to avoid the alignment of ministerial responsibilities with departmental functions (Cole et al, 2003), with Welsh ministers expected to work across structures and avoid compartmentalism (Rawlings, 2005).

Scotland moved from the model of distinct departments as a basis for effective government to a system of Scottish government directorates (Elvidge, 2011). These were organised under five core strategic objectives: wealthier and fairer; healthier; safer and stronger; smarter; and greener. The actual number of directorates, around 36, is subject to change and a key advantage is the flexibility that using directorates as building blocks can provide. This structure does encourage cross–cutting approaches. Health and Social Care is the largest grouping of directorates and three groupings are responsible for most of social services, as indicated in Box 2.2.

Box 2.2: Scottish directorates dealing with social welfare services

Health and Social Care
- Finance and Information
- Finance, eHealth and Analytics
- Performance and Delivery
- Population Health Improvement
- Healthcare Quality and Strategy
- Health and Social Care Integration
- Children and Families

Learning and Justice
- Learning
- Employability, Skills and Lifelong Learning
- Education, Analytical Services
- Safer Communities
- Justice

Communities
- Local Government and Communities
- Housing, Regeneration and Welfare
- Digital

The Welsh government has retained a structure of seven formal departments but they operate in a strongly cooperative and integrated way. The configuration of departments is described in Box 2.3. Four departments have major social service responsibilities, with the others having some role.

Box 2.3: Government structures for social welfare in Wales

- Health, Social Services and Children
- Education and Skills
- Local Communities and Local Government
- People, Places and Corporate Services
- Sustainable Futures
- Strategic Planning, Finance and Performance
- Business, Enterprise, Technology and Science

The configuration of departments in Northern Ireland remained similar between 1999 and 2015, with the addition of the new Department of Justice as the only alteration. Each department has a separate statutory status. The extensive configuration of 12 departments has a strong representation of social services. In 2015, agreement was reached on reducing the number of departments to nine, as indicated in Box 2.4, but the basis of departments remained the Whitehall model.

Box 2.4: Government departmental structures for social welfare in Northern Ireland

Structures 1999	Structures from 2016
• Health	• Health
• Education	• Education
• Employment and Learning	• Economics
• Social Development	• Communities
• Office of the First and Deputy First Minister	• The Executive Office
• Justice	• Infrastructure
• Regional Development	• Justice
• Agriculture and Rural Development	• Agriculture, Environment and Rural Affairs
• Finance	• Finance

Delivering devolved services

The mechanisms for the delivery of social services under devolution were originally similar to those used by the UK government and this raised the question of whether changes would result as devolution became embedded. The traditional role of national government departments had its major focus on policymaking, financial allocations and scrutiny of the effectiveness of provision by other bodies. Devolution raised the possibility of the more direct involvement of devolved central government in the actual delivery of services. It also raised the general question of a continuing reliance on quasi-autonomous non-governmental organisations (quangos) in delivering services, with political narratives emerging of the culling of quangos and of bonfires of quangos. Particularly in Scotland and Wales, local government had had a major role in the delivery of social services, but with local government as a whole a devolved matter, it was possible that local government's role in social services could alter. There were the further questions of whether the devolved administrations would follow a path to greater partnership and joined-up working, whether they would encourage more participative approaches, and the whether the trend in England towards reduced state involvement and more use of the private sector would be copied. The pattern of the trends that did develop is examined for each of the major areas of social services.

Delivering the NHS in Scotland

Following devolution, the Scottish government moved to abolish the purchase–provider split and quasi-market that had been introduced in the 1990s in Great Britain. The primary and secondary sectors were unified in a single system under area health boards, which meant the abolition of the existing NHS trusts that had functioned as commissioning bodies. By 2004, the establishment of 15, later 14, territorial NHS boards had been completed. They have significant powers for local provision and the delivery of acute, primary and community health care, with powers of strategic development, resource allocation, the implementation of local health and delivery plans, and performance management (Robson, 2011). The area NHS boards were appointed quangos, with a membership of up to 23. In 2010, a pilot study was held into the direct election of board members but this innovation was not pursued. Significant powers were delegated to the area health boards to empower them to determine the pattern of local care provision, set local priorities and manage the health service at the local level. The devolved department remained responsible for the 14 area health boards and for monitoring health delivery, and the area health boards were directly accountable to the cabinet secretary. The Scottish government continued to base the structure on the principles of unified and integrated health services and public and patient participation. After 2007, the SNP reaffirmed this approach, as well as ideas of mutuality, cooperation and public ownership. An essential feature of the system for delivering health is the use of quangos, as set out in Box 2.5.

Box 2.5: Structure of the health system in Scotland

Delivery bodies	Bodies with Scotland-wide responsibilities
• 14 regional NHS Boards	• NHS Health Scotland
• Integration Authorities	• Health Care Improvement Scotland
	• National Health Scotland
	• Scottish Ambulance Service
	• NHS Education for Scotland
	• NHS 24
	• The State Hospitals Board for Scotland

NHS National Services Scotland provides advice and support to the rest of NHS Scotland and works closely with the health boards. It employs some 3,600 staff spread over six locations and is a non-departmental public body. This body does directly provide some services, including the Blood Transfusion Service, but it mainly offers business services, health information and statistics, supplies, and support. The Special Health Boards are responsible for a range of services thought best provided on an all-Scotland basis. NHS Scotland covers public health and each area has a public health department and a director. NHS Healthcare

Improvement Scotland gives guidance on clinical practice and the quality of care, and sets standards, although it cannot enforce its advice. It has contributed to improving delivery through assessing quality, spreading best practice and empowering people. It also regulates the independent health sector. A number of other advisory quangos exist, including the Scottish Medicines Consortium, akin to the National Institute for Clinical Excellence (NICE), which advises boards on the effectiveness of new licensed medicines. The Scottish Intercollegiate Guidelines Network produces guidelines on clinical practice.

As well as a commitment to health integration, there is a strong commitment to performance management and public participation underlying the delivery system (Steel and Cylus, 2012). Local delivery plans are a contract between the Scottish government and NHS boards. The details of the delivery plan include the calculation of demand, the model of care, the location of care, workforce requirements, costs and funding (Audit Scotland, 2014a, p 137). Measures have also been taken to improve public accountability and the health boards are regularly reviewed by ministers, with the public given an opportunity to put questions, and with stakeholders also involved. The private health sector in Scotland is small, involving mainly 900 beds in seven hospitals, and the NHS in Scotland only contracts out services to a very limited extent. Private involvement in the NHS is officially discouraged (Smith and Hellowell, 2012). NHS boards are required to meet a number of performance targets that cover: health improvement; efficiency; and access and treatment, including waiting times (Scottish Government, 2011). Most NHS boards met their targets in 2013/14 but four required additional funding to fill gaps (Audit Scotland, 2011, p 10). Significant demand and financial pressures have delayed progress in changing the balance of care and home- and community-based settings (Audit Scotland, 2015a).

Delivering the NHS in Wales

Originally, NHS Wales made less radical changes but was to follow Scotland in eliminating the market based on GP fund-holding. However, the new system of 22 local health boards commissioning from NHS trusts did not operate effectively, proving inefficient and expensive. In 2009, the system was simplified with an end to the separation into health service providers and commissioners. The model of a single specialist national health authority was rejected as undesirable as it would create an arm's-length relationship between the minister and the NHS. At the centre of the new system were seven local health boards responsible for the planning and delivery of all health services within their geographical boundaries, including primary, secondary, tertiary and community services. There was a continuing commitment to a model of health delivery in Wales based on a localised and holistic approach. The local health boards were responsible for local planning based on a full assessment of local needs, covering services, financing, infrastructure and workforce (Longley et al, 2012). There were also three special delivery boards with all-Wales functions, a single ambulance board, a public health body and a special Cancer Services Trust, the Velindre Trust. The redesign of the delivery of the NHS in Wales was seen as providing a seamless unified health system comprising local health boards, Public Health Wales and partnerships with local authorities, based on cooperation, collaboration and partnership working (Hart, 2009). The Welsh devolved department relates closely to the local health boards, particularly in discussing how resources are to be used. The government, the department and the main boards can also take advice from a number of bodies: the National Advisory Board on developing and delivering policy; and the Bevan Commission, which also provides advice but is not part of the NHS. In addition, guidance is accepted from NICE and advice can be taken from the All Wales Medicines Strategy Group. Box 2.6 includes the quangos that provide the NHS with advice or perform special tasks.

Box 2.6: Structure of the health system in Wales

Delivery bodies	Bodies with Wales-wide responsibilities
• 7 Local health boards	• NHS Wales Shared Services Partnership
• 3 NHS Trusts	• All Wales Medicines Strategy Group
• Wales Ambulance Service	• NHS Wales Informatics Centre
• Velindre (Cancer) Trust Hospitals	• NHS Centre for Equality and Human Rights
• 22 local authorities	• Healthcare Inspectorate Wales
	• National Advisory Board

The Welsh government has been committed to delivering high-quality services (Welsh Government, 2012a) and to key objectives, including reducing inequalities and ensuring services are safe, effective, accessible, affordable and sustainable. In practice, the delivery of health care in Wales has been subject to some difficulties. The management of the operation of ambulance services in Wales has attracted criticism. There have also been difficulties with waiting lists for hospitals. The Williams Commission (Williams, 2014) reported views that the health boards were too remote, difficult to engage and difficult to hold to account, and that appointments to boards did not reflect the need for local accountability and understanding. Funding for the Welsh NHS has fallen and there have been attempts to increase cost-efficiency across acute hospitals (Roberts and Charlesworth, 2014). As in the rest of the UK, a major priority has been to move services out of the acute sector into primary and community sectors. A new initiative, *Delivering Local Health Care*, was launched with a focus on strengthening locally led service planning and delivery, rapid intervention, integrated care, and support for people with long-term conditions (Welsh Government, 2013a). Public participation is another value and is reflected mainly in Wales through a localised structure of seven community health councils also operating with area associations.

Delivering health in Northern Ireland

The devolved configuration of health services in Northern Ireland has an overall significant difference from Scotland, Wales and England in that, since the 1970s, there has been an integrated structure of health and personal services. The health component operates within the principles of the NHS and with a similar range of health provision. As in Scotland and Wales, there is a very small private health sector. Health services had developed in a decentralised management and delivery structure, and at the reintroduction of devolution, there was four health and social service planning boards and 11 health and social service delivery trusts, seven hospital trusts, and one ambulance trust. The overall structure of 37 public bodies, all operating under the quango model, came under scrutiny and pressure in the Review of Public Administration. The structure was also under pressure from a review of the effectiveness of the system, which proposed a clear commissioner–provider split in order to incentivise improvements in performance (Appleby, 2005). The outcome was the creation of a pan-Northern Ireland commissioning body, the Health and Social Care Board, and five delivery health and social care trusts, plus the one ambulance service. A restructuring in 2007 meant that primary and secondary health care were fully integrated alongside social care (Gray and Birrell, 2012). This created very large bodies in terms of population size and range of functions. The devolved department is responsible for policy development and legislation and holding the other bodies to account, although the Health and Social Care Board, as well as commissioning, was responsible for performance management, service improvement and resource management. As in the other devolved administrations, there are a number of other centralised quangos with key roles. These are: the Public Health Agency, responsible for health promotion and contributing to commissioning; the Business Services Organisation, providing a range of support and specialist services; and the Regulation and Quality Improvement Authority, with duties relating to the regulation and inspection of health and social care bodies, including hospitals, and the carrying out of themed inquiries. A single quango for the whole of Northern Ireland, the Patient and Client Council, is responsible for representing the views of the public. Some other functions are carried out by other specialist quangos, including the Northern Ireland Blood Transfusion Service, the Northern Ireland Medical and Dental Training Agency, and the Northern Ireland Practice and Education Council for Nursing and Midwifery. The overall direction of the delivery of health services has largely copied Great Britain in promoting a shift in focus from acute care to community-based care (DHSSPS, 2011). The structures, set out in Box 2.7, have been criticised for over-centralisation, and O'Neill et al (2012, p 16) describe the model as provided and administered under a centralised command-and-control system. Significant criticism was also made in a commissioned review of the failures of the commissioner–provider structure (DHSSPS, 2015). It is now planned to abolish the Health and Social Care Board, with functions transferred to the department and trusts.

Box 2.7: Structure of the health system in Northern Ireland

Delivery bodies	Bodies with Northern Ireland-wide responsibilities
• 5 Health and Social Care Trusts • Northern Ireland Ambulance Service	• Health and Social Care Board (until 2016) • Public Health Agency • Regulation and Quality Improvement Authority • Patient and Client Council • Blood Transfusion Service

Social care

In the delivery of social care and social work services, there are significant differences between Scotland, Wales, Northern Ireland and England. A major similarity in Great Britain is the role of local government in that, since 1968, local authorities have been responsible for comprehensive social services. This has covered domiciliary, residential and day care for elderly people, services for people with mental illness, services for people with physical and learning disability, rehabilitation and respite care, child protection and services for children and families, adoption, fostering, residential care and newer service developments in reablement, and direct payments. In the Northern Ireland delivery system, there is no local government involvement and delivery responsibilities are allocated to bodies structurally integrated with health.

Developments in England following the Laming report on child abuse had originally led to a division within local authority social service departments between adult social care and children's services, with child protection aligned with education. This was a widely imposed trend (Birrell, 2006) that, as time went on, began to be reversed. Such a division was not repeated in Scotland or Wales or within the Northern Ireland structures. Social work departments in Scotland have a distinctive approach to work with children, retaining responsibility for criminal justice (Dumbleton and McPhail, 2012). Social care is the responsibility of 32 local authorities that have a statutory duty to provide social care, assess needs, provide or pay for services, and determine eligibility. Social work services cover residential services, day services, home care, services in health, children and families services, probation and supervising offenders in the community, community development, welfare rights, and aspects of employability services. A majority of core services are now outsourced to the private and voluntary sectors. A declining percentage of residential provision remains with statutory bodies, some 12%. Overall, the private and voluntary sectors have overtaken the local authority sector as the largest social services employer (Scottish Social Services Council, 2015). The use of direct payments is still at a low level but the personalisation agenda has impacted upon delivery through the promotion of self-directed care. This offers users a choice of direct payments, the person directing statutory services, the local authority arranging services or a mixture of methods. The Scottish Social Services Council is responsible for the registration of the workforce and regulating their education and training. Social Care and Social Work Improvement Scotland inspects, regulates and supports the improvement of care and social work and child protection services across Scotland and is separate from the health improvement body.

In Wales, 22 local authorities are responsible for social services, covering both services for children and adult care, including support for carers. Although the number of local authorities will reduce, perhaps to 12, it is likely that social services will continue to be at the centre of local government. Under devolution, social work has been seen as developing with distinctive features driven by social policies emphasising rights and equality and the central role of the public sector (Scourfield et al, 2008). The Social Services and Well-being Act 2014 puts social care legislation in a single framework and is part of a project for *Sustainable Social Services for Wales* (Welsh Government, 2011) in order to improve care and support.

The aim of the Act is to keep together children's and adults' social services, make service delivery more responsive, and give greater control and choice for citizens (Welsh Local Government Association and NHS Confederation, 2013). The Act, implemented in 2016, provides a right to assessment for people with needs and also carers, and, if eligible, people are entitled to a care and support plan. As in the other administrations, there has been a shift towards the majority of care being delivered by the private and voluntary sector. There has been a low rate of take-up for direct payments as the Welsh government believed the strategy was too closely associated with market-led models of social care. A number of centralised quangos have a role in the delivery of social care. The Care Council for Wales, renamed Social Care Wales, carries out the registration of staff and promotes training and standards of conduct. Legislation has established a new system for the regulation and inspection of social care that makes provision for the registration and regulation of providers of care (Welsh Government, 2016a). A special initiative to ensure that the voice of the citizen is heard was the creation of a National Social Services Citizen Panel for Wales.

The delivery of social care in Northern Ireland is markedly different in that it has been delivered through an integrated structure with health under the department and a centralised Health and Social Care Board. From 2016, the department will directly commission, that is, plan and fund, health and social care and the five health and social care trusts will continue to deliver both health and social care. In practice, the five trusts can also act as commissioning bodies for some social care services, for example, domiciliary care. Unlike Great Britain, there is no local government involvement in delivering social care. The range of social care provision is largely similar to Scotland and Wales and does include children's services as well as adult social care. The role of statutory services has been decreasing, with plans in place to end all statutory provision of residential care except for some specialist homes while domiciliary services are increasingly outsourced to the independent sector.

Box 2.8: Bodies with responsibility for social care in Scotland

Specialist bodies:	The Social Care Council and Social Care Improvement Scotland
Delivery bodies:	32 local authorities (social work departments)
	Integration authorities (from 2016)

Box 2.9: Bodies with responsibility for social care in Wales

Specialist bodies:	Care Council Wales
	Users Panel
Delivery bodies:	22 local authorities (to be reduced) (social work departments)

Box 2.10: Bodies with responsibility for social care in Northern Ireland

Specialist bodies:	Council of Social Services
	Regulation and Quality Improvement Authority
Delivery bodies:	5 health and social care trusts
	(17 integrated care partnerships)

Integration of health and social care

As indicated, Northern Ireland has a largely distinctive and long-standing system of structural integration of health and social care. The system had been established in the early 1970s, almost as a matter of administrative convenience as part of a major reorganisation of local administration, although it was anticipated that benefits could accrue from comprehensive planning, the better use of resources and improved joint working and understanding between the professions. Since 2007, there has been a Health and Social Care Board for planning and commissioning all health and social care, and five delivery trusts, with responsibility for primary health care, all hospitals, tertiary care, community health care, adult social care and children's services. Key features of this structural integration are: a single employer; one source of funding and one budget; integrated programmes of care; integrated teams; and integrated management and commissioning (Gray and Birrell, 2012, p 112). It has been argued that the full potential of the integrated structure has not been fully realised and problems remain with delayed discharges, inter-professional cooperation and dominance over resources by the acute health sector

(Heenan and Birrell, 2009). A *Transforming Your Care* (DHSSPS, 2011) review of health and social care in 2011 suggested that the integrated delivery of services could be improved and proposed the creation of 17 integrated care partnerships. These partnerships, better understood as networks, came into existence in 2015 but are built in or nested within the five trusts, with no independent status, and their relationship to the overall integrated structure causes some ambiguity. The main rationale for this development was to engage GPs more fully in integrated working, to set up a more localised format of networks and to focus on more project activities (Birrell and Heenan, 2014).

Scotland developed its own distinctive partnership model for joining up health and social care. After devolution in 1999, a 'Joint Futures' initiative was launched on the basis of formal partnerships between NHS boards and local authorities, aimed initially at improving care for older people. Legislation was introduced in 2002 to remove some of the barriers to collaboration, including sharing functions and pooled budgets. Each NHS board had to submit a scheme to establish Community Health Partnerships (CHPs) to link clinical and care teams and work with local authorities, as well as to extend to areas other than older people. A total of 39 CHPs were created but the degree of integration varied between largely health-only CHPs and partially integrated CHPs with some social care services (Evans and Forbes, 2009). This initiative did not remove statutory responsibilities from the parent bodies and criticisms were made of their lack of powers of partnership, the lack of clarity about their role, operational differences between health and social care, and limited progress in shifting the balance towards more community care (Audit Scotland, 2011). Such criticisms led to the Scottish government deciding to require NHS boards and local authorities to integrate health and social services for all adults through health and social care partnerships. They would be jointly accountable to their NHS board and local authority. They would also be required to integrate budgets for the joint strategic commissioning and delivery of services (Robson, 2013). A Change Fund was also set up to assist the 32 planned partnerships to adjust to more integrated working (Ham et al, 2013, p 51). The Public Bodies (Joint Working) (Scotland) Bill was passed in 2014, confirming that there were two options for integration, either the health board and the local authorities delegating the planning and resourcing service provision to an integration joint board, or the health board or local authority taking the lead responsibility. All 32 local NHS partnerships have prepared for the 2016 start and set up integrated joint boards, with authorities required to integrate budgets, including adult social care, primary health, community health and some aspects of acute health care, with parity in voting members from the NHS board and the local council (Audit Scotland, 2015a).

In Wales, there has been a similar focus on integration between the NHS and local authorities but with less formal arrangements. For a period after devolution, there was coterminosity between the 22 local health boards (LHBs) and 22 local authorities. The LHBs had a comprehensive responsibility for primary, secondary and tertiary care but problems with the small size of many LHBs led to their reduction to seven. Local health boards used a mechanism of local service boards to improve cooperative working through multi-agency working, arrangements for joint working, challenging underperformance and reviewing progress (Ham et al, 2013, p 60). These local service boards were not statutory bodies and Wales can be seen as lacking in a single strategy or plan to implement integration. An independent report covering all of social services (Independent Commission on Social Services in Wales, 2010) noted recent innovations in joint teams, joint appointments and integrated services but none of this had been easy to achieve. There was a strong recommendation that social services for adults and children should remain together. The Welsh government's response built on this paper, *Sustainable Social Services for Wales* (Welsh Government, 2011a), proposed picking up the pace on integration and the use of resources in a more integrated way. Of major significance was new legislation, the Social Services and Well-being (Wales) Bill 2013, as a single Act for Wales that would provide the statutory framework to deliver the commitment to integrate social services to support people of all ages. Under the legislation, ministers could prescribe partnership arrangements and require local authorities and local health boards to work together and integrate key services (Welsh Government, 2013b). The Act offers an opportunity for the Welsh government to shape the integration of social services and health in a way that has not been done in Wales since devolution (Welsh Local Government Association and NHS Confederation, 2013, p 20).

Housing services

Housing is a devolved matter and the Scottish Housing and Regeneration Directorate and the two government departments in Wales and Northern Ireland have major policy and financial responsibilities but their role in the direct provision of housing services is limited. The trend over time during the recent period of devolution has been a decline in owner-occupation and an increase in private renting, with the level of social housing maintained, as Table 2.3 indicates. Overall, housing is seen as a key devolved function. In Scotland, getting housing right has been seen as enabling all of Scotland to flourish, with accessible, affordable housing helping to achieve the country's potential and to tackle poverty and inequality (Scottish Government, 2011).

Historically, the main delivery structure for social housing in Scotland and Wales was the local authority sector and this provision was on a large scale. Even in the 1970s, almost half the housing stock in Scotland was local authority housing. In Northern Ireland, a single quango, the Northern Ireland Housing Executive (NIHE), performed this role. The responsibilities of these statutory bodies were to be dramatically reduced when they were largely stopped from building new houses. The main responsibility for the building of new social housing passed to housing associations throughout the UK. Much of the statutory stock was sold under the Right to Buy provisions. The Right to Buy scheme for council housing was responsible for dramatically boosting home-ownership in Scotland

Table 2.3: Changes in housing tenure by country

	Housing tenure by country (%)		
	Owner-occupation	Local authority/ social housing	Private rented
2009–10			
Scotland	66	23	9
Northern Ireland	69	14	16
Wales	72	16	12
England	68	18	14
2014			
Scotland	61	23	13
Northern Ireland	67	12	17
Wales	70	16	14
England	63	19	17

given the existing large public sector (McKee and Phillips, 2012). The SNP government scrapped the Right to Buy for new social housing and new tenants but subsequently announced that the Right to Buy would end for all council housing association tenants on 1 August 2016.

Local authorities were encouraged to transfer their housing stock to registered social landlords, mainly housing associations. A number of housing functions remain with local authorities in Scotland and Wales and with the NIHE. Unlike England, there has not been a complete transfer of the housing stock and housing management functions in the devolved countries. Only five local authorities have transferred stock in Scotland, and the Housing Act (Scotland) 2014 ends the right to buy in Scotland, giving social landlords more flexibility in the allocation and management of their housing stock. In Wales, 11 of the 22 local authorities have retained their housing stock and the Welsh government is consulting on ending the Right to Buy provisions. Almost no public housing stock has been transferred in Northern Ireland and the NIHE continues to manage some 80,000 properties, although the government department is attempting to produce mechanisms to accomplish this. The transfer of NIHE housing stock to a configuration of housing associations is politically divisive and controversial given the positive reputation of the NIHE. After some years of restrictions, local authorities in Scotland and Wales have begun to build houses again but on a small scale. Local authorities in Scotland were allowed to borrow money for capital expenditure. Between 2004–05 and 2008–09, 336 houses were completed and 250 started. In 2014, Cardiff City Council launched a large house-building programme of some 1,000 new council houses, the first for 30 years.

Local authorities also carry out a range of other largely similar direct functions across each country, supervised by their respective departments. Local authorities in Scotland and Wales and the NIHE produce local housing strategies, supported by assessments of need, and set out plans for the delivery of housing services. In

Scotland, while councils draw up plans to meet housing need, the councils have few direct powers to meet the need. There was a post-devolution consensus on delivering means to prevent homelessness and provide housing support (Wilcox et al, 2010). Legislation has placed extensive duties on local authorities in relation to homelessness. In all three jurisdictions, the housing authority is responsible for providing advice and help to prevent homelessness and also providing temporary and permanent accommodation where homelessness cannot be prevented. In Scotland, all those assessed as unintentionally homeless by local authorities are entitled to settled accommodation as a legal right. The Housing Act Wales 2014 placed more responsibility on local authorities and their partners to help people who are homeless or at risk of homelessness (Mackle, 2015). Some local authority services are directed at owner-occupiers, including addressing disrepair and giving financial assistance in loans, grants, practical assistance and advice, or local authorities can take a more flexible area-based approach to improving poor-quality housing. This may cover private rented accommodation as well.

The promotion of affordable housing for purchase, schemes of initial financial assistance and assistance with mortgage arrears usually lies with the devolved department. Local authorities and the NIHE are also involved in housing support services, primarily involved in assisting vulnerable people in living independently in the community, usually in partnership with social care services or voluntary organisations. In Wales, it is estimated that around three quarters of a million vulnerable people have obtained help from Supporting People programmes providing housing-related care, which has helped to ease pressure on the already-strained NHS and social services in Wales. All the authorities are empowered to take action to adapt properties to meet the needs of disabled people. The devolved administrations have all continued with Supporting People programmes despite the ending of the scheme in England.

Welfare reform has also had an impact on the housing functions of local authorities. A discretionary payments scheme is designed to minimise the effects of changes to housing benefits. Local authorities can top up welfare payments to claimants entitled to housing benefit where they need further financial assistance towards their housing costs in the private and social rented sectors, and in Scotland, councils have had to deal with rapidly increasing numbers of applications (Berry, 2014). Local authorities in Scotland and Wales took action to mitigate the impact of the under-occupancy charge or spare room subsidy, often called the 'bedroom tax'. The Welsh government, local authorities and housing associations have worked closely to develop clearer protocols for awarding the discretionary housing payments to mitigate the impact of housing benefit reform.

Since the 1970s, housing associations have moved to the centre of the system for the delivery of social housing. While housing associations, as registered social landlords (RSLs), have largely replaced local authorities in England, in the devolved administrations, they have developed to share the delivery of social housing with the statutory housing bodies and build, let, manage and repair social housing. Unusually, housing associations constitute a hybrid form of governance.

Originally part of the voluntary sector, they can be seen as part charitable not-for-profit organisations, with voluntary board members, and as part public body, with substantial public funding, public regulation and quango-type structures. Housing associations vary in size and mergers are not uncommon. They number around 246 in Scotland, 76 in Wales and 24 in Northern Ireland. The devolved government departments exercise regulatory and financial controls over housing associations. In all three countries, housing associations have a representative organisation, the Scottish Federation of Housing Associations, the Community Housing Cymru Group and the Northern Ireland Federation of Housing Associations. They relate sector-wide issues to government departments, the Assemblies and Parliament, local government associations, social care and voluntary umbrella groups, builders' organisations, and trade unions.

Delivery of social security benefits

The delivery of social security benefits in Scotland, Wales and Northern Ireland presents a different scenario from the other main services. The administration of social security and benefits is not devolved to Scotland and Wales, although it is formally devolved to Northern Ireland. A further distinguishing characteristic is that the Whitehall Department for Work and Pensions (DWP) is responsible not only for policy throughout Great Britain, but also for the direct delivery of benefits. Her Majesty's Revenue and Customs (HMRC), responsible for the administration of revenue and customs, has a relevant direct responsibility for tax credits, Child Tax Credit and Working Tax Credit, in this case, throughout the whole UK, including Northern Ireland. The DWP was brought into existence by the Labour government in 2002, bringing together parts of the Department for Social Security and the Department for Education and Employment (Carmel and Papadopoulos, 2003). The DWP has four delivery sections: Jobcentre Plus for delivering working-age benefits and moving people from benefits into work; the pension service; the disability and carers service; and the Child Maintenance Group. The whole benefits system is delivered through some 1,000 local Jobcentre Plus offices, including in Scotland and Wales. The DWP is responsible for about 28% of all public expenditure, and in 2013, the DWP was responsible for £14.4 billion of expenditure on benefits in Scotland (Phillips, 2013). As social security is devolved in Northern Ireland, a devolved Department for Communities is responsible for policy and administration. In practice, Northern Ireland has largely followed the practice of maintaining parity in benefits but leaving some administrative differences. There is still a separate department with responsibility for skills and training, although integrated local offices for jobs and benefits have been created. Northern Ireland also has its own Social Security and Child Support Commissioners.

As noted, the DWP has drawn up concordats with the Scottish and Welsh governments as an agreed framework for cooperation on all matters arising from the DWP's responsibilities that impact directly or indirectly on the functions of the Scottish and Welsh governments, and vice versa. There are many interactions between the DWP's areas of responsibility and services for which the two devolved administrations are responsible. The largely similar concordats cover the exchange of information, good communication, finance, access to services and dispute resolution for Scotland. The main link is between the Devolution Policy team in the DWP and the Social Inclusion Division in the Scottish government. The concordat for Scotland lists all the main issues about which good communication is necessary, covering the areas of health, housing, employment, learning and skills, and such matters as European initiatives on social exclusion. In addition to the concordat, there are service-level agreements and working-level agreements covering such matters as job search and support and job-related training and training allowances (DWP, 2010). For Wales, the arrangements for liaison are taken forward initially between the DWP and the Department for Education and Skills. Housing policy and local government finance are areas of devolved responsibility that interact closely with housing benefit and council tax benefit, which are the responsibility of the UK government. Separate agreements set out agreed responsibilities in areas where there are concurrent powers, including job search and support and job-related training. A concordat again establishes an agreed framework for cooperation and lists the matters on which the DWP and the Welsh government will establish good communications (DWP, 2012). The corresponding concordat for Northern Ireland is a statement about the way the DWP and Department for Social Development (since 2016 renamed the Department for Communities) (DSD) will work together to ensure good communications and efficient cooperation. It recognised that the devolution legislation in 1998 transferred most responsibilities for social security, child support and pensions matters in Northern Ireland to the Assembly, and other aspects of relations between the two departments are affected by a number of statutory agreements. The concordat specifies the range of services provided by each to support the other. Liaison on EU and international matters remains the responsibility of the UK government. Where the Northern Ireland social security system is delivered via the DWP infrastructure, that is, computer systems, the Northern Ireland department with responsibility pays a pro rata contribution towards the cost of providing the service. A number of areas that are covered by service- and working-level agreements are listed, including policy development and compliance with human rights, and adjustments between the National Insurance Agreements of Great Britain and Northern Ireland.

The introduction of welfare reform in Great Britain had some immediate effects on the delivery system. The Welfare Reform Act 2012 included the devolution of the discretionary elements of the Social Fund, community care grants and crisis loans for living expenses and household items. The Scottish government set up a Scottish Welfare Fund as a national scheme that determined the details and rules, being delivered by local authorities. The Scottish government could supplement the budget to meet anti-poverty objectives or reduce the need for institutional care. The Welsh government set up a discretionary assistance fund that would be managed by Northgate Public Services, the Family Fund and Wrexham County Borough. The Social Fund was already devolved to Northern Ireland but this was seen as an opportunity to design a discretionary support system with government strategies in mind. This would also include discretionary housing payments and there would be a common scheme for the whole of Northern Ireland, to be operated by the Social Security Agency as an executive agency of the department. The housing discretionary assistance provided by the DWP to ease reductions in housing allowances is administered through local authorities in Scotland and Wales but it was open to the devolved administrations to give further financial support to discretionary housing assistance.

Apart from these direct consequences, the devolved administrations have also reacted to UK welfare reform plans by introducing measures to mitigate adverse effects on populations. The most direct action was taken by the Scottish government to top up discretionary housing benefits allocated through local authorities. The amount of the discretionary housing payment top-up in Scotland for 2013–14 was £20 million or 53% of the total compared to £18 million or 47% from the UK government. Apart from this top-up, there was also expenditure by the Scottish government of £38 million to the Social Welfare Fund and £23 million for council tax reductions and to fully mitigate the 'bedroom tax'. Wales is also able to make up support for low-income families with council tax reductions. Both devolved administrations have taken action to help mitigate the impact of welfare reform in areas where they have responsibility, including free school meals, blue badges, legal aid and emergency food funds. Scotland created a Welfare Reform Resilience Fund to make local services stronger and more resilient to the impacts of welfare reform. In Northern Ireland, the first response to the UK proposal for welfare reform was the negotiation of flexibilities within the system before Northern Ireland enacted its own version of the legislation. The outcome was agreement on three concessions related to the delivery of the reform: that universal credit could be made on a twice-monthly basis instead of being a monthly payment; that payment could be split between two parties in the household instead of a single payment; and that the housing element of universal credit will be paid to the landlord rather than the claimant, with an opt-out option (Birrell and Gray, 2014). Further agreement was reached on a four-year reprieve to the introduction of the bedroom or under-occupancy tax in Northern Ireland, with the Northern Ireland Executive meeting the costs, some £17 million.

The original thinking of the SNP was to advocate some degree of devolution of benefit arrangements but asserting that for effective devolution, Scotland would have to be fully responsible for financial measures (Scottish Government, 2009a). The Scotland Act 2012 was passed to come into effect in 2015, even though it was criticised for a rather limited increase in devolved powers (McLean et al, 2013). The Scottish referendum was to have considerable impact, with the UK parties agreeing to devolve further powers in the event of 'no' vote. Most significant was the proposed devolution of responsibility for a range of benefits including the regulated Social Fund and discretionary housing payments.

Box 2.11: New devolved welfare responsibilities for Scotland

- Benefits for disabled people and carers: Disability living allowance, carer's allowance, attendance allowance, severe disabled allowance, personal independence payment, industrial injuries.
- Discretionary housing payments: Powers to support housing benefit and help for universal credit claimants with housing costs.
- Regulated Social Fund: Includes winter fuel payments, cold weather payments, Sure Start Maternity Grants, funeral payments.
- Discretionary welfare payments: Power to legislate for discretionary payments in any area of welfare.
- Supporting people back into work: Power to set up employment programme to help long-term unemployed and disabled people into work.
- Contracting of providers for work programmes.

Source: Scottish Government (2015a)

Box 2.12: Continuing responsibilities of the UK Department for Work and Pensions

- Universal credit
- State pension
- Child benefit, guardian's allowance
- Maternity allowance, statutory maternity pay
- Statutory sick pay
- Bereavement allowance, bereavement payment
- Widowed allowance

Education services

Education is almost entirely a devolved service and has become an area not only of major policy divergence, but also of administrative difference. The areas of devolved responsibilities are similar to each other and to England, covering the main areas of school administration, curriculum development, school inspection, further education, higher education, early years provision and the related area of skills. Wales and Scotland retain a strong involvement of local government in education administration, which now contrasts with developments in England and with structures in Northern Ireland.

Local authorities in Wales are responsible for the planning, organisation and funding of schools in their area, as well as ensuring the right number of schools, which are funded through the local government revenue settlement. Two particular difficulties have arisen over poor educational performance and the large number of small local authorities exercising education functions. Action was taken to establish a framework for school improvement, based on a national model for regional working. Four consortia or groupings of local councils were established, North Wales, South-West-Mid Wales, Central South Wales and South East Wales, with the tasks of monitoring performance, identifying areas for improvement, setting targets and advising on statutory interventions. However, a major review of the future delivery of education services in Wales (Hill, 2013) found: variation in understandings of the scope of activity that should be undertaken; that the consortia were weakly organised structurally; that system leadership was not working; and that functions were duplicated with local authorities. It noted that nearly a quarter of education services in Wales had been placed in special measures by inspectors from the Welsh Inspectorate and that the existence of so many small local authorities was a major contributory factor. The review proposed that the 22 education authorities should be cut by a third, and this is still under discussion.

The system for the administration of schools in Scotland strongly reflects the influence of local government, as in Wales, and also the influence of professional groups. Mandatory powers to provide schools for 5–16 year olds are exercised by 32 local authorities who plan and manage resources, develop the local education infrastructure, and seek to improve the quality of education. It is almost wholly accepted that overseeing and managing schools should be a local matter. This is notwithstanding criticism of the performance of some local authorities regarding the need for more coordinated approaches and more recorded information (Audit Scotland, 2014b). The focus of attention for change has been not on the administrative structure, but on performance management arrangements, school self-evaluation, reforming the curriculum and avoiding top-down approaches (Arnott and Ozga, 2012). The influence of professional organisations is seen in the role of a number of centralised bodies: Education Scotland, which develops the curricula; the Scottish Qualifications Authority, which awards qualifications; the Inspectorate of Education, which examines schools; and the Central Teaching Council, which promotes and regulates the professions.

Northern Ireland displays two major differences in the system of education administration that are fairly long-standing and represent local socio–political circumstances and culture (Donnelly and Osborne, 2005). Since the early 1970s, local government has been excluded from a role in the administration of schools and this task has been carried out by appointed quangos, although with some local government representatives on the various boards. Second, the administrative structure reflects the division between Catholic schools (representing 51% of the school population) and state schools, which are mostly attended by the protestant population and contains former church schools. Until 2015, five education and library boards were the employer bodies for controlled (state) schools, with boards of governors for each school. A Council for Catholic Maintained Schools performed this function for Catholic schools but the education and library boards were also responsible for equipment, maintenance and running costs of maintained schools. The introduction of devolution and a review of public administration produced a lengthy and divisive discussion of a proposal for a single centralised quango to become responsible for all education administration, including youth services and early years, although agreement was reached by the Assembly in 2015. A major area of divergence in the UK schools system has emerged with none of the devolved administrations copying the development in England of Academies or Free Schools.

Early years strategy became a priority area for the new Welsh government and an innovative approach to provision was to continue (Wincott, 2005). The early years and childcare plan spanned from pregnancy to seven years old and a partnership approach for delivery was taken. Among the initiatives was Flying Start for the under fours, with additional services for disadvantaged communities. In Scotland, early education and childcare was also a priority area and early intervention was a hallmark of the approach. The delivery of the early years framework was based on partnership arrangements involving multi-agency collaboration and programmes linking social services, health and education, and this was seen as a key factor in preventing poverty. Steps taken to develop early years provision lagged behind in Northern Ireland, partly delayed by disagreement over which department should be responsible.

The administration of further education displays quite a degree of similarity between the three countries. Two specific developments can be noted. First was the process of merger between colleges: in Scotland, from 37 to 20; in Wales, from 25 to 13; and in Northern Ireland, from 22 to seven. Second, in Scotland, colleges were classified as public bodies, leading to additional financial reporting and reduced autonomy. In Wales, colleges were classified as further education institutions (National Assembly for Wales, 2013) and financially seen as part of central government. In Northern Ireland, there is a current proposal to make colleges public bodies and, as such, subject to more central control and accountability.

Higher education is an area of significant policy divergence, with different tuition fee arrangements in the four countries. Scottish universities are funded via the Scottish Funding Council (SFC), which is responsible for distributing funding to individual institutions for teaching, research and associated activities. The Scottish government has also passed recent legislation to prescribe the composition of governing bodies and to uphold academic freedom. Universities Scotland is a representative body that can draw up policies on topics such as widening access, values and achieving efficiencies. A new framework relationship was introduced in 2012 between the SFC and higher education institutions, to be based on outcome agreements on such objectives as improving employability, retention, entrepreneurship, collaboration with industry and knowledge transfer. In Wales, the Department for Education and Skills is responsible for funding and policy. Universities Wales represents university interests and negotiates with government on behalf of universities. It collaborates with government in developing strategies on enhancing employability, developing international links, Welsh-medium teaching and cooperation with further education. A Higher Education Funding

Council for Wales looks after funding, while Student Finance Wales is a Welsh government-led partnership responsible for administering student financial support. In Northern Ireland, there is a more direct relationship between the devolved department and the universities and there is close control over funding and caps on student numbers.

Devolved strategies for tackling poverty

Delivering strategies and services to tackle poverty and deprivation, especially among children and older people, has been a matter of importance for the devolved administrations since their inception. There has been a strong motivation to deliver measures using devolved levers, social policy powers and the allocation of public expenditure. The dominance of left-of-centre parties in government in Scotland and Wales has resulted in programmes of government containing policies to tackle poverty. Until 2010, it was accepted that powers reserved to the UK government were usually more important than devolved powers and the evidence on what had been delivered for low-income groups was patchy and mixed (McCormick and Harrop, 2010). The coming of the period of austerity and welfare benefit cuts imposed by the UK government meant that developing responses became a priority for the devolved administrations. Lodge et al (2015) found that each of the devolved administrations has taken different approaches to using a package of devolved powers to prevent and tackle poverty. Wales had a fully coordinated anti-poverty programme, embracing three key initiatives: Communities First, Flying Start and Families First. Scotland had several substantial measures to address deprivation, including free personal care, no tuition fees and a council tax freeze. In Northern Ireland, a cross-departmental Delivering Social Change framework was introduced as the key policy focus to tackle poverty and social exclusion. By 2016, this initiative had involved a number of fairly small-scale projects on such issues as literacy, family support and local job creation. Common measures across the three administrations can be identified, for example, education maintenance allowances and free prescriptions. A typology of diverse actions to reduce living costs has been produced by McCormick (2013), covering: abolishing costs, freezing costs, reducing costs, limiting increases and giving financial support. The approach to reducing health inequalities had shown a degree of convergence in concern with social and economic determinants but differences later appeared with a degree of a shift in emphasis to lifestyle behaviours (Smith and Hellowell, 2012, p 168). The use of devolved levers became more important after the introduction of welfare reforms in Scotland and Wales as a strategy to mitigate the effects of the Welfare Reform Act. Devolved action in this area has major political and policy dimensions (Hay and Wincott, 2012). After the referendum in Scotland, the planned further devolution of powers in the area of welfare benefits raised the possibility of Scotland being able to deliver more effective measures to counter poverty.

Devolved intergovernmental cooperation on services

Cooperation between the devolved administrations in service delivery is limited, with contact mainly restricted to exchange of information, a degree of policy copying and comparing practice. Some important examples of policy copying include the establishment of Children's Commissioners in all four countries and the copying of an Older People's Commissioner, except in Scotland. Subsequently, the commissioners maintain communication and cooperation with each other. Several formal structures have emerged at governmental level that promote cooperation, clarification of overlapping powers and exchange of views and practices. The Joint Ministerial Committee (JMC) has a liaison role between the four governments in the UK and operates through three formats: plenary, domestic and Europe. The JMC can resolve disputes and examine issues straddling the division between devolved and non-devolved matters but any influence on delivery or provision is indirect. The British–Irish Council (BIC) was set up as part of the Good Friday Agreement for Northern Ireland and consists of ministerial representatives of the governments of the UK, Northern Ireland, Scotland, Wales, the Republic of Ireland, the Isle of Man and the Channel Islands. It has become established as a forum for collaboration and exchanging information and launching some service-related initiatives. A permanent secretariat was set up in Edinburgh and a number of BIC work-streams examine areas of common interest and potential cooperation, for example, on dealing with substance abuse, telemedicine and social exclusion. Other largely formal cooperative structures include quadrilateral meetings on finance and agriculture. The quadrilateral meetings on finance involve the finance ministers and the secretaries of state and have focused on the UK government's spending review and welfare reform plans. There can be more ad hoc intergovernmental working groups between two or more administrations (Paun and Munro, 2015), for example, dealing with criminal justice matters in Wales or a joint programme board in Scotland between the UK and Scottish governments to oversee the implementation of welfare reform. Most intergovernmental cooperation that is linked more closely to delivery takes place at the level of bilateral relations between UK and devolved departments. The top tier of relationship involves the territorial departments – the Scotland Office, the Wales Office and the Northern Ireland Office – with the Treasury also falling into this category. Regular cooperation may take place between departments and all UK departments have a devolution lead or devolved coordinator to give advice on relationships with departments (Paun and Munro, 2015, p 34). In practice, some devolved areas may have little contact with their equivalent Whitehall departments and this can be the situation regarding education, health, social care, housing, youth services and local government in general. It may only be in special circumstances, such as an inter-country inquiry or a conflict between departments, that inter-departmental contact is necessary. An example of such a conflict in Scotland occurred over the care of children in immigration procedures. Some quangos have a UK remit and may have to make special collaborative arrangements for their operation in Scotland, Wales or occasionally Northern Ireland. An important example is the Equality and Human Rights Commission, which has a special structure in Scotland and a special committee in Wales.

Developing devolved perspectives

The devolution delivery systems were marked by the initial use of the traditional inherited systems of central devolved departments, quangos and local government. As devolution settled in and developed, reviews of the delivery systems were undertaken. Developments in Scotland were centred on the abolition of government departments and creating directorates as components of a single coherent government organisation. There was also a major development in the relationship between government and local authorities through concordats and arrangements for partnerships in the pursuit of national outcomes. A major review did not call for a substantial restructuring of local government, only for enhanced partnership working (Christie, 2011). A reduction and streamlining of the quango sector received attention but rather faded to leave a quango sector with a still substantial role in delivery and administration. The Welsh Assembly Government had taken early action to reform the structure and delivery of public services and make it work together, with the citizen as the centre. Following the Beecham Review (Beecham, 2006), the WAG produced an implementation plan to improve service delivery through more involvement of citizens, closer relationships between bodies and better value, and with the Welsh Assembly Government driving change. By 2014, a further commission on public service governance and delivery (Williams, 2014) reported on overhauling how public services are governed, led and delivered. There was a belief that delivery mechanisms were improving too slowly and an initiative to cull the number of quangos had rather run out of steam. The Williams Commission recommended reducing the complexity of the delivery system, more structured performance management and, more radically, a reduction in the number of local authorities. Northern Ireland has had a very lengthy review of public administration that resulted in some mergers of quangos involved in delivery but little change in the functions of the sector, and also in a reduction in the number of local councils but with only a small increase in functions. Discussion on a wider public sector review did reach agreement on a reduction in the number of central government departments. A review by the OECD (OECD, 2016) called for more joined up government but the model of separate ministerial departments remained. Overall, the systems and structure for the delivery of social services remain similar between the three devolved administrations, not radically changed under devolution, but displaying increasing divergence from structures for social welfare delivery in England.

THREE

The role of UK government departments in welfare provision

Introduction

The main areas of social services are allocated to UK central government departments, operating under the principle of ministerial departments. The minister, usually called a secretary of state, is the political head of the department and a member of the cabinet. Most departments have a ministerial team consisting of three to five junior ministers who are given specific responsibilities for a topic or sub-area of the department's activities. A number of small departments or offices are not headed up by ministers and are classified as non-ministerial departments.

In this chapter, three important contextual dimensions to the operation of UK government departments in delivering social services are identified:

- the territorial dimension;
- the separation of the delivery function from the policy functions; and
- the allocation of services into departments.

Also identified are three areas of major policy changes that have had an impact on departmental functions:

- the impact of efficiency and austerity cuts;
- radical changes in social policies that impact upon delivery; and
- civil service modernisation and reform agendas.

The organisation of departments

The territorial dimension

The establishment of devolution and its operation from 1999 had major implications for the role of UK government departments. Major areas of social services, health, social care, children and young people, education, and housing and planning are all devolved, as discussed in Chapter Two. This means that Whitehall departments with these responsibilities cover only England in their territorial coverage. The main exceptions in relation to services are benefits, pensions and employment, where the UK departments' responsibilities include Scotland and Wales, although not Northern Ireland. It is only in the case of a few more peripheral areas of social policy that some Whitehall departments have

UK-wide responsibilities, for example, the Home Office for immigration and asylum seekers.

The post-devolution scenario was not a totally radical departure for the delivery of government services in Scotland, Wales and Northern Ireland. A strong territorial dimension had existed in a different format before 1999 through the operation of the Scottish Office, the Welsh Office and the Northern Ireland Office. In Scotland, education, health, social services and housing were administered from the Scottish Office in Edinburgh. This had its origin historically in separate education and legal systems, and delegated administration had grown into other areas (Lynch, 2001), allowing for Scottish distinctiveness as a form of central administration (Mitchell, 2009). The Scottish Office was not seen as a strongly innovative institution and while it had a wide range of responsibilities, it often copied implementation from other UK departments (McGarvey and Cairney, 2008). It has been noted that although administrative matters were organised separately in Scotland in a form of administrative devolution, there was very little policy autonomy (Keating, 2005). It did, however, leave a legacy and the new devolved institutions inherited a system of devolved administration in health, social work, education and housing. The administrative powers of the Welsh Office developed much later than in Scotland, largely from 1966, starting with housing and planning. It was not until the 1970s that major functions transferred to the Welsh Office, including health, social services, education, local government, economic development and the Welsh language. The steady accumulation of administrative functions signified the acceptance of a distinct Welsh administration (Mitchell, 2009, p 66). Administrative devolution was more advanced in Northern Ireland, which had experienced political devolution between 1922 and 1971 and had a continuing system of separate government departments and a separate civil service. A form of administrative devolution existed during the period of Direct Rule from 1972 to 1999, when the political leadership of the structures passed to UK ministers in the Northern Ireland Office (Birrell, 2010). Although changes in the administrative and delivery systems did take place, the new arrangements for devolution readily fitted into the existing administrative systems.

The three territorial governments had administrative systems that largely reflected the practices of the UK government system. There are clear reasons

Table 3.1: UK departments: territorial coverage

UK coverage	GB coverage only (England, Scotland, Wales)	England only	Territorial offices
• Home Office • Revenue and Customs • HM Treasury • Cabinet Office	• Work and Pensions	• Health and Social Care • Education • Communities and Local Government • Business, Innovation and Skills	• Northern Ireland Office • Scotland Office • Wales Office

for this. Historically, there were the established traditions of the UK home civil service, which had laid down the Whitehall department model in Scotland and Wales, and this model had also been followed in Northern Ireland despite having a separate civil service (Birrell, 2009). When the new devolved administrations were establishing their central administrations or creating structures for new services or policy changes, there was an inclination to follow or adapt UK government practices. The home civil service continued to operate in Scotland and Wales and pressure for similar approaches comes from regular meetings of UK senior permanent secretaries, which includes representatives from the devolved administrations. Despite these influences, the devolved administrations in Scotland and Wales developed a degree of autonomy over the structures of their central administration. In part, this was a response to new policies, local policy communities and cultures of openness and participation (Cairney, 2011).

UK departments have very limited responsibility for the delivery of social welfare services in Scotland, Wales and Northern Ireland but it is necessary also to note the somewhat complex role of the territorial offices under devolution. The Scotland Office, the Wales Office and the Northern Ireland Office are all UK government departments and their secretaries of state are members of the cabinet. Their statutory duties are now quite limited and are mostly general in nature rather than specific. All three represent the interests of each country within the UK government, represent the UK government in each country, have a role in advising UK government departments on devolved matters and have a general duty to support the working of the devolution settlement. The respective secretaries also make the annual funding grants to the devolved administrations, although the calculations are made by the Treasury, mainly on the basis of the Barnett Formula.

Separation of policy and delivery

The main functions of UK government departments are in the area of policymaking, and this has been emphasised in most departments through a separation of policymaking, budgets and parliamentary liaison from the task of delivering services. Any general delivery role has been largely transferred to executive agencies in a process that was initiated by Mrs Thatcher. This process, known as the *Next Steps Initiative*, was continued by successive governments, and by 1997, only one quarter of civil servants worked in departments as opposed to executive agencies. Executive agencies remain part of the parent department and are staffed by civil servants. They operate in relation to areas of social welfare services concerned with the implementation of strategies, the direct provision of services and direct contact with the public (see later). A few departments retain some responsibilities for direct service provision and some have taken back functions from established executive agencies. Even where there is a separation of responsibilities, this does not mean that departments have no responsibility for delivery. UK departments' responsibilities for delivery can be described under four headings: financial allocations and responsibilities; formulating policies on delivery, including such matters as user participation and joined-up working with other bodies; monitoring delivery; and assessing delivery performance.

Configuration of services into departments

The configuration of departments and services can change between administrations and during administrations. The power to make allocations and make changes rests formally with the prime minister. A relatively small number of departments are responsible for the core areas of social welfare services while some areas may constitute a small part of a department with other responsibilities. While health, education and social security historically tended to make up a distinct department, this has become subject to some variation, reflecting thematic developments in government strategies. Cognate programmes have become an overarching criterion for creating departments, to an extent replacing client group or traditional service configurations. The actual outcomes will represent government policies and strategies. In recent years, changes have been made to even the more long-established departments, for example, the Home Office. The actual mechanics of realigning departments can be readily classified as in Box 3.1.

Box 3.1: Changing the allocation of departmental functions

- Collaboration: Promoting collaborative activities between departments.
- Mergers: Bringing together two existing departments.
- Abolition: Abolishing a department and distributing the functions to other departments or government bodies.
- Start-up: Creating a new department with new functions or transfers from other departments.
- Transfer: Moving one service from one department to another.
- Division: Dividing a department into two.

Substantial changes can occur between administrations to the structures of central government departments and can affect quite a number of departments. Usually, there are between 22 and 25 ministerial departments. Out of 24 departments, the administration of Tony Blair made changes affecting 19 departments and changes by Gordon Brown affected 11 departments. The reasons for invoking the mechanisms described earlier mainly fall into several categories: a long-term programme of policy changes drawn up by government; a response to political events and criticisms of government performance; a response to internal political factors; or coming about through inter-party negotiations. The Labour government introduced some reshaping of department responsibilities that reflected major policy decisions. In the second term in office, it combined the

Departments of Social Security and Employment into a new Department for Work and Pensions (DWP). This was a means of implementing the new Welfare to Work policy, which was a priority area. In 2007, major changes occurred involving social care and education. Children's care was moved from the health department and separated from adult social care. The Department for Education became a department with responsibilities for schools, families and children's care, including child protection. This was a response to the findings of investigations into deficiencies in childcare procedures and an acceptance of the need for the better coordination of all children's services, under the Every Child Matters agenda (Burnham and Horton, 2013). In 2007, the Home Office was divided into two, with courts and prisons transferred to a new department, the Ministry of Justice, leaving policing and immigration with the Home Office. Gordon Brown created a new Department of Energy and Climate Change to reflect a shift in policy priorities. Internal party considerations were a factor when John Prescott, in the Office of the Deputy Prime Minister, had his portfolio expanded to include housing. When Mr Clegg was appointed Deputy Prime Minister, the only main power given was a general role related to devolution.

There has been little change in department configuration in recent UK administrations. The Coalition government made very few changes to the configuration of central departments in 2010 (see Table 3.2). The change of name from the Department for Children, Schools and Families to the Department for Education did represent a shift away from a broad child and family support focus to a narrow focus on educational achievement (Bailey and Ball, 2016, p 134). Some existing configurations, such as the DWP, accorded with Coalition thinking. One reason for the lack of change was the greater interest of the Coalition government in reshaping the delivery structures for services outside the central departments (Burnham and Horton, 2013, p 56). The Conservative government in 2015 made almost no changes. Some limited changes were introduced by Prime Minister May relating to preparations for plans for the UK to exit from the EU. It has been suggested that changes in departments and the allocation of functions is

Table 3.2: Changes of names of departments

2010 Labour	2010 Coalition	2016 Cameron (Conservative)
Health	Health	"
Children, Schools and Families	Education	"
Work and Pensions	Work and Pensions	"
Communities and Local Government	Communities and Local Government	"
Government Equality Office	Government Equality Office (Education)	"
Business Innovations and Skills	Business Innovations and Skills	"
Justice	Justice	"
Home Office	Home Office	"

not always well planned, often takes place at short notice, is poorly managed and is always costly (Dunleavy and White, 2010). A calculation has been made that the direct costs of 90 changes between 2005 and 2009 was £780 million while there was little evidence of value for money.

The impact of efficiency and expenditure cuts

Drives for greater efficiencies in government departments have been a significant context since Mrs Thatcher's initiatives and have usually been judged in terms of reductions in the numbers of civil servants. The goals of greater efficiencies continued by the Labour administration were accompanied by other measures related to the contracting out of services and the transfer of services to other parts of the public sector. Privatisation, the removal of services and the transfer of services have expanded and have been combined with substantial cuts in budgets and operating costs within departments, which led to reductions in the civil service workforce. The outcome is that the civil service is the smallest that it has been since 1939. In 2015, the numbers were 23% smaller than in 2010.

With savings of £5.5 billion in 2012 and £3.75 billion in the year before, this was reflected in a reduction of 54,000 civil servants. Joining up departments has reduced jobs, with the merger of Inland Revenue and Customs and Excise removing 3,000 civil servants. The scale of reductions varies between departments with 5–6% in the Department of Health and the DWP but much higher figures of 16% in the Department for Business, Innovation and Skills (BIS) and near 20% in the Department for Communities and Local Government (DCLG). The actual cuts in expenditure by department have also varied since the 2010 comprehensive expenditure survey, at –22% in the DWP, –12.9% in the Department for Education and –21% in the DCLG, but in the Department of Health, there was a 1% increase (Stephen et al, 2013). The pattern of cuts also has to be set against the actual number of civil servants in departments. The largest department is the DWP, representing 20% of the total number of civil servants, followed by the Departments of Justice and Defence, while the Department of Health has only 3,190 staff and the Department for Education has only 2,670 staff. There has been a decrease of 6.6% in the number of civil servants in the DWP, but increases of

Table 3.3: Home civil servant numbers

Year	Number of home civil servants
1979	739,000
1997	516,000
2009	527,000
2010	480,000
2012	424,220
2015	406,000

Source: Office for National Statistics (2014).

5.3% in the Department of Health and 10.6% in the Department of Justice due to the transfer in of probation staff (Allen, 2015). Of all civil servants remaining in central departments, some 70% work in operational delivery.

Radical changes in social policies that impact upon delivery

Social policies introduced by the Coalition and by the Conservatives have contained many changes in principle and content. The scale of these has been described as a massive restructuring programme, impacting on nearly every area of public provision (Taylor-Gooby, 2013). The main themes of these radical changes can be categorised as less state provision, reductions in social service provision, and cuts in the scope of welfare state, as specified in more detail in Box 3.2.

Box 3.2: The changes in social provision

- Reshaping the role of central state departments from direct provision, with functions transferred to other public bodies and the independent sector.
- Change to the commissioning and funding role of central government departments.
- Increased privatisation, marketisation and outsourcing to the private and voluntary sectors.
- Development of government departments' role in relation to regulation, inspection, scrutiny and monitoring.
- Commitment to bottom-up approaches, personalisation and choice.
- Commitment to raising standards.
- Promoting a localism agenda.
- Promoting the Big Society agenda related to the role of the voluntary sector, empowerment and participation.

The programme of cutbacks and restructuring has been seen as aimed at an entrenchment of a permanent neo-liberalism, with the restructuring programme leading to fragmented and restricted state services and a larger role for the private sector (Taylor-Gooby, 2013, p 43).

The Coalition's programme for government was reflected in the content of the key areas of social policy through two general commitments: to cut expenditure and to reduce the fiscal deficit; and to promote markets, choice and competition. The programme, agreed by the Conservatives and Liberal Democrats, also made commitments to delivery, to ending top-down control and centralisation, and to the radical redistribution of power away from Westminster and Whitehall to councils, communities and households (HM Government, 2010). It is possible to note the major social policy changes and their implications for the delivery systems in the core areas of social policy (see Table 3.4). The Conservative government, free from Liberal Democrat influence, focused its programmes more strongly

Table 3.4: Changes under Coalition and Conservative governments

Social policy area	Major policy changes	Delivery and restructuring implications
Benefits, work and pensions	• Radical overhaul of all benefits, encourage people to work, end existing welfare to work programmes • Jobcentres to move people from benefit to work, reassess claimants for incapacity benefits, amend child support and child maintenance	• Extend delivery functions of department • Jobcentres lose executive agency status • Child maintenance moved into core department
Health	• Improve local commissioning of health • Shift resources from acute health care to community-based care • Contract health care to any qualified providers • An independent board to allocate finance • Improve standards of care and inspection • Local rather than central control over public health	• Introduce clinical commissioning groups, GP-led • Abolish Primary Care Trusts (PCTs) and strategic health authorities • Set up NHS England as a quango • New regulatory and inspection bodies • Public health becomes local government function • Structures to promote integrated care • More engagement with communities/users • Health and social care scrutiny bodies created
Adult social care	• Promote integration of health and social care • Help elderly people to live in the community • Promote personal budgets and direct payments • Review funding of residential care • Promote workforce development • New legislative basis and entitlements	• Break down barriers between health and social care functions • Promote partnership working within NHS and between NHS bodies and local authorities • Local authorities given public health role • Health and well-being boards created
Housing	• Continuing stock transfer • Increasing housing outputs • Reducing housing benefit costs and changing eligibility to social housing	• Local authorities in England not building or managing social housing • Promotion of affordable housing • Increased role for housing associations
Education and children	• Develop and promote free schools in England • Raise educational attainment • Increase tuition fees • Increase early years and childcare provision • New arrangements for inspection and standards in early years	• Local government losing functions • Developments with children's departments in councils • New governance for free schools and academies

on reducing the deficit, cutting income tax and changing eligibility criteria for social security benefits and some welfare services. Since Mrs May became prime minister in 2016, there has also been a focus on exiting the EU and further changes to education.

Civil service and modernisation and reform agendas

There have been a number of key themes in the ongoing processes and proposals for civil service reform, most of which have had some significance for service delivery by departments. The 1979 election of Mrs Thatcher heralded major changes to the traditional role of central Whitehall departments as the mechanism to control and deliver core social services. The commitment to marketisation, privatisation, compulsory competitive tendering, internal markets and performance indicators led to what was identified as 'new public management'. This was reflected in the introduction of radical policy changes in the sale of council housing, internal markets in the National Health Service (NHS), contracting out residential care and the control of schools but also in the challenge to the traditional bureaucratic and administrative model in government departments. The most significant change in civil service departments was through the Next Steps programme to break up service delivery and policymaking, with the aim of improving the efficiency and performance of the civil service. This was to have a major impact on the delivery of social security benefits and other services. The Conservative Party approach to the themes of efficiency, marketisation and decentralisation were extended by the administration of John Major but with a new emphasis on user accountability (Commission on 2020 Public Services, 2009).

The continuation of reform under the Labour administration of Mr Blair built upon the work of previous governments and embraced the principles of taking power from central government monopolies and giving it to consumers, with a particular focus on service delivery. Additional commitments were made to private–public partnerships, improving quality and diversity, devolution, and the involvement of all stakeholders. More specific reform measures were published in 1999 with the White Paper *Modernising Government* (Cabinet Office, 1999). While this included general commitments to improved policymaking, the use of new technology and valuing public service, it also contained commitments regarding delivery: to deliver responsive services, to meet the needs of citizens and to set targets to improve the quality of services. There was a strong civil service reform element, advocating strong leadership, better business planning, sharpening performance management, greater diversity, being more open to people and ideas, and with a better deal for staff. This White Paper led to a new Delivery and Reform team in the Cabinet Office and further actions to introduce private sector structures, decentralisation and more joined-up government (Driver and Martell, 2002).

A specific policy document published in 2004 was significant in addressing civil service reform and delivery issues (Cabinet Office, 2004). It was produced by the then Cabinet Secretary and Head of the Civil Service and it flagged up two aspects of the changing environment: public expectations and the wider public sector. People had higher expectations concerning their personal needs, were more willing to challenge authority and not accept inadequate provision, while delivery was under greater public scrutiny from the media and other bodies. Departments also had to see themselves as leading a process of public service delivery made up of a wide network of public sector organisations. For departments that operated through other bodies, this required accepting responsibility for outcomes, setting frameworks and standards, and promoting integrated working, for example, in relation to children's services (Cabinet Office, 2004, p 12). The core of the document went on to discuss the components of civil service reform to improve services as experienced by their users, in terms of professionalism, leadership, performance, careers and development. Implementation-wise, the Gershon Review was to have a more direct impact, with a focus on efficiency and proposing initiatives on common backroom functions, information technology (IT) handling, procurement improvement and relocations from London. This was to provide a background to the merger strategy, which linked Inland Revenue and Customs and Excise and created the DWP.

Gordon Brown largely continued the work of his predecessor in public sector reform and also continued policies on contracting out, for example, of employment services to private and third sector providers (Commission on 2020 Public Services, 2009, p 37). Two major government papers were produced with a major emphasis on users but, in practice, there was little opportunity for implementation. *Excellence and Fairness* (Cabinet Office, 2008) developed a model based on increasing the professionalism of the workforce, strategic leadership and citizen empowerment. This did make a contribution to the developing policy of the personalisation of services. The second paper, *Working Together* (HM Government, 2009), expanded upon the theme of placing power in the hands of those who used public services. The last of Gordon Brown's three papers, *Putting the Frontline First* (HM Treasury, 2009), was focused on producing three action plans to deliver excellent front-line services for lower cost.

Box 3.3: *Putting the Front Line First*, actions

- Action 1: Strengthen the role of citizens – including: guaranteeing high-quality services; digitalised public services; opening up data; encouraging personal responsibility through technology; building a strong civic society.
- Action 2: Recast the relationship between the centre and front line – including: letting local areas have more control; reducing burdens on the front line; using comparative data.
- Action 3: Streamline central government for sharper delivery – including: equipping the civil service; rationalising quangos; improving back-office processes; managing assets effectively.

Source: HM Treasury (2009)

In June 2012, the Coalition government published *The Civil Service Reform Plan* (HM Government, 2012). This was based on a vision of the civil service responding to the public's desire for services to be delivered better. It was designed to align with new policies and it has been noted that the document had no obvious inputs from the Liberal Democrats (Pyper, 2013, p 377). The aims were couched in the managerialism principles of a drive for efficiency, productivity, digitalisation, more accountability, building capacity and better performance. The Head of the Civil Service stated that the service will work differently to improve delivery of policy and services. Referencing the context of civil service reform, he stated that the civil service will have to do less centrally and commission more from outside. The actual plan was based on six specific items, mostly couched in general terms (see Box 3.4).

Box 3.4: *Civil Service Reform Plan*

- A specific commitment was made that the civil service would become smaller and more strategic, down in numbers from 480,000 to 380,000, a 23% reduction.
- A commitment to more efficiency through digitalisation and shared services for finance, payroll, human resources and procurement.
- Improving policy capability.
- A specific commitment that a new reform implementation would be created in the Cabinet Office.
- Capability was to improve through measures including appointing heads of professions and secondments.
- The workforce had to be engaged in the reform process.

Source: HM Government (2012)

The reform plan noted that effective delivery was critical for the government's most important and high-value projects but it was strongly criticised by parliamentary bodies. The Public Administration Select Committee (2013) suggested that more fundamental action was needed. The proposed reforms were seen as incremental and likely to lead to only superficial change. It was argued that failed organisation was very evident in some departments as there was a failure to learn from mistakes. The Select Committee report went on to make only one recommendation: the establishment of a parliamentary commission to conduct a comprehensive review of the nature, role and purpose of the civil service. This recommendation did not meet with government approval. The House of Commons Public Accounts Committee (Public Accounts Committee, 2013a) supported the broad aims of the attempt to reform central government operations but it found that the government had not set objective measures to assess the impact of its reforms and did not have a clear idea of the specific outcomes from the implementation of its plan. There was particular criticism that the procedures for the oversight of major projects were not strong enough.

An assessment of the progress of reform noted that the implementation had been held back (Cabinet Office, 2013) and described what had been achieved as significantly off the mark. Success was claimed in some areas close to delivery, particularly relating to new models for delivering services, matching administrative resources to government priorities and developing department improvement plans. There was a response to criticisms in that the 'One year on report' (Cabinet Office, 2013) set out five further reform actions designed to pick up the pace on promoting the reform programme. Two were of a more political nature: strengthening accountability and supporting ministers. The others were: the further integration of corporate functions to secure efficiency savings; further improving the delivery of major large-scale projects; and building capability.

The reform agenda moved on to develop further priorities for cultural change, new digital skills and project and contract management, with a call for all civil servants to think about the services they deliver (Cabinet Office, 2014) and develop skills on risk taking and leadership. A key theme has remained the tight centralised control over cross-departmental activities and rolling back the state. For 2015–20, all Whitehall departments are to follow a programme of transformational change in key areas, as described in Box 3.5.

Box 3.5: Departments working collaboratively, 2015–20

- Developing digital solutions.
- Rationalising their estate in joined-up work.
- Delivering savings in commercial relations.
- Delivering a proportion of spend to small- to medium-sized enterprises.
- Working to deliver changes in arm's-length bodies.
- Reducing losses through fraud and error.

Source: DfE (2016)

The main departments dealing with social welfare services

A range of UK departments deal with the delivery of social services. Tables 3.5 and 3.6 compare the current configuration with the previous Labour administration.

Some departments have a much more central role than others and Table 3.5 gives some indication of the core departments and those with more peripheral engagement with social services.

In setting out the role of central government departments it is useful to make a distinction between the following:

- the departments dealing largely exclusively with social services;
- those which include a social services function among other responsibilities;
- the role of the main coordinating departments;

Table 3.5: Labour government departments with aspects of social welfare services, 2009

Departments
Health
Work and Pensions
Children, Schools and Families
Communities and Local Government
Business, Innovation and Skills
Justice
Home Office
Energy and Climate Change
HM Treasury
Cabinet Office

Table 3.6: Departments and main welfare services responsibilities, 2016

Departments	Social service responsibilities
Health	Health, social care and support, public health, quality issues
Work and Pensions	Pensions, employment, welfare reform, disabled people
Education	Schools, equalities, apprenticeships, higher and further education
Communities and Local Government	Housing, local government, planning, communities
Justice	Policing, criminal justice, prisons and rehabilitation, justice and civil liberties
Home Office	Immigration, justice and victims and crime prevention
Environment, Food and Rural Affairs	Rural affairs
Energy and climate change	Energy costs
Cabinet Office	Civil society, civil service reform, constitution
HM Treasury	Finance

- the more minimal role of non–ministerial departments; and
- delivery through executive agencies.

Departments dealing exclusively with social welfare services

The three exclusively social service departments cover: benefits and work; health and social care; and education and children. The focus in this description of these departments is on the delivery function as it operates alongside the policy and financial functions in central government departments in Whitehall.

Department responsible for benefits, work, pensions and social security

A department, the DWP, also operated under the last Labour administration, the Coalition government and the Conservative government. The range of functions that it covers are laid out in Box 3.6.

Box 3.6: Functions of the DWP

- Working-age benefits.
- Pensioner benefits.
- Disability and carers' benefits.
- Housing benefits.
- Child maintenance.
- Labour market procedures.
- Employment and support allowance.
- Income support.
- Council tax benefit.
- The new universal credit.
- Health and safety.

The DWP has been described as the biggest public service delivery department in the UK and serves over 22 million customers. The significance of its delivery role is demonstrated in DWP statistics for 2013 (see Box 3.7).

Box 3.7: Activities of the DWP in delivery

- Processing 7.4 million benefits and pensions claims;
- Paying £166 billion in benefits and pensions;
- Carrying out 24.5 million adviser interviews;
- Supporting 3.6 million people to move off Jobseeker's allowance; and
- Collecting/arranging £1.2 billion of child maintenance.

Source: DWP (2014)

The internal structure of the department reflects both traditional administrative tasks as well as current operational priorities. Thus, the DWP currently has four traditional sections for finance, IT, human resources and legal services, plus three sections dealing with the general day-to-day delivery of services, strategy across the department and universal credit. The major delivery role has resulted in decentralised administration through localised Job Centre Plus offices. These were an arm of the DWP, established between 2001 and 2003, responsible for out-of-work benefits and providing employment support. The creation of the new delivery agency reflected Labour policies of work-first and active labour market interventions (Wiggan, 2007). The network of 700 Job Centres has two main roles: the first is to administer working-age benefits; and the second is to provide a public employment service for the unemployed, providing advice and support, ensuring claimants look for work and ensuring the operation of the labour market. The DWP Select Committee has conducted an inquiry into how the Coalition government's welfare reforms are affecting the way services are delivered by staff in Job Centres. The general conclusion was that Job Centres had responded effectively to change and were giving value for money (House of Commons Work and Pensions Committee, 2014a). The Select Committee recommended that Job Centres should continue to provide a public employment service for the unemployed and also take steps to monitor the experience of financial hardship caused by benefit sanctions. Another important structural change was made in 2012 when the Child Maintenance Commission was abolished as a quango and its functions brought back into the department as the Child Maintenance Group. The localisation of a number of payments to local authorities, the Social Fund, council tax benefit and discretionary housing payments has resulted in some reduction in the decentralised work of the DWP and Job Centres (SSAC, 2015).

Reorganisation of delivery systems for work and pensions was a clear response to changes in social security policy. The special delivery role of this department is also acknowledged in that departmental plans have specified delivery principles that should govern their activity, as separate from fulfilling policy objectives. Seven are mentioned (see Box 3.8).

Box 3.8: DWP delivery principles

1. Putting claimants and customers at the heart of activity;
2. Promoting flexibility in delivery;
3. Tailoring local services to meet local needs;
4. Delivering change in a continuous way;
5. Providing digital services;
6. Continuing the importance of service delivery; and
7. Delivery by commissioning services and working in partnership.

Source: DWP (2013)

The influence of the three main contextual changes has been highly significant for this department through cuts, service transformation and civil service reform. There has been a 7% year-on-year efficiency saving. The operational costs baseline was £1.9 billion lower than in 2009–10. Staffing has reduced from 127,000 in 2009 to 90,000 in 2013, a 21% reduction (DWP, 2013), the largest staff fall across Whitehall. The department has been implementing the most fundamental reforms to social security legislation for 60 years and there are 45 different projects paving the way for universal credit, personal independence payments, benefit caps, state and private pension reform, reform to the discretionary element of the Social Fund and council tax rebate, and child maintenance changes. The many changes have involved a combination of processes and IT design, testing, training and communication. This has been done at such a pace and across such a wide swathe of the department's business that it has almost inevitably stretched the department's capability and capacity. The development of an IT system for universal credit has proved difficult and posed problems, and the House of Commons Public Accounts Committee has been critical of poor programme management, oversight and financial control, with a need for redesigning software support in several departments (Public Accounts Committee, 2016).

Department of Health

The Department of Health is a major social service department and its overall areas of responsibility have remained consistent during recent administrations, covering the NHS, social care, public health and related areas such as public safety and emergencies. The Department of Health has not had direct responsibility for the delivery of services and this substantial task falls in the case of the NHS to a system of centralised and localised quangos, and in the case of social care in Britain to local government councils. In 2013, the reforms introduced by the Health and Social Care Act 2012 made significant changes in how the department carried out its responsibilities by removing the day-to-day strategic management of the NHS from the department's direct control. Consequently, the department can be seen as no longer the headquarters of the NHS and is no longer directly managing any NHS organisation. It remains responsible for national policies and legislation, providing funding and overall financial control, supporting improvements and research, and delivering the reforms and restructuring. However, a key role is played by NHS England, a quango, with a major commissioning and allocation role, and other quangos with regulatory functions. In a somewhat confusing division of responsibilities, the department has been seen as remaining responsible for the stewardship of the system as a whole (National Audit Office, 2014a). The limited role of the department is reflected in the relatively small number of civil servants in the department (2,160), standing against the 1.35 million people employed in health and social care. The internal structure of the department reflects a very wide range of policy topics, covering such major headings as the office of Chief Medical Officer, adult care, the health workforce, medical and pharmaceutical benefits, primary and mental health, rural health, eHealth policy, change and adoption, therapeutic goods administration, and corporate services. The department has become leaner, with the number of Directors-General reduced from 12 to six, with the six areas giving some indication of the department's revised role (see Box 3.9).

The emphasis of the department for 2015–20 will be on shared delivery, between the NHS, public health and adult social care, working with patients and other partners (DoH, 2016).

> **Box 3.9: Organisation of the Department of Health**
>
> 1. Strategy and external relations.
> 2. Information and department operations.
> 3. Public health.
> 4. Social care, local government and care partnerships.
> 5. Finance and the NHS.
> 6. Research and development.

The department has also had to respond to cuts and the civil service reform agenda. The Department of Health is the second biggest-spending government department, and although funding for the NHS has been maintained in real terms in the last two spending reviews, it had to make efficiency savings to keep pace with demand. Efficiency savings have been sought of up to £20 billion in the four years to 2014–15 (National Audit Office, 2014b, p 8). The reforms in the health and social care system have been described as involving the largest-ever changes to the department and management infrastructure of the NHS and public health (DoH, 2014a). The National Audit Office (2014a) concluded that the transition to the reformed health system was successfully being implemented, although not everything was operating as intended. The department has also faced major challenges arising from inquiries into serious failings in the delivery of care relating to Winterbourne View and the Mid-Staffordshire NHS Foundation Trust. The department acted to introduce changes relating to expert inspections of hospitals and appointing chief inspectors of hospitals, adult social care and primary care. The controversies on standards of care led to the adoption of the Connecting Initiative, through which all senior staff will spend four weeks a year connecting with the front line of health and care, seen as a unique development in Whitehall (DoH, 2014b).

Department for Education

The Department for Education has responsibility for policy, legislation and the funding of teaching and learning at primary, secondary, further education and university levels. Some significant changes have occurred in the last two governments. In 2007, the department assumed responsibility for children's services, including child protection, residential care and adoption. These services were transferred as part of the Every Child Matters agenda, which was based on the principle of integrating all children's provision and services. The department still had a limited direct delivery role, with services mainly delivered through local authorities and non-departmental public bodies. A change in this process has occurred with the development of new forms of governance by the Coalition and Conservative governments to academies and free schools, as responsibility for funding and oversight was removed from local authority education committees.

There was a shift from a predominantly local authority-maintained system of schooling to a more autonomous system through the creation of academy trusts to manage this sector. However, academies and free schools are publicly funded schools and legally have central government public sector status (DfE, 2014). This programme of education reforms has, in practice, had a more centralising outcome, with more schools within the direct orbit of the department and with direct department intervention. An executive agency was established within the department to deal with the funding of academy trusts, including meeting their maintenance needs, meaning a more direct management role for the department. The removal of controls over schools by local councils has led to a new layer of governance made up of regional commissioners appointed by and responsible to the central department and minister. Education reform is a department priority, with other major areas being curriculum and qualifications reform, initiatives to increase grammar schools, teacher training, performance, and early learning and childcare. The Department for Education has only three directorates in its structure: education strategies; children, young people and families; and infrastructure and funding – plus a financial and commercial group for corporate services (DfE, 2014). Actual budget cuts to the department have been limited to a 1% reduction for 2015–16 in resource expenditure and a zero approach to capital expenditure, with protection for core schools budgets. The Department for Education embraced the civil service reform programme by launching a departmental review in 2012. This found the fundamental structure fit for purpose, having successfully delivered big changes, but the review indicated room for improvement through removing further barriers to efficiency and focusing resources on priorities (Page et al, 2012). The Department for Education will follow other UK departments in having for 2015–20 an emphasis on working collaboratively across government on digital solutions, rationalising their estate and delivering savings in commercial relationships (DfE, 2016a).

Departments with a social service responsibility among other responsibilities

Social welfare services may be one responsibility of a department but not its only or major responsibility. Four services are considered noteworthy under this heading. Housing has tended to be located within departments with a wider range of functions. At present, housing is only one of the responsibilities of the DCLG, although a major responsibility. Local government itself is important for the organisation and delivery of a range of social services, including adult social care, planning, social housing, aspects of family intervention, community development and regeneration. The department can have a funding and mentoring role over these services. Other than housing and local government, the department is responsible for planning, fire and rescue, local enterprise promotion, and decentralisation and the Big Society agenda. Again, the department has a very limited direct provider role, mainly responsible for policy and strategy, legislation, funding, and reform, and consists at its core of only 1,600 civil servants. The department is organised into three main groupings, covering: localism, neighbourhoods, and finance and corporate services, with a strategy division and a special initiative team for a 'troubled families' programme. Housing is administered in two of five sections within the neighbourhoods directorate, covering housing growth, affordable housing, homelessness and building standards. The other three sections deal with planning, the planning inspectorate and local economies. The actual delivery of housing provision rests with a range of providers, local councils, housing associations, quangos and the private sector, and through partnerships. The department has had a wide-ranging funding role for many initiatives, but has been fundamentally changing the way it operates, moving away from a predominantly grant-giving role to a commercial and enabling role. This operating model relies largely on others to deliver policies and priorities (DCLG, 2013a). The impact of cuts has been to produce a smaller department, bringing down administrative spending by more than 40%, and a planned office move will save £39 million per year, a faster rate of reduction than in any other department since the spending review (DCLG, 2014). The department has also reduced its headcount by 37% since April 2010. While the department has managed major changes in housing and policy initiatives, planning system reforms, and reforms in financing local government, these have not been on the same scale as other radical changes in social welfare services.

Higher and further education occupies a more minor, though still significant, role in the work of BIS. The overall objective of this department is to deliver economic growth but it has responsibilities for higher education, further education and skills, and science and research. These comprise a fairly small part of the overall duties of the department, which also covers the economy, trade and investment, Europe, employment, business and enterprise, consumer rights, financial services, and regulation reform. Only one of the eight Directors-General had dealt with higher education, as part of a wider Knowledge and Innovation section. However, one of the six ministers is designated as the Minister for Universities, which was quite a high-profile position. The department devolves most of its delivery to a diverse set of partner organisations, with the Higher Education Funding Council for England, the Student Loans Company and the Research Councils among the largest spending bodies in the department (National Audit Office, 2014c). Responsibility for higher education was transferred to the Department for Education in 2016. Apart from policy, performance and legislation, a major activity of the department involves paying out grants. The department has been subject to cuts and a reduction in the resource budget of 25% and capital spending of 44%, and these savings primarily came from the reforms to higher and further education. A reduction of £2.9 billion was made in the higher education budget and a reduction of £1.1 million in the further education resource budget. Plans to reduce administrative costs were achieved mainly through closing regional developmental agencies. Some major reforms in higher education were also introduced during this time. It can be said that higher education has been able to maintain a distinct identity, although within a department covering a wide range of responsibilities.

Some traditional areas of social provision may be located in a more minor and even isolated position within a large department. Probation services for England and Wales are part of the responsibilities of the Ministry of Justice. The major responsibilities of this department relate to the administration of the courts, prisons and legal aid, and include probation as part of the National Offender Management Scheme. The Ministry of Justice as a headquarters is in charge of policy, legislation, funding, regulation and monitoring, but the delivery of services rests with a number of large executive agencies, quangos and independent providers. The ministry has been committed to making spending cuts and a linked programmes of reforms. Spending cuts required were in the region of 23% in services, and administrative costs are to be lowered by 50%. This has resulted in restrictions in the scope and eligibility for legal aid and criminal injuries compensation, as well as the privatisation of prisons. A new strategy for probation services has involved replacing public sector provision of probation services for low- and medium-risk offenders with independent contractors. This strategy differs from Scotland and Northern Ireland and reflects a different model of probation and rehabilitation of offenders from an approach based on social work practice and skills.

The role of the main coordinating departments: the Cabinet Office and Treasury

Two departments – the Cabinet Office and the Treasury – have always had an important coordinating role over the whole UK machinery of government and have the potential for influencing delivery and administrative systems. The Cabinet Office has a critical role in fostering cooperation and communication between departments and between the prime minister and departments, as well as in countering trends towards departmentalism. While the Cabinet Office has a specific task, providing the secretariat to serve the cabinet, its meetings and committees, and, in practice, also the Prime Minister's Office, it has also developed as the host department for special units. These special units tend to be used to facilitate better cross-departmental coordination or to perform a special cross-departmental task. This does mean that changes readily occur between administrations in the responsibilities of the Cabinet Office. The responsibility for civil service reform was given to the Cabinet Office in recent times. The importance of this section was strengthened by the creation of a new post of Chief Executive of the Civil Service, leading this part of the Cabinet Office and separate from the post of Cabinet Secretary. The position of Permanent Secretary of the Cabinet Office is now a third separate post. A main special unit functioning within the Cabinet Office has been an Efficiency and Reform Group. This was set up to encourage efficiency across departments through such measures as: sharing common services, procurement, IT, and property; the reform of public bodies and the diversification of the range of public sector provision; digitalisation, using the principle that if a service can be delivered online, it should be; and more open transparency. The group has also been responsible for a wide range of cost-reduction initiatives across government, including central controls on recruitment, pay and certain types of spending (National Audit Office, 2013a). A major infrastructure Projects Authority gives advice and assurance on the implementation of large projects. Other parts of the Cabinet Office have functions relating to greater integration and coordination. The Economic and Domestic Affairs Secretariat of the Cabinet Office has a policy coordinating role and has an Implementation Unit that monitors the implementation of important public programmes across government. Officially, the Cabinet Office has a key role in resolving inter-ministerial disputes arising between departments. It also has responsibility for increasing openness and transparency and has continued with its role in coordinating civil service reform, supporting transforming delivery and supporting departments in delivering savings.

Special units in the Cabinet Office have at times addressed social service issues that have a significant cross-departmental dimension. In the first Labour administration under Tony Blair, a Social Exclusion Unit was established focused on an interdepartmental approach. A new Performance and Innovation Unit reflected Labour's concern with the management and delivery of public services (Driver and Martell, 2002, p 160). A Delivery Unit was later established to facilitate the effective implementation of the government's priorities, although it was transferred to the Treasury in 2003. Other special units included a Women's Unit and a Drugs Control Unit, which reflected a commitment to a more collaborative approach requiring the active involvement of several government departments (Dorey, 2014). The Cabinet Office has been used to drive efficiency and reform agendas across departments, which has had a major impact on the delivery of services. A few other cross-cutting themes are located in the Cabinet Office, including the Big Society agenda, an initiative for youth social action, community organisations and the National Citizen Service to promote volunteering opportunities, and a section to promote social mobility (Cabinet Office, 2016).

The Treasury's functions cover national finances, taxation, funding allocations, public sector pay, pensions, investment appraisal, risk management and deficit control, financial services policy and oversight of the UK tax system, which puts it in a strong financial coordination position. The Treasury also has the capacity, through its Public Services Directorate, to oversee major public service expenditure and departmental spending, including in the key areas of health, housing and education. The Treasury can have the final say in departments arguing with each other over Treasury-imposed cuts in public expenditure. However, it has traditionally struggled to impose tight settlements with such departments as the Department of Health, with its protected status and public support.

Role of non-ministerial departments in the UK government

This is a rather unusual class of department; as the name implies, they are departments in their own right but they do not have a minister. Their status is usually set out in legislation rather than as an administrative decision. There are some 23 non-ministerial departments, although there is a lack of clarity about the status of a few (Institute for Government, 2013). It might be thought that these departments are small with insignificant responsibilities, and while some fall into this category, not all do. Their activities cover a wide range of matters and specialisms, and while relatively few fall into a social service category, some important departments do. The main rationale for departments with this status is the desirability of a degree of independence from direct ministerial control for the function. They are led by a Chief Executive and by a Board. Most of the new non-ministerial departments are regulatory bodies, for example, the Office for Standards in Education, Children's Services and Skills (Ofsted) and the Office of Qualifications and Examinations Regulation (Ofqual). Ofsted delivers its inspection regime on a regional basis of eight offices throughout England. Her Majesty's Revenue and Customs (HMRC) is a non-ministerial department but is one of the largest of all government departments, employing some 63,850 full-time staff and operating in local offices throughout the whole of the UK. HMRC is responsible for the payment of tax credits, the administration of child benefit and statutory payments such as sick pay and maternity pay, and for enforcing the national minimum wage. Most non-ministerial departments are directly funded by the Treasury, but they are accountable to Parliament through a sponsoring minister in a mainstream department. It has been argued that in such cases as the HMRC, it is a ministerial department in all but name (Institute for Government, 2013, p 14). HMRC is responsible to Parliament through a Treasury minister who oversees spending. The Treasury leads on policy but HMRC leads on implementation. Other non-ministerial departments have no direct oversight by a mainstream department and occupy a more independent position. The UK Statistics Authority is directly accountable to Parliament rather than through ministers, in order to 'safeguard the production and publication of official statistics and serve the public good' (UK Statistics Authority, 2014). The Charity Commission stresses its freedom from specific ministerial control and influence and its independence from the sector it regulates, although the commissioners are appointed by a minister in the Cabinet Office.

Inter-departmental working

UK government departments may cooperate with each other directly rather than through Cabinet Office mechanisms. This usually takes the form of cooperation between two or more departments on a specific cross-cutting problem or initiative. The idea of joined-up action and delivery between government departments was a strong feature of Labour's modernisation agenda. It was seen then as a response to challenging problems that did not fit traditional Whitehall structures and also as a way of reducing fragmentation and the duplication of resources. Subjects that received attention for a joined-up approach included Sure Start, welfare to work, health action zones, neighbourhood renewal and local strategic partnerships. Public service agreements were used to promote joined-up working, which meant setting joint performance targets for the departments involved. The National Audit Office (2013b, p 7) found that departments varied in their commitment and ability to work collaboratively. In the 17 business plans published in 2012, 24% of the actions listed referred to joint working with other departments and some departments gave a higher priority to collaborative working than others. Reduced costs and improved services were the main attractions. A number of strategies have been based on a collaborative approach. The Department for Education and the DWP cooperated in establishing a commission to reduce child poverty and improve social mobility, with the Department for Education taking the lead role. A Troubled Families Programme has been set up to address 120,000 families that have social problems or have caused problems that have a high public cost. The Troubled Families Programme team is based in the DCLG but is drawn from across government departments. The other main departments involved are the Department for Education, the DWP, the Department of Health, the Ministry of Justice and the Home Office. In 2013, a joint delivery agreement was signed to boost the employment component in the programme, and in 2016, a further 400,000 families were included. A number of initiatives have taken a cross-departmental approach to improving the way Whitehall works (McCrae et al, 2015). The Major Projects Authority, renamed the Infrastructure and Projects Authority, is an initiative by the Cabinet Office and the Treasury in collaboration with other departments to help deliver major projects more successfully. This could include several departments and also complex private procurement agreements. Apart from infrastructure developments, the projects included: in health, flu vaccinations for children and a health visitors scheme; and in education, a priority schools-building project. The whole initiative is based on collaboration between the Cabinet Office, the Treasury and other departments to improve the successful delivery of major government projects. There is still support for the view that the effectiveness of the government delivery of services is hampered by the tendency of civil service departments to work in departmental silos. It has been suggested that joined-up governance between Whitehall departments can be difficult and joining up front-line services provision is more important (Page, 2009). Another view is that as long as service provision remains structured around different departments, with ministers responsible for their patch, effective collaboration will remain difficult to achieve (McAnulla, 2006). However, it has also been argued that the acceptance and commitment to collaborative and joined-up working may increase with the digital revolution, which makes access to information so immediate and may render a silo approach out of date (Dunleavy, 2010). The Government Digital Service and the Behavioural Insights Team have driven forward new collaborative ways of working (McCrae et al, 2015, p 1).

Delivery through executive agencies

The proposal for the creation of executive agencies came from the *Next Steps* report (Efficiency Unit, 1988) to Prime Minister Margaret Thatcher. This initiative was based on the argument that government departments were too large and diverse to manage as a single unit and there was a case for smaller delivery-focused units to improve efficiency, economy and effectiveness. These units, termed 'executive agencies', would be based on a distinction between policy, handled by the department, and operations/delivery, handled by an executive agency. Legally, executive agencies remained part of the ministerial department and were staffed by civil servants. Executive agencies began to develop rapidly and were seen as representing a major transformation in the delivery of government services (James, 2001). A major aspect of their organisation was that the management would have an area of discretion detached from traditional civil service constraints and the executive agencies would have flexibility to focus on delivering specific services efficiently and effectively. Agencies would be headed by chief executives, possibly recruited from outside the civil service, and recruitment and pay could differ from existing civil service regulations. Reorganisation of executive agencies can take place quickly and respond to policy and administrative and political requirements. A calculation has been made that between 1988 and 2010, a total of 217 agencies were created and 131 terminated (James et al, 2011). The advantages of the agency model or 'agentisation' initiated by Mrs Thatcher were largely accepted by the Labour government, although the evidence concerning the performance of agencies was mixed. James (2003) found that agencies and departments made positive assertions in their annual reports and reviews. The performance of agencies such as the Benefits Agency met the expectations of those introducing them but evidence and information about their efficiency and effectiveness were limited or missing in a significant proportion of annual reports. An agency policy review concluded that the model had been a success, meeting 75% of performance targets but with problems of becoming disconnected from departments.

Box 3.10: Benefits of executive agencies

- Agency staff are directly involved in delivery operations – are customer-oriented.
- Can give informed feedback on outcomes to policy sections of departments, making department have a greater focus on delivery.
- Contributed to radical culture change in departments of customer first.
- Able to adopt innovations to improve delivery and customer satisfaction.
- Allowed a smaller civil service group to concentrate on policy issues.
- Increased transparency of delivery processes.
- Created opportunities to achieve administrative savings.

> **Box 3.11: Difficulties with the use of executive agencies**
>
> - May not always be easy to separate delivery from policy.
> - Creates an organisational divide, leading to poor coordination.
> - Can lead to fragmentation if there are a large number of executive agencies in a department.
> - Can lead to the executive agency adopting a silo mentality within the department.
> - Can lead to poor communication.
> - Work may become disconnected from the aims of ministers.
> - Agencies may not develop with the appropriate area of discretion from the department and ministers.
> - May make it more difficult for departments to collaborate with each other.
> - Weak system for executive agencies being held to account by Parliament.

The identification of a number of such problems as set out in Box 3.11 led to the Cabinet Office producing a *Guide for Departments* (Cabinet Office, 2006). The criteria for establishment were given as threefold:

- undertaking the executive functions of the department, as distinct from giving policy advice, and sufficient in size to justify their structure;
- capable of having agency-specific targets and independently accountable within their department; and
- adequately resourced to attain targets in a business plan (Cabinet Office, 2006).

Agencies are required to have a framework document setting out the relationships between the chief executive, permanent secretary, ministers and the Treasury. Departments deviating from the central guidance on framework documents had to consult the Cabinet Office and Treasury. It was accepted that the variety of agencies meant that departments had some discretion regarding the governance system. The sponsor departments were tasked with keeping under review the effectiveness of the processes, and departments could decide that an executive agency was no longer supporting the objectives of the department, government or customers, and should be dissolved (Cabinet Office, 2006, para 20). Its functions could be transferred or returned to within its sponsor department (de-agencification) or converted into another type of public body.

The number of executive agencies involved in delivering social services is now quite small. The Department for Education has the largest usage of the model, with three executive agencies. The Standards and Testing Agency sets the curriculum tests for children from early years to the end of stage 3, supports schools to carry out testing and manages teacher assessments. It is small, employing 100 staff spread over four sites. The National College for Teaching and Leadership has the status of an executive agency and has 350 staff on four sites. Its main function is to improve the quality of the education workforce, ensure the quality of training, take responsibility for the allocation of teacher training places, recognise awards, promote continuous professional development and deal with professional misconduct. However, the most high-profile executive agency is the Education Funding Agency (EFA), which is responsible for allocating and delivering the majority of departmental funding. It is responsible for managing some £54 million of funding to all state-funded education, including the direct funding and monitoring of academies, some 2,108 academy trusts covering 2,283 schools, free schools and university technology colleges. The EFA also allocates funding to 152 local councils for maintained schools, and 4,000 voluntary-aided schools and general further education colleges, and looks after building maintenance programmes for schools, overseeing capital projects. It has the specific tasks of ensuring that academies follow funding agreements and for intervening quickly where institutions are failing. The EFA was created in 2012 from three parts of the existing department, the Partnership for Schools and Young People's Learning Agency, along with a section of the department that was responsible for funding local authority schools. It has 730 staff working on seven sites. In its annual report, the EFA has claimed to have introduced a simplified system, reduced bureaucracy and made significant cost savings (Education Funding Agency, 2014). A major value of the flexibility afforded by executive agency status has been in meeting the complex challenge of consolidating academy accounts into departmental budgets and accounts.

The Department of Health, although working through numerous arm's-length bodies, now has only two executive agencies: one a regulatory body for medicines and health-care products; and the other an important new executive agency for public health. Public Health England was established in 2013, with 5,500 staff in a decentralised structure of four regions and 15 local groups. As the actual delivery of public health services has been given to local government, Public Health England was to have a more strategic role, originally covering: advising government and supporting action by local authorities to improve public health; reporting on improvements in public health; sharing information; and providing an evidence basis. There was a specific duty to ensure arrangements nationally for health protection, including emergencies. The precise role of this executive agency and its diffuse origins caused some debate as to whether it had established and built authority and credibility. In 2014, the Minister for Public Health clarified its role as leading the public health system at the national level, fully aligned with its core purpose.

Under the Coalition government, there was a further reduction in the number of executive agencies, with a considerable decline to a total of 47 executive agencies. The majority focus on delivery but a small number carry out regulation or research. The executive agencies in the main departments dealing with social services are listed in Table 3.7.

The National Offender Management System (NOMS) is one of the largest executive agencies. Located in the Ministry of Justice, it is responsible for the direct management of all public sector prisons, contracting out a range of

Table 3.7: Departments and executive agencies

Departments	Number of executive agencies	Title and function
Education	3	e.g. Education Funding Agency Standards and Testing Agency
Health	2	Public Health Agency Medicines and Healthcare Products Regulatory Agency
Work and Pensions	0	
Communities and Local Government	2	e.g. Planning Inspectorate
Ministry of Justice	6	e.g. National Offender Management System Legal Aid Agency
Environment Food and Rural Affairs	5	e.g. Rural Payments Agency
Other departments	29	
Total	47	

provision, probation trusts and services, attendance centres, and other provision. The complex commercial work, extending privatisation, opening up services to a range of providers and collaborating in partnership with a large number of bodies, including police, local councils and the voluntary and private sectors, all attract a great deal of political and media attention. This provides a rationale for the department having the more arm's-length approach of an executive agency while NOMS has also been seen as achieving value for money in maintaining performance but delivering savings (Public Accounts Committee, 2013b).

Overall, the number of executive agencies has continued to fall and there have been several key reasons for this. This process was, in part, a response to the growth of demands for more joined-up government as executive agencies could be seen as contributing to fragmentation. In 2006, the Pensions Service was joined up with the Disability and Carers Service for these reasons. The reduction and closure of executive agencies has been achieved by a mixture of mergers, some privatisations and reintegration into the department (Elston, 2013). Two reasons have particularly influenced the approach of the governments: first, as a way of reducing expenditure and making savings – the scrapping of all executive agencies in the DWP was claimed to generate 40% savings; and, second, to ensure clear political leadership and direction for executive agency activities, which became more significant with the radical impact of many policies on delivery. The history of executive agencies did produce problems with clear lines of accountability. Serious problems with the Prison Service, Identity and Passport Service, Child Support Agency and Rural Payments Agency highlighted the existence of blame games between ministers and officials (Flinders and Skelcher, 2011). It is not clear that creating more monolithic delivery-related structures back in departments will accomplish major savings and more political accountability while maintaining service standards. It has been suggested that it should not be difficult for ministers to exercise control over the activities of executive agencies if they wish (James, 2003). It is unlikely that all executive agencies will disappear. The Department for Education created executive agencies in 2012 for the first time and executive agencies remain a delivery option for government services that are judged to require some degree of operational distance from the policy and management core of departments.

FOUR

Local government: the changing scene

Background

Local government welfare provision developed strongly in the post-war period (Butcher, 1995, p 40), particularly in education, housing and social care. The Education Act 1944 established local education authorities as the sole education providers of state education. The responsibilities of local government for the planning, building, allocation and management of social housing go back to the pre-war period but continued, and by 1979, almost one third of all dwellings in Great Britain were in the local authority sector. Social care had developed in a more fragmented fashion. The National Assistance Act 1948, which provided residential accommodation for the elderly, and the Children's Act 1948 established care services within local government. The Seebohm review in 1968 led to the establishment of comprehensive social services departments for each responsible local authority, mainly bringing together children's authorities and welfare departments with additional family and mental health services (Hill, 2000). This growth in responsibilities in social services was marked in the same period by a decline in some of the traditional public utility functions of local government – for gas, electricity and transport. Consequently, education, housing and social care and related services became the key services of local government and accounted for the majority of local government expenditure. Reforms and changes in local government throughout the UK were to be subsequently linked to change and reforms in social policy provision. These included changes in role, structure, functions, finances, internal management and relationships with central government. The close interaction between social welfare services and local government meant that major policy changes by central government could have major implications for local government.

Value of local government delivery

Local government consists of local statutory bodies covering a geographical area and exercising powers laid down by central government. The characteristic of being locally elected bodies makes them distinctive in public governance. Local government has generally been valued as a delivery vehicle for services for a number of reasons:

- it means that the delivery of major services can be tailored to suit local needs and variation in need;

- it gives local areas and populations a degree of discretion over the nature and details of provision;
- it provides a diversity in service response, avoiding a single centralised solution;
- councils can seek or claim a democratic mandate for locally determined provision;
- local councils have a clear accountability to their local electorate for issues related to delivery;
- it means that local bodies responsible for multifunctional delivery are easily known and accessible to the local population;
- local government can be seen as a form of self-government for communities;
- local councils can foster participation by local people in decision-making by councils;
- local government normally has an area of financial independence, allowing them freedom of choice on some service priorities;
- it may produce economic resource utilisation by reducing waste in applying aspects of national provision that are unsuitable or unnecessary;
- local government facilitates the coordination and integration of a range of services in the locality through the wide range of powers councils have;
- local councils can enter into partnership arrangements with other public bodies, other councils, voluntary bodies and private sector bodies, and develop overseas links, in order to provide forms of joined-up services; and
- councils can lobby other agencies, locally and nationally, on behalf of their local area and community on issues related to delivery.

Changing role of local government

One consequence of Conservative governments under Mrs Thatcher was their influence on the traditional role of local government, with an erosion of many of the established powers of local government amounting to a rolling back of the local welfare state (Butcher, 1995). For social policy, one of the most obvious implications was the lessening of the role of local government in the direct provision of services (Bochel and Bochel, 2004, p 114). This was to be exemplified in a number of radical policies and strategies, including compulsory competitive tendering (CCT) for some services, the removal of services from local government, the sale of council housing and reduced scale of provision.

The role of local government continued to change under subsequent governments. There was a fundamental refocusing of the role of local government from provider to enabler. The Labour government extended the mixed economy of local service delivery inherited from the Conservatives and continued the refocus on enabling services to be delivered rather than necessarily delivering services themselves (Laffin, 2008). The Labour government also introduced a modernisation agenda, a wide-ranging programme comprising some 20 different initiatives, described as mainly embracing modern public services, democratic renewal and community leadership (Sullivan, 2005). An analysis of the reform agenda (Downe and Martin, 2006) identified six key themes: executive governance, strong leadership, partnership working, strengthening performance, community engagement and social inclusion and restructuring. It has been suggested that some of the swathe of initiatives in the local government modernisation agenda contradicted each other, for example, service improvement, participation, Best Value and partnerships (Leach, 2010). Over time, the development of the agenda seemed uneven and lost its focus. Other main developments include devolution, a localism agenda, the impact of austerity and the devolution of powers to cities.

Devolution in Scotland, Wales and Northern Ireland

The implementation of devolution in Scotland, Wales and Northern Ireland was to influence developments in local government, raising the possibility of changes in the role of local government in all three countries and divergence from the system in England. The devolution settlement raised questions about the relationship of local government to the devolved institutions, the distribution of powers, structural reform and change in delivery systems. In practice, it was to be some time before major changes were discussed (see later).

Localism

The modernisation agenda of the Labour government had included some commitment to stronger community involvement and local leadership by local government in England (Ellison and Ellison, 2006). The Conservative Party had committed itself to a new localism to revitalise democracy and community life, with reference to freeing local government from central control, giving local government financial rewards and giving local people more power over local government (Conservative Party, 2010). These ideas were reflected in a new Localism Bill introduced by the UK Coalition government in 2010, aimed at ending the hoarding of power within central government and promoting locally authored solutions, with greater powers and freedoms to councils and neighbourhoods to help build the Conservative idea of the 'Big Society' (HM Government, 2010). However, the measures were also argued to reinforce existing inequalities and justify fiscal restraint (Padley, 2013). Under the Coalition, relatively few new powers were proposed for local government in England, with more focus on greater powers for local people to hold their councils to account through rights to veto excessive council tax rises by referendum, to challenge to take over services and to buy local assets. Local residents were to be given powers to instigate local referendums on any local issue via a petition. Referendums would also be held to enable 12 cities to have mayors, although only one city was to vote for such a measure. More financial openness was planned, with local authorities required to publish every item of expenditure over £500. This package of reforms has been seen as attempting to shift powers from local government to local individuals, driven by ideological belief in the role of the state and having the potential to deliver a radically different form of local governance (Lowndes and Pratchett, 2012).

Austerity

Measures introduced by the Coalition government to tackle the budget deficit had a major impact on local government. In 2010, the overall budget cut was 27% in England and large-scale cuts were to continue. By 2015/16, local authorities had seen a 25% cut in spending power (National Audit Office, 2014d). These cuts were more severe in pace and depth than any previously experienced by local government (Bailey et al, 2015). Compounding the impact of the cuts on social services was a rise in demand for services reflecting demographic change, and policy changes reflecting the government's neo-liberal and reform agenda (Levitas, 2012). Some service areas have been given a degree of government protection, including education, social care and public health, and there were variations in cuts between local council areas (Bailey et al, 2015, p 575). Local government has had to respond to unprecedented budget gaps and their worst financial settlement in living memory. Councils have tried to protect those services that they have a statutory duty to provide, such as adult social care assessments, and to restrict reductions to discretionary services, such as Supporting People (Local Government Association, 2014a). Local authorities have had a history of resilience to radical central government demands (Shaw, 2012) and innovation has been a local government characteristic. It was argued that local councils displayed the capacity to act to reinvent institutional forms (Lowndes and McCaughie, 2013) and adapt new commissioning arrangements, cross-service working and external partnerships. Early research has identified three strategic approaches to managing austerity: efficiency – through back-office services and sharing between councils; retrenchment – through reducing the level of services, targeting, charges and restricting eligibility; and prevention, assisted by training and integrating services (Hastings et al, 2015a). The main mechanisms were through the adaption of budgets, new ways of delivering services and more targeting of provision (Hastings et al, 2015b). The National Audit Office (2014d, p 18) concluded that local authorities had dealt with the reduction in funding mainly by reducing spending on services, but for 2016/17, councils would be looking at a combination of cuts in front-line services and increasing charges for services (Local Government Information Unit, 2016).

Devolution of powers to cities

The principle of devolving greater powers to groups of councils in city areas in England came to the fore as a major government strategy. The idea of merging groups of councils in England had been promoted by the Labour government to coordinate planning and delivery for more strategic cross-boundary services relating to economic development, planning, housing and transport. This led to the creation of multi-level agreements in 2007 drawing together cities (Smith and Wistrich, 2014, p 8). Legislation in 2009 enabled two or more councils to form a combined authority (CA) and take collective decisions with parliamentary approval. The criteria used is that the CA will improve the exercise of statutory functions. By 2016 seven CAs had been set up and although most envisaged the functions of regeneration, economic development and transport, a few were considering including health and social care and community safety (Local Government Association, 2016). The option of a city region as a Combined City Authority had first emerged, with Manchester and Leeds as the first examples, apart from the earlier example of the Greater London Authority. The Coalition continued to look to cities as a major engine for growth, with reports by the Liberal Democrats on 'Unlocking Growth in Cities' and the Conservative peer Lord Heseltine on promoting growth through combined local council areas (Fenwick, 2014). A measure to further empower cities was included in the Localism Act 2011. A number of city deals were agreed for additional powers and resources to enable cities to better support economic growth in their areas (Smith and Wistrich, 2014, p 69), although there was opposition to the idea from some local councils and sections of the public (Gash et al, 2014). A major impetus to the policy followed the Scottish referendum, when the prime minister announced that the wider debate on improving governance in the UK would include how to empower the great cities (Sandford, 2015a). What were described as devolution deals would confer new powers and additional budgets, and create combined authorities for Greater Manchester, Cornwall, Sheffield and West Yorkshire. After the 2015 general election, a Cities and Local Government Devolution Bill was introduced, offering city areas and council groupings greater control over local transport, housing, skills and health care. The rapid rise of the combined authority and the underlying principles has been described as one of the most remarkable aspects of the recent government's policies (Carr-West and Diamond, 2015). City deals are normally negotiated with the Treasury and have tended to relate to infrastructure, transport and planning, the functions of regeneration, economic development and transport (Randall and Casebourne, 2016) An agreement in 2015 was to have major implications in terms of devolution of health responsibilities to Greater Manchester. This will involve local boroughs, clinical commissioning groups and hospital and community services taking over an annual budget of £6 million. Although described as devolution, NHS England will remain in control (Westminster Health Forum, 2016). There will be minimal institutional change. Half of the 38 city devolution applications made have proposed forms of health and social care.

Changes in the delivery role of local government

Since 1979, the change from the traditional delivery role of local government to a reduced role in welfare provision has taken different forms and has been promoted by a number of mechanisms, including: legislation; strategies and guidelines; the withdrawal of resources; financial incentives; and the threat of sanctions by central government. A number of principles can be identified in terms of the changing delivery role of local government, including contracting out, the removal of functions and the selling off of assets.

Contracting out, outsourcing and commissioning

The traditional practice of local councils having responsibility for delivering and organising their own services underwent a major alteration by Mrs Thatcher's Conservative government with the introduction of CCT. This meant that the services previously provided by the public sector provider were put out to competitive tender. This strategy was promoted by a desire for efficiency and by ideological beliefs in promoting a competitive market and reducing state provision. The Local Government Act 1998 specified that if local authorities wished to retain a service in-house, they must put the service out to tender (Cutler and Waine, 1997). CCT required a comparison of in-house provision with those of private providers. The government view was that local authorities should be looking to contract out work to whoever can do it more efficiently and effectively, normally to the lowest bidder (Wilson and Game, 2006, p 354). Initially, CCT was restricted to areas such as refuse collection, cleaning, catering and maintenance, but it was extended to school meals and housing management, and later to information technology (IT), finance and human resource services (Cutler and Waine, 1997, p 90).

Originally, the majority of contracts under CCT were won in-house by direct service organisations for cleaning, refuse collection and maintenance, but the market share gained by private contractors increased in most areas (Cutler and Waine, 1997, p 98). The politically polarised context of CCT was demonstrated when the Labour government replaced CCT with Best Value in 2000. Best Value was more flexible, allowing consideration of quality benchmarking, degree of improvement and reduced costs, and did not require that contracts go to the lowest bidder. The distinction between Conservative and Labour approaches has been described by Baekkeskov (2011) who sees the Conservatives in power from 1979 to 1997 as framing the contracting out policy narrowly to focus on saving money and boosting privatisation. Under the Labour government contracting out was framed as part of welfare modernization, as a means to improve services and promote social justice. Neither party took the position that contracting out was a new management technique that had no political implications.

The principle of contracting out was to develop into the wider concept of commissioning. This was set out in the government White Paper *Strong and Prosperous Communities* (DCLG, 2006), emphasising the need for local councils to move away from simple service delivery towards a commissioning role that would involve identifying needs, planning, designing, purchasing and monitoring delivery and outcomes. A further broader context was to be added by the Social Value agenda. This was an approach looking beyond the price of individual contracts to look at the collective benefit to the community in terms of economic, social and environmental well-being. The Public Services (Social Value) Act 2012 gave scope to incorporate social issues relevant to contracts (Edmonds et al, 2010), and related to, for example, employment impact upon marginalised groups.

The Coalition government declared its preference for outsourced services through its Open Public Services agenda and also the Community Right to Challenge policy (Murray, 2014). Under the latter, local authorities must respond to expressions of interest from voluntary and community groups, staff, and others to run services and put the service out to tender, although this option was rarely taken up. Originally, the outsourcing of local government responsibilities was seen as more problematic in social housing and education but the extension of outsourcing to these areas further weakened the role of local government as a provider of care. Also under discussion by the Conservative government was the contracting out of children's social care services.

The sale of local government assets

The selling off of local government assets has been an aspect of the privatisation agenda and also a cause of a reduction in local government capacity in welfare services. The most significant example has been in local authority housing through the implementation of the Right to Buy strategy. Introduced on a statutory basis in the 1980s, over the next 25 years, over 2 million council houses were sold to qualified tenants at a substantial discount, and between 1971 and 2001, local authority housing as a percentage of the total declined from 31% to 14% (Mullins and Murie, 2006). The policy has continued at much lower levels of sales and the Scottish and Welsh governments have taken action to stop all sales. In 2012, the government introduced a Right to Bid, which allows communities in general to initiate action around the sale of places and spaces, although, to date, in only a few cases has the community purchased the asset directly. New rules introduced in 2016 in England allow local authorities to spend any revenue they generate from selling surplus assets or property, shares, and bonds to fund the cost of improvements in areas such as housing and children's services.

The removal and transfer of local government functions

Councils were also encouraged to transfer their social housing stock mainly to housing associations, existing or newly formed, or to special arm's-length management bodies of the council. Between 1988 and 2005, half of English local authorities had transferred their stock. The procedure involved the availability of funding for estate-based transfers and linked housing improvements to encourage take up, and there was a requirement for a tenant ballot. The building of council homes, a traditionally key function of local government in Britain, was largely removed and house-building slumped from 150,000 per year in the late 1970s to around 1,000 from the 1990s. It was not until 2012 that financial caps and restrictions were lifted and some local council house-building began again. The role of building new social housing had been transferred to housing associations, which have become the main delivery agents for building and managing social housing. Local government had been forced into a much-changed role: to focus their attention on strategic decision-making and support services for housing rather than the direct delivery of services (Murray, 2014, p 20).

In the area of education, there has been a dominant agenda since the 1980s to separate schools from local authority control. This was based on an underlying view that schools performed best when operated independently of local education authorities (Burton, 2013, p 205). In 1988, the introduction of grant-maintained schools in England and Wales meant that school governors were allowed to opt out of local authority control following a ballot of parents. They received funding direct from the government department, managed budgets, appointed staff and agreed admissions policy. The Labour government abolished this status but there was a continuing focus on the role of school leadership in delivering and implementing schools policies (Gunter, 2012) and more centralised control of performance and standards (Goodwin, 2015). A new initiative related to the creation of academies, originally underperforming secondary schools in deprived areas, with the support of private sector sponsors and free from direct control by the local authority. The number of academies rose dramatically under the Coalition from 203 to 2,309 by 2012 (Burton, 2013, p 208) and expanded to 4,500 by 2015. The process of undermining and removing local government was to continue with the free schools initiative. Free schools can be set up by private organisations, parents and charities, and are state funded, non-selective and outside local government control. The continuing expansion of academies and free schools in England means that there is a contracting middle tier of education delivery and administration.

Impact of funding reductions on service delivery

Since 2010, central government funding for local government has reduced by 37%, a 25% fall in spending power up to 2015/16 (National Audit Office, 2014d) leaving councils facing a 1.4 million black hole in their budgets with the possibility of all central government grants axed in the future. Local councils have had to take action to mitigate the pressures and risks threatened by the cuts and the pace at which they are being imposed (Local Government Association, 2014b), with the main responses being reductions in spending and more efficiencies to try and protect their statutory and main services, particularly adult social care and children's care. Reductions in staffing and expenditure on services have been widespread but it has been recognised that the scope for efficiencies may become exhausted (Hastings et al, 2015a, p 610). A major risk has been seen as the reduction in organisational capacity to deliver core services or develop new approaches, and local councils have taken approaches that have been seen as 'rewiring service delivery' (Local Government Association, 2013a) in order to ensure as far as possible that services remain fit for purpose. The impact on delivery can be categorised under a number of headings: more efficiencies in delivery; priorities between and within services; innovations in delivery: and sharing provision between councils.

Outsourcing arrangements have been seen as important to improving the efficient use of resources through the redesign of contracts and modifying costs and conditions. In some cases, this has resulted in less use of outsourcing, for example, to the voluntary sector. On the other hand, there has been increasing use of large-scale outsourcing (Sandford, 2015b, p 9). A wide range of other measures have been introduced to promote efficiencies in delivery, including establishing a single administrative centre for services and public access as well as prioritising services, with councils scaling down services that they do not have a statutory obligation to provide. Many councils have moved to only cater for more substantial or critical adult social care needs, while participation by councils in the Supporting People programme of housing-based community support has been much reduced. Some programmes have been abandoned, for example, the neighbourhood renewal programme. New approaches to protect delivery have ranged from self-help schemes, for example in relation to libraries, to the involvement of mutual and social enterprises. Overall, many local councils have demonstrated an adaptive capacity to maintain core services (Hastings et al, 2015b, p 610) and have displayed resilience in maintaining services but there is concern that in the immediate future, councils may not have the resources to meet all their strategic requirements (Fitzgerald and Lupton, 2015).

Delivering services through collaboration has been a feature of local government delivery for some time. A major focus, reflecting central government priorities, became the integration of social care services with NHS services through partnership working. Collaboration could be based on different formats. The tri-borough councils, Hammersmith and Fulham, Westminster, and Kensington and Chelsea, combined their social care budgets; in London, a tri-borough partnership combined the delivery of children's services (Sandford, 2015b). Councils have also taken the lead in launching Multi-Agency Safeguarding Hubs or the joined up Troubled Families programme, where local authorities provide 60% of the funding (Wilson et al, 2015). Austerity measures have prompted attention to the possibilities of other partnership working, for example, with the police. The majority of councils have set up sharing arrangements with neighbouring councils and moved on from back-office services to shared staff and actual joint service provision, for example, in community services, transport and regeneration programmes. While joined-up working has been promoted to reduce costs, it can also have the aim of better service. Collaboration and sharing services has been particularly important between county councils and district councils in two tier areas where building relationships can protect services. Such collaboration can cover joint procurement, apprenticeships, vulnerable communities and social care integration (Parker and Mansfield, 2014).

There have been funding cuts to local government in Scotland and Wales but the impact has not been quite so dramatic. In Scotland, between 2010 and 2014, government funding for councils decreased by 8.5% in real terms, alongside rising demand for services (Audit Scotland, 2015b). Most councils report funding cuts and have responded with staff reductions and management restructuring. To meet the challenge of making further savings, councils are planning to make services more efficient and considering new service delivery models, working with other bodies and setting up arm's-length organisations (Audit Scotland, 2015b, p 24). Other suggestions include user involvement to help determine priorities and more prevention strategies, such as reablement services. Welsh councils have faced an average cut of 3.4% in cash terms in their support grant from the Welsh government. Annual increases in council taxes are allowed in Wales, unlike Scotland and, in practice, England, and have helped reduce the level of cuts. Notwithstanding this, in 2014, some £150 million has been cut from council budgets and it is anticipated that some key services may struggle, particularly as education expenditure has been protected, leaving the other major service, social care, in some difficulty. Social work services have also been facing a crisis in Wales in being sustained at an acceptable level (Jordan and Drakeford, 2012). A survey (Wilkes, 2014) found that 84% of councils reported that they were currently involved in integrating resources, organisation capacity, leadership and the loss of autonomy.

New functions

While recent developments in the powers of local government have focused on the removal and reductions in powers, some new powers have been allocated to local councils. This process has varied between the four countries of the UK. In England, a major development has been the transfer to local government of the public health function. A review in 2010 (Marmot Review) recognised that the main aspects of public health strategies related to local government functions: housing, planning, licensing, the local economy and leisure (Heath, 2014). In 2013, public health teams transferred to local authorities and began to operate in a network partnership model with the main service areas (Kingsnorth, 2013). Local authorities in England had a limited health role in overseeing and scrutiny but this has developed into a more significant role through the establishment of health and well-being boards. These were set up in England in 2012 on a localism basis with a membership representing local councils, clinical commissioning groups, NHS England and Local Healthwatch.

Somewhat unexpected powers were allocated to local councils in England as part of welfare reform. Provisions in the existing national Social Fund for community care grants and crisis loans for living expenses were abolished. Instead, a grant would be paid to local authorities to provide locally determined assistance in cash or in kind to vulnerable people. Councils were given the flexibility to redesign the emergency provision in what is a new role for councils. This power was devolved to Scotland, Wales and Northern Ireland, and in Scotland, it was decided to allocate the delivery to local authorities. Councils would have the discretion to provide support in different ways and discretion on where in their organisations applications would be processed. While the localisation has been seen as enabling councils to be flexible and innovative (SSAC, 2015), there were concerns that the budget allocations would be cut. Following welfare reform, funding was made available to local authorities in Great Britain to pay discretionary housing payments to help people in difficulties. It is also planned to have a local support system for the introduction of universal credit.

Developments in working in various formats have taken place, most significantly, in joined-up economic planning and strategic development, where, in England, local strategic partnerships, total place initiatives and community budgets can be seen as involving new powers. Councils have also been given a lead role in the coordination of services delivery through a community planning process in Scotland and Northern Ireland and a similar process in Wales through local service boards. The effectiveness of such measures has been disputed but the various forms of partnership working do increase the scope and scale of local government activity.

Local government structures

Structures of local government have developed differently over time in the separate parts of the UK. In England, a diverse and complex structure has emerged that has been subject to a rather frenetic succession of changes over the last 40 years (Hill, 2005). Scotland, Wales and Northern Ireland have had less change and have a simpler configuration. The most major changes to the whole system throughout the UK took place between 1972 and 1974, with a two-tier structure devised for most of England, consisting of county councils and district councils with a division of functions. Six main urban areas also had a two-tier system with a different division of functions, but in 1986, this was reorganised into a single tier of metropolitan district councils, covering Greater Manchester, Merseyside, West Midlands, Tyne and Wear, and West and South Yorkshire. London also had a single tier of 32 London boroughs, but in 2000, the Greater London Authority was created as a strategic body for the whole of London. Changes in the 1990s allowed the transformation of the two-tier system in England of county and district councils into single unitary authorities. A total of 46 new unitary authorities came into existence across England between 1995 and 1998 (Wilson and Game, 2006, p 69), with a further nine created by 2009 (Chisholm, 2010). Plans had been announced for the remaining. Two-tier areas of England but the Coalition government revoked this and new legislation prevented the implementation of further unitary proposals. Metropolitan councils and London boroughs are forms of unitary authorities. There is a view that too much re-organisation damages public service performance in the short term (Parker and Mansfield, 2014). In England, as of 2016, 27 two tier areas remain.

Two-tiered structures in Scotland and Wales were replaced in 1994 with 32 unitary single-tier authorities for Scotland and 22 for Wales in order to foster greater identity, efficiency and accountability. Since devolution, there has been no major proposal in Scotland for any restructuring (Christie, 2011). The situation in Wales was similar until recent years, when proposals have emerged to reduce the number of councils, possibly to eight or nine (Welsh Government, 2015a), following recommendations from the Williams (2014) Report. The restructuring of local government in Northern Ireland in 1971 led to a single tier of 26 district councils but with very limited functions. The restoration of devolution in 1999 was accompanied by a review process of local government structures but political agreement was slow. A reformed structure of 11 new district councils only came into operation in 2015.

In practice, England, Scotland and Wales also have another community-based tier of local government. Some parts of England have parish or town councils, numbering nearly 10,000, while all of Scotland has a system of community councils and all of Wales a structure of community and town councils.

The nomenclature adopted by councils can be confusing in relation to their type and functions and arises because district councils, unitary authorities and metropolitan authorities may call themselves district councils, borough councils or city councils. The position of the new city regions or combined authorities in England raises questions concerning their classification. Up until 2015, there were four such bodies for Greater Manchester, Sheffield, West Yorkshire and Cornwall, with five other proposals for deals and possibly for London boroughs as well (Sandford, 2015a, p 19). Combined authorities may be classified as similar to the Greater London Authority, with elected mayors. Yet, the combined authorities do not have an elected assembly and may be more similar to groupings of councils formed to deliver a number of specific services and strategies rather than a distinct category of local government.

The processes of reorganisation in England and the nature of changes in local government structures have clear implications for the effectiveness of service delivery in the area of social welfare services (Bochel and Bochel, 2004, p 179).

Table 4.1: Local government structures, 2015

England	Scotland	Wales	Northern Ireland
• 27 county councils • 201 district/borough councils • 55 unitary authorities • 36 metropolitan district/ borough councils • 33+1 London boroughs • 1 other • 10,000 town and parish councils	• 32 unitary authorities • 1,200 community councils	• 22 unitary authorities • 730 community/ town councils	• 11 district councils

Source: Based on Sandford (2015c).

Restructuring itself can substantially affect service delivery and there is evidence that restructuring has at least short-term negative consequences for performance (Andrews and Boyne, 2012). A study on the impact of reorganisation on social services found evidence of a loss in staff morale, the dismantling of partnership arrangements, gaps appearing in service provision, more meetings and procedures, and confusion for users and carers who had to adjust to new patterns of service delivery (Craig and Manthorpe, 1999) or the role of partnership boards.

Central–local relations

Changes made by central government to local government functions suggest that local government in England is in a subordinate position. Historically, a number of different models have been put forward to describe and explain the nature of central–local relations. The agency model sees local councils as agencies delivering locally what they are instructed to do by central government and given little discretion – sometimes also referred to as a control and command model (Jones and Stewart, 2012, p 29). A contrasting model would be an autonomous model, with considerable freedom in decision-making for local councils. This is not seen as prevalent and is more usually described as a model involving partial autonomy (Wilson and Game, 2006, p 159). The most popular alternative model has been a partnership model, with central and local government as equal partners, dependent on each other. Local government cooperation is necessary to central government for the delivery of national policies and national standards. Implicit in this model may be the idea of bargaining and negotiation but the partnership model has been criticised as overlooking the control of resources by central government (Chandler, 2001, p 88). The nature of the relationship may vary according to a number of intervening factors, including the fact that local government is a multifunctional enterprise; in England, for example, while the Department for Communities and Local Government has overall responsibility, other Whitehall departments have policy, financial and delivery relationships with local councils, particularly the Departments for Health and Education. The degree of central control may vary with the specific nature of the service and the relationship may vary according to the alignment of party-political control of councils with the party in power nationally.

Central government direction is formally exercised through a number of mechanisms, including legislation and regulations. More frequently, it is through the issuing of circulars containing advice, guidance and instructions (Jones and Stewart, 2012, p 354). Financial incentives or the withdrawal of funding may be powerful controls and it is open to a number of central Whitehall departments to intervene to force local councils to act in certain ways or change delivery processes. As a last resort, central government may use stronger sanctions: the disqualification of councillors, the removal of a service from a council or the suspension or even abolition of a council, such as the replacement in 2015 of Rotherham Metropolitan District Council by commissioners appointed by the department following a sexual exploitation scandal. Official reviews of central–local relations, including the Layfield and Lyons Reports, were sympathetic to greater autonomy, as were some government narratives, but a House of Commons report found that central direction and control remained unchanged or had even increased (House of Commons Communities and Local Government Committee, 2009). The localism agenda used some of the language of promoting greater autonomy but, in practice, was set in a centralist framework and led to greater central control and direction. The devolution agenda is the latest initiative to make promises about increasing local autonomy for large metropolitan areas, but it again appears to be under central government direction and approval.

The relationship between central and local government is a devolved matter, and in Scotland and Wales, there appears to be a strong commitment to partnership working, mainly implemented through a partnership between the devolved central administrations and the representative local government bodies. The Scottish Executive signed a partnership framework with the Convention of Scottish Local Authorities (COSLA), which has impacted on the financial settlement and performance outcomes. COSLA has also had influence on policy development, statutory guidance and joint activities with the Scottish government on issues such as disability and planning for refugees. In Wales, a statutory Partnership Council was established between the devolved administration and the Welsh Association of Local Authorities (WALGA). The work involves cooperation on strategic priorities, joint working in delivering services and community leadership and liaison. A partnership arrangement was introduced in Northern Ireland with the Northern Ireland Local Government Association but central government and departmental control over the limited functions is substantial. The degree of central control and direction can also vary in the devolved settings according to the nature of the service. In Scotland, it has been noted that there is stronger central control of education and community care but more decentralised control in other services (Gallagher et al, 2007).

Conclusions

The local government system in the UK has been subject to considerable change, particularly in England, mostly imposed by central government in London. This has had significance for the role of local government in providing and delivering social services. Local government has been increasingly viewed by the UK government as for the delivery of services in accordance with national policies, as almost an arm of national government. The scope of change has been wide-ranging in England, including: increasing unitary structures; an enabling or commissioning role rather than a direct provider role; the whole or partial removal of functions; and the allocation of some new functions. New financial arrangements and reduced funding; and internal organisation and performance management have had major impacts. There has been an increase in central government control over finance for local government, as regards central grants, local council tax powers, council tax increases and the use of financial sanctions. There has been conflicting approaches by central government. While there has been a major loss of powers in education and a limited increase in housing powers, local authorities have seen a significant increase in health powers. The localism agenda has been judged in practice to have actually increased centralism and it remains to be seen what impact on local government powers the new city devolution initiative will have. The loss of more financial independence has had an impact on the discretion that local councils have available to them in delivering local services. In practice, the scope of such discretion for local councils has always been determined by central government legislation and ministerial and departmental direction.

Local government systems differ from England in Scotland, Wales and Northern Ireland. There has been less radical change in the devolved administrations, with recent restructuring in Northern Ireland but with little change to the limited responsibility for delivering social services, as seen in Chapter Five. The structures in Scotland and Wales remain unchanged, although a reduction in the number of councils is pending in Wales. There has been less major change in the financial arrangements in the devolved countries, apart from the impact of overall UK Treasury allocations. Some of the trends to outsourcing have also been applied to adult social care and housing in Scotland and Wales but less so to education.

FIVE

Local government responsibility for social welfare services

The degree of change in welfare provision by local government makes it important to identify those services that are the responsibility of local authorities. The major welfare services still lie within local government, as Table 5.1 indicates.

This broad–brush approach does not convey the degree of change and the allocation of responsibilities for sub–areas or components of service areas, or the precise nature of local government involvement in the delivery of welfare services. It is therefore necessary to examine each major functional area in more detail. The main local government services in the area of welfare services generally fall into three groups: adult social care and aspects of health care; children's services or sometimes education and children's services; and housing. For the purposes of identifying and describing the main welfare services, especially in a time after much change, a larger number of categories are used but with the acceptance that there are some areas of overlap and acknowledging that configurations within councils can vary. The groupings of services set out in the following relate to: adult social care; education; housing; children and young people; public health and other health services; and welfare assistance. As noted, the exact role of local government in service provision has altered and become diverse, covering: remaining services that are directly provided; the commissioning or contracting of services; self–directed support or personal budgets; advice and information; assessments of need; capacity building of alternative providers; internal joined–up provision; and direct provision through partnerships and joint commissioning. Each area of functional activity presents a mixed scenario for the funding, organisation and nature of its service delivery.

Adult social care

Adult social care is the biggest single area of local government expenditure, representing some 35% of total expenditure in England (ADASS, 2015). The Care Act 2014 for England imposed more functions on local councils, including rights to personal budgets, support for carers, national eligibility criteria for care, integration with health, statutory safeguarding, the general promotion of well–being, giving information and advice and provider failure. Direct provision of the main services has declined substantially. The majority of councils no longer own and operate residential homes and the majority of domiciliary care is commissioned. Personal budgets have increased dramatically, covering 62% of

Table 5.1: Council responsibilities for social welfare services

Service	England					Scottish councils	Welsh councils	Northern Ireland councils
	County councils	District councils	Unitary councils	Metropolitan districts	London boroughs			
Education	✓		✓	✓	✓	✓	✓	
Adult social care	✓	✓	✓	✓	✓	✓	✓	
Children's services	✓	✓	✓	✓	✓	✓	✓	
Social housing		✓	✓	✓	✓	✓	✓	
Public health	✓		✓	✓	✓	✓	✓	
Youth services	✓		✓	✓	✓	✓	✓	✓
Planning	✓	✓	✓	✓	✓	✓	✓	✓
Leisure and recreation		✓						✓
Community safety		✓	✓			✓	✓	✓
Licensing			✓	✓		✓		✓
Emergency planning		✓			✓		✓	
Environmental health			✓	✓	✓			
General well-being			✓					✓

Box 5.1: Adult social care services

- Residential and nursing care.
- Domiciliary/home care, day care, meals.
- Reablement, intermediate care, hospital discharge.
- Support for carers.
- Assessment of needs.
- Personal budgets and direct payments.
- Advice and information and advocacy.
- Special services for vulnerable groups:
  - the elderly, frail elderly;
  - people with physical disabilities, learning disabilities;
  - mental health needs and asylum seekers; and
  - innovative services, for example, telecare.
- Safeguarding.

service users, up from 29% in 2001 (Local Government Association, 2015a, p 19). Needs assessment for eligibility for adult social care is the responsibility of councils in England, as is the assessment of applicants' assets and income to determine financial contributions. Some 90% of successful applicants are categorised as being in critical or substantial need (ADASS, 2015, p 6). From 2008/09 to 2013/14, local authorities reduced the total amount of state-funded care provided through individual packages of care every year (National Audit Office, 2014e), and local authorities' spending on individual packages of adult care services, home care, care homes and day care has fallen significantly (National Audit Office, 2014e). A 2016 report (Humphries et al, 2016) reported that gross spending by local authorities on social care for older people fell by 9% between 2009/10 and 2014/15. Providing adequate adult social care poses a significant challenge for service providers. A great many of the main services – reablement, intermediate care and rapid response care – involve partnership working and commissioning rather than direct delivery, as do many of the more specialist services for vulnerable groups, for example, mental health recovery services and dementia services. Adult care needs are multiple and related to other public services and support, for example, housing and welfare benefits. Personal budgets, self-directed support and direct payments are all being pushed forward by governments but questions have arisen as to whether councils can make the required changes in delivery without financial and organisational difficulties.

Scottish councils have similar features to England, with an increasing proportion of care services organised by councils but delivered by voluntary and private bodies. Only around 12% of places in care homes and 49% of home care is directly delivered by councils (Audit Scotland, 2012). Councils assess needs and draw up personal care plans, but in Scotland, everyone over 65 is entitled to free personal care. Scottish authorities have been cautious about private providers in relation to risks and sustainable delivery and have also been keen to involve users and carers in commissioning processes. There has also been a significant shift from buying services from external providers to an emphasis on self-directed care, individual budgets and supporting people to take direct control, with a planned strategy for expansion between 2010 and 2020. Councils have responsibility for identifying needs and the kind of services and support that people want. Individuals are given four alternatives: direct payment; budget managed by others, the council or another provider; traditional care management; or a combination of these options for parts of their care (Audit Scotland, 2014c). This has brought significant change but progress has been slower in some areas, which reflects differences in political attitudes between regarding it as an extension of individuality, choice and control, and seeing it as based on individualist and consumerist values (Ferguson and Lavelette, 2013). Implementing the delivery of self-directed support does seem to require significant support for users. Power (2014) notes that promoting self-directed support in a time of austerity has made it appear as a cost-saving measure. Glasby (2014a), writing of England, suggests that pursuing the goals of more personalised services and integration at the same time is incredibly difficult.

Box 5.2: Local council spending on social care in Scotland, 2012/13

- Older people – 45%.
- Children and families – 27%.
- Adults with learning difficulties – 17%.
- Adults with physical difficulties – 7%.
- Adults with mental health needs – 3%.
- Other – 1%.

Source: Audit Scotland (2014c, p 31)

The Social Services and Well-being (Wales) Act 2014 is fairly similar to the care and support legislation in England and was seen as transforming the way social care is delivered, supporting more control for people, more integration and a renewed focus on prevention and intervention. In contrast to developments in England, it was the intention in Wales to keep the delivery of services for adults, children and carers closely aligned. Local authorities have to provide and keep under review care and support plans for people. A certain reluctance to opt for private providers saw the Act introduce new duties on local authorities to promote the development of new models of delivery in local authority areas through social enterprises, cooperatives and user-led and third sector services. A cooperative has been launched to help people manage their direct payments. This Act also enhanced the function of councils to provide information, advice and assistance on the care and support system as a central tenet, as well as improve the investigation of local data (Welsh Local Government Association and NHS Confederation, 2013). There has been a strong emphasis in Wales on connecting up public service delivery but an inquiry ruled out any change in formal responsibility for health and adult social services (Williams, 2014).

Education services

As noted earlier, the role of the local authority in relation to schools has changed dramatically in England since 1988. All schools are now largely self-governing, and academies and free schools are directly funded and overseen by the Department for Education and have little contact with local councils. Although no longer providers of schools, local councils continue to supply a range of statutory and non-statutory services to maintained schools and can enter into agreements to deliver services to other types of schools. Local councils in England are responsible for the oversight of around 1,700 community, voluntary-aided and foundation schools. Between 2010 and 2015, some 4,500 schools converted to academies through an academy trust structure, representing nearly half of all state-funded secondary schools. In 2016, the Conservative government stated its intention that all schools should become academies, but later announced that academisation would not be made compulsory. In September 2016 the Conservative government led by Theresa May published a consultation document proposing that new selective schools should be allowed to open and allowing existing schools to become grammar schools (DfE, 2016b).

Box 5.3: Local council services to schools

- School admissions.
- School-age benefits – free school meals and travel.
- School transport, school dinners.
- Special educational needs.
- Education welfare.
- Pupil referral, learning clubs, bullying.
- Education improvement.
- Minority ethnic achievement.
- Children in care education.
- Administrative assistance, human resources, IT, insurance, legal.
- Arts and cultural services, sport.
- Buildings maintenance.

Admissions remain an important function for councils in England. Despite having control over admissions only for community schools, councils are responsible for coordinating all school admissions in a common application process. Following the Education Act 2011, new schools have to be built as academies or free schools, with councils left only with a power to expand those schools under their control. The role of councils in producing improvements has also changed and few statutory responsibilities remain. Most of the powers of intervention by councils have been restricted or removed but councils retain a role in identifying the performance of maintained schools that require improvement and intervention (Local Government Association, 2015a). Councils can issue maintained schools with a notice to improve but governing bodies can appeal against the notice to the inspection body, the Office for Standards in Education (Ofsted), and councils have no power to remove school governors. Councils have responded by supporting more innovative approaches to promote improvements in school–to–school schemes or by a partnership company, such as 'Herts for Learning', to deliver school improvement services, and councils may have school intervention advisors (Local Government Association and Solace, 2013). The relationship of schools to local authorities has become highly fragmented in England, with much divergence, for example, all but three secondary schools in Brighton are local authority maintained but in North East Lincolnshire, all secondary schools are academies. In the light of this, some councils moved to a relationship of cooperation, influence and support for all schools in their area (Local Government Association, 2015b, p 16). Local councils have also maintained responsibility for special educational needs (SEN), for assessing needs and making provision for them. As part of the Children and Families Act 2014, local councils revised SEN statements and local councils must now arrange SEN support in schools and also produce an education, health and care plan (Long, 2015). Although councils are in the lead role in ensuring that plans for children with SEN are delivered, councils have no powers to intervene if they are not satisfied with the provision.

In Scotland and Wales, local authorities still largely function as comprehensive education authorities with responsibility for the planning, organisation and funding of state schools. Almost all schools are state-maintained schools owned and operated by local authorities. There are only a small number of private schools in Scotland and a very small number in Wales, and there are no academies or free schools. There are some differences between state schools in details of management. In Wales, in voluntary and foundation schools, the governing body employs staff and controls admissions but they are maintained by the local authority. Such differences usually relate to faith schools. Otherwise, the actual main services supplied by councils cover similar matters to those outlined in Box 5.3, including the planning of places, transport, free school meals, SEN, school welfare, referral units and the implementation of measures arising from special strategies on standards, performance, better environment, early years schooling and languages. Wales is moving to an administrative change, with local authorities required to work through four regional educational consortia to improve the efficiency of school improvement arrangements (Wales Audit Office, 2015).

Children's services

The positioning of children's services within local government in England has undergone changes and reorganisation that have created differences with the rest of the UK. Following the Laming inquiry into the death of Victoria Climbie, the government evolved a strategy for the creation of children's trusts that would bring together children's social services with education services within local authorities (Birrell, 2006). These developed into local authority children's services departments (Purcell and Chow, 2011) with a director of children's services for each upper-tier council. Scotland and Wales were to maintain unified adult and children's services, separate from education but still within the same local council. Northern Ireland continued with unified adult and children's services, also integrated with health services but outside local government. By 2016, the actual organisation of children's services as distinct from schools in 152 local authorities in England does demonstrate a number of diverse configurations (see Box 5.4). There has been a trend towards moving back to reunifying children's and adult social care.

Box 5.4: Children, youth and family services

- Child and family assessment.
- Child protection and safeguarding.
- Children in care, looked-after children.
- Family support services, social work teams, family support workers.
- Early years provision and funding early intervention, Sure Start Children's Centres.
- Fostering and adoption.
- Youth and young people's services.

Child protection, care for vulnerable children and support for families has been an area of growing demand and referrals to local councils. This reflects earlier intervention in safeguarding and instigating child protection measures, more children with complex needs and disabilities, higher rates of domestic abuse, and action against sexual exploitation. This has meant increased expenditure by local councils on child protection and looked-after children – in 2015, 69,504 looked-after children were cared for by local councils, an increase of 6% since 2011, some 60% under care orders (Zayed and Harker, 2015). This has to be set against other reductions in children's services budgets while the related schools funding in England has been ring-fenced (Local Government Association, 2015b). In practice, children's care funding has been given some protection but at the expense of youth services. Local councils have adopted measures to make the best use of resources, particularly in developing and strengthening work with and through schools in the integrated council organisation in England. Local initiatives have included groups of up to 15 local councils, as in Yorkshire and the Humber, working together to create bigger children's social work teams. An additional responsibility placed on local councils has been a government initiative – the national Troubled Families programme, with funding for 129,000 families with multiple problems. Councils are allocated a target number of families. The programme is aimed at behavioural change related to work, schooling, poor health and anti-social behaviour, dealing with family problems as a whole and joining up local services to make better use of resources. The programme has attracted criticisms, specifically that interventions do not target the complexity of troubled families, in particular, health needs, and are taking place as key local services are cut (Boddy et al, 2016).

Fostering and adoption have been major and growing areas of local government responsibility. There was a 9% increase in fostering between 2010 and 2015 and adoption between 2011 and 2015, rising year on year. New legislation has been introduced by the government that extends to Wales as well as England. The intention is to enable local authorities to place children with prospective adopters more swiftly and remove requirements for local authorities to seek a perfect or partial ethnic match. The legislation also promotes the ability of a local council to place children in other local council areas or with voluntary adoption agencies (Roberts and Jarrett, 2015), and already councils have been using regional consortia. A controversial provision subject to parliamentary approval would require local authorities to outsource adopter recruitment, assessment and approval to an adoption agency. It has also been suggested that high-profile media cases relating to child protection have fostered a culture of risk aversion (Devine and Parker, 2015) and that such caution has been an obstacle to new delivery models, for example, an integrated or combined approach to children, youth, early years and specialist services.

A further important area of children's services has been early years services for children under four. Free early years entitlement is provided by councils and other providers, and is supervised by councils. Sure Start was a programme of play, advice, childcare and outreach services to deprived communities. Eventually, this led to Sure Start Children's Centres, with greater local authority oversight through integration into existing children's services. Ring-fencing of Sure Start funding was removed in 2011, which was expected to result in a decline in provision in England (Bates and Foster, 2015).

The delivery and commissioning of children's services and the oversight of services has become increasingly fragmented, with parts more subject to central control. This is reflected in variations in school autonomy, in local council control and in the providers of children's services, residential care and potentially child protection. The complex scenario of provision has increased the need for more connected leadership and partnership working and delivery (ADASS, 2014).

Scotland has continued with a system of unified children's and adult social care within local authority social work departments. Consequently, there is a separation from education services and, for example, residential care for children is inspected by a care inspectorate and not by an Ofsted-type organisation. One of the unique aspects of children's services in Scotland has been the children's hearings system, which regards those requiring care and protection as being as equally deserving as those who offend (McPhail, 2006). Children's hearings represent a holistic approach to the delivery of care and justice, a major transformation process for improving and reshaping care for children enacted through the Children and Young People (Scotland) Act 2014. This embraces a consistent way working with children and young people, known as Getting it Right for Every Child (GIRFEC). Key elements are a named person, a lead professional and child well-being at the centre (Scottish Government, 2015b). Implementation is based on a community partnership basis but led by local authorities in a process of the realignment of children's services. The Welsh child protection system is similar to England's, but in 2011, Wales took the lead in incorporating the UN Convention on the Rights of the Child into domestic policy. A national adoption service was started in 2014, run by five regional consortia aimed at pooling resources and becoming more efficient. Between 2014 and 2015, there was a reduction in the number of children looked after by local authorities and an 11% increase in adoptions. Welsh programmes aimed at keeping families together, Flying Start, targeting families with children under 5 in deprived areas, and Integrated Family Support, a service targeted at families with complex issues, have seen continuing investment. New legislation in Wales, the Social Services and Well-being (Wales) Act 2014, includes support for changes, covering: a renewed focus on prevention and early intervention; giving individuals a stronger voice; a common process for every safeguarding board; new eligibility criteria for children, focusing on need with portable assessments; and a national outcomes focus.

Public health

Under the Public Health and Social Care Act 2012, some public health functions were transferred to upper-tier and unitary local authorities in England from April 2013 (see Box 5.5).

Box 5.5: Public health responsibilities

- Providing/commissioning smoking cessation services, tackling obesity, alcoholism, drug abuse, sexual health.
- Carrying out research on how to improve health.
- Giving advice and information to adults and children.
- Working with local bodies to mitigate risks to health.
- Using financial incentives to encourage individuals to adopt healthy lifestyles.

Source: DoH (2012a)

A central public body, Public Health England, provided advice and support during the transformation stage and NHS England provided £546 million to local authorities to fulfil their public health obligations as a ring-fenced budget (NHS England, 2015), particularly with regard to improving health, health protection functions, reducing health inequalities, and providing health-care advice. Each local authority has to appoint a director of public health. Some variations have appeared between councils. In some areas, the directors are placed under the control of the director of adult services; while in others, the role of directors of public health was expanded into environmental health, social care, housing and planning. Rather than a discrete set of services, the public health function is normally integrated and joined up with the main service areas – housing, education, transport, leisure and community safety – although there has been a focus on some specific topics such as childhood obesity. There is also a close relationship with local government health and well-being boards. Local council areas are seen as a catalyst for this joined-up approach across local government and are in a position to introduce existing services and programmes to emphasise public health goals (Thraves, 2012), for example, child health programmes, early years programmes and drug and addiction programmes (Local Government Association, 2015c, 2015d).

They can provide special public health support to local authorities in matters related to public health and a wide range of local government services impinge on public health, including social services, community centres, leisure facilities, environmental health, home insulation, air quality measures and transport passes.

Local government has also taken on wider health scrutiny functions in England, originally with a health overview and scrutiny role since 2003 to enable councillors to monitor and connect on local health issues and more significantly, in partnership with health and well-being boards in upper-tier councils, to promote integrated planning and commissioning. Local government is not directly involved in delivering public health functions in Scotland, Wales and Northern Ireland, where centralised and specialist boards carry out this function.

Housing

Local councils are still responsible for a range of housing services, mostly but not entirely covering social housing, despite the reduction in the size of the local authority housing sector.

The direct responsibilities of local councils for providing, owning and managing social housing has been in a downward decline due to house sales, stock transfer and the virtual end of council new-build (DCLG, 2012) but in 2016 council housing is still at the substantial number in England of 1.69 million dwellings. House sales have declined and stock transfers have continued, but slowly, in England. In Scotland, house sales have been stopped, with Wales likely to follow suit. The transfer of housing stock has only applied to about half of public dwellings in Scotland, around 53% is still owned by local authorities, and in Wales, only half of all the local authorities have transferred their stock to new social landlords. This does not mean that all local councils still carry out housing management functions and deliver services directly. Since 2002, arm's-length management organisations (ALMOs) have had a major role in the management of council housing in England and Wales. ALMOs are a way of achieving social housing investment without having to pass the ownership of housing stock out of council control. They now manage about 564,000 council homes across 43 local authorities (National Federation of ALMOs, 2015). They have demonstrated a high level of performance, provided good services to tenants, promoted participation and improved housing standards and community services. Diversity in housing management has also seen the growth of tenant management organisations (TMOs) to administer services on estates, as well as other providers contracted for services, particularly for specialist extra care and sheltered accommodation (Reeves, 2014).

Box 5.6: Housing services

- Assessment of housing need.
- New house-building.
- Allocation policy.
- Management of council housing stock, rent collection, rent arrears, repairs, tenant participation.
- Supervision of arm's-length management organisations (ALMOs).
- Transfer of housing stock.
- Sheltered housing, extra housing, on-site support.
- Homelessness.
- Repair grants to housing, including owner-occupied housing.
- Registering houses in multiple occupation.
- Housing data collection.
- Adaptations to housing stock to assist people with disabilities.

Local government responsibility for housing received a boost when a new Housing Revenue Account (HRA) framework for England was introduced through the Localism Act 2011. This allowed for the self-financing of council housing, replacing a centralised subsidy system. A survey has reported that 93% of councillors in stock-retaining councils said that they had plans to build new council homes (Smith Institute, 2013) using mainly the HRA borrowing headroom. Councils have been giving priority to new-build but the total planned per council is around 1,000 and this development has to be seen against 1.85 million households on local authority waiting lists. A number of other housing services are the direct responsibility of local councils, including homelessness and the provision of temporary accommodation, the energy efficiency of homes, capital repair works, the administration of housing benefit and forms of support for independent living.

Welfare assistance

Local authorities have normally had a limited or indirect role in the delivery of cash benefits and welfare support, but this has changed somewhat in recent years in the context of welfare reform. Again, there are differences between the four countries of the UK.

Box 5.7: Welfare and financial assistance

- Local welfare provision replacing the Social Fund.
- Discretionary housing payments.
- Universal credit and council support.
- Council tax support.
- Independent living fund.
- Other impacts of welfare reforms on councils.

The Welfare Reform Act 2012 abolished the discretionary Social Fund but transferred the responsibility for crisis and emergency support to local councils in England and the devolved administrations. Legally, provision was allowed to be tailored to meet the needs of local communities but was expected to be concentrated on those facing greatest difficulty in managing income through a mix of cash and goods. Most local councils in England provide emergency support not usually through cash, but through vouchers, fuel cards and furniture. It has been anticipated that councils may struggle to meet increases in demands (SSAC, 2015) and there has also been criticism of variations in eligibility criteria used by councils in distributing crisis funds, as well as high administrative costs. The Scottish government has delegated the scheme, called the Scottish Welfare Fund, to local authorities and has put in funding additional to the Department for Work and Pensions (DWP) allocation. In Scotland, there will be continuing use of the two traditional forms of support: crisis grants to help people in emergencies, and community care grants to help people stay at home, including one-off items like cookers. Wales has opted for a discretionary assistance fund to be nationally administered by a partnership involving one council. Northern Ireland will have a scheme administered by the Department for Communities. In 2015, the UK government announced its withdrawal of funding for local welfare support, which would mean the scrapping or scaling back of this support. In 2013/14, there were 400,000 local welfare awards made by local authorities in England and councils have fears that reduced support will lead to an increase in social problems.

Discretionary housing payments were introduced to help those whose housing benefit does not cover the rent. Funding was made available from central government to provide transitional cover following welfare reform changes, particularly the introduction of the underoccupancy/bedroom tax. Local councils in England, Scotland and Wales are responsible for delivering these and have the discretion to set the criteria. The DWP originally set aside £390 million to fund discretionary housing payments over four years and the Scottish and Welsh governments created their own funds. The amount that councils can spend has been set by the government.

Universal credit is the key feature of welfare reform, bringing together a collection of working-age benefits into a single streamlined payment, and the roll-out of the scheme has commenced. Local authorities are seen to have a part to play in the effectiveness of the programme of work to introduce the scheme and eight councils in England were chosen as pilot sites to test out different elements of support offered to claimants during their universal credit claimant journey. A review of these pilots suggested that there was a vital role for councils in initial questioning and advice, leading or commissioning partnerships to deliver support for claimants, and working to deliver more joined-up services. The review also highlighted that local councils could apply for European Social Fund support for initiatives to help move people towards employment.

The UK has operated with a council tax benefit and reduction scheme for categories of claimants, but in 2010, the UK Coalition government announced that it would abolish council tax benefit and give responsibility for developing replacement arrangements to local authorities in England and to the devolved administrations. The funding transferred for council tax support was cut by 10%. Each local authority has to adopt its own council tax reduction scheme regulations and has some area of discretion to take the needs and priorities of their local area into account. There were concerns that councils might be discouraged from promoting take-up of the benefit (Adam and Browne, 2012). In England, the scheme was to become partly funded through business rate retention, absorption from other budgets or reductions in claimants (Local Government Association, 2015e). The Scottish and Welsh governments have acted to try and reduce the impact of the UK government cut in funding and the devolved administrations have the power to make the regulations but the local authorities administer the scheme. A similar system of rate relief exists in the Northern Ireland system. Overall, approximately £31 billion of funding has been removed from council tax benefit in the three years up to 2015/16.

Financing local government services

Finance for local government is a key factor in the operation of councils and the range of services they can deliver. The main sources of funding for local councils are set out in Box 5.8.

Box 5.8: Categories of local authority income

- Local government taxation: council tax and non-domestic rates.
- Local government charges, fees, sales.
- Central government grants – general and specific borrowing and investment.
- Other sources, for example, the European Union.

Charges and fees have always been a small component of financing, ranging from council house rents to admission to recreational facilities, and are not subject to much change. Central government funding through general and specific grants has been the most significant component and has traditionally constituted around 60% of total income. In England, there has been a significant reduction in the level of central government grants in recent years, falling from 65% in 2010/11 to 58% in 2013/14. In Scotland, Wales and Northern Ireland, the devolved administrations act as the central government for funding purposes. Local government has historically had its own form of taxation contributions through a local property tax, since 1993, called local council tax in England, Scotland and Wales, which has a domestic and non–domestic property application. This locally funded income has traditionally comprised around 25% of total income, as discussed later. The total income for local authorities in England in 2013/14 was £158 million, down from £165 million in 2010/11 (the percentage breakdown is shown in Box 5.9).

Box 5.9: Local authority income, 2013/14

- Revenue Support Grant – 10%.
- Specific grants – 26%.
- Other grants – 21%.
- Charges, fees, sales – 13%.
- Council tax – 15%.
- Non-domestic rate retention – 7%.
- Other income – 8%.

Source: DCLG (2015a)

Local council tax

Local councils in England, Scotland and Wales can raise finance through a local council tax, while a similar tax in Northern Ireland is still called 'rates'. Local taxation paid depends on the value of properties: per household on domestic properties, with discounts for single-person households and those with lower incomes; and also on non-domestic properties and called in this case 'rates'. All domestic property in Great Britain was fixed in one of eight bands and the amount of council tax paid depends on the valuation band as set in 1991, ranging from £40,000 to £320,000. Council tax is inherently regressive as those in lower bands pay a higher percentage of their income. Dissatisfaction with the apparent unfairness of council tax and the lack of a revaluation did lead to each country in the UK reviewing local taxation but coming to different conclusions. The final report of the Lyons inquiry into local government in England recommended adding new bands at the top and bottom and revaluation but this was rejected by the government (Lyons, 2007). A review in Scotland recommending replacing the council tax with a new local property tax, calculated on the market value of each house with regular revaluations, was also rejected by the Scottish government (Burt, 2006). In Wales, there was a revaluation and new council tax bands, with a new maximum of £424.001. The review for Northern Ireland maintained a different system of individual property values, with no bands and no maximum cap (Birrell, 2007). The income from rates in Northern Ireland is divided into two components: a district rate to support district councils; and a regional rate, centrally determined, to support services such as education, social care and housing, which are local government services in Great Britain but a central responsibility in Northern Ireland.

Since 1984, local council taxation has been subject to capping by central government through a ceiling imposed on the planned budget of any local authority that is regarded as excessive, and this was applied selectively and proved politically controversial (Wilson and Game, 2006, p 209). UK governments have taken stronger powers to restrict local councils increasing local council taxes and limiting their spending on services and their ability to compensate for reductions in central government grants. Since 2012/13, local authorities in England have been required to determine whether the amount of council tax they plan to raise is excessive using a departmental formula. Any authority proposing such an increase had to hold a referendum to obtain a 'yes' vote. For 2015/16, local authorities could not raise council tax by 2% or more without a referendum. Only one such referendum has been held by a Police and Crime Commissioner and the proposal to increase council tax was defeated. More significant was the decision by the new Conservative government to freeze council tax over the lifetime of the Parliament. The government, as part of the general spending round, provides additional grant funding to support councils that freeze council tax but keeping council tax low meant a loss of revenue of some £3.7 billion (Local Government Association and ADASS, 2014). In Scotland, council tax has been frozen annually since 2007/08 and the freeze has been funded by providing an extra £70 million each year in the local government finance settlement. The Welsh government has taken a different approach in allowing each council to decide with no national freeze, and it can be noted that council taxation is lower in Wales than in England, as it is in Northern Ireland, where the regional rate is frozen but the district rate is not. In 2015, financial pressures on adult social care led to councils in England being permitted to raise council tax by up to 2% for expenditure on adult social care only.

Local government in the UK is very dependent for any discretionary expenditure on the local council tax, whereas in most developed countries, local government has access to a range of local taxes, including local sales taxes, local income tax, hotel taxes and others. Since 1990, most non-domestic properties in England are liable to nationally set rates, which are also known as 'business rates'. There were a number of exemptions, for example, for small businesses and discretionary reliefs. The rates were collected by local councils and the receipts were passed to central government, which pooled and redistributed the income to local councils. Variation of the system of business rates operated in the devolved administrations. From 2013, the system in England was reformed through the introduction of the business rates retention scheme, which allowed local authorities to keep half of the proceeds in business rates revenue to invest in local services. This was seen as a way of encouraging councils to promote business growth. Further reforms announced in 2015 will mean that local councils can retain 100% of business rates by 2020, some £26 million of revenue. At the same time, the main grant from Whitehall would be phased out, ensuring that the reform was fiscally neutral. Areas that choose to have city-wide elected mayors would be able to increase rates for spending on local infrastructure projects as long as they had the support of local business. Such a change will create difficulties for local authorities in poorer areas with a low tax base and raises issues of compensation.

Central government funding

A range of funding grants has formed the basic core of local government. Grants may be general in nature and devised to take into account the needs of local areas, or specific to services. Central funding may cover the cost of services or encourage local councils to deliver services but leave some discretion. The Department for Communities and Local Government negotiates the amount of central government funding for local authorities with the Treasury and assesses the impact on local services (National Audit Office, 2014d, p 28). Historically, the main revenue grant in England was the Revenue Support Grant (RSG), which was the core element of the local government finance settlement. Prior to 2013/14, this was distributed through the local government finance settlement based on the socio-economic and demographic characteristics of authorities and the councils' council tax-raising capacity. From 2013/14 local councils general revenue expenditure consisted of the RSG and the Business Rates Retention Scheme. Under this new system, local authorities keep half of local business rates revenue and the other half is used to fund the majority of RSG (DCLG, 2015a, p 36). Basically, this revenue can be used to finance revenue expenditure to deliver any local government service. In 2013/14, central government grants amounted to £75.3 billion, decreasing by 3.8% to £72.4 billion for 2014/15. This has meant that more grant-dependent authorities in England, generally poorer ones, have seen their spending power reduced more than less grant-dependent councils – by as much as 40% for some councils. Specific grants are allocated mainly by individual government departments and are usually ring-fenced for specific services and projects, for example, nursery education and Hull's celebration as UK's City of Culture. The Housing Revenue Account, funded by rents and other income, is a ring-fenced account, which means that rents cannot be raised to support council tax levels. The UK government has announced the introduction of a national funding formula for schools from 2017/18 so that local authorities will no longer determine how much funding schools are allocated. It is the intention that local authorities will retain all business rates revenue, leading to the end of the central government grant, which may disadvantage councils in weaker economic areas.

In Scotland, the local government finance settlement is a single-year settlement and provides councils with revenue funding and support for capital expenditure. This is negotiated with the Convention of Scottish Local Authorities as far as possible. Specific funding has recently been included to fund the council tax freeze, pay discretionary housing payments and to compensate for business rates reductions and for specific government spending commitments, including free school meals and a teachers' induction scheme. The Welsh government provides around 80% of the money allocated annually to local authorities in Wales through a revenue support scheme, government grant programmes and capital grants. Again, the financial settlement involves negotiations with the Welsh Association of Local Authorities and a feature of the Welsh system has been a financial distribution using a needs-based formula, carried out by a joint Welsh government and local authority working group. This has involved the use of 50 social indicators. The existing system is under review by an independent commission on local government finance in Wales.

Other sources of finance

The delivery of some services by local government results in income for local authorities through sales, fees and charges. Since 1989, local councils in England have been able to charge for any service except education and emergency services. They receive income from fees and charges from over 100 different service areas. The total income is around £12.6 million, a figure that has not altered much between 2009 and 2014, and represents only 2% of total income. Older people, including older mentally ill people, is the service area with the highest sales, fees and charges, having receipts of £2.2 million (DCLG, 2015a, p 39).

Capital funding is that used by local authorities for buying, constructing or improving physical assets, mainly in the areas of transport, housing or regeneration, and education. Local authorities can use their own revenue funds, capital receipts or receive central government support for specific projects for a major part of their capital programmes. Since 2003, local authorities in England, Scotland and Wales, and since 2011, in Northern Ireland, can also borrow to fund additional investment in capital infrastructure as long as they follow a prudential code and can service the debt. They may also attract funds from other sources, such as the national lottery. About a quarter of capital expenditure is financed through self-financed borrowing.

Expenditure on services

Local government expenditure in the UK accounts for approximately one quarter of total government expenditure. Statistics for net current expenditure show that education, social care and housing dominate (see Table 5.2).

Local government total expenditure in England has dropped in recent years, from £160 billion for 2011/12 to £157 billion in 2013/14, largely reflecting a major reduction in core funding from central government in line with strategies to reduce the UK deficit. The Local Government Association has reported that core funding has reduced by over 40% in the five years up to 2015. Council tax has reduced by 5.8% in real terms between 2010 and 2015 (Local Government Association, 2015f) and it has been estimated that there has been a 25% real-terms reduction in local authority income between 2010 and 2015 (National Audit Office, 2015a). Local government in England has been faced with the worst financial settlement in living memory (Hastings et al, 2015a) and potentially the biggest cuts. Adult social care has been under extreme financial pressure and has had to find savings of £3.5 billion over the four years from 2011 to 2015. Local authorities have tried to protect social care by measures such as cross–subsidies, use of resources and investment (Local Government Association, 2015e). The situation of local government can be contrasted with the ring-fencing of health

Table 5.2: Net current expenditure in England, 2013/14

Services	Percentage
Education	32
Social care	19
Housing, including benefits	20
Police	10
Environment and planning	7
Highways and transport	5
Public health	2
Fire and rescue	2

Source: DCLG (2015a, p 43).

expenditure. Other services hit have been early intervention grants, children's centres and youth services. Local authorities have acted through efficiencies to attempt to continue service provision but fear not being able to provide all core services. The scale of reductions does vary between geographical areas and there is evidence of disproportionate cuts in more deprived areas (Bailey et al, 2015). For many councils, it has become more difficult to deliver their statutory services to a sufficient standard (National Audit Office, 2014d, p 5). The UK government announced in a spending review that local authorities in England dealing with social care could apply a social care precept of a 2% rise in council tax (Communities and Local Government Committee, 2016, p 3). Apart from funding pressures, there are cost pressures due to the ageing population, public health duties and social housing support, as well as the impact of welfare reform. In Scotland and Wales, reductions in services have also occurred but the devolved administrations have been able to shelter local councils to an extent.

Organisation and political management

The internal organisation of councils has also undergone significant change in recent years, particularly in England. Whatever the internal organisation, a continuing important context is the political composition of local councils. The political balance in councils is subject to frequent change, especially because of the roll-on electoral process in many councils. The breakdown for 2015 for England showed that the Conservatives controlled 52% of councils, Labour 29%, the Liberal Democrats 2% and Other 1%, with no party in overall control of 21% (Local Government Information Unit, 2015). Political parties in control are in a position to influence council policy and aspects of expenditure and service delivery. Political party groupings on councils may differ in interests and capacities and take differing approaches, from the highly active to the more mechanistic (Copus, 2004). Many councils, however, operate their internal structures on the basis of the power-sharing of posts. For more than a century, local government was run by a committee system, with major decision-making vested in large groups of elected councillors. The committee system was changed by the Local Government Act 2000, prompted by a trend away from the tradition of separate committees for each discrete area – housing, education, planning and so on – to more broadly defined responsibilities – lifelong learning, children and young people, and health and well-being (Fenwick and Elcock, 2004). The new arrangements allowed for a choice of three options: a leader chosen by the council and cabinet, with cabinet members responsible for a particular section; an elected mayor and cabinet following a referendum to approve the change; and the option of the old committee system for councils with a population below 85,000.

By 2015, only 15 councils had arranged for the elected mayor and cabinet model. The main format was the council leader and a cabinet of two to 10 members. The cabinet as a whole could advise on policy and monitor the processes of service implementation. Cabinet members can have extensive delegated powers and operate with considerable autonomy or the cabinet could work in a more collective way. Cabinet members were advised by the council's professional staff but did not require committee approval for all decisions. It became usual practice for councils to have overview committees through which the non-executive councillors could challenge and question the cabinet members. The council budget had to be passed by the full council. Local councils had a range of statutory and regulatory committees outside this organisational structure. Special statutory committees have included health overview and scrutiny committees and, more lately, health and well-being boards. Regulatory committees include licensing, planning and audit committees. The most common management model, leader and cabinet, did begin to appear in various hybrid formats. A typical example was Birmingham City Council, with cabinet leads for: health and social care; children's services; inclusion and community safety; neighbourhoods and housing; learning and culture; development; and two leads for commissioning and sustainability. Another council had only four cabinet leads and called them deputy mayors. There were also criticisms of the organisational systems placing too much power in a small number of councillors. A change was eventually allowed in the system under the Localism Act 2011, allowing councils more freedom to create their own organisation and hold a referendum to revert back to a committee system.

Local government in Wales has followed a similar pattern to England, using the model of a leader and cabinet. The cabinets in larger areas, Cardiff and Swansea, have nine members, but in smaller councils, there may only be a few cabinet members. The configuration does indicate cabinet members for the main social service areas – children's services, health, social care and well-being, communities and housing – and in Swansea, there is also an anti-poverty cabinet lead. A system of scrutiny committees also operates. Scotland is rather different in that it has adhered to the traditional committee system. A distinction is also made between the council leader and the mayor or provost. Local authorities in Scotland can devolve most decision-making to a structure of committees and subcommittees. Glasgow has a very extensive committee structure, including area subcommittees. There is no requirement for councils to adopt a particular decision-making and scrutiny structure, and in recent years, some councils have altered arrangements in the interests of efficiency and accountability. Local government in Northern Ireland has also kept to a committee structure for its more limited functions.

Conclusions

In recent years, central government policies have had a major impact on core social services, especially through developing privatisation and outsourcing, and deregulation in areas of social care, education, housing, youth services and planning. The state of flux in delivery functions is also highlighted by the allocation of new functions in public health, health scrutiny and welfare assistance. It has been forecast that by 2020, health and local government integration will have progressed substantively and to such an extent that there will be a case for considering how departmental responsibilities at Whitehall might be best divided to enable integration (New Local Government Network, 2016).

Local government has developed new approaches and policies. These include a broad commitment to the well-being of individuals and communities, partly using general competence powers and covering social, economic, environmental, cultural and physical dimensions. There has also been an adoption of anti-austerity approaches by many councils throughout the UK, using the powers and resources available to them to mitigate the impact of austerity measures and welfare reform. The UK government has been keen to promote a new culture and emphasis in the operations of local government on business growth and economic development. In recent years, all councils have also had to pay attention to performance management, value for money, better value and improved outcomes. There has also been a growth in shared services as a delivery model between councils, which may be more attractive to councils than outsourcing as they can exercise more control (Sandford, 2015a).

A further shared and dominant trend has been the growth of partnership working, with the most important and widespread partnership working between local government, social care services and health services, often leading to formal partnership arrangements, as in Scotland. However, partnership working is evident across a range of local government services in areas such as supported housing, community safety, public health, family services, services for immigrants and urban and rural regeneration. This large and growing volume of partnership working links local government with UK government departments, devolved departments, quasi-autonomous non-governmental organisations (quangos), the private sector, the voluntary sector and social enterprises. It has been argued that this has led to a more fragmented structure of governance and delivery which has become confusing for users and the public, and clouds where accountability lies (Jones and Stewart, 2012). At the same time, the increase in partnership working and provision has increased local government activities and compensated for some loss of functions.

SIX

Delegated governance: 'quangos' and services

Introduction

Public bodies, other than government departments and local government, are usually referred to as 'quangos' (quasi-autonomous non-governmental organisations) or increasingly as 'arm's-length bodies' (ALBs). Despite a historic tendency to neglect their status as a third arm of public administration, they constitute a permanent and very significant aspect of delivery and have been described as fundamental to the efficient running of the British state (Gash et al, 2010). Quangos developed rapidly as an important feature of the establishment of the welfare state in the post-war period and played a major role in the organisation of welfare services and the delivery of services to the public (Butcher, 1995). They are now responsible for between a quarter and a third of central government expenditure, a higher proportion than local government expenditure. Following changes by the successive governments across the UK, they have become closer to replacing local government as the main vehicle for delivering social services.

The definition of and the identification of quangos has been a somewhat elastic exercise given their large numbers. A House of Commons Select Committee used a definition of quangos as all bodies responsible for developing, managing or delivering public services or policies, or performing public functions, with a membership of wholly or largely appointed persons (Public Administration Select Committee, 2001). The official listing of what are termed 'non-departmental public bodies' (NDPBs) by the UK government uses the following definition: 'an NDPB is a body which has a role in the processes of national government but is not a government department or part of one and therefore operates to a greater or lesser extent at arm's-length from the minister' (Cabinet Office, 2012, p 1). The bodies classified as NDPBs do not include all apparent quangos and a wider definition can be used that states what they are not, that is, that quangos are all public bodies outside government departments and local government. A House of Commons Select Committee (Public Administration Select Committee, 2011) suggested adopting the term 'arm's-length bodies' to describe the totality of public sector organisations.

Quangos make up a sector created mainly through the allocation of functions by government departments, and, as such, are a form of delegated governance, managed by an appointed board, not by an elected body. The rationale for their use relates to a number of key factors, which are listed in Box 6.1.

Box 6.1: Rationale for quangos

- Administration by a board representing expertise and skills, whether, commercial, managerial, professional or legal.
- Upholding impartiality and independence and depoliticising decision-making. This may be of value in contentious areas or where more freedom from political interference and ministerial inputs is desired.
- The promotion of efficiency through a focus on a single issue in contrast to the multifunctional operation of departments and local authorities, which provides a clear focus, public clarity and a board with specialist knowledge.
- The promotion of flexible approaches through greater autonomy to innovate, exercise discretion to take more entrepreneurial approaches and increase operational independence in areas of recruitment, management, advertising, public relations, partnerships and delivery operations.
- The promotion of diversity, with a board representing diverse backgrounds and views.

Apart from these rationales, the development and size of the quango sector can be explained by reference to more theoretical considerations. Processes of the hollowing out of the central state can result in delegation to quangos in a format where a level of delivery and decision-making may function in practice almost outside the formal political organisations. A further trend to depoliticisation has also encouraged the use of more ALBs, aligned with a need for growing expertise and scientific knowledge in implementing policy initiatives. A third development has been that of multilevel governance, with quangos established by and responsible to devolved governments.

Types of quango

Lists of classifications of quangos are largely in agreement but demonstrate some differences in interpretations. The Cabinet Office (2012) lists four types of NDPBs, as outlined in Box 6.2.

Box 6.2: Classification of quangos

Executive NDPBs
- These are normally established by statute and carry out directly executive, delivery, administrative, regulatory, funding and commercial functions.
- They operate with a board appointed by a minister.
- They have a parent or sponsoring department.
- They employ their own staff who are not civil servants.
- They have their own budget.

Advisory NDPBs

- These provide expert advice to ministers on a wide range of issues.
- Their focus is on policy issues rather than delivery, but, on occasions, the advice may relate to delivery matters.
- Advisory NDPBs are usually small in size with little funding.

Tribunal and quasi-judicial NDPBs

- These have jurisdiction in the specialist field of administrative law and their quasi-judicial role is focused on individual complaints.
- These include inspection and regulatory bodies.
- Independent monitoring boards are listed by the Cabinet Office as covering prison watchdogs but this category can be extended to include a range of regulatory and inspection bodies, many of which relate to aspects of social services.

Public corporations

- Historically, public corporations have been a distinct category with responsibility for the running of nationalised industries and combining commercial freedom with public accountability.
- Few public corporations remain in existence.

Health-related quangos are, on occasions, listed separately as bodies authorised to provide NHS services or as specialist health bodies. However, these bodies are in most respects akin to an executive NDPB, have the Department of Health as their parent department and can be considered as executive quangos. Executive NDPBs and other executive quangos are the most significant bodies for the delivery of social services. The role of regulatory and monitoring bodies is discussed further in Chapter 10. There are a number of grey areas in the definition and classification of public bodies and confusion with other public bodies (Walker, 2014). The boundary with voluntary bodies can also cause some confusion. Thus, housing associations have traditionally been seen as part of the voluntary sector and have management boards not appointed by ministers. Another relatively new category are departmental taskforces, usually set up to give advice or undertake some action on a short-term and ad hoc basis, which are a somewhat hybrid category of quango. Examples set up in Scotland are taskforces on health inequalities, fuel poverty, early years and refugees. There can be arbitrary distinctions. The Care Quality Commission is a quango, a non-departmental public body, but the Office for Standards in Education (Ofsted), also an inspectorate, is a non-ministerial department, for reasons that are not clear (Public Administration Select Committee, 2014).

A further important divergent aspect of quangos relates to their jurisdiction within the UK. Quangos may differ in their constitutional and geographical jurisdiction (see Box 6.3).

> **Box 6.3: Jurisdiction of quangos dealing with social welfare services within the UK**
>
> - Cover England only.
> - Cover Great Britain only, that is, England, Scotland and Wales.
> - Cover England and Wales only.
> - Cover the whole UK, including Northern Ireland.
> - Devolved quangos covering Scotland, Wales or Northern Ireland only.

Government policies on the use of quangos

The landscape and the number of quangos reflects contradictory policies, a process of uncoordinated growth of quangos in some areas and comprehensive attempts by successive government administrations to reduce overall numbers, as well as the lack of a strategic approach to the governance of quangos.

The numbers in the official list of public bodies does not represent all quangos and a number count does not convey the significance of the continuing core of executive quangos in delivering services. It has been noted that nearly 80% of NDPB expenditure was located in just 15 NDPBs (Gash et al, 2010, p 10).

The attention of the Conservative government led by Mrs Thatcher was drawn to the large number of public bodies and the incompatibility with government policies on increasing efficiency and reducing the state. Action was taken to abolish many advisory bodies and a major review of autonomous executive public bodies was launched. However, the review was to recommend the abolition of only 30 out of a total of 489 bodies examined (Pliatzky, 1980). This review was also to introduce the term 'non-departmental public bodies'. The Conservative government went on to abolish public corporations with the end of almost all nationalised industries. However, between 1979 and 1991, the number of executive quangos and other quangos did not significantly drop as the

Table 6.1: Number of executive and advisory NDPBs

Year	Executive NDPBs	Advisory NDPBs
1979	492	1,485
1980	489	1,561
1997	305	610
2000	276	460
2005	211	458
2009	192	405
2012	185	215
2013	175	170
2014	154	149
2015	111	146

government sought to achieve efficiency gains and to tackle problems by moving from multifunctional bodies to more single-purpose bodies.

The incoming Labour government also made a promise to reduce the number of quangos and to create new bodies only if they were cost-effective. A government review, *Opening the Doors to Quangos* (Cabinet Office, 1998), stressed the positive attributes and benefits of quangos and recommended improvements by opening them up to greater scrutiny. This would involve annual open meetings, consultations with stakeholders, bringing them under the Freedom of Information Act and the remit of the ombudsman, and opening up public appointments. These policies meant only a small reduction in the number of quangos. Nearly 200 new quangos were established in the 10 years from May 1997, replacing almost as many as were abolished or merged, and total expenditure increased in real terms (Flinders, 2008). A range of new and powerful executive quangos were created and many reflected new policies in health, social care, education and other areas of social policy (see Box 6.4).

Box 6.4: Examples of new quangos established by the Labour government

Health and social care (35 in total)
- National Institute of Clinical Excellence.
- Health Development Agency.
- General Social Care Council.
- Council for Quality of Health Care.
- Commission for Public and Patient Involvement.
- Health Protection Agency.
- National Patient Safety Agency.
- NHS Appointments Commission.
- NHS foundation trusts.
- Monitor.
- National Care Standards Committee.
- Independent Reconfiguration Board.

Education (13 in total)
- Qualifications and Curriculum Authority.
- School Funding Agency.
- Learning and Skills Council.
- Office of Fair Access.
- Sector Skills Development Agency.

(continued)

Social policy (11 in total)
- Low Pay Commission.
- Youth Justice Board.
- Children's Commission for England.
- Independent Pension Commission.
- Disability Rights Forum.
- New Deal Taskforces.

Further major changes to the quango landscape and the sponsorship role of Whitehall departments occurred following the establishment of devolution for Scotland, Wales and Northern Ireland (see later). The Labour administration under Gordon Brown saw some further reform processes aimed, in part, at the abolition of more bodies (Maer, 2011, p 4). A report on the reform of ALBs (Cabinet Office, 2010b) recommended that proposals for any new quangos should be subject to a value-for-money assessment and there should be a sunset clause for new bodies.

Continuing review of quangos

Prior to the 2010 UK election, all the parties had spoken of a need to reduce the complex quango landscape. The UK Coalition's programme for government contained a commitment to reduce the number and costs of quangos. It was suggested that the range of responsibilities handed to public bodies and the amount of money they received was at an all-time high of some £38 billion, and that the sector had grown out of control (Cabinet Office, 2010b). Shortly after taking office, the Coalition government, with both parties in agreement, undertook a major review of all quangos sponsored by government departments. The original objective was to achieve savings and ensure value for money, and a number of departments quickly announced some abolitions and mergers. As the Maude review got under way, the principal objective changed to increasing the accountability of quangos in order to ensure that bodies would be subject to direct democratic accountability (Public Administration Select Committee, 2010, p 27). In this major review, each quango was subject to several tests, as follows: 'If the body carried out highly technical functions requiring precise expertise; If the body required the freedom to be politically impartial; If it needed to act independently to establish facts' (Cabinet Office, 2010b, p 34).

Quangos that passed one test were to be retained but reforms could be introduced to increase their efficiency and accountability. Otherwise, if a quango failed one test, it faced abolition, and it was a major intention to bring quangos back within departments. The government expected to make savings of some £2.6 billion. The Select Committee on Public Administration was to argue that, in practice, the judgements made were not precise, with the application of the three tests being 'hopelessly unclear' and a consistent approach not being applied (Public Administration Select Committee, 2010, p 10).

The government response to the criticisms by the Select Committee on Public Administration did expand upon the objectives of their strategy, referring to streamlining the public bodies landscape, saving taxpayer's money and removing duplication and waste, as well as contributing to cutting the fiscal deficit (Cabinet Office, 2011). In responding to criticisms of the use of the three tests, the government asserted that the test framework had to be consistent but also sufficiently flexible to allow individual ministers to make decisions in the context of wider reforms to key aspects of public policy. The initial review process was undertaken in a short timescale, covering 904 organisations, with advice and a toolkit supplied by the Cabinet Office. This amounted to a major restructuring of the machinery of government. It has been suggested that some departments used the public body reform process to aid the delivery of policy objectives by streamlining work and clarifying responsibilities, while, in other cases, reforms were driven by deficit-reduction objectives (Skelcher et al, 2013). The outcome of the review process was to specify the action to be taken for each NDPB, as outlined in Table 6.2.

While the number of abolitions seemed large, quite a few were actually not operating or incurring costs. The specifications for reform and changes were quite significant in some cases, for example, the Equality and Rights Commission. The number of bodies involved varied across departments and was somewhat unbalanced by the large number of bodies sponsored by the Ministry for Justice.

The overall numbers of NDPBs in each category were affected by the multiple numbers of bodies in some classes of quangos, for example, eight regional development agencies, 15 agricultural wages committees and the merger of advisory committees for Justices of the Peace falling from 101 to 49 (Skelcher et al, 2013, p 8). The recommendation for abolition covered a range of options: confirming that some bodies had ceased to operate; the abolition of a few bodies that did operate, for example, Standards for England; the transfer of functions to government departments, such as child support and qualifications and curriculum development; the transfer of functions to charities and the voluntary sector; and a few transfers to local government. The vast majority of abolished bodies were very small advisory bodies and few of the large executive NDPBs were affected (Dommett et al, 2014, p 140). Many small advisory quangos were reconstituted as department committees of experts (Rutter, 2014).

Table 6.2: Outcome of the review of public bodies

Outcome	2010		2015	
	Number	Percentage	Number	Percentage
Abolished	192	21%	195	22%
Merged	118	13%	101	11%
Retained	380	42%	398	44%
Retained and reformed	171	19%	132	15%
Under review	40	4%	10	1%

Source: Cabinet Office (2010b, 2015).

Table 6.3: Outcome of review, by core social policy department

Department	Abolished	Merged	Retained	Retained and reformed	Under review	Total
Health	30	–	10	–	–	40
Work and Pensions	3	2	8	–	2	15
Education	6	–	3	–	8	17
Communities and Local Government	11	4	35	–	1	51
Home Office	2	1	10	–	3	16
Ministry for Justice	29	105	209	4	3	350
Cabinet Office	7	–	6	–	2	15
Business and Skills	21	6	20	1	9	57
Total (core social policy departments)	109	13	301	5	28	361
Total (all departments)	192	118	380	171	40	901

Source: Cabinet Office (2010b).

A major vehicle for the reform process was the enactment of the Public Bodies Bill 2011 as enabling legislation allowing ministers through an order in council to abolish, merge or transfer the functions of public bodies (Maer, 2011). A clause in the Bill requires ministers to consider that rules passed under clauses to improve the exercise of public functions have regard to efficiency, effectiveness, economy and securing appropriate accountability to ministers but there was concern about the arbitrary use of powers by ministers (Pearson et al, 2015, p 4). A number of other pieces of legislation have contributed to the reform process. The Health and Social Care Act 2010 included plans to cut the number of health bodies to help meet the government's commitment to cut NHS administrative costs, including the abolition of primary care trusts (PCTs) and strategic health authorities. The Education Act 2011 incorporated plans to abolish: the General Teaching Council for England; the Training and Development Agency for Schools; the Qualifications and the Curriculum Development Agency; and the Young People's Learning Agency. The Localism Act 2011 took forward plans to abolish the London Development Agency and the Tenants' Services Authority (Cabinet Office and Efficiency and Reform Group, 2014).

The Cabinet Office and departments reported good progress in reducing the numbers of public bodies (Cabinet Office, 2015). By December 2013, 283 (92%) of the planned reduction of 308 in the number of bodies through abolition or merger had been completed. By the end of the reform programme, there would be 598 quangos, 306 fewer than in 2010 (National Audit Office, 2014a). This would represent the largest restructuring of public bodies in decades. As noted, a key aim of the review was to improve direct accountability by bringing functions closer to elected representatives. The National Audit Office (2014a, p 7) found that departments had not yet produced evidence on public value. It has been pointed out that the process of change was not all one-way as some important new quangos came into existence, for example, the Office of Budget Responsibility and NHS England (Pearson et al, 2015).

Triennial reviews

A new system by the UK government of triennial reviews of quangos was instituted as a second phase of the reform process. The new system of triennial reviews for NDPBs commenced in 2011/12, based on guidance issued by the Cabinet Office. The review would examine the key functions of an NDPB, the contribution to the work of the sponsor department, whether the functions were still needed, whether a quango was the most appropriate delivery model and then the body's control and governance arrangements (Cabinet Office, 2014, p 7). In round one of the reviews, 156 NDPBs were to be reviewed, and by December 2013, departments had completed 30 reviews covering 77 bodies (National Audit Office, 2014a). Only four of the first 30 reviews, covering 38 out of the 77 bodies involved, recommended that the bodies concerned should no longer continue and 35 of these were probation trusts (National Audit Office, 2014a, p 7), which involved wider policy considerations. Although most reviews made recommendations for improvements to governance arrangements, they tended not to make explicit recommendations on improving performance or achieving savings. The Cabinet Office has not set out measurable objectives in terms of value for money for the triennial review programme (National Audit Office, 2014a, p 35). It has been suggested that there is a danger that triennial reviews will become an administrative burden rather than contributing to the departments' approach to delivery (Skelcher et al, 2013, p 11). A House of Commons inquiry found that the aims of triennial reviews have expanded over time and include aims around efficiency, transparency and contribution to economic growth (Public Administration Select Committee, 2014, p 21).

Composition of boards

A number of issues concerning the composition of appointed boards that governed quangos had attracted major attention by the 1990s. The issues that emerged related to: the representativeness of the membership of boards; the exercise of political patronage; the nature of appointment processes; and the appropriateness of the skills of board members. In 1996, only 24% of the membership of the boards of executive quangos were women (Skelcher, 1998, p 63) and there was a major under-representation of minority ethnic groups. There was also a predominance of people from a business background, which generated another debate as to what skills were necessary for board members. Evidence relating to the London bias of the membership of national quangos was also noted. The major attempt to tackle these issues came through the establishment in 1995 of the Office of Commissioner for Public Appointments. This followed a recommendation from the Nolan

Committee, which had examined current concerns about the standards of conduct of holders of public office and noted problems with quangos. It recommended an independent public appointments commissioner to monitor, regulate and approve departments' appointment processes. The Commissioner for Appointments has continued to regulate the processes by which ministers make appointments to the boards of public bodies for England and Wales, with Scotland and Northern Ireland having separate commissioners for public appointments. It has to be noted that appointments to a number of bodies are not regulated. Commissioners operate through a code of practice, monitor compliance, conduct regular audits and investigate complaints. Their main role has been described as firmly establishing appointments to public bodies on the basis of merit (Commissioner for Public Appointments, 2014) and maintaining a system free of political and personal patronage. The other major task that developed was the promotion of diversity and equality of opportunity, aimed at producing a more diverse field of candidates. A Centre for Public Appointments was also established in the Cabinet Office to promote best practice across departments. Progress with producing more diversity has been slow but published statistics show some progress. For 2013/14 in England, the proportion of women appointed had increased to 39.3%, the proportion from an minority ethnic background increased to 7.7% and of people with disabilities to 7.7%. The age profile remains skewed against younger people, with only 12% aged under 45 and only 1.6% under 35. While the merit principle operates, there has been some questioning of what constitutes merit in terms of decision-making abilities on the boards of quangos (Macleavy and Gay, 2005). In Wales, the criticism has been made that in focusing on serving specific professional skills and knowledge, board members may not sufficiently reflect the need for stronger local accountability and knowledge (Williams, 2014, p 46).

The appointment system has become a more independent system and parliamentary involvement has developed through pre-appointment hearings (with the relevant select committee), where scrutiny is exercised over some 50 posts. Overall, there have still been criticisms that public appointments are not sufficiently transparent, representative or accountable. An independent review made a recommendation, accepted by the government, for the use of more diverse assessment techniques (Grimstone, 2016).

Role in core social policy areas

Even with the reforms of quangos, the sector of delegated governance plays a major role in the delivery of social services in England (see Table 6.4).

Benefits/social security

The delivery of benefits is not a major area of quango responsibility. One of the more significant executive NDPBs in the area, the Independent Living Fund, ceased to exist in 2015. This had been set up in 1988 to deliver financial support to

Table 6.4: Quangos, by social policy area

Area of social policy	Executive NDPBs	Advisory NDPBs	Tribunal	Public corporation	Other	Total
Work, pensions, social security	6	2	2	2	1	13
Health and social care	7	8			6	21
Education	1/9	2			1	13
Housing	3	1				4
Employment	1	1				2

disabled people to enable more to live in the community rather than in residential care. As part of the programme of welfare reform, this function will transfer to local authorities in England and to the devolved administrations in Scotland, Wales and Northern Ireland. The remaining quangos sponsored by the Department for Work and Pensions (DWP) are somewhat marginal to social security. However, an advisory NDPB, the Social Security Advisory Committee (SSAC), is significant and much of its work can have an impact on the delivery of social security. The SSAC has existed since 1980 as an independent statutory body to provide advice and assistance to the secretary of state in response to a specific request or on its own initiative, and also to perform mandatory scrutiny of most of the proposed social security regulations. Advice offered formally by the SSAC in relation to proposals for legislation must be published by the secretary of state, along with the government's response to the advice and recommendations. The government is not obliged to act on other reports and recommendations produced by the SSAC, although, in practice, it normally does. A DWP–SSAC framework sets out relationship principles that enable the SSAC to provide independent, expert, well-informed and impartial advice. The department is committed to respecting the operational independence of the SSAC and it is specified that both bodies should regard each other as trusted partners (SSAC, 2014a). The SSAC also has a role in offering advice to the Treasury and HM Revenue and Customs on issues relating to tax credits, National Insurance and child benefit. The board of the SSAC has 13 members, although the staffing resource is small. The work of the SSAC also covers operational and delivery matters and has included a programme of visits to local offices to ensure that the board understands operational aspects of benefit delivery and the impact of reforms on the ground. The large scale of the implementation of welfare reform and the political controversy that it has produced has placed pressure on the framework relationship and some reports have been very critical of aspects of the implementation of welfare reform (SSAC, 2013a). A study on the cumulative impact of welfare reform on vulnerable groups such as disabled people highlighted the lack of analysis by government (SSAC, 2014b), but the minister for welfare reform refused to accept the accompanying recommendations. Work by the SSAC on the details of regulations will often produce more positive responses in looking afresh at detailed and technical aspects of, for example, universal credit and related regulations (SSAC, 2013b). The SSAC has evolved as an influential body in monitoring the delivery of social security and it can be noted that the SSAC's role and remit has no precise equivalent elsewhere in government (Saunders, 2007).

Health and social care

Health, in particular, is an area where delivery is dominated by a range of quangos. They can be divided into five categories (see Box 6.5).

Box 6.5: Categories of health quangos

1. Executive NDPBs – includes a number of quangos with significant functions, for example, NHS England.
2. Advisory NDPBs – reforms have reduced this category to eight specialist bodies, for example, the NHS Pay Review Body.
3. Other executive quangos – these are technically not NDPBs, but are similar in format and functions, for example, NHS Blood and Transplant.
4. Other regulatory quangos – for example, the General Social Care Council.
5. Structure of sub-national quangos – these are front-line delivery bodies and are extensive in number, for example, NHS foundation trusts.

In England, the delivery of the NHS is now effectively in the hands of quangos (Rutter, 2014, p 150). In 2013, NHS England replaced the NHS Commissioning Board, which supported and developed the commissioning of services. The major commissioning task continued as NHS England, with the largest budget of all quangos in England, allocates resources to the new clinical commissioning groups (CCGs), which had replaced another set of localised quangos, Primary Care Trusts (PCTs). A related task for NHS England is the commissioning of specialist services, primary care, offender health, armed forces and aspects of public health, including national immunisation and screening programmes (NHS England, 2015). NHS England has the normal NDPB structure of a board of non-executive directors, and the executive posts include some key to the whole delivery of the NHS. The chief executive of the NHS, the national medical director and the chief nursing officer are located in the quango, at arm's length from the Department of Health. The extensive nature of the functions performed by NHS England are demonstrated by a decentralised system of administration through four regional teams for the North, Midlands and East, London, and South and South-West, and 27 area teams. The Department of Health has described a complete working relationship with NHS England, with regular dialogue and clarification of delegated responsibilities from the department (Public Administration Select Committee, 2014, para 26).

NHS Improving Quality (NHSIQ) is part of NHS England and is not a separate quango, but is best considered a hybrid organisation. It was established in 2013 through a collaborative agreement between the Department of Health and NHS England to deliver improvement programmes and develop improvement capability and capacity. The work covers five domains: living longer, long-term conditions, acute care, positive experiences of care and patient safety. It was formed through bringing together a number of previous improvement bodies, some of whom had operated as separate quangos, including NHS Improvement, the NHS Institute for Innovation and Improvement, and bodies such as the National Cancer Action Team and NHS Diabetes and Kidney Care. Transfer into NHSIQ was part of the public bodies reform programme. The hybrid management structure has a five-person senior management team and a board, called a programme board, which includes representatives from NHS England, NHSIQ and the department (NHS Improving Quality, 2013).

Monitor was established in 2004 as an independent regulator for NHS foundation trusts. Its role was expanded in 2012 to become a sector regulator, with a remit to make the system work better for patients. The original responsibilities remained for approving application for foundation status, overseeing 147 foundation trusts, placing problem trusts in special measures and working with 40 trusts that were in financial difficulties in 2013/14 (Monitor, 2014). Monitor formerly had to act to ensure essential services are maintained if a trust is in difficulty. The troubled Mid Staffordshire NHS Foundation Trust was disbanded. In 2012/13, Monitor found 19 trusts in significant breach of their terms of authorisation, and in 2014, eight were in special measures. The expansion of Monitor's work saw it taking a major role in the promotion of integrated care and supporting pioneer schemes in making health and social care work better together. The board of Monitor largely followed normal practice, but was rather small in members, with only a chair, four non-executive directors and two directors. It also had four advisory groups, including a medical advisory group. The work of Monitor did attract some criticism, with the House of Commons Public Accounts Committee expressing concern at pressures and conflict between the traditional role of Monitor and its new responsibilities, mainly outside hospital settings. A further specific criticism was made concerning the level of clinical experience within Monitor (Public Accounts Committee, 2014). A major feature of Monitor's operation was its formal agreements with other quangos, which recognises the possibility of overlaps in responsibilities. It had an agreement with NHS England as there could be overlaps in commitments to work to produce better outcomes for patients and therefore a need to cooperate and work together to remove barriers to improvements.

The National Institute for Health and Care Excellence (NICE) is probably the most high-profile health quango. Its origins go back to 1999 and it developed as a national advisory body, but in 2013, it was established as an NDPB in legislation and its remit was extended to social care. Although having official advisory functions, it is classified by the department as an executive public body, really for the reasons that recommendations from NICE tend to be fully accepted and implemented and are regarded as binding. NICE is officially an England-only body but it does provide some advice and services for Scotland, Wales and Northern Ireland. NICE produces evidence-based guidance on a range of areas but mainly concerning: guidelines on managing specific conditions; technical appraisal of the clinical effectiveness of new drugs and products; guidance on diagnosis; and interventional procedures. These programmes are supported by online evidence resources for all health and social care professionals. The scope of NICE's activities was extended to cover social care. The composition of the NICE board is set down in legislation, and the membership largely reflects scientific expertise. The board is currently constituted to consist of eight non-executive members and four non-executive directors. An unusual innovation is the existence of a Citizens Council of 30 members, whose task is to provide a public perspective on overarching moral and ethical issues. This council operates through an open discussion process at a biennial session and publishes a report of its views. Much controversy has surrounded decisions by NICE on its assessment of new cancer drugs. Kadcyla is a drug that extends survival by around 5.8 months and could affect 1,500 people per year. NICE concluded that the high price of the treatment was still unaffordable for use on the NHS. NICE has stretched the top of an especially extended range of effectiveness for cancer drugs, and representations have been made to pharmaceutical companies to reduce the costs of new drugs. Judgements by NICE on blocking drugs it deems to be poor value for money has been criticised on the grounds that the drugs have been made available in other countries, including in Scotland.

Specialist health bodies

The Department of Health sponsors special health quangos that are formally not executive NDPBs, but, in practice, they function in ways akin to executive boards. These are of relatively new origin and have mostly been created through the merger of existing quangos, being part of the structural reforms introduced by the Health and Social Care Act 2012.

Box 6.6: Specialist health quangos

- NHS Blood and Transplant.
- Health Education England.
- Health Research Authority.
- NHS Litigation Authority.
- NHS Business Services Authority.
- NHS Trust Development Authority.

All six quangos play a role in delivering the NHS and may have some advisory functions. They all contribute to the operation of the NHS in England but may have some roles extending to Scotland, Wales or Northern Ireland. NHS Blood and Transplant supplies safe blood to hospitals in England and provides tissues and organs to hospitals across the UK. Associated tasks relate to increasing the number of blood donors and collecting, testing, processing, storing and delivering blood. Increasing organ donation is a further task, along with matching, allocating and analysing organs across the UK. Health Education England was established in 2012 to provide leadership in developing the education and training system to ensure a skilled workforce and a supply of professionally qualified workers. It is also responsible for producing high-quality education and training, promoting innovation, and allocating training resources. Health Education England works through 13 local education and training boards, which have the status of statutory committees. The Health Research Authority was established in 2011 to streamline procedures for approving health research and protecting the interests of patients. It has delivered a uniform system for approving research applications. The work of the Health Research Authority is carried out through a series of committees for special areas and some 1,000 people participate in committees, such as the research ethics committee.

The NHS Litigation Authority has existed since 1995 to manage negligence and other claims by patients against the NHS in England. From 2013, another quango, the National Clinical Assessment Service, became an operational division of the Litigation Authority. In practice, the Litigation Authority has attempted to resolve most claims out of court. A further function of this quango is to share lessons from dealing with claims to improve practice. The NHS Business Services Authority is somewhat different in providing a range of centralised backroom services to a number of NHS organisations, NHS contractors and the public. This includes payments to dentists, pharmacists and other contractors, the administration of prescription charges, and the administration of the European Health Insurance Card. This quango was set up in 2005 to take over the functions of five existing small quangos. The sixth of the specialist health bodies, the NHS Trust Development Authority, had a more specialised function: to monitor and support the non-foundation NHS trust sector. There are still 99 NHS trusts managing hospitals. The Trust Development Authority monitored the performance of the trusts, assured the quality of the work of the trusts and the governance arrangements, assessed risk, and also managed the appointments process to trust boards. From 2016, the NHS Trust Development Authority was merged with Monitor to form a new regulatory body, NHS Improved.

These special quangos operate under the normal procedures for executive quangos, with a framework of understanding setting out relationships with the relevant department. Health Education England is different in that the department published a mandate to guide the work of the quango and also published an education outcomes framework. Many of the functions are specialist and benefit from a clear arm's-length approach, but in a few cases, it is not so clear why a quango is especially necessary for delivering a service.

Sub-national health structures

The delivery of the NHS in England lies with an extensive structure of localised sub-national quangos, both for commissioning and for providing primary and secondary care. These structures have been subject to much change over the last decade. The delivery of acute and community health care has been the responsibility of a localised structure of NHS trusts. The traditional model of NHS acute trusts was of a hospital or hospitals in a geographical area, possibly plus community health services, managed by an appointed board and responsible to the Department of Health. Since 2004, this system has been subject to a process of transition to a new concept of foundation trust status. NHS foundation trusts are part of the NHS and subject to NHS inspection but have more operational freedoms to raise revenue from patients other than NHS patients and could work with local communities. The benefits were anticipated as: freedom to develop new ways of working, with less central control from the Department of Health; more involvement of local people in taking decisions; three-year commissioning contracts; the facility to carry forward surpluses; managing its own capital investments; and responding quickly to local needs. There were concerns about ownership passing from government, with foundation trusts entering into agreements with private companies, and with departure from national staff agreements. Existing NHS trusts had to apply for foundation status and be able to meet the main conditions. It was anticipated that all the NHS bodies would become foundation trusts by 2014, but by this time, 99 NHS trusts had still not changed status, with 123 NHS foundation trusts in existence. The outcome has been a dual system of local NHS quangos. In terms of the governance of quangos, there are three main differences. First, the board members of non-foundation trusts are appointed by an NHS Development Authority. In foundation trusts, there is still a board of executive and non-executive members but the non-executive members and the chief executive are appointed by a council of governors. The governors are elected by members of the trust, who register as local residents or users of services, and by nominees of stakeholder groups. Second, in terms of government control, that task for non-foundation trusts was undertaken by the NHS Development Authority (subsequently merged into NHS Improvement), which oversaw and held the trusts to account. They combined what was described as the hard edge of accountability over quality, finance and sustainability with support and development (NHS Development Authority, 2014). The overall aim was to get applications from the NHS trusts for transition to foundation status up to speed. Monitor, prior to 2016, oversaw the foundation trusts and ensured that they complied with the terms of their licence. Third, in terms of public accountability, the innovative method of the council of governors applies, as with their advisory, strategic and guardianship role, they can hold the foundation board to account. They can also develop relationships with local communities and have a legal duty to hold annual meetings with their members. Non-foundation trusts can operate a members' scheme to encourage accountability. A study of foundation trusts found it difficult to identify directly if the governors system had produced more social ownership or democracy and reported problems related to low voting and their ability to represent their constituencies (Bojke and Goddard, 2010), although 79% of governors said that they were clear about their role.

NHS health trusts are listed by the Department of Health in four categories, as detailed in Table 6.5. In each category, trusts may have the status of either a foundation or non-foundation trust. Acute trusts make up the largest category and the largest number of foundation trusts. Acute trusts are responsible for one or more hospitals and some may also provide services in the community. Ambulance trusts are the second category and four of the ambulance trusts now have foundation status. The third category is mental health NHS trusts, with responsibility for hospitals and community mental health care, and, in places, involved in integrated work with local authority social services. The name may indicate differences in focus, for example, Manchester Mental Health and Social Care Trust, Somerset Partnership NHS Trust, Mersey Care NHS Trust and Oxfordshire Learning Disability Trust. The fourth category is health and social care trusts or community health and social care trusts. These tend to be providers of community health services with community hospitals and some collaborative working with adult social care.

The commissioning and delivery of primary health care has undergone a significant change through the provisions of the Health and Social Care Act 2012. Previously, since 2002, a conventional structure of localised quangos had operated in the form of PCTs in England to take responsibility for both commissioning hospital care and delivering primary care. PCTs covered all GP practices in a geographic locality and their boundaries became coterminous with local authority boundaries, which facilitated joint working between health and social care. This system represented a collective approach to commissioning, replacing GP fund-holding. The adoption of a local quangos model facilitated the extensive involvement of local interests. PCTs had a board consisting of a chair and five non-executive members who could be drawn from GPs, other health professionals, local authorities and the community. The creation of PCTs was an attempt to engage local stakeholders as well as health professionals in the

Table 6.5: Categories of NHS trusts

Type	Non-foundation trusts	Foundation trusts	Total
Acute/hospital NHS trusts	57	92	149
Ambulance trusts	6	4	10
Mental health NHS trusts	14	38	52
Community health and care NHS trusts	22	4	26

Source: NHS Choices (2013).

governance of the NHS, decision-making and the allocation and management of resources, through a local quango model (Dowling and Glendinning, 2003). The PCT system found it difficult to meet the government's desire for greater commissioning from a variety of providers in order to ensure value for money and higher clinical standards. The granting of foundation status to hospitals also weakened the position of PCTs (Baggott, 2004). Some PCTs also began to delegate budgets to GP practice-based commissioning groups. Such pressures on the system were a factor in the Coalition government proposing a new structure for clinical commissioning in England.

The new government's view was that GPs were best placed to improve commissioning and should play a much more prominent role than was given to them with PCTs. From April 2013, PCTs were abolished and replaced by a new system of CCGs and this was essentially the main component of the Coalition government's reforms to the health and social care system. CCGs were seen as different from any predecessor NHS organisations. They were built around GP practices in a locality and have a governing body of appointments made by the membership of the CCGs. The main responsibility of CCGs is to commission secondary and community care services for their local population, that is, covering hospital care, rehabilitation care, emergency care, community health services and mental health services. CCGs do not commission primary care services or specialist services, or directly deliver services. Around two thirds of the NHS budget is under the control of the new bodies. The commissioning task involves measuring the needs of the local population, assessing which services are needed to meet these needs and then purchasing the appropriate services on behalf of patients (Naylor et al, 2013). A second major role for CCGs is to support quality improvement in general practice through more effective management of long-term conditions and better integration of primary, community and secondary care. The CCGs are NHS statutory bodies and have been referred to as membership bodies, but, in practice, they have many of the characteristics of quangos and can be seen as such.

Box 6.7: Composition of clinical commissioning groups

1. GPs or other health-care professionals.
2. Chair and accounting officer, chief finance officer and possibly chief operating officer.
3. Two lay members for governance and public involvement.
4. Two clinical members from secondary care and nursing.
5. Other directors.

Source: NHS Commissioning Board (2012)

A degree of discretion is left with the CCG over the exact composition (NHS Commissioning Board, 2012) and the actual number of governing body members can vary from 10 to 20. The number of GP members can vary, usually between three and six, there can be more lay members and the number of executive directors can vary. With 211 CCGs and considerable variations in size and the delegation of powers to localities, there is not a formal, hierarchical relationship between CCG leaders and member practices (Naylor et al, 2013, p 31). Overall, CCGs are accountable to NHS England. The composition and operating mode therefore suggests a model close to a quango model, except for the method of appointment, and they readily fall into the category of a form of delegated governance. Although the aim of the structures was to expand the role of GPs in commissioning, a study has shown that levels of GP engagement on CCGs are highly variable (Naylor et al, 2013, p 28). The introduction of CCGs has produced substantial criticism on a range of grounds, including the cost of the restructuring, redundancy and re-employment of staff, the facilitation of increased privatisation in commissioning, and expenditure on management consultants. The composition has been criticised as being dominated by GPs rather than other health professionals. Furthermore, many GPs do not have the time or knowledge to participate in service planning and funding and are not attracted by involvement in commissioning at a time of economic recession. Another major criticism has centred on the structural separation of primary commissioning from that for acute and community services and the lack of a whole-system approach in England (NHS Clinical Commissioners, 2014, p 3).

Given the complex structure of newly set up bodies, and in the context of the large number of bodies involved at the level of NHS trusts and CCGs, attention has also turned to the Department of Health offering support to bodies that wish to contemplate mergers. It is something of an anomaly in the context of government drives to reduce the number of public bodies in England that the number of CCGs exceed by far the number of PCTs they replaced. It has been argued that it has proved difficult to find a fit between separate commissioning quangos and provider quangos seeking to improve NHS services (Checkland et al, 2012).

Education quangos

The Department for Education sponsors very few quangos and the period of public body reforms was used to centralise some core functions under the direct control of the department. Three new executive agencies were created for funding, standards and testing, and teaching and leadership, in part drawn from previous quangos, while Office of Qualifications (Ofqual) and Ofsted are non-ministerial departments rather than quangos. This left only one NDPB, two advisory NDPBs and one other small quango. All of these quangos shared the characteristic of requiring a major degree of independence to operate at a clear arm's-length from the sponsor government department. This clearly applies to the deliberations and advice from the School Teachers' Review Body, which, since 1991, has made recommendations on teachers' pay, professional duties and working time. With restrictions on public sector pay increases, the minister has used powers to issue directions to the Review Body, thus limiting its room for manoeuvre. The Office of the Schools' Adjudicator is a small quango but makes sensitive decisions in responding to objections about possible breaches of schools' admission policies. The Social Mobility and Child Poverty Commission is technically an advisory NDPB but has some unique characteristics: it works with the DWP and the Cabinet Office, as well as its sponsoring Department for Education; it was established with 10 commissioners; and it has a former Labour minister as the chair and lead commissioner. Giving advice and undertaking social mobility advocacy could lead to possible conflict with government policies but the Commission has published research and analysis reports that have had some impact in government evaluation of services. Reports have covered: attainment gaps and social mobility in London; high-attaining children from disadvantaged backgrounds; higher education; and fair access and continuing elitism.

Since 2010, there has been a major transformation in the governors of schools, from 200 to some 4,500 by 2016, with the UK government's intention being that all maintained schools in England will transfer to academy status. Each school becomes the responsibility of an academy trust and the usual pattern is to set up multi-academy trusts to run a number of academies; over half of academies are in academy chains, but the majority have only three or four. Academy trusts are charitable companies with a board of trustees, thus resembling a type of quango. They can delegate functions to a local governing committee. The Public Accounts Committee found that the Department for Education did not have the resources to oversee the transformation, and criticised the lack of accountability for performance, financial probity and the effectiveness of academy sponsors (Public Accounts Committee, 2015). In 2016, 18 academy chains were 'paused' over concern about their performance. A controversial development in education administration has been the creation of eight regional school commissioners (RSCs) to perform departmental functions allowing schools to convert to academies, having intervention powers for underperforming academies and free schools. Each RSC gets support from a head-teacher board, which can be seen as hybrid quango model.

In relation to higher education, with a different sponsoring department, there are actually nine executive NDPBs. Seven are research councils with a research funding remit for mainly funding university research, covering medicine, the arts and humanities, engineering and physical sciences, the natural environment, the biological sciences, science and technology facilities, and the economic and social research council. Two NDPBs have significant delivery functions. The Higher Education Funding Council (HEFC) allocates public money to universities and colleges in England and monitors the quality of teaching and research. A range of other initiatives includes the National Student Survey, widening participation and administering a higher education innovation fund. HEFC has a governing board of 15 members. The Student Loan Company pays loans and grants to students and operates for the whole of the UK. Part of its function is to pay the tuition fees to colleges and to work with Revenue and Customs to collect loan payments. The Student Loan Company has a small but conventional board, consisting of five non-executive members and three executive directors. The Office for Fair Access has executive status, but, in practice, it is more advisory. It is an independent quango to promote and safeguard fair access to higher education and acts through approving and monitoring access agreements and forms of financial support. The main focus is on encouraging the acceptance of students from under-represented groups and low-income groups. The Office has a single director in the commissioner model who works with an 11-person advisory group.

Housing quangos

The use of government-sponsored quangos in the area of housing has been limited as delivery increasingly became a function of the private sector, as well as including the traditional involvement of local authorities and the voluntary sector. The department responsible for housing sponsors only three NDPBs, one of which is the Housing Ombudsman and the second is a small quango, the Leasehold Advisory Service. This NDPB does not as such advise the government, but gives free advice to leaseholders, landlords and financial advisers. However, the other NDPB, the Homes and Communities Agency, performs key delivery functions. Despite the agency's name, it is an executive quango with two areas of responsibility: first, as the national housing and regeneration agency for England; and, second, as the regulator of social housing providers. In practice, the Homes and Communities Agency delivers the government's affordable homes programme, increasing private housing supply through market interventions, bringing surplus land to the market and operating a Help to Buy equity loan scheme. Funding is provided for affordable home-building, mainly through housing associations. The main board of 10 members is responsible for this focus on delivering affordable homes and can work with advisory groups, for example, on rural housing (Homes and Communities Agency, 2014). A separate board of six members is responsible for the second main function of regulating the providers of social housing through maintaining a register and setting a regulatory framework with standards, but with an overall focus on economic regulation covering financial viability and value for money.

The main vehicle for delivering new social housing and managing the major part of social housing in England now rests with housing associations, sometimes referred to as registered social landlords. A large number of local authorities have transferred all or part of their housing stock to registered social landlords. Housing associations have their origins in specialist housing and social care charities but they have emerged as the main deliverer of social housing, replacing local authorities. This has given rise to a lack of clarity about the status of housing associations: should they be considered as public bodies and a form of quango or rather as part of the voluntary sector? They are independent bodies with a board, but not appointed by the department, and there is only limited remuneration for members, with overall funding from government, private sources and rents. They are not accountable directly to the department or minister but to the national quango, the Homes and Communities Agency. The composition of boards is in some respects similar to the conventional quango model, representing a range of interests and expertise with the use of non-executive directors, but housing associations are also under pressure to adopt a style more similar to governance outside the public sector (Hutchinson and Ward, 2010).

Employment matters

A range of quangos operate in the area of employment matters and two are of interest in social policy considerations. The Commission on Low Pay is an advisory body with a specific remit of advising the UK government on the national minimum wage. Its scope, therefore, covers the whole UK. It has adopted the commissioner model, with nine commissioners, including three from trade unions. The government uses the Commission to carry out detailed research and analysis and can request advice on specific issues, for example, the contribution of the minimum wage to the employment of young people. It is in a position to have determining impacts on changes in provision. The UK Commission on Employment and Skills is an executive NDPB, although it also has advisory functions. The Commission produces a large number of policy and research papers, most contributing to an advisory role, but also directly invests funding in employer-led projects in an executive function. Somewhat unusually, it covers the whole of the UK. Again, it uses the commissioner model, with 30 commissioners appointed on a representative basis from, specifically, large employers, trade unions, education, the voluntary sector and the devolved administrations.

Relationship with departments

All quangos have a relationship with at least one government department in their delivery role. There has not been a consistent approach between departments and bodies carrying out similar functions may be treated in different ways by departments. An analysis of 41 large quangos in England found that many aspects of the sponsorship arrangements were left undefined (Public Administration Select Committee, 2011). A number of reasons have been identified for the confusing nature of the relationships and the variation between largely hands-off and micromanagement approaches (see Box 6.8).

Examples can be given of poorly functioning relationships causing problems. Following problems over exam testing, an investigation found that there was a range of difficulties in the relationship between the then Department for Children, Schools and Families and the Qualifications and Curriculum Authority. There was a confusion of responsibilities and poor communication, and the department attempted to micromanage delivery (Children, Schools and Families Select

Box 6.8: Issues in relationships with departments

- A lack of clarity as to where the boundaries of responsibilities are drawn between a department and a quango, with departure from the presumption that quangos are given clear objectives but with operational freedom to deliver results. Insufficient clarity can lead to tensions over roles and responsibilities with the sponsor department and can lead to the duplication of functions.
- Weak mechanisms for maintaining productive institutional relationships between sponsor departments and quangos, and poor communication principles and systems.
- The hasty creation of some quangos can mean that little attention is paid to setting out relationships.
- Insufficient focus on developing the skills necessary for operating relationships. A specialist skill set is seen as desirable. These tasks may be handed to junior staff or staff at too low a level in departments and problems may be accentuated by a high turnover of staff.
- No agreed best practice on how to organise sponsorship, whether through a core team to relate to all quangos or whether through the policy groupings in a department.
- A tendency for some departments or sections of departments to involve themselves too closely in day-to-day delivery issues that are the responsibility of the quango.

Source: Adapted from Gash et al (2010)

Committee, 2008). In 2011, a similar problem was identified in the relationship between the Department of Health and the Care Quality Commission, with ineffective performance monitoring and inadequate staffing assessments (National Audit Office, 2011). In 2010, a review of the Youth Justice Board found a lack of clarity about its role, both within the board and the sponsor department (Gash et al, 2010). The lack of clarity can give rise to core delivery problems, with the duplication of functions, neglect of some issues, failing responsibilities, neglect of the role of quangos in the department and extra costs. It has been reported that the majority of executive quangos or delivery quangos are given less freedom from departments. Government departments or ministers tend more readily to get the blame for failures in the performance of major quangos.

An Institute for Government study, despite the identification of difficulties, did find that more than two thirds of those leading large NDPBs describe their relationships with sponsor departments as good. However, sponsor departments often appeared to have difficulties in avoiding either micromanagement or the neglect of quangos, both of which impeded cost-effectiveness (Gash et al, 2010). The issue remains of finding the balance between freedom and control. Proposals for departments supplying back-office functions for quangos may produce cost benefits but, again, raise questions of reducing the freedom, responsibilities and specialist approaches of quangos. The Institute for Government, along with the Public Chairs' Forum, has suggested a framework with recommendations for more effective relationships with departments. A dynamic differentiated approach to managing their portfolio with quangos was proposed based on the degree of required independence of the quango and the riskiness to the achievement of department and government objectives (Rutter et al, 2012, p 8). Among the other recommendations suggested were: that the Cabinet Office and Treasury agree a standard data set for quangos in consultation with sponsor departments; that quangos should be involved in the development of a long-term controls framework; and that the Cabinet Office should produce guidance to ministers on the expectations for their role in respect of their departments' quangos. The report, *It Takes Two*, concluded that departments must recognise the important functions performed by quangos/ALBs and the importance of effective sponsorship, while quangos must understand how best to contribute to department objectives (Rutter et al, 2012, p 9). A standard set of principles or practices, or a one-size-fits-all approach, may be untenable in determining the balance between department control and a quango's freedom to perform its functions. Gash and Rutter (2011, p 99) note that the independence requirement is not uniform. Regulatory bodies and bodies preventing discrimination, adjudicating or hearing appeals, or making scientific judgements need more formal independence than those delivering services or grants within frameworks or strategies set by ministers. In response to criticisms of weaknesses in the guidance on public bodies published by the Cabinet Office, the government agreed to produce a new set of principles of good corporate governance for executive NDPBs, including a requirement to consult ministers on business plans, but the principles were not a rigid set of rules and regulations (Cabinet Office, 2011, p 20). The Cabinet Office (2014) has specified conditions for ALBs to check expenditure, deliver value for money and ensure governance reform; it has been suggested that the new tough conditions represent a shift from loose–loose to tight–tight management (Dommett et al, 2014).

The government proceeded to set out guiding principles for relationships between sponsors in departments and quangos, including that the outcomes of departments allowing bodies to develop and implement delivery mechanisms should be consistent with the department's objectives, and that there should be a balance between control and quangos operating independently day by day (Civil Service, 2014). A House of Commons inquiry suggested that departments should report on the effectiveness of their sponsorship of ALBs and each department should set as a goal the improvement of its relationship with ALBs (Public Administration Select Committee, 2015, para 43).

Accountability to Parliament and the public

Scrutiny over NDPBs has increased, with departmental select committees able to monitor their work and make reports. The Public Accounts Committee looks at individual quangos when issues of efficiency and effectiveness arise. The expansion of the remit of the National Audit Office to cover all NDPBs allows the Public Accounts Committee to assess whether quangos are meeting value-for-money criteria. The scale of parliamentary scrutiny differs between quangos, and some quangos, for example, the National Institute for Clinical Excellence, have been investigated several times. There is not an annual process of parliamentary oversight over individual quangos, so this form of accountability is more episodic. The role of parliamentary select committees also increased when they were given the power to scrutinise major appointments. Changes in the composition of quangos have facilitated the participation of a range of members of the public in decision-making. A wider range of people are enabled to engage in the processes of governance, although there are still issues about the representativeness and size of board membership. A further measure that promotes accountability to the public is the requirement that board meetings are open to the public.

The outcome of reforms in England

The Coalition government adopted the position that the primary reason for the reform of quangos was to ensure that accountability rests in the right place. Strong arguments were advanced in favour of bringing functions back into departments. As has happened with the DWP and Department for Education, the argument was essentially seen as claiming that some existing quangos were performing functions that did not require independence from ministers (Public Administration Select Committee, 2011, p 31). It has been argued that the tests used in the reform audit of quangos offer no obvious basis for differentiating how much freedom individual quangos have in light of their different functions. Also, the Public Administration Select Committee noted evidence it received that questioned whether transferring functions from public bodies back to departments would actually mean more accountability and transparency. The counterargument refers to the structure whereby the board, chief executive and chairman can be held to account in a more transparent way than civil servants within a department. Quangos have their own separate structured profile, annual reports, business plans, public identity and links with community groups, which facilitates greater accountability than if a quango was a small part of a large department (Public Administration Select Committee, 2011, p 32). The Public Administration Select Committee concluded that bringing functions back into sponsor departments may undermine the other channels of accountability, leading to less attention being paid to the work of the quango. The reform process led to action by the Cabinet Office, with stronger controls over expenditure, although the extent to which departments see accountability issues as driving reform varies between departments (Skelcher et al, 2013, p 9). The accounts given by Whitehall departments to explain reforms and restructuring tend to emphasise the aim of reducing the cost of quangos, and, rather than accountability, refer to the configuration and nature of quangos as assisting the achievement of departmental aims. Some more radical ideas have been debated through the mutualisation of quangos or joint ventures with the private sector (Tonkiss and Noonan, 2013) but have not been acted upon.

Use of quangos in the devolved administrations

Following the establishment of devolved governments, each administration inherited a large set of devolved quangos, especially in the area of health. This raised issues about the distribution of functions between the devolved departments and devolved quangos. To an extent, they were in competition for the same administrative space (Birrell, 2008). Pre-devolution, quangos had been seen as contributing to a democratic deficit. Each of the devolved administrations was to make a commitment to rationalise the number of quangos involved in the administration and delivery of services, and to improve their accountability. Another objective was to bring key activities under the direct control of the devolved ministers and Parliament/Assemblies and build greater capacity through decision-making powers.

The Scottish Executive carried out a major review, resulting in the announcement of the planned abolition of 52 public bodies out of 186 identified (Flinders, 2011). The Welsh Assembly Government also made a commitment to review all the major Assembly public bodies, including the National Education and Training Council, the Tourist Board, the National Development Agency, Health Professions Wales and the Curriculum and Assessment Agency. Effectively, 10 out of 34 bodies were reviewed. A review of quangos in Northern Ireland was part of a wider review of public administration and the focus of the review was on reducing the number of quangos and cutting costs, objectives pursued by all the devolved governments and the UK government.

Despite the use of florid language of bonfires and culling, the actual outcome was more modest. The main outcome in Scotland was amalgamations, particularly of 43 health bodies into 15 new unified health boards, although the Scottish Homes quango was to transfer to a Government department as an executive agency. Overall, there was no large bonfire or wholesale change (Denton and Flinders, 2006). The main outcome in Wales was for three major quangos to transfer into the Welsh Assembly Government. Again, this hardly matches the language of extensive culling (Osmond, 2004). Progress at absorption was slow, with the Welsh Development Agency and Tourist Board only transferred in 2006/07. A significant change did occur in 2007 when 22 health boards were reduced to seven boards, along with three other boards, to deliver the NHS. The process in Northern Ireland had a focus on health and education quangos, with one commissioning board and five delivery trusts replacing 18 existing trusts in health and social care, and a large single education authority replacing five delivery boards. Few proposals were mooted to transfer bodies to central departments. In all, the review claimed that the number of quangos had been reduced from 99 to 50, although largely through mergers (Birrell, 2012, p 179). Knox (2010) suggests that bold claims to reduce the number of quangos in the review of public administration began to unravel.

The SNP government continued the commitment to reduce the number of quangos but through a more measured approach, although controversies arose over some quangos, for example, Sports Scotland and Creative Scotland. A practice was introduced of using ad hoc taskforces to give advice, instead of setting up a new quango (Cairney, 2012, p 134), although a number of new quangos appeared. A new government strategy was developed of *Simplifying Public Services*, aimed at streamlining the complex landscape of public service organisations (Scottish Government, 2008), and this included reducing the number of quangos. By 2010, some 162 public bodies had been reduced to 115, but the sector was still responsible for 40% of Scottish expenditure, while the number of employees actually increased. Merger was the main form of simplification, with 32 separate local children's panels replaced by one national panel, while the restructuring of health delivery resulted in 12 local health boards and eight specialist bodies. New quangos included Health Improvement Scotland and Social Care and Social Work Scotland. The simplification strategy was expected to improve the delivery of services, create an improved user focus, instil more cohesive leadership, lead to more coordination and enhance the link between policy development and delivery. The Christie Commission on the future delivery of public services (Scottish Government, 2011) recognised that there was a continuing complexity of organisations and systems, undermining their effectiveness by complicating joint working, generating costs and delays, and causing difficulty for people in navigating through the system of public services (Christie, 2011, para 7.35). The Commission, however, did not see wholesale reorganisation as an end in itself as it might prove costly and fail to impact upon service outcomes. Recommended was a rolling programme of reforms related to streamlining functions, exploring organisational mergers and sharing services, and simplifying governance (Scottish Government, 2011). It also called for more local integration of public services, more transparency and for services to be encouraged to pursue preventative approaches, tackle inequality and promote equality.

The Welsh process of absorbing quangos into devolved government proceeded slowly. Overall, the number of Welsh government-sponsored bodies has reduced from 38 in 1999 to 33 in 2014, which, of course, also indicates the continuing creation of new bodies, as with Qualifications Wales in 2015. The Commission on Public Service Governance and Delivery (Williams, 2014) noted that the Welsh sector of public bodies was still overcrowded and relationships were highly complex in terms of accountability, governance, funding regulation and policy implementation (Williams, 2014, para 7.8). The emphasis was on streamlining collaboration and removing duplication, and on promoting the co-production of services with a focus on outcomes but not on the transfer of functions. Principles for reform included ensuring simplicity, building trust, respecting diversity and clarifying accountability (Williams, 2014, para 7.37). A follow-up strategy, *Improving Public Services for People in Wales* (Welsh Government, 2014a), was again written largely in general terms in relation to quangos. It had a focus on performance improvement and leadership, and while discussing a 'one public service', this was in relation to sharing service capability across the public sector. Quangos were only treated separately in connection with public appointments.

After the completion of the review of public administration, attention to further reform of the quango sector faded in Northern Ireland. Agreement on establishing a very large centralised Education Authority was reached in 2015 to deliver schools and youth provision. A thorough review of all quangos was announced but reports were only published on two bodies, the Social Care Council and the Consumer Council. A proposal to abolish the advisory Housing Council was dropped. Some new quangos came into existence and the Stormont House Agreement, in recommendations for dealing with the past, proposed several new quangos. Public sector reform has remained a government objective in Northern Ireland, although with no direct emphasis on the reform of the large quango delivery sector. The role of the quango sector in Northern Ireland was largely ignored by the OECD review of public sector reform (OECD, 2016).

Conclusions

Quangos are a significant feature of governance across the UK, but in all jurisdictions, efforts have been made to reduce their number and role. Despite an increase in scrutiny over quangos and their members, as well as measures to ensure greater accountability, concerns remain about their reach, representativeness and transparency. As has been shown, however, there are few clear indications that simply transferring power back to government departments would effectively address these concerns. The main benefits to the use of quangos to deliver services and their appropriateness within devolved administration remains a matter of some dispute. In terms of the delivery of welfare services, there is increasing emphasis on collaboration between quangos and other statutory, voluntary and private bodies, with a strong focus on outcomes.

SEVEN

Developments in partnership working

This chapter explores the role of partnerships in the delivery and governance of welfare. It examines the types and nature of partnerships and reasons for the growth of partnership working, and their status as a distinct mode of governance. Using examples from a number of areas, including education and health and social care policy, it examines the rationale for partnership working. The chapter also assesses the evidence relating to the impact of the use of partnerships.

Terminology and definition

A number of terms are used alongside or instead of 'partnership', including 'joined-up working', 'inter-agency working', 'inter-agency collaboration', 'multidisciplinary partnerships' and 'hubs'. Petch et al (2013, p 624) note that it is easy to become 'mired in issues of definition' when discussing partnerships. The Audit Commission (1998, p 16) referred to 'partnership' as 'a slippery concept that is difficult to define precisely' but suggests that partnerships can be seen as 'joint working arrangements where parties who are otherwise independent bodies agree to cooperate to achieve common goals, create new organisational processes or structures, implement a joint programme or share relevant information'.

The development and growth of partnerships

A number of factors account for the increasing focus on partnerships and more formal cooperation in the governance and delivery of welfare. These include calls to ensure the better integration of services to users and changing thinking about how public services should be organised and delivered, and by whom. While responsibility for welfare services was traditionally placed across a range of organisations, all with separate governance and funding systems and different cultures, the needs of users frequently crossed these organisational boundaries. Issues relating to fragmentation in service provision for health and social care users received particular attention. The disjointedness of provision between NHS health services and local authority social services created problems for users, which became even more apparent with the growing emphasis on care in the community from the 1980s. Although there were some attempts to achieve coordination of care through legislation by placing a duty on local authorities and health authorities to cooperate and through structural reorganisation (Challis et al, 1988), these had little impact. One writer talked of local authorities and health authorities acting as 'micro-political systems ... with their own organisational imperatives ... and professional and political perception of priorities' (Allsop, 1984, p 114).

The ideological shift in thinking about how welfare should be financed, governed and delivered in the UK from the 1980s paved the way for an expansion of partnerships. It was seen by Conservative governments as a way of unlocking the dominance of the public sector (Newman, 2001, p 5). The growth of neo-liberalism in welfare planning and delivery and the ascendency of new public management in the 1980s involved an organisational split between policy and administration, which saw the administration and delivery of services as often being dealt with outside government, largely by the private sector (Pollitt et al, 2007). It advocated the adoption of private sector management techniques within public service organisations and the outsourcing of services on the assumption that this would result in greater efficiency and effectiveness. The lack of evidence that this was more cost-effective contributed to a reanalysis in a number of areas of social and public policy that resulted in more of an emphasis on partnership working. Partnership emerged as a central theme in 'third way' politics was seen as moving beyond old ways of organising public services (Clarke and Glendinning, 2002). Osborne (2010) talks of the emergence of new public governance or network governance as a decentralised and more flexible form of management, where needs were assessed and mutually agreed and coalitions of public, private and third sector organisations were established to meet those needs. Rhodes (1996, p 60) refers to governance as being characterised by 'self-organising, inter-organisational networks' as a consequence of the hollowing out of the state. Partnerships have also been said to represent a growing acknowledgement on the part of government that addressing increasingly complex and multidimensional issues could be better achieved by disparate systems working together in a spirit of cooperation and inter-professional collaboration (Sullivan and Skelcher, 2002).

Rhetoric about partnerships also came to focus on issues of user choice and how greater diversity in supply would provide users with more options with regard to such things as where they had their operation or how their social care was provided (Petch, 2011). This would represent a devolution of power to users and enable them to hold providers to greater account. Partnerships were seen to be a way of empowering communities and increasing community capacity by enabling more involvement in decisions about their local areas through representation on the new joined-up bodies making those decisions and, in more recent years, through 'co-production' (Bovaird and Loeffler, 2014). The appeal of partnerships crossed party-political boundaries, and by 2010, public sector organisations were involved in approximately 5,500 different partnerships, with a direct and indirect expenditure of £15–20 billion (Perkins et al, 2010). As seen later in the chapter, the added value of partnerships was somewhat assumed, with little empirical evidence about positive outcomes, but that has not resulted in a diminution of their use.

The nature and types of partnerships

Petch et al (2013, p 64) point to a continuum of partnership working, ranging from tentative collaboration between specific individuals, to formalised joint delivery, to full integration. The size and nature of partnerships vary considerably, with some very large partnerships set up by the state to deal with substantive policy issues, while others may be non-statutory community-based partnerships. Partnerships can be intra-sectoral, that is, between organisations in the same sector, or, less commonly, cross-sectoral. Intra-sectoral partnerships have been common within local authorities and between quangos. Partnerships between local authorities revolve around the delivery of services where there are benefits in a joined-up or 'group' approach, for example, making better use of staff and financial resources. In the third sector in the UK, intra-sectoral partnership is a fairly recent phenomenon, with most third sector organisations that are involved in partnerships being in cross-sector partnerships (Kara, 2014). Petch et al (2013) identify how partnership working takes place at a number of levels (see Box 7.1).

Box 7.1: Levels and forms of partnership working

- Macro – structural level.
- Meso – service system level.
- Micro – service user level.

Forms of cross-sectoral partnership:
- *Public–third sector partnerships* such as children's centres for early years provision or Supporting People in housing.
- *Public–private sector partnerships*, such as the private finance initiatives (PFIs) in health and education.
- *Private–third sector partnerships*, such as consortia set up to bid for and deliver government welfare-to-work contracts or probation services in England.
- *Private–public–third sector partnerships*, such as local strategic partnerships (LSPs).

(Kara, 2014)

Partnerships can also be organised around specialist services and activities, for example, youth offending teams or supported housing partnerships. Other partnerships are generalist in that they seek to address a range of issues, such as the LSPs discussed later in the chapter. Many partnerships are created around service delivery for a specific group, such as children's centres; others may be organisational, for example, partnerships that aim to integrate the delivery of health and social care to a range of users. Glasby (2003), referring to partnerships in health and care, looks at the level at which partnership working is being addressed:

the individual level, where professionals work together; the organisational level, which is about providing a seamless service; and the structural level, which relates to the planning of health and social services in a holistic way. He argues that all three levels are essential for effective partnership working. A distinction has been made between facilitating/strategic partnerships and implementation partnerships (McQuaid, 2010, p 128). The format of partnerships is variable and can be broadly categorised as follows:

- as loose collaboration;
- through a written agreement and protocols;
- through formal contractual arrangements; and
- as a structural framework.

The basis on which partnerships are established is of key importance. This is a particularly salient point given the growth in mandatory 'partnerships', those imposed or legislated for by government to meet particular objectives. The inherent contradiction in legislating for what can be specifically defined partnerships has been described as undemocratic and disempowering (Ferguson, 2003), sending a message that communities, usually disadvantaged communities, need to have 'solutions' imposed on them, are deficient and have to be coerced. The extent to which partnerships have achieved participation from local communities has also been questioned, with Sabry (2015) arguing that even area-based partnerships purporting to be community-led can be criticised for marginalising the interests that they are purporting to support. The point has been made that while policymakers have been keen to engage communities in partnerships, communities themselves are often more concerned that the services they need should be delivered by institutions that they are comfortable working with (Matthews, 2012). Other concerns relate to equality, power and control in the governance of partnerships (Newman et al, 2004) and the degree to which partnerships generally benefit the most powerful partner (Rummery, 2002). However, partnerships are also seen to have the potential to facilitate stronger bottom–up community action (Postle and Beresford, 2007).

The growth of partnership working is evident across the UK. In Scotland and Wales, as in England, there has been an expansion of partnerships at the local government level. This is not so evident in Northern Ireland, where local authorities do not have responsibility for major social welfare provision. A particular feature of the Northern Ireland partnership landscape has been the partnerships set up as a result of European Union funding and, in particular, the European Union Special Programme for Peace and Reconciliation. The aim of the programme was to achieve cohesion between communities involved in the conflict in Northern Ireland and the border counties of Ireland, as well as to build economic and social stability. The first phase of the programme between 1995 and 1999 was implemented through 26 district partnerships set up at the local authority level. The membership of these partnerships was cross–sectoral and included representatives from local councils, the community and voluntary sector, the private sector, and trade unions. Subsequent analyses of the impact of these did point to some positive outcomes with regard to cross-community collaboration, the sharing of services and the facilitation of local grass-roots involvement in local decisions (Harvey, 2003; Racioppi and O'Sullivan, 2007). As part of the review of public administration, which saw the number of local authorities being reduced from 26 to 11, some opportunity for partnership working is being seen by the requirement on local authorities to develop community planning for their areas involving a partnership approach (Department of the Environment (NI), 2013).

Public–private partnerships

Governments in many parts of the world have turned to private sector involvement in both the private sector financing and provision of public infrastructure and services. The rationale for this has tended to be couched in terms of combining the strengths of both actors and promoting greater efficiency through competition and the diversity of providers. The UK Treasury defined public–private partnerships (PPPs) as an arrangement between two or more entities that enables them to work cooperatively towards shared or compatible objectives and in which they have some degree of shared authority and responsibility, joint investment of resources, shared risk taking, and mutual benefit (HM Treasury, 1998). The policy of governments since the 1990s regarding marketisation, competition and the outsourcing of welfare services has seen the development of PPPs in a number of areas of service delivery. There was obviously private sector interest in the business opportunities presented by the contracting out and outsourcing of services, and this is discussed in greater detail in Chapter Eight. In a number of policy areas, the rhetoric relating to outsourcing policies has included a focus on the benefits of mixed-economy partnerships. An example of this can be seen with the welfare-to-work provisions. While early welfare-to-work initiatives, such as Pathways to Work, in the late 1990s saw government contract with a range of organisations, including voluntary sector organisations working with specific groups, such as lone parents or disabled people; since the late 1990s, the move towards contracting along a prime contractor model has seen many voluntary organisations unable to compete for contracts. The model that has been endorsed is of consortia, often led by large private sector organisations, bidding for contracts. They can then subcontract to other providers, including voluntary sector organisations, which has led to some concern about how the voluntary sector has fared in this process (Damm, 2012).

A review of the literature on PPPs in health between 1990 and 2011 found that effectiveness depends on a number of factors, including the roles assigned to each partner and especially the regulatory role of the state and contract arrangements (Torchia et al, 2015). The evidence suggests that greater efficiency cannot be assumed and that despite the widespread adoption of PPPs in the UK and internationally, there are substantial gaps in the scholarly and practitioner understanding of some elements of PPPs, including how the concept is understood and applied (Roehich et al, 2014).

The PFIs introduced by the Conservative government in 1992, and enthusiastically embraced by the 1997 Labour government, became the form of public–private 'partnership' most often used in the UK. PPPs are based on a contractual relationship and competitive tendering. The use of PFIs was at its highest in the UK in 2007/08 and has since declined. They were established to engage the private sector in the design, building and operation of public infrastructure based on the premise that engaging private sector commercial expertise would secure better value for money by ensuring that infrastructure projects were delivered on time and within cost. Under PFIs, private investors take on the risk of building and operating new infrastructure such as hospitals or schools. In return, they receive payments usually spread over 25–30 years, which usually far exceed the original cost of the project. By 2012, over 700 PFI projects had been established, with total capital costs of £54.7 billion (HM Treasury, 2012). Projects covered a broad range of sectors, including schools, hospitals, roads, prisons, housing, defence and waste facilities.

The use of PFI contracts has always been controversial, with a lack of consensus on whether projects offer value for money (Barlow and Köberle-Gaiser, 2009). Studies on PFIs in hospitals have raised questions about cost-effectiveness, quality, the lack of flexibility and complexity, with claims that hospital building costs have frequently been underestimated (McKee et al, 2006) and that value for money in hospital builds has been lower than for non-PFI hospitals (Pollock et al, 2009). A National Audit Office (2009) report found that, generally, PFI projects were built close to the arranged time frame and within budget and specification, but that the PFI system was overly complex and inflexible, with difficulties making alterations to projects and high compensation payouts if contracts needed to be terminated. A later National Audit Office (2013b) report found that while departments had to conduct a value-for-money assessment before agreeing to PFIs, the model used by the Treasury was not sufficiently robust. The Foreword to a Treasury review of PPPs in 2012 (HM Treasury, 2012) noted that: 'The Private Finance Initiative (PFI), the form of PPP used most frequently in the United Kingdom, has become tarnished by its waste, inflexibility and lack of transparency'. This review led to the reform of the PFI with the introduction of Private Finance 2, with measures to achieve greater transparency in relation to the financial performance of the project company, more efficient procurement processes and more appropriate risk allocation. Booth and Starodubtseva (2015) summarise what are argued to be the benefits and limitations of PFI projects (see Box 7.2).

PFIs are frequently justified on cost-efficiency grounds but there are clear fiscal reasons for governments pursing PFIs. Many PFIs are not included on the public balance sheet and do not count as part of public borrowing totals. Although the official line has been that PFIs should not be used for accounting reasons, there are clearly incentives to do so. The House of Commons Treasury Committee (2011, p 13) concluded that 'If Departments or public bodies do not have a capital

Box 7.2: Benefits and limitations of PFI projects

Potential benefits

- Risk transfer to the private sector from the public sector.
- Provides an opportunity to deliver on assets that may be difficult to finance or procure conventionally.
- May encourage ongoing maintenance.

Limitations

- Higher cost of finance.
- Inflexible contracts.
- Ultimate risk lies with the public sector.
- Prone to over-complexity and inflexibility.
- Problem of excessive returns relative to risks.

budget large enough to allow for desired capital investment, there is currently a substantial incentive to use PFIs which are not included within Departmental budgets'. Office for National Statistics (ONS) analysis (Hayes et al, 2015) sets out wider contingent liabilities and obligations, which are not included within the national accounts framework, but are published separately by the ONS or within HM Treasury's Whole of Government Accounts. As PFIs and some PPPs are classified as 'off-balance-sheet', there is no debt liability recorded in the government balance sheet and so no direct impact on national accounts and public sector finances debt measures. The scale of this is illustrated by the national accounts and public sector finances debt measures. At March 2015, these included approximately £5 billion in finance lease liabilities relating to on-balance-sheet PPPs compared to approximately £31 billion in off-balance-sheet PPP liabilities at the same point in time (Hayes et al, 2015).

The controversy and concern about the lack of transparency of PFI and PPP initiatives has resulted in some attempts to reform the system. In March 2015, the Treasury reported that £2.1 billion worth of savings had been secured and announced new arrangements to strengthen scrutiny and place a £70 billion control total on future Private Finance 2 contracts for five years from 2015/16 (HM Treasury, 2015a). However, despite reforms, the criticism of PFI has continued. In April 2015, the *Independent* newspaper reported that, based on an analysis of Treasury data, the UK owed £222 billion to banks and business as a result of PFIs (Owen, 2015).

What evidence is there about how citizens and users view a wider provider mix and the impact it has had on them? The involvement of private sector organisations has been controversial and hotly debated, with some arguing that the ideological hostility creates a 'comprehension gap' in relation to the performance of partnerships. Analysis of the effectiveness of PPPs is not well developed and research findings are mixed but they do suggest that PPPs that have PFI as their focus are not appropriate for every setting and they are not always cost-effective (National Audit Office, 2009; Andrews and Entwistle, 2015). There continues to be distinct differences in theoretical and empirical opinion, with division between those who see involvement of the private sector as always leading to efficiency, and those who argue that disadvantages outweigh benefits, with no evidence that they were more efficient or effective. While governments have accepted the need for reform to the management and accounting processes, especially around PFI, there continues to be a strong policy commitment to partnership with the private sector. Scotland has moved away from PFI and has introduced Non-profit Distributing (NPD) as an alternative to a PFI model, funding private sector contributions from revenue budgets once an asset is built. NPD has been used mainly in health, education and transport projects.

Local government and partnerships

Measures to strengthen partnership working at the local government level were a strong feature of the Blair and Brown Labour governments and were argued to represent a shift from a contract culture to a partnership culture (Balloch and Taylor, 2007). They were seen as having a pivotal role within the context of structures and processes established to strengthen the leadership of local authorities with regard to improving economic, social and environmental well-being, and to modernise public service delivery (Glendinning et al, 2002; Perkins et al, 2010; Baggott, 2015). Local authorities were charged with, and at times mandated with, leading on the development of partnerships between local authorities and other public agencies and between public sector, private sector and voluntary sector organisations. This emphasis on partnerships, albeit with changes to rationale and focus, continued under the Coalition and the Conservative governments. This section of the chapter looks at a number of partnership initiatives at the local government level. The focus is mainly on the initiatives in England but reference is also made to partnerships specific to the devolved jurisdictions, such as community planning partnerships in Scotland and Wales. Local government in Northern Ireland does not have major responsibilities for social welfare services but reference is made in the chapter to partnerships involving local government and to proposals for local authority-based community planning.

Area-based partnerships

The use of area-based partnerships to address specific social and economic issues and multiple disadvantages in the UK has a long history. Examples in the 1960s and 1970s include housing action trusts, urban and rural regeneration partnerships, and the Home Office-sponsored community development projects (Burton et al, 2004). Poverty was a strong focus of area-based partnerships in the 1980s, with many being developed in the areas of employment initiatives and economic regeneration, such as the Making Belfast Work Partnership. Linked to this was the influence of the European Union, with partnerships a strong feature of European Union spatial anti-poverty programmes in many countries in the 1980s and 1990s (Haase and McKeown, 2003).

Under the 1997 Labour government, area-based partnerships were seen as instrumental to the objectives of the Social Exclusion Unit. Partnerships aimed at tackling poverty and social exclusion were rolled out in quick succession. Education action zones, health action zones, the early years Sure Start partnerships, employment zones, criminal justice community safety partnerships and the New Deal for Communities were among those set up with the objective of securing collaboration between businesses, local authority providers and users in multi-agency partnerships. These partnerships were to collaboratively address inequalities, improve social and economic outcomes, and modernise public service delivery in areas of social deprivation. The composition and use of area-based partnership initiatives to address poverty and disadvantage have provoked contesting views, with some seeing opportunities for community participation and others arguing that they are a diversion from the fundamental causes of poverty and inequality (Muscat, 2010). Under the Conservative and Blair's Labour governments, they shifted from innovation-based local partnerships to increasingly facilitating and implementing neo-liberal policies – as, for example, in the area of welfare to work (Jones and Gray, 2001).

Evaluations of area-based partnerships show varying degrees of success but identify a number of common concerns, including the overambitious setting of targets, the pressure for early 'wins' and the difficulty of measuring impact – especially in the short term (Ofsted, 2003; National Evaluation of Sure Start, 2008). The health action zone programme was abandoned in 2003, and in evidence to the House of Commons Health Select Committee, Professor Ken Judge, who led the evaluation of health action zones, reported that 'Health Action Zones were conceived and implemented too hastily and without clear direction to enable them to make a significant contribution to reducing health inequalities in the time that they were given' (House of Commons Health Committee, 2009).

The more broadly defined LSPs were to be a major aspect of local government activity. Set up by the Local Government Act 2000 as overarching bodies to exercise a broad strategic oversight across service providers and other partnerships, their representation was to include representatives from local authorities, public service providers, the voluntary sector, politicians and the police. Established in most local authority localities in England, their key aims were closely linked to a number of central government initiatives. Their core tasks (DETR, 2001) are set out in Box 7.3.

There was to be local discretion about how LSPs should be organised and what issues they should focus on. Having said this, national policies, especially on health, crime, education and children, determined the context in a number of specific areas of work, raising questions over the extent to which this constrained LSP discretion. The complexity of LSPs and the challenging agenda set for them

Box 7.3: Core tasks of local strategic partnerships

- The introduction of statutory community strategies – intended to improve the economic, environmental and social well-being of each area, and to contribute to the achievement of sustainable development.

- The rationalisation and simplification of existing partnerships within LSP areas – to reduce duplication and unnecessary bureaucracy and to make it easier for partners, including those outside the statutory sector, to get involved. LSPs were tasked with the rationalisation of local partnerships within their area.

- The launch and rolling out of the National Strategy for Neighbourhood Renewal – to narrow the gap between the most deprived neighbourhoods and the rest of England, with common goals of lower unemployment and crime, and better health, education, housing and physical environment. In those LSPs containing the most deprived neighbourhoods, eligibility for government funding from the Neighbourhood Renewal Fund was conditional on the existence of an LSP.

- Work with local authorities to develop public service level agreements – to tackle key national and local priorities (on health, education, crime, employment and transport), with agreed flexibilities, pump-priming and financial rewards if improvements were delivered.

was reflected in an interim evaluation (Office of the Deputy Prime Minister, 2005), which raised issues of the limits to the resources available to many LSPs in relation to the scale of their tasks and the danger of excessive and premature demands from government, particularly in the context of competing national priorities. Difficulties also emerged regarding duplication with the myriad of existing partnerships and coordination strategies (Burgess et al, 2001).

While many of the partnerships set up by the Labour governments were time-limited or were abolished, the faith in area-based partnership approaches did not diminish and continued to be linked to an agenda about improving performance in localities, with initiatives such as local area agreements, multi-area agreements and the Total Place Initiative. Initially established across 13 local authority areas in England, these were to take a whole-area approach involving chief executives and leaders from each local authority, primary care trusts (PCTs), Jobcentre Plus, the police, and all other partners in the LSP. Their aim was to achieve efficiency and successfully tackle problems in areas such as children's services, aged care, drugs and alcohol, housing, crime, and mental health services. Other partners outside the LSP, for example, the Courts Service, were also to be involved where a project was focusing on a particular theme. A core thread running through these area-level projects was to encourage joint planning, pooled budgets and a whole-area-focused approach.

Concern about partnerships such as LSPs has centred not just on their efficiency, but on the extent to which they are compatible with, or undermine, democratic processes. Given the, at least theoretical, degree of autonomy devolved to LSPs, they could be considered to be a form of governance network, thereby giving rise to similar concerns as those raised by Klijn and Skelcher (2007, cited in Rees et al, 2012). They have suggested that there are four possible ways of looking at the role and impacts of governance networks:

- The implicit rules of governance networks conflict with those of representative democracy.
- Governance networks complement democracy because they are more adaptable to complexity and fragmentation. They therefore open up opportunities for greater citizen engagement around the edges of traditional liberal democracy.
- Such networks may represent a transition from representative government to network governance.
- Networks are instruments used by dominant actors to structure social reality and reinforce their interests and power base.

Such debates are similar to those aired in relation to quangos and the democratic deficit, but as Rees et al (2012, p 28) point out, suggestions that the election of LSP members would increase the democratic legitimacy and accountability of LSPs were not taken forward and the wider governance issue of how democratic decision-making can influence partnerships remains unclear.

Local authority place-based partnerships continued to predominate under the Coalition government in the form of its pilot Whole-Place Community Budgets in four areas. These were to reduce duplication in public services primarily in the fields of families with complex needs, health and social care, economic growth, work and skills, and early years. The programme of Community Budgets established in 14 neighbourhoods was extended in 2013 through a £4.1 million funding package from the Department for Communities and Local Government to support 100 more Community Budget programmes in addition to the Whole-Place Community Budget areas. The initial focus on so-called 'troubled families' with complex needs was replaced in the second phase of the Community Budgets by a focus on public service transformation. To support the wider adoption of Community Budgets, a new multi-agency network, the Public Service Transformation Network, was announced by the Chancellor in the 2013 Budget, which was to 'spread innovation from the Whole-Place Community Budget pilots and What Works Centres to support other places at key stages to provide advice and support on co-designing local public service transformation' (Pollock, 2014).

Sandford (2015d, p 4) sees Community Budgets as:

> the latest incarnation of a policy issue which has been in existence for
> at least twenty years – how to reduce policy and spending based on

government functions ('silo government') in favour of spending on people and areas (policy and spending based on territory).

Views on the success or likely success of these projects are mixed. While it has been suggested that over £1 billion of fiscal and social benefits will be achieved by 2020 (DCLG and HM Treasury, 2015), the House of Commons Communities and Local Government Committee was more circumspect. In two inquiries, noted that the pooling of budgets was not widespread (House of Commons Communities and Local Government Committee, 2012) and that the main focus of Community Budgets had been on redesigning services rather than saving money (House of Commons Communities and Local Government Committee, 2013). It did however conclude that Community Budgets demonstrated that through joint working between agencies and local and central government, there was a potential to facilitate cheaper and more integrated public services. This, however, potential was contingent on a number of factors: overcoming cultural barriers at all levels of government in the context of the current financial conditions; the need to secure a framework for agreement on sharing the benefits of investment between local authorities' partners and central government; and addressing concerns about financial accountability arising from the way in which the projects could make their own arrangements for monitoring spending.

Under the Coalition government (2010–15), there was also evidence of a shift in focus towards the integration of some services, particularly in relation to health and social care services (discussed later). This included pursuing more integration of services through joint commissioning and achieving greater efficiency through joint management and joint service provision between councils. Building partnerships with the private sector continued to be a priority. The requirement on local authorities to lead on LSPs was removed but new Local Enterprise Partnerships (LEPs) were set up as voluntary arrangements between local authorities and businesses with the aim of determining local economic priorities. They have generally not included the social sector (with some exceptions regarding the involvement of social enterprises) in their structures and are not organised to meet any particular social objectives, focusing on the 'hard' end of development (Doyle, 2013). By 2013, these LEPs were accessing £370 million-worth of funding (Johnston, 2015). Table 7.1 summaries the key area/place-based partnerships established at the local authority level in England.

In Scotland, Community Planning is the key overarching partnership framework at the local authority level. It was introduced by the Local Government in Scotland Act 2003 (following the introduction of pilots in 1995), which placed duties on local authorities to initiate, facilitate and maintain Community Planning Partnerships as an integral part of the Scottish government's reform of public service delivery and a main mechanism for involving local communities through the representation of voluntary sector organisations on the partnership boards. Other partnerships, such as local employability partnerships, sit within the Community Planning Partnerships. Core partners in the 32 established

Table 7.1: Key area/place-based partnerships established at the local authority level in England, 2005–13

Date	Partnership	Aim
2005	Local area agreements	To work to an agreed set of area-based priorities and indicators
2009	Total Place pilots	To be a bottom-up approach to achieving efficiencies and improving outcomes
2010	Community Budgets	To facilitate the development of an area-based approach to tackling complex social problems, including the pooling of budgets
2010	Whole-Place Community Budget pilots	Bring together all local public services to achieve cost efficiencies in the delivery of services
2010	Local enterprise partnerships	To determine local economic priorities
2011	Our Place	Evolved from 12 neighbourhood Community Budgets with the aim of enabling communities to control local services
2013	Public Services Transformation Network	To build on Community Budgets by identifying, disseminating and supporting innovation and good practice
2013	Better Care Fund	Local authorities and NHS bodies to achieve the integrated planning and delivery of services

Community Planning Partnerships also include health boards, the enterprise networks, police and fire, and regional transport partnerships. They also involve a range of other organisations, such as Jobcentre Plus, further and higher education institutions, and business representatives.

The achievements of Community Planning have been seen as limited, particularly in relation to the integration of services, the lack of focus on preventative approaches and the limited extent to which there has been community involvement in policymaking and public service delivery (Audit Scotland, 2014a; Escobar, 2015). The Community Empowerment (Scotland) Act (Scottish Government, 2015c) placed additional duties on the partnerships around the planning and delivery of local outcomes. A 2016 update on Community Planning by Audit Scotland recommended a range of actions to be taken by the Scottish government, local authorities and Community Planning Partnerships to improve Community Planning and enable it to be up to the job of addressing the challenges set out in the Christie Commission review of the future delivery of public services (Christie, 2011). Some of the deficiencies identified in the Audit Scotland report reflected problems with leadership and national structures, and key measures advocated included stronger national leadership and the establishment of a national forum with the credibility and authority to address national and local barriers to effective community planning; other measures related to the measurement and monitoring of performance and the need for partnerships to prioritise preventative actions (Audit Scotland, 2016).

As discussed later in the chapter, the Well-being of Future Generations (Wales) Act 2015 established statutory public service boards in each local authority area in Wales. These replace the non-statutory local service boards that had been tasked with developing and delivering a single integrated plan based on a common understanding of long-term local needs and priorities. The Williams Commission had identified limitations and shortcomings with the governance of and outcomes from the local service boards, pointing to 'the need for a much clearer and more concise set of outcomes on which partnerships in general, and local service boards in particular, must focus' (Welsh Government, 2014b). The remit of the new public service boards includes assessing economic, social, environmental and cultural well-being in their areas, and they have a legal mandate from the Welsh government to make sure that local bodies work together. Membership is largely from public sector bodies but each board has representation from the voluntary sector.

Children's social services

Local authorities have overarching responsibility for safeguarding and promoting the welfare of children and young people. In addition to place-based initiatives such as Sure Start and children's centres set up to address disadvantage and promoting well-being, collaboration and partnership working around children at risk has had a pivotal place in social policy and legislation in the UK and in most modern welfare states. Partnership working was identified as a core principle and important element of work with children in the 1989 and 2004 Children Acts. Guidance on implementing partnership working to safeguard children, *Working Together*, was first published in 1999, revised in 2006 and 2010, and reissued in 2015 (HM Government, 2015c). This guidance focuses on the core legal requirements on a range of agencies with regard to their role in ensuring that there is effective collaboration through joint working around the assessment of needs, the coordination of support and the processes and principles in place for sharing information.

Discussion of partnership working in the literature on childcare and child protection has largely been of the failure in collaborative working. The importance of, and need for, better partnership working has been consistently raised in major reviews of children's services, which have repeatedly outlined problems relating to the failure of agencies to share information and the fragmentation of services. In his review of the murder of Victoria Climbié, Lord Laming (Laming inquiry, 2003, p 42) stated that despite measures implemented by government to reduce the impact of organisational boundaries, 'there was little or no real investment in developing an effective inter-agency child protection partnership'. His recommendations included proposals for strengthening multidisciplinary teams involved in the care and protection of children and he advocated a structure, reinforced by statute, which would be responsible for ensuring the implementation of multi-agency plans (Laming inquiry, 2003, p 361). Strong emphasis was placed on the joint training of staff working in services such as health, education, housing, police and social services, and to achieve this with a proposal that each training body should be required to promote training specifically designed to bring together staff from different agencies on working with children and families (Laming inquiry, 2003, p 367). The *Every Child Matters* agenda (Department for Education and Skills, 2003, 2004), developed in the wake of the Laming Inquiry under the Labour government (1997–2010), did attempt to shift the focus from a narrow child protection approach to a more holistic and preventative model of child well-being, which included a major focus on inter-agency partnership work (Woodman and Gilbert, 2013. The Children Act 2004 sought to enhance the integration of health, education, social care and others, including by establishing children's trusts. It also placed a statutory duty on local authorities to establish local safeguarding children boards with powers to investigate and review inter-agency failings. The Common Assessment Framework (CAF) introduced in 2006 saw common assessments carried out by schools, childcare providers, children's centres, health services and the voluntary sector with the aim to improve inter-agency working and avoid families having to provide information to different agencies (Collins and McCray, 2012; Rogowski, 2015). However, despite other major reviews recommending better inter-agency communication and work, including the *Munro Review of Child Protection* (DfE, 2011), more than a decade later, the Jay *Independent Inquiry into Child Sexual Exploitation in Rotherham* (Jay, 2014) pointed to continuing failings in partnership working and concluded that while there were inter-agency policies and procedures, members of the safeguarding board rarely checked if they were working.

Despite the challenges surrounding various models of partnership working, they continue to be regarded by government as a mechanism for reforming and improving what are viewed as failing public services. In December 2015, the Conservative government announced that underperforming children's services would be removed from direct local authority control to be run by partners – including high-performing local authorities, child protection experts and charities, who have formed trusts in what it described as an academy-style system (Stevenson, 2015).

Partnerships and schools

As indicated earlier, the Labour government's establishment of education action zones was focused on addressing educational disadvantage through the development of schools working with local partners. However, since 2000, the scale of the expansion of school partnerships has seen a myriad of different models emerging, with a strong focus on improving educational attainment and the performance of schools, addressing disadvantage through partnership and collaboration initiatives to enhance engagement and motivation, and achieving efficiencies through the sharing of resources (Hadfield and Jopling, 2006; Chapman and Muijs, 2014). Much of the literature on partnerships in education uses the term 'collaboration' to refer to different models of working together between schools (Armstrong, 2015). In England, in addition to education action zones, initiatives have included the 1998 beacon schools project, where improvements were to be achieved through schools working together to share good practice. City Challenges, introduced in 2003, were to improve schools in London by developing a model of inter-school collaboration, where struggling schools would be partnered with high-performing schools. The initiative was later extended to several other regions. Partnership-based developments include network learning communities, focused on schools becoming professional learning communities by working interdependently in a network. Between 2002 and 2006, 1,500 schools in England were involved in a network learning community (Greany and Allen, 2014). The Education Act 2002, which allowed local authority schools to collaborate with other schools in a variety of arrangements, resulted in federations becoming a common mechanism for partnership between two or more schools. A typology of the governance of federations was developed by Lindsay et al (2007), who distinguish between what they describe as 'hard governance' federations, where the federation has a single governing body shared by all schools and one executive head teacher, and 'soft governance' federations, where each school retains its own governing body. The structural arrangements for the main inter-school partnerships have been defined by Woods and Simkins (2014) as:

- Local federations – developed initially among groups of local authority schools where groups of schools are encouraged to work together in partnership.
- National chains – non-profit charitable ownership and management of a number of schools where there is a shared leadership and management structure, such as the chains governing academy schools.
- School-led chains – initiated and led by successful schools.

Under the Coalition government, the number of academy schools, started by the Labour government, increased significantly. These are state-funded schools, independent of local authority control, which receive funding directly from the Department for Education. They were encouraged to federate by joining an academy chain or a sponsored multi-academy trust. Most chains are small local or regional groups of academies. However, there are several large chains that cover a number of different regions across England, such as Oasis or E-ACT. This encouragement by the Coalition government included a financial incentive of £25,000, with non-academy federations not entitled to this support.

Greater collaboration and partnership working as a mechanism for improving standards has also been a feature of policy in Wales and Scotland. Since 2010 in Wales, regulations have allowed governing bodies of schools to choose to federate. In 2014, the Federation of Maintained Schools (Wales) Regulations enabled local authorities to federate schools, following an Organisation for Economic Co-operation and Development (OECD, 2014, p 77) report recommending the development of a Welsh strategy for school-to-school collaboration as an effective measure for developing professional and social capital among teachers and leaders. In Scotland, the government has also taken the view that strengthening partnerships between schools and across local authorities is a core aspect of improving the quality of the learning experience and addressing attainment challenges. Education Scotland has led the development of the School Improvement Partnership Programme, involving schools in the most deprived catchments in each of the local authorities, with evaluation identifying some positive impact on attainment (Chapman et al, 2014). In Northern Ireland, school partnerships have also been a feature of the education landscape but they have largely been developed to address the particular contextual challenges of the region. Education in Northern Ireland is largely divided by denomination in a region still dealing with the legacy of conflict. School partnerships have been designed to address the impact of a divided society by developing cross-sectoral shared education partnerships. More recently, a Contested Space Partnership (Duffy and Gallagher, 2015) has been piloted, where a number of schools have formed a unitary partnership with a new governance and organisational structure, which is also focused on addressing social need and economic disadvantage.

In England, many of the initiatives in education have resulted in a reduction in the power of local authorities with schools, often structured around a variety of partnerships, having a direct relationship with central government. There has been little research specifically on the impact of partnerships on educational outcomes. Of the research that has been conducted, findings are mixed (Armstrong, 2015). Research on the city challenges initiative (Hutchings et al, 2012) indicated some positive impact on student outcomes. Chapman and Muijs (2014), comparing federations of different sizes, academy federations and faith federations, found that, after controlling for a range of factors, being in a federation was positively related to performance. Although federations are relatively new in Wales, a 2015 Estyn report concluded that nearly all federations had resulted in financial benefits from the pooling and sharing of staff and expertise, and that there was some link to improved educational outcomes. As with much of the research on partnerships generally, there is difficulty identifying what can be attributed directly to the partnership rather than other factors. The conditions necessary for effective collaboration are identified as similar to those for other partnerships, including agreement by partners regarding underlying need and mutual benefit.

Health and social care and partnerships

Although partnerships have been a dominant feature of the health and social care landscape for some time, here, again, there is little robust evidence showing that they have a positive impact on users' experience or outcomes. Despite this, they are seen as an important mechanism in tackling problems with disjointed care services, improving coordination, reducing health inequalities and enhancing safeguarding, and there has been a sustained focus on partnerships since the 1990s. In establishing new PCTs, the Labour government indicated a shift from market-based competition to collaboration. These PCTs were to build ties with local government, especially in relation to health improvement and social care. In England, the Health Act 1999 aimed to advance partnership through a new statutory framework placing a duty to cooperate on NHS bodies and local government. The legislation also allowed for the creation of flexibilities, such as pooled budgets. The Health and Social Care Act 2001 legislated for the care trust model whereby separate trusts could be formed to deliver both health and social care services where there was agreement between the partners. The plan was that within five years, all adult social care services were to be delivered by a care trust (Petch, 2011). However, ten years later, less than 20 had been established. Most of these had a focus on mental health.

The drive to build partnerships continued and under the Coalition government, initiatives were established that required or encouraged partnership working. There was a particularly strong focus on the integration of services, which was seen as integral to reducing the need for acute care. The Care Act 2014 placed a new duty on local authorities to promote integration not just with health services, but with housing and other services. The Better Care Fund, essentially ring-fenced pooled budgets, was set up to promote integration through funding drawn from NHS commissioners and local authority social care, plus other NHS money. The Fund, to be introduced in 2016, is allocated through local plans, where clinical commissioning groups (CCGs) set out how they use their allocation. A performance pot is part of the Fund, mainly set against a reduction in total emergency admissions, and other targets are set against admissions to residential homes, effectiveness of reablement, delayed transfers and user experience (DoH, 2014b). The promotion of integrated partnerships in England has continued with the Better Care Fund strategy since 2013, entailing a shift of activity from hospitals to community-based health and social care integrated service delivery through an integrated better care plan (Bennett and Humphries, 2014).

Integrated care was also to be encouraged through the working of the new CCGs, set up following the Health Act 2012 (DoH, 2012b). These replaced the PCTs, which had operated from 2001 to 2013. CCGs are legally required to involve local government health and well-being boards in developing their commissioning plans (Baggott, 2013) and also have a duty to engage patients and the wider public. Interim research on the commissioning practices of CCGs (Addicott, 2014) found larger partnerships being developed, with two models in use: either a 'prime contractor model', where the CCG contracts with a single organisation or consortium that takes responsibility for the day-to-day management of other providers that deliver care; or else an alliance contract that sees a set of separate providers enter into a single agreement with a CCG to deliver services. While a key aim of joint commissioning between CCGs and local authorities involving health and well-being boards was to more effectively identify needs and result in integrated delivery, evaluations and research on the working of joint commissioning in Britain has highlighted major difficulties. These can be categorised as problems arising from: organisational and structural differences;

cultural and value differences; separate funding systems; and partnership isolation. Ten years after joint commissioning initiatives were first introduced, Dickinson and Glasby (2013) note the struggle to cite examples of its impact. In England further initiatives have been introduced to promote integrated practice. The Pioneer initiative explore new ways of delivering integrated and co-ordinated care and bring services together in 25 sites (NHS England, 2016a). This initiative has been augmented by a Vanguard Programme of 29 sites aimed at redesigning health delivery and includes multi-speciality community provider vanguards. Even in Northern Ireland, where health and social care services are formally integrated, problems are similar to those experienced in Britain. Accounting for this, Williams et al (2010) draw attention to the influence of the context of decision-making between separate health and social care bodies and differences in values, particularly between health and social care models and perspectives. Evidence also suggests that, in Britain, different funding regimes in local government and NHS bodies are a significant barrier to integrated commissioning (Thraves et al, 2012) and there have been difficulties in establishing a single integrated health and social care budget (Humphries and Wenzel, 2015). Additionally, in the setting up of joint commissioning there has often been a tendency to focus on the policy and procedures of partnership working, seeing this as an end in itself (Dickinson and Glasby, 2013).

Both the Coalition and the Conservative government have made wide-ranging changes to public health that have had important implications for partnerships. The leading national health and care quangos in England that deliver and oversee services have come together to publish 'Delivering the Forward View', setting out steps to help deliver what they call a sustainable transforming health service and improve the quality of care. The partnership issuing this guidance includes NHS England, NHS Improvement, the Care Quality Commission, Public Health England, Health Education England and the National Institute for Clinical Excellence (NICE) (NHS England, 2015).

As discussed in Chapters Four and Five, local authorities have acquired new responsibilities for public health that require them to work across different local authority departments and with external bodies. Statutory health and well-being boards were established as local authority-led boards with responsibility to lead on partnership working in the development of local health and well-being priorities. They aim to achieve better integration of health and social care through local authorities working in co-governance with a range of partners, including the NHS, children's services, housing services and elected representatives from Healthwatch. Health and well-being boards and CCGs were allocated joint legal responsibility for conducting joint strategy needs assessments and for the formulation of joint health and wellbeing strategies, describing how those needs are to be met (Baggott, 2015). While the potential of the transfer of public health duties to local authorities was acknowledged, especially given the local authority experience in developing partnerships, some concern has been expressed about the capacity of local government to take on these new roles, especially in the context of austerity. There has been some suggestion that the impact of health and well-being boards has been limited (Perkins and Hunter, 2014; Humphries and Wenzel, 2015). Baggott (2015) points to their weak statutory powers, their reliance on what he describes as 'soft' powers of persuasion and building consensus. Another significant development with the potential to impact on delivery has been the beginning of what is termed the devolution of health and social care powers and funds to large city areas of England through partnership working. The Greater Manchester Health and Social Care Partnership board consists of 10 local councils, 12 CCGs and 15 NHS providers and brings together £6.2 billion in budgets (McKenna and Dunn, 2015).

In the devolved administrations, there has been a similar emphasis on partnership working in health and social care. In Scotland, the NHS Reform (Scotland) Act 2004 required NHS boards to establish one or more Community Health Partnerships in their areas. The membership was defined by the Scottish government and included NHS stakeholders and members of the local public partnership forum. They were to coordinate planning and the provision of certain services, and contribute to joint working between health and social care. In subsequent assessments of the partnerships, it was observed that although they had considerable demands placed on them, 'these responsibilities did not come with the necessary authority to implement the significant changes required' (Audit Scotland, 2011, p 10) and they lacked the financial and human resources and key personnel from relevant organisations (Perkins et al, 2010). Audit Scotland statements about issues relating to the context of the partnerships have wider resonance and its reference to a 'cluttered partnership landscape' (Audit Scotland, 2011, p 11) where there was duplication, lack of coordination with these new partnerships and existing health and social care partnership arrangements, and the lack of evidence of impact have also been raised in other evaluations and studies. Steps towards formal integration in Scotland were taken with the setting up of integrated health and social care partnerships, giving NHS boards and local authorities shared responsibility for those people who use both services. New statutory partnerships operationalised from April 2016 will manage £8 billion of health and social care resources. The partnerships are to be initially supported through a special allocation of £300 million over three years (Scottish Parliament, 2014). The legislation requires the integration of adult health and social care services but the statutory partners, local authorities and NHS boards, can decide locally to include children's health and social care services in their integrated care plans. The objective is that services should be planned and delivered seamlessly from the perspective of the service user.

In Wales, there is a formal commitment to partnership, public participation and citizen engagement in the design of public services. The Social Services and Well-Being (Wales) Act 2014 enhanced the duties of local authorities and local health boards to work together to improve the well-being of people with care and support needs. The legislation made provision for partnership arrangements to be prescribed by ministers. A system of eight community health councils, with membership coming from the voluntary sector and local and central government, is seen as representing the voice of users and the public. The health councils have statutory powers to be consulted and also powers to inspect NHS premises. There has been a strong focus in Wales on ensuring public bodies work towards a set of common aims. The Wellbeing of Future Generations (Wales) Bill 2014 requires public bodies to pursue the 'common aim' of improving the economic, social and environmental well-being of Wales. The Bill established new partnership bodies, public service boards, in each local authority from 2016. They have a statutory duty for assessing local well-being and developing local well-being plans. Their membership must include representatives from the local authority and local health board, the police and crime commissioner, the chief constable, a representative from the probation service, and a representative from at least one voluntary organisation.

In Northern Ireland, while the full structural integration of health and social care facilitates a degree of formal partnership, there has been less emphasis on developing partnerships with organisations outside of health and social care. There are examples of issue-based partnerships between health and social care trusts and other statutory agencies and voluntary sector partners on areas such as the health and well-being of the Traveller community, children and young people's services, and tackling health inequalities. The local commissioning groups were intended to facilitate partnership working through their membership, but in practice were controlled by the parent central body, the Health and Social Care Board. In addition, given that local authorities do not have any statutory responsibility for health or social care, the extent to which there can be genuine partnership working is a moot point. A recent development is the creation of 17 integrated care partnerships (ICPs). Described as collaborative networks, they are really more like project boards with limited powers that enable them to develop business cases that identify the resources needed to better integrate services but not to commission those services. Part of the rationale for the ICPs was to achieve a more integrated approach to service planning and delivery but their work to date has largely been on acute care issues with an added objective of encouraging greater involvement of GPs (Birrell and Heenan, 2014).

Petch (2011, p 14) talks of 'enhanced partnership' in health and social care being achieved through a system-wide commitment where there is shared vision and integration across most strategic and commissioning functions in order to achieve integrated working and better outcomes for users. Examination of the main aims of partnerships in health and social care shows that these have been to achieve more holistic approaches, including earlier and more appropriate intervention and the integration of care. However, expectations that partnership working and integration will deliver financial savings are not supported by robust evidence (Weatherly et al, 2010).

The voluntary sector and partnerships

While partnership between the state and the voluntary sector is not a new phenomenon, since the 1980s, the voluntary sector has increasingly been seen as a partner in the governance of and delivery of welfare services (Rees et al, 2012). A number of reasons have been put forward to account for this. First, new public management and the rhetoric of choice and competition in public services saw governments seek a greater diversity of providers, especially in health and social care, housing, employment services, and youth services. Given the goal of increasing efficiency linked to new public management, it is argued that governments have viewed partnership with the voluntary sector through contracts as more cost-efficient, in part, due to the use of volunteers by organisations (Edwards, 2009). Second, writers have pointed to the view that partnership working would enable the voluntary sector's record of and skills in involving users and innovation in service design to be applied more widely to public service delivery (Pestoff et al, 2010). Third, the reputation and respectability of the voluntary sector have been argued to be important factors in increasing the legitimacy and acceptance of the outsourcing of provision to large private sector contractors who work at a local level with voluntary organisations (Rees et al, 2012; Kara, 2014).

Attempts have been made to categorise the various state–voluntary sector partnerships. Bode and Brandsen (2014) refer to Coston's (1998) configurations of voluntary sector–state partnerships, where he makes a distinction between collaboration, cooperation and contracting and commercial competition. The latter has been criticised for distorting the aims, strategies and internal organisation of voluntary sector organisations as they adapt to the requirements of contracts (Edwards, 2009; Buckingham, 2012). The increasing role of the voluntary sector in contract service provision has caused some blurring between what could be considered partnership working and outsourcing, contracting and privatisation. The emphasis on outcome-based commissioning and the introduction of a different model of provision through prime contractors in some areas of welfare provision programmes has favoured larger private sector organisations and, in some cases, larger more formal voluntary organisations. The procurement processes of local authorities have also been argued to present challenges, especially for smaller organisations (Osborne and Strokosch, 2013; Kara, 2014). Tensions have arisen in the relationship between the state and the voluntary sector, with debate about the extent to which the state sees the voluntary sector as an equal partner. The Charity Commission (2007) statement that the public sector needed to improve its capacity to work with the voluntary sector in a meaningful and effective way is just one indication of the difficulties.

Given the highly contextualised and issue-specific nature of partnerships, there is a perhaps surprising lack of information about how to achieve success in cross-sectoral partnerships or the extent to which voluntary organisations can carry the costs associated with partnership working. While much is expected from partnerships, a context of austerity and cuts is likely to impose constraints on the ability of partnerships to be innovative (Hastings et al, 2013). There is evidence that a lack of resources means that partnerships can be weak and unsustainable in the long term; as agencies comes under increasing pressure in their own areas of work, partners can withdraw or reduce their contribution, thereby diminishing previously positive outcomes (Payler and Georgeson, 2013).

Impact of partnerships

Evaluations of partnerships have overwhelmingly focused on process rather than outcomes. The Wanless Report in 2004 noted the gap between evidence and practice in partnership work and recommended evaluation of the emerging ways in which NHS organisations and local authorities were working together with regard to public health. Evidence on better outcomes as a result of partnership working is weak (Dowling et al, 2004; Glasby and Dickinson, 2009; Weatherly et al, 2010; Boydell, 2015).

There has been much discussion in the literature of the challenges of partnership working. These could be described as cultural, procedural, professional and financial. Some of the main issues are summarised in Box 7.4.

Box 7.4: Challenges of partnership working

- Issues of governance – where partnerships are ill-defined with confusion about issues and responsibilities; the state may retain strong control over the working of the partnership, resulting in an unequal 'partnership'.
- Problems stemming from national policies – tensions/contradictions as a result of conflicting national policies or restrictions on the ability of partnership to pool resources; performance frameworks can create professional 'silos'.
- Lack of agreement about purpose – individual partners have different perceptions about the role of partnership and outcomes.
- Different organisational cultures and professional boundaries – can be rooted in historical and institutional arrangements of individual partners; can also give rise to issues of status and power between partners; existing professional boundaries can impede partnership working.
- Resource issues – partnerships being insufficiently resourced with regard to the partnership process and the work of the partnership; evidence of cost-effectiveness may be hard to demonstrate in the short term.
- Difficulty attributing positive outcomes to the partnership – given the range of variables, it can be difficult to identify success due to partnership working.
- Loss of clarity for service users – partnerships could result in a loss of clarity for users and potentially lengthier decision-making process.

Dimensions of process success have been identified as: the level of engagement and commitment of partners; agreement about the purpose and need for partnership; high levels of trust and reciprocity; sound accountability and governance arrangements; and good leadership and management (Dowling et al, 2004; Audit Scotland, 2011; Jones and Barry, 2011; Johnston, 2015). What would outcome success look like? One argument is that a requirement for good outcomes is quality at every level of the partnership, including through co-governance. Johnston (2015, p 18) defines co-governance as 'consensual regulation shared by public, civic and professional actors in the delivery of public services. The importance of genuine engagement with stakeholders is also seen as important to outcomes, which may lengthen decision-making (Bovaird et al, 2015). In the area of health and social care, better outcomes for users is seen as an important goal of partnerships: changes in the level and delivery of services; improvements in individual and population health status; more equitable access to services; and improvements in the efficiency and effectiveness of services.

Conclusions

While successive governments have advocated partnership working, some issues divide researchers and academic commentators. There is much agreement that better partnership/joined-up working is a desirable goal, a 'self-evident good', but when identifying when the conditions are right for partnership working, strategy and operation both remain problematic (Allen, 2003; Johnston, 2015). There are challenging governance issues and tensions between a bottom-up approach and the control imposed by policy direction, with debate about whether partnership working acts to extend state power through a network of governance structures (Newman, 2001). Partnerships carry costs and risks for individual partners. While they can be inclusive in terms of sectoral membership, it has proven very challenging to break down organisational and professional silos and representatives, including from the voluntary and community sectors, who are often from a professional class (Johnston, 2015). The preventative agenda of partnerships such as those set up to address disadvantages in health, education and early years means that outcomes will be realised over the long term, so the short-term nature of some evaluations creates difficulty. One of the key aims of partnerships is often to achieve greater cost efficiency, but if partnerships are not adequately supported or have sufficient flexibility over resources, this is likely to limit impact. A context of austerity makes the future partnership landscape a challenging one.

EIGHT

The mixed economy: privatisation and welfare delivery

This chapter examines the theme of provision of welfare by agencies other than the state by looking specifically at privatisation and welfare services. It considers issues of terminology and definition and the mechanisms used to transfer provision from state to non-state entities, sometimes referred to as the 'independent sector'. The background to the development and expansion of privatisation is discussed, identifying the influence of the Conservative government under Margaret Thatcher and the policy of successive UK governments. The chapter includes a review of the scope and degree of privatisation in a number of policy areas and an assessment of the impact of privatisation.

Terminology and definition

The complexity of definition in relation to the term 'privatisation' has been well documented, with 'marketisation', 'commercialisation' and 'privatisation' often used interchangeably. Powell and Miller (2014) refer to the range of views on what constitutes privatisation, pointing to Starr's (1988) definition of privatisation as a shift from the public to the private sector but not shifts within sectors (eg the conversion of a state agency to an autonomous public body would not constitute privatisation, but commercialisation). Dunleavy (1986) views privatisation strictly as the permanent transferring of the production of services or goods from the public sector to private firms or voluntary organisations. Others, however, see it as a multifaceted set of processes involving not just the transfer of functions or commissioning of services to the private sector, but the privatisation of governance (Whitfield, 2006), a decline in state provision such as charging for public services previously paid for out of taxation, and a reduction in state subsidies (Le Grand and Robinson, 1984). Crouch (2003) considers that privatisation occurs when ownership of a previous public resource is transferred to a private firm but also includes the transformation of managerial practices in the public sector, including through the use of technocratic assessment of performance, such as school or hospital performance targets and league tables (Crouch, 2011).

While marketisation and privatisation are not coterminous, marketisation, through public–private partnerships and outsourcing for example, has been seen as creating the ideological and economic conditions for further privatisation (Whitfield, 2006, p 4). Ideological privatisation could be seen as fostering a belief that the values and principles of the private sector are superior to and should replace public values, and requiring public sector institutions to operate like those in the private sector. These have been termed 'quasi-markets' (Le Grand, 1991), which are seen as operating differently from conventional markets in a number of ways. While they put in place a separation between purchaser and provider, the state continues to finance services; providers can be private, voluntary or social enterprises, and services are not always bought by those using them, though quasi-market policies are often couched in a rhetoric about user choice. Quasi-markets also differ from conventional markets in that they allow for a strong role for government, particularly with regard to regulation and performance management. The form that a quasi-market takes can vary substantially depending on how policymakers structure the intersection of competition and choice (Greener, 2008), but they have been viewed by some as enabling new forms of privatisation, whereby both private finance and private provision are increasingly brought into public services (Whitty and Power, 2000).

Box 8.1: Terms used in discussions about the use of markets in welfare delivery

- Privatisation: The transferring of responsibility for services from the state to non-state entities such as private sector companies, voluntary organisations, social enterprises or individuals. Privatisation can also include the adoption of private sector managerial practices.
- Marketisation: Creating a set of conditions to facilitate or extend the privatisation of welfare services.
- Outsourcing: The contracting out of responsibilities previously carried out 'in-house' – mostly to non-state providers.
- Commissioning: Assessment of needs followed by decisions about how services needed should be provided. Often, emphasis is on achieving value for money.
- Quasi-markets: A type of market that places a separation between purchaser and provider. They often allow for a regulatory role by the state.
- Procurement: Processes related to the buying of services where there is strong emphasis on value for money and achieving efficiency.

Source: Adapted from Gash et al (2012)

Gingrich (2011), in her analysis of three policy areas – health, education and elder care – in England, Sweden and the Netherlands, set out six types of market based on how access to services are allocated and how services are produced. Allocation includes the financing and regulation of services; where there is strong regulation, the scope of providers to maximise profit is limited. The production dimension looks at how choice and competition in the market is structured and the degree of control held by providers and by users to advance their preferences. She links different types of market reform to the positioning of right and left political parties, arguing that political actors construct their preferred market configurations but that their actions are also tempered by the public perception of services. For example, the public are more likely to resist producer–driven markets in popular universal services, so political parties pursuing such an approach my face potential electoral costs (Powell, 2015). This can be observed in the Thatcher government's initially more cautious approach to introducing market reforms in health care and in the 2015 Conservative government's reversal on the decision to require all schools in England to become academy schools. The following section of the chapter sets out key developments in the privatisation of welfare by different political parties and governments in the UK.

The context and development of privatisation in the governance and delivery of welfare

Privatisation can be looked at on two levels: policies that aim for fundamental change and the removal of entire parts of welfare service delivery from government; and policies that aim to influence management and delivery through embedding market values and mechanisms to improve efficiency in public structures. Elements of both can be seen in the policies of the Conservative government elected in 1979. The social policy of the Thatcher government was strongly influenced by a neo–liberal economic agenda and characterised by a set of objectives linked to reducing the role of the state in welfare provision, which included the privatisation and marketisation of welfare services, most notably, pensions, housing provision and health and social care. The political legitimacy for this course of action was based on arguments about how the expansion of the welfare state could be linked to economic decline, the wastefulness and inefficiency of public services, and their unresponsiveness to users (Corbett and Walker, 2012). The solution, as Thatcher saw it, was: to reduce public expenditure and to increase the outsourcing of public services to private and voluntary sector organisations, which, it was argued, would promote economic efficiency and innovation; to introduce internal markets in education and health; and to subject public services to market disciplines through an emphasis on managerialism (Bochel and Bochel, 2004; Taylor Gooby et al, 2004).

Privatisation and marketisation measures introduced by the Thatcher government included the privatisation of areas of welfare provision and welfare governance. With regard to housing, a 'Right to Buy' policy saw the percentage of housing in Great Britain owned by local authorities decrease from 32% in 1978 to 19% in 1995 (Hills, 1998), and a policy on stock transfer in the 1980s resulted in housing associations taking over housing estates from local authorities (Jones and Murie, 2006). There was a strong focus on the outsourcing of service provision. The Local Government Act 1988 required local authorities to open up many of their services to competitive tender. In 1983, a programme of contracting out ancillary services was imposed on health authorities (DHSS, 1983), despite a lack of evidence about cost efficiency (Cousins, 1988). In long–term care provision, there was a marked shift from public to private provision. A policy change in 1993 resulted in people being able to choose private or voluntary sector nursing or residential care and have the fees paid from the social security budget. While voluntary sector homes could have clients paid for in this way – and some did – the greatest beneficiary was the private sector, with a major expansion of new corporate care home operators (Player and Pollock, 2001). While the implementation of the community care legislation (DoH, 1990), with the introduction of needs assessment and caps on charges, did change the landscape somewhat, the private sector has continued to be the main provider of care homes. In the area of pension provision, there was a significant shift to the private sector. The Social Security Act 1986 reduced existing state provision and incentivised private pension alternatives (Pemberton et al, 2006), with people encouraged to move to private sector pensions rather than state or occupational schemes. Quasi-markets were developed in education, with measures to allow schools to opt out of local authority control and to compete with each other for pupils, as well as in health care through the introduction of GP fund-holding and the purchaser–provider split.

Assessment of the impact of such policies suggests that between 1979 and 1997, there were deliberate policies to increase private provision, which represented a gradual rather than a rapid privatisation of welfare (Hills, 1998). Burchardt's (1997) analysis of public/private welfare activity shows that between 1979/80 and 1995/96, there was a fall in purely public activity (from 52% of the total to 49%) and a rise in purely private activity (from 24% to 29%), and over a number of welfare areas, the role of the private sector in the provision of services increased during the years of the 1979–97 Conservative governments.

Privatisation post-1997

The Labour government

Since 1997, the Labour governments under Blair and Brown, the Coalition government, and the Conservative government elected in 2015 have all maintained an energy for privatisation in the governance and delivery of welfare services. In a departure from traditional Labour Party policy, the Blair government strongly embraced the mixed economy of welfare and the idea of local authorities as enablers rather than providers of services. There was a stronger narrative and emphasis on quality, and on the state regulation of quality and on performance, with the introduction of payment by results in some areas of provision. In adult social care policy, there was a new emphasis on the individual as the commissioner of their own care through the use of personal budgets (DoH, 2007). The reduction in the social housing responsibilities of local government started by the Thatcher government continued through stock transfer to housing associations and the establishment of new arm's-length management organisations (ALMOs) to take over the day-to-day running of local authority housing (DETR, 2000).

While the Labour Party had expressed a commitment to abolishing the internal market in health care while in opposition, in power, the privatisation agenda was observed by some as constituting new dimensions in privatisation (Pollock, 2005; Lister, 2008). It maintained a purchaser–provider split, contracted out clinical services and made extensive use of private finance initiatives (PFIs). Powell and Miller (2014, p 587), identifying the range of different views on the Labour Party approach to the National Health Service (NHS), note that while some see significant privatisation, others 'see the New Labour reforms not as privatisation *per se* but rather on the basis of developing a market in which patients choose providers from any sector, and point to the limited degree of provision by private providers'. Burchardt (2013) assessed that by 2007/08, the tax-financed, publicly provided services under public decision-making accounted for just under half (48%) of expenditure, which was only slightly smaller than the corresponding proportion in 1979/80 (52%).

The Coalition government and the Conservative government

While all the indications were that the Coalition government was going to expand the mixed economy of welfare, seeing tendering and commissioning as fundamental to greater efficiency (Bochel, 2016), the rhetoric about the Big Society initially seemed to indicate a key role for voluntary organisations and for social enterprises in replacing state welfare provision. Bochel (2016, p 60) discusses how the Coalition government support for the development of mutuals (staff-owned companies that can bid for public services), including the setting up of a Mutuals Taskforce, may have been to address concerns about the privatisation of services. However, as he points out, provision by mutuals has been limited and mainly confined to some provision in children's services and health and social care.

Two key policies published in 2011 suggested that the Coalition's approach to welfare delivery was to include a strong focus on non-state providers. The *Open Public Services White Paper* (HM Government, 2011, p 6) included the statement that 'the old centralised approach to public service delivery is broken', advocating a new approach of opening up the delivery of these services to new providers. How this was to happen was through a 'new presumption in favour of individual choice and control' (HM Government, 2011, p 9), being facilitated through mechanisms such as personal budgets in adult social care, personal health budgets for those with long-term conditions, the proposal for personal budgets for families with children with special educational needs, and more use of direct cash payments and vouchers. The Localism Act 2011 (DCLG, 2011b) also contained measures to accommodate the agenda of 'opening up' public services. Here, discussion was of ensuring a wider range of providers, again, under the rationale of choice, by giving voluntary and community groups, parish councils, and local government employees the right to express an interest in taking over the running of a service, with local authorities required to respond by running a procurement exercise for the service in question. It also set out new community 'rights', such as the right to bid for community assets such as libraries, post offices or community centres threatened with closure or up for sale. Outlining the aims of the Localism Bill, Minister of State for Decentralisation Greg Clark stated that 'Our default position is that all public services should be open to diverse provision, with monopoly provision justified on an exceptional basis' (HM Government, 2010, p 9). The Act was viewed with some scepticism, with questions as to whether public procurement processes under these measures would make it easier for voluntary sector organisations to successfully bid for services (Bovaird, 2012) or whether it was based on an underlying assumption that public provision had failed to deliver quality services and that the private sector was seen as the solution. Others argued that little attention had been given to whether the market would respect the principle of subsidiarity and ensure that users would have a greater say and control (National Coalition for Independent Action, 2012). Such concerns were seen as particularly pertinent because of the impact of the austerity measures being imposed by the Coalition government on local government, leading local authorities to prioritise cost reduction over other issues. Bovaird (2012, p 11) refers to a comment by the Labour MP Hazel Blears that if the Act:

> simply opens the door for more externalisation, so that large-scale commercial firms end up being the main gainers ... then it will not only be seen as an act of trickery but may also result in significantly worse public services being delivered than previously by the public sector.

With regard to housing and health (discussed later), the Coalition government pursued very direct privatisation and marketisation policies. The *Housing Strategy for England* (DCLG, 2011a) included a revival of the Right to Buy through the raising of discount caps from £38,000 to £75,000 (Hodkinson, 2012). The 2015 Conservative government went a step further by extending the Right to Buy to housing association tenants in England (Wilson and Bates, 2016). While ministers sought to allay fears about a reduction in the housing stock by suggesting that additional houses sold would be replaced by new-build, only half of those sold under these new Right to Buy measures would be replaced, and in a further development, the rules for those holding social housing tenancies were to be changed through the introduction of new 'flexible' tenancies instead of lifetime tenure (Somerville, 2016).

Among the most controversial proposals by the Coalition government was that children's services should be outsourced to private companies. Following lobbying, this was changed and the amendments to the Children and Young Persons Act 2008 in 2014 (The Children and Young Persons Act 2008 [Relevant Care Functions] [England] Regulations 2014), included plans for the majority of children's services to be outsourced to not-for-profit providers. There has been resistance to this from some local authorities, who have argued that it is better to deliver services in-house, but many have been financially unable to do so (Stevenson and Schraer, 2015). Where functions have been outsourced, they have tended to be in the area of children's homes, children's centre provision and leaving care services.

The structure and nature of outsourcing under the Coalition government meant that for-profit organisations dominated in many areas of welfare provision, including in prison provision, probation, employment services and health and social care, as discussed later in the chapter. This was a trend continued by the 2015 Conservative government. The debate about the privatisation of welfare also moved on under the Conservative government as it reignited debates about the role of the state, the division of responsibility for welfare between individuals and the state, and how welfare services should be governed and delivered. Privatisation was to impact upon a number of areas of provision: health and social care; prisons and the probation service; housing provision; and employment services.

Health and social care

The expansion of the use of non-state providers and the influence of managerialism and new public management can easily be seen in the area of health and social care. The introduction of the purchaser–provider split in 1993, the policy of 'money follows patient' in 2000 (with government paying hospitals on the basis of work they attracted through competition with other hospitals), the establishment of foundation trust hospitals in 2003, the publication of *Our Health, Our Say* (DoH, 2006) (which required primary care trusts to put their provider services out to tender) and the Labour government's tendering of Hinchingbrooke Hospital in 2007 can all be seen as expanding the market in health and social care. Across successive governments and a range of NHS policies, there was a rhetoric of promoting greater patient choice and control and improving quality (eg DoH, 2006, 2007, 2011a), with assumptions that this required more non-state providers competing with each other to provide services. The Coalition government's 2011 White Paper *Equity and Excellence: Liberating the NHS* (DoH, 2011b) and the resulting legislation, the Health and Social Care Act 2012, abolished the secretary of state's duty to *provide* comprehensive health services and required the clinical commissioning groups, responsible for about two thirds of NHS spending, to put services out to competitive tender. The monetary value of NHS services contracted out increased from £6.6 billion in 2009 to £10 billion in 2014 (out of a total budget of £113 billion), although the extent of contracting out was evident in some areas of provision more than others. While the rate of spending on non-NHS acute services was less in real terms in 2012/13 than in the previous year, spending on community health services provided by the private sector rose from 12% in 2010/11 to 18% in 2012/13 (The Kings Fund, 2015). It is difficult to determine exactly the value of the contracted-out services provided by the private sector. Baggott (2016, p 115) notes that after the new competitive clauses contained in the 2012 Act came into effect in April 2014, over half of new contracts went to the private sector. Greener (2015) estimates that about 6% of all NHS contracts by value go to the private sector, and that in 2013/14, around one third of all commissioned care contracts were private. This, he notes, is not a big increase from the situation in 2010 but is double that of 2006/07; a BBC report put the money spent by the NHS on private sector providers in 2013/14 at £6.5 billion (The Kings Fund, 2015).

Klein (2015, p 622) has argued that 'talk of the privatisation of the NHS seems at best premature and at worst a misuse of language', a view supported by The Kings Fund (2015), which concluded that there has been growth in non-NHS provision but that there has been no wholesale privatisation of the NHS. There are very differing views on this (Hunter, 2013; Powell and Miller, 2014, 2016; Pollock, 2015), though as Greener (2015) points out, the debate needs to be looked at in terms not just of the principles of the NHS, but also of the provision of public care – the NHS was created through a nationalisation of care providers, especially hospitals, and so the 'public' bit is clearly important. He concludes that if it is unravelling, it is doing so slowly, and that the process began not under the Coalition government, but under their Labour predecessors.

Outsourcing of employment services

In the UK and in many other countries, activation measures aimed at getting more people into paid employment have been a feature of the policy landscape since the 1990s. Many of these schemes have been characterised by marketisation and contracting out, where the provision of services is outsourced and the role of the state is increasingly focused on process requirements and regulation. Carter and Whitworth (2015) identify strong cross-party agreement in the UK on the marketisation and contractualism of employment services. Labour governments post-1997 supported the marketisation of employment services and this was a key element of employment support programmes under the leadership of Blair and Brown (Freud, 2007). The New Deal programmes rolled out in 1998, the Pathways to Work approach introduced in 2007 and the Flexible New Deals in 2009 were all based around contracting with the private and voluntary sector, and to a lesser extent social enterprises. Increasingly during the period of the Labour governments, a prime contractor model was developed whereby the nature of contracts, procurement processes and high transaction costs favoured large well-resourced organisations (Struyven and Steurs, 2005), and this has been a tendency in many welfare markets (Heins and Bennett, 2016).

This approach was extended by the Coalition government in its 2011 Work Programme. In Great Britain, this meant that delivery would take place through contracts with large-scale and mainly private providers, who can deliver services but also subcontract them. This was facilitated through conditions in the tendering process that restricted eligibility for bidding to be a prime contractor to organisations with an annual turnover of £20 million or more, which meant that many smaller organisations and voluntary organisations that had previously been involved in providing specialist services could not bid (Lindsay et al, 2014).

Delivery of the programme is structured around contract package areas, with two or three prime contractors in each area. While prime contractors could include subsidiary suppliers in their bids, following the award of the contract, there were no requirements placed on prime contractors regarding the use of suppliers (Simmonds, 2011).

While the rationale of the Work Programme was to personalise services according to user needs, Newton et al (2012) suggest that rather than this being the case, a 'procedural' personalisation became more common, with Department for Work and Pensions (DWP) imposing few requirements on the prime contractors awarded tenders. Fuertes et al (2014) conclude that the type of marketisation applied to the Work Programmes did not have the result of increasing competition or choice except between a small number of large providers – and then only at the point of the granting of the contracts.

In addition to contracting out employment services, assessment of fitness to work and eligibility for incapacity benefit, and, from 2008, employment and support allowance (ESA) assessments, were also outsourced from 2005. After years of controversy and allegations that high numbers of people were wrongly judged by the contractor, ATOS, as fit for work, ATOS bought its way out of its £400 million contract with the government. It also had to make a financial settlement to the DWP for the early termination of the contract. The government indicated that it would maintain outsourced provision but would move towards contracting with multiple providers (Penning, 2014). The contracting out of health and disability assessments had been the subject of a number of critical reports (House of Commons Work and Pensions Committee, 2014; House of Commons Committee of Public Accounts, 2014), and a Work and Pensions Committee inquiry in 2016 expressed concern that previously identified failures had not been tackled by the government (House of Commons Work and Pensions Committee, 2016). These included 'unacceptable' regional and local variation in the performance of contractors, concern about the inappropriate and inadequate treatment of those with fluctuating and especially mental health conditions, and risk about value for money given the increasing cost of assessment but no notable benefit to claimants.

The evidence about the impact of contracted-out work programmes on employment outcomes in Britain is patchy. Some research (Carter and Whitworth, 2015, p 279) suggests that outsourced provision is not more efficient than public services in achieving job outcomes but that claimants do tend to be more satisfied with outsourced provision. The nature of contracts, the system of prime contractors and payment by results have been linked to a less holistic approach to users and a tendency towards selection bias (Newton et al, 2012; Carter and Whitworth, 2015). Referred to as 'creaming' and 'parking', this suggests that providers prioritise claimants with fewer barriers to work, they are therefore more likely to move into paid work and allow the provider to receive the outcomes-based payments while deliberately 'parking' and neglecting to give those users with most barriers to work time and resources. The Work Programme has sought to reduce creaming and parking through the introduction of 'minimum services guarantees' from prime providers, with differential payments across the groups of claimants. However, Finn (2012) points to weaknesses in the substance and enforceability of the impact of these measures and also to the fact that the payment methods do not take account of the variability within groups.

Both social security and employment policy are the responsibility of the Northern Ireland government. While scope for divergence in social security policy has been limited by the financial implications of a break with parity with Great Britain (Birrell and Gray, 2014), there has been greater scope for divergence in employment policy. Unlike in Great Britain, where social security benefits and employment policy is the jurisdiction of a single government department (DWP), in Northern Ireland, responsibility falls to two separate departments. In respect of work activation programmes, since 2008, there has been greater convergence with policy in Great Britain in terms of the outsourcing of provision. The Steps to Work programme introduced in 2008 saw the number of contracts with external providers reduced from 147 (which had included a large number of voluntary sector providers) to 10, with each of the 10 providers being responsible for delivering services in a single contract area. Under a new Steps to Success programme in 2014, the 10 contract areas reduced to three, each led by a single contractor (with subcontractors) (Department for Employment and Learning, 2013). Up to 2014, most of the prime contractors had been based in Northern Ireland but they were not perceived by the department as having the resources necessary for upfront investment or the capacity to manage the risks, so one of the aims of the new structure was to attract large contractors from Great Britain. Wiggan (2015, p 122) describes how in the post-2014 model, local contractors were relegated to subcontractor status, being replaced by large British contractors such as EOS Works and Ingeus. This meant that large for-profit organisations enjoyed 'a relatively privileged position in the activation market which did not exist under Steps to Work' (Wiggan, 2015, p 122). However, he concludes that developments post-2014 in Northern Ireland saw the state relinquish some control over the content of the programme. There continued to be some differences, which he attributes to lesson learning from market failure in Britain. These included the maintenance of minimum service standards and greater public regulation than in Great Britain.

Prisons and probation services

Prisons

The privatisation of prisons was first introduced in the late 1980s by the Conservative government under a tendering process that the public sector was barred from participating in. It was announced in 1993 that all new prisons would be privately built and operated under PFI. Despite opposing the policy while in opposition, the Labour government continued with the PFI initiative for prison building. The Coalition and subsequently the Conservative governments expressed continuing commitment to the contracting out of prison services. In May 2016, there were 14 private prisons in England and Wales (17% of the prison population) managed by SERCO, G4S Justice Services and Sodexo (Department of Justice, 2016), and two out of 15 prisons in Scotland have been contracted out to private companies. Prison provision is not outsourced in Northern Ireland. The privatisation of prisons has been controversial, generating debates about efficiency and standards. The National Audit Office (2003) noted that the PFI initiative with regard to prisons had brought 'success and failures', and government claims about cost efficiency have been questioned on the grounds that publically available financial data do not include the full costs of prison building (Mills et al, 2010). Poor standards with regard to procurement and to service provision have been raised. In November 2013, the privatisation of three prisons in Yorkshire was abandoned, with the leading bidder under investigation for overcharging (Grimwood, 2014). In September 2015, G4S secured a five-year contract worth £50 million to run a facility for young offenders. This was awarded despite strong criticism by the Office for Standards in Education (Ofsted, 2015) of the firm's poor management of a young offender centre in Rainsbrook. Following a BBC *Panorama* investigation in January 2016 into staff assaults on children at Medway Secure Training Unit in Kent, a government investigation resulted in the National Offender Management Service taking over the running of the unit from the private company G4S (BBC, 2016a). Shortly afterwards, G4S announced that it was in the process of selling its UK children's services business, including 13 children's homes and two young offender centres (G4S, 2016). In 2015, its revenue from this business was £40 million.

Probation

In 2015, more than half of the probation service in England and Wales was privatised. Probation services had been delivered by 35 self-governing probation trusts working under the National Offender Management Service. Under the Coalition government's 2013 *Transforming Rehabilitation* reforms (Ministry of Justice, 2013), the probation service was to be reconfigured with public sector probation staff to be transferred to either a public National Probation Service, which would deal with high-risk offenders, or one of 21 community rehabilitation companies (CRCs) working with low- to medium-risk offenders (Robinson et al, 2015). The stated aims of the *Transforming Rehabilitation* reforms included a new mix of providers with a set of incentives including an element of payment by results (Ministry of Justice, 2013, p 9). The policy document assumed savings, stating that these would be used to extend rehabilitation and achieve more effective services, including more integration of provision from custody to the community.

Two companies (Sodexo and Ingeus) won half the contracts, worth £450 million a year. Most of the other contracts were also won by private sector companies but three were awarded to a private–voluntary company, Working Links, which was to run the services with a mutual of former probation staff. In addition to criticism that there was little evidence that these developments would secure greater effectiveness or cost efficiency, they were seen to threaten the fundamental ethos and identity of the probation service, shifting it from a social work value base to a culture of 'compliance and enforcement' (Teague, 2013, p 17). A National Audit Office (2016a) report on the implementation and working of *Transforming Rehabilitation* identified failings across a range of processes, concluding that it was not possible to judge value for money. While 77% of service users said that they had not noticed any change in the services they personally received, the National Audit Office (2016a, p 25) found that the performance of CRCs and the National Probation Service was unclear because of poor data quality and availability. Performance varied significantly across CRCs, various information and communication technology (ICT) systems created severe inefficiencies, and the way in which CRCs are paid for completing specified activities with offenders rather than reducing offending risked hindering innovative practice.

Education

Chapter Seven included examination of the increasing role of public–private partnerships in education but it is useful to draw attention to some specific aspects of private sector involvement in education. Ball (2007) argues that, in England, there has not been one single policy or set of policies that have supported the entrance of private interests into the operation and delivery of schools. Rather, there has been a steady flow of reforms that have had an accumulative effect. Higham (2014) believes this to have been so extensive that, over time, what was once unimaginable has been normalised, so that now an array of private interests operates in state education, including in the provision of back-office services (ICT, human resources and accounting), school buildings and school improvement services. The Coalition government sought to open up the system to new providers by expanding the Labour government's academies programme (discussed in Chapter Seven). Alongside the extension of academies, the Academies Act 2010 allowed for the creation of 'free' schools – schools that could be established by a range of proposers, including groups of parents, charities and businesses. These, the secretary of state for education asserted, would drive social mobility – particularly in areas where deprivation was high (Gove, 2011). To others, these developments are in keeping with the Conservative Party reform programme by securing a power shift away from central government and by creating further environments for a free market and the 'possibility of schools run by large corporations' (Bailey and Ball, 2016, p 139). The idea of free schools as a mechanism for social mobility has been challenged. Experience in Sweden, albeit where free schools can be profit-making bodies, suggests that they were more likely to be located in more affluent areas (Higham, 2014), exacerbating inequities. Higham's empirical work concluded that the proposal process largely weighed against disadvantaged communities due to the expertise and access to resources needed to be successful. The 2015 Conservative government proposed what were viewed as even more radical reforms to education which would mean that local authorities would no longer maintain schools. Instead, an all-academy system would exist with schools becoming part of multi-academy trusts and the role of local authorities limited to ensuring the sufficiency of school places and some responsibilities for vulnerable pupils (DfE, 2016a). This was a proposal that proved highly controversial (Long and Bolton, 2016), including among Conservative backbench MPs, and on 6 May 2016, Secretary of State for Education Nicky Morgan announced that plans to compel all schools in England to become academies was being abandoned (BBC, 2016b).

The success or failure of welfare markets

The experience of a stronger role for private markets in welfare provision has given rise to a number of issues and questions. Primary among these is whether an increasing role for the private sector in the governance and delivery of welfare has resulted in market effectiveness or failure. Relevant to this question are debates about: the extent to which there is a diversity of providers; whether more outsourcing has resulted in the fragmentation of provision and made coordination and integration more difficult to achieve; whether the state has transferred responsibility for fundamental aspects of welfare; whether a greater role for non-state actors has resulted in better value for money; the extent to which users have been provided with greater choice; and whether standards and quality have improved.

Some of the problems with the outsourcing of prisons discussed earlier in the chapter illustrated failures with contract design, management and the monitoring of the quality of provision. Similar issues arose with the one example of an NHS hospital franchised to a private sector provider. In November 2011, Hitchingbrooke Hospital in Cambridgeshire was taken over by a private company, Circle Health. In January 2013, the Committee of Public Accounts expressed concerns that Circle Health's bid to run Hitchingbrooke had not been properly risk-assessed and was based on unachievable savings projections (House of Commons Committee of Public Accounts, 2015). It was rated 'inadequate' by the Care Quality Commission in 2014 (Care Quality Commission, 2015), and by January 2015, Circle Health announced that it was handing back management of the hospital to the NHS, citing problems with funding cuts. In an update on Hitchingbrooke Health Care NHS Trust, the Committee of Public Accounts noted the failure by the various parties who had oversight and responsibility to respond to previous warnings about risks, as well as the lack of accountability, with no one being held accountable for the consequences (House of Commons Committee of Public Accounts, 2015, p 5). It went on to express concerns that lessons from managing major contracts will not be learnt and that 'public bodies will not achieve value for money from these contracts until they become more commercially skilled' (House of Commons Committee of Public Accounts, 2015, p 7).

The case of Southern Cross, the UK's largest private provider of residential care services, which went into insolvency in 2011, illustrates the risk to users when one provider is allowed to be so dominant in the market and oversight systems are not sufficient to monitor and identify threats to quality and sustainability. With 750 care homes and an 8.7% share of the market nationally when Southern Cross became insolvent, the government had to step in to ensure that a crisis was averted (New Economics Foundation, 2015). A subsequent report into Southern Cross (National Audit Office, 2012) found no effective system in place to minimise the impact of provider failure on users. The growing number of insolvencies in the residential care sector is a result of unsustainable expansion, but also since 2010, of funding cuts to local authorities. The number of care homes going out of business rose by 23% between 2014 and 2015, with a 23-fold rise since 2010 (Tovey, 2016). An emerging issue for markets in public services may be the lack of demand from non-public providers (Dalton, 2014) because of the financial pressures and as it becomes perhaps less possible for companies to focus on short-term profit.

The issue of problems caused by large dominant private providers has also arisen in health-care provision. In 2014, CCGs in Staffordshire announced that they would be seeking bids for a £1.2 billion 10-year contract for cancer and end-of-life care. This gave rise to considerable controversy, including a 70,000 named petition opposing the move. With one bidder left in the process, a consortium including the Royal Wolverhampton Hospital and private sector company Interserve, NHS England asked the CCG to suspend the process following the setting up of a review into the collapse of the procurement of a £800 million contract held by Uniting Care for elderly care in Cambridge and Peterborough (NHS England, 2016a).

A common criticism of the outsourcing of services has been a lack of transparency that compromises accountability. In law, an authority that arranges for services to be delivered by another entity remains accountable and there is an argument that marketisation increases accountability, for example, public–private partnerships and PFIs are often premised on the transfer of financial risk to the private sector contractors, who are theoretically responsible for any increased cost. However, as discussed in Chapter Seven, substantive issues have been raised about the transparency and nature of PFI contracts.

When services are outsourced to other bodies, contractors are not covered by Freedom of Information legislation, although contracting bodies can specify that they comply with certain standards of transparency in contracts. While governments have promoted some forms of accountability through contracts, there has been resistance to incorporating human rights obligations into contracts, and Donnelly (2011) has identified the reluctance of courts to intervene to impose public law obligations on private welfare providers. There have also been well-documented concerns about contract management, with questions about the ability of public organisations to develop the form and content of contracts to allow them to secure value for money and to manage and monitor them robustly (Field and Peck, 2004; National Audit Office, 2014f). In 2013/14, there was a series of government contractor and contract management failures in the contracting of public services but government committees had been raising concerns over a number of years. A National Audit Office (2014f) report reflected on the, by then, fairly long history of contracted-out services across government. It notes a list of reviews by the Home Office, DWP and the Ministry of Justice that had shown widespread problems in the administration of government contracts, including overbilling, poor governance and capacity issues, and contributing to a crisis of confidence in the contracting of public services. While the various reviews had all included recommendations, the National Audit Office (2014f, p 6) was critical of the weak government response, criticising the government for acting as if 'the firms were too important to fail'.

Impact on the workforce

There are contesting views on whether the outsourcing of care work has led to a uniform 'race to the bottom' in pay and conditions. The shift towards large-scale providers in tendering and outsourcing has resulted in private sector companies dominating the market, with many former public sector employees being employed by private sector organisations or, as has increasingly been the case in adult social care provision in England, by individuals. In adult social care, for example, the majority of services are now delivered by the private sector, with more than a million workers employed by 30,000 employers, individuals and small businesses (Local Government Association, 2013c). While the focus in terms of the cost of outsourcing has largely been on value-for-money issues and cost efficiency, the impact of outsourcing on the workforce has received some attention (Cousins, 1988; Rubery and Urwin, 2011), with differences in opinion about the impact on pay and conditions (Baines and Cunningham, 2015). The Smith Institute (2014) found evidence that some employees, especially those in managerial and professional roles, benefitted from progression opportunities in the private sector. For lower-paid employees, the evidence is to the contrary and progression opportunities declined. It also found that the successive re-tendering of contracts has produced an array of different terms and conditions among employees providing the same service. The context of austerity has led to renewed debate about the role and value of the private sector, with a view that it is the scale of public expenditure cuts that is primarily setting the objectives of public service outsourcing (Smith Institute, 2014), with saving money being the main purpose. This, in turn, impacts on the terms and conditions of employment of workers whose jobs have been contracted out of the public sector, with them being more likely to work excessive overtime, have greater job insecurity, be on short-term contracts and have lower pay. In some areas, for example, in social care and in childcare provision, there are also differences in the qualification levels of workers (Greer et al, 2011; Cunningham and James, 2014).

A code of practice regarding the workforce in relation to local authority contracts was adopted in 2003. It aimed to ensure that workers in the same service were similarly contracted (New Economics Foundation, 2015). Where contracting out results in local authority employees being transferred to a private sector provider, they have to be covered by the Transfer of Undertakings (Protection of Employment) Regulations (TUPE). In 2014, new regulations (HM Government, 2014b) amended the original TUPE rules, resulting in fewer rights to workers where there is a change of employer. Under the new regulations, activities carried out under outsourced or tendered work must be 'fundamentally the same' for TUPE to apply and dismissal is no longer automatically unfair because of a change in the workplace location.

Quality, trust and privatisation

Since the 1990s, with regard to the main political parties in the UK, there has been a cross-party political consensus that privatising aspects of welfare services is desirable. The public, though, have seemed less convinced and are particularly apprehensive about the role of private companies in the delivery of public services (Worth, 2012; Defty, 2016). There may be some scepticism about the motivation for privatisation. Hood (2011) suggests that the contracting out of public services delivery by government could be seen as a strategy by politicians to avoid blame for potential service failure through the delegation of the management of delivery. The perception of the public to outsourcing may depend to an extent on the type of organisation contracted for the provision. Using the example of street maintenance in the UK, James et al (2015) found that the public were more likely to see not-for-profit organisations in a more positive light but this would be much less the case with health or social care services. There is also some variance in opinion within the UK when it comes to the delivery of public services, with the public in Scotland being much more likely to feel that public authorities do the best job (54%), compared with 30% in England and Wales. When asked about what sector would provide the best quality of service for the money, 50% of Scots said the public sector compared to 25% in England and Wales (Ormston and Reid, 2012; Diffley, 2013).

Devolution and privatisation

Arguably, the devolved jurisdictions have taken a somewhat different approach than Westminster governments to privatisation, which has been linked to their 'more expansive visions of welfare' in the pre-2007/08 period (Chaney and Wincott, 2014, p 775). And although all of the devolved jurisdictions have adopted a mixed-economy approach to the delivery of services, as is very evident with social care provision, the use of the private sector to reduce hospital waiting lists and employment services, Scotland and Wales can be seen to be to the left of the political dimension and have rejected some of the market-based policies introduced in England (Birrell and Gray, 2016). For example, there has not been the same approach to prison privatisation in Scotland, and both Scotland and Wales abolished the internal market in health care. The devolved countries also have small private health sectors; less than 1% of the budget in Scotland in 2010 was spent in the private sector compared to 5% in England (Timmins, 2013). As in England, there has been strong and increasing reliance on private provision for older people's residential and nursing care and home care provision in all the devolved jurisdictions, with most care not provided by the state. In Scotland, the volume of home care directly provided by local authorities fell from 82% in 2000 to 44% in 2011 (Rummery and McAngus, 2015). In Northern Ireland, while the use of private and voluntary sector providers has been growing and is set to increase, the statutory sector still delivers 32% of domiciliary care contact hours and the independent sector 68%; by comparison, in England, the split is 11% and 89% (Health and Social Care Board, NI, 2015). Taking into account these differences, there has been substantial marketisation in the provision of services in all parts of the UK.

Conclusions

Since the 1980s, there has been a distinct shift in the relationship between the state and the market in many advanced Western welfare states, with welfare services increasingly being delivered within a mixed welfare market. While public service outsourcing was initially for processes considered to be 'non-core', it now extends to a wide range of welfare services. The *Outsourcing Yearbook* (National Outsourcing Association, 2016) states that in the third quarter of 2015, the total value of local government outsourcing contracts more than trebled when compared with the previous quarter, meaning that local government outsourcing accounted for 21% of all outsourcing contracts across the UK between July and September 2015. Bode (2006) discusses that underpinning these changing welfare markets are ideas that go beyond economic developments and need to considered in the context of a moral economy. For example, the focus on offering people choice over the kind of service they use may be more and not less costly than traditional services provided by the state and therefore may not be in keeping with an agenda of welfare state retrenchment. Although personalisation of services such as adult social care, as designed and implemented in England, has characteristics of new public management it also has civil rights elements as a result of the demands of the disability movement (Needham, 2011). The growing focus on choice and co-production is seen as having been positive for some users but the state's linkage of these ideas to a rise of welfare markets has been seen as problematic. Concentration on fewer, larger providers with a for-profit motive has often limited the mix of provision and reduced choice in terms of location, sector and approaches to delivery (Shutes and Taylor, 2014).

As discussed earlier, the expansion of non–state provision does not mean total withdrawal of the state and the risks associated with for-profit delivery markets may have been constrained by the state retaining and strengthening an oversight over outputs and standards. Analysis of the experience of privatisation in UK welfare services points to a number of problems. The premise that a shift to private providers is always more efficient has been challenged (Farnsworth and Holden, 2006). There have been examples of poor standards due to a lack of understanding of the needs of users or the services required. While governments have theoretically retained often considerable control through oversight and regulation, they have also often responded weakly to problems of poor provision. Weaknesses in the tendering and contracting process have allowed 'gaming' by providers and the kind of creaming and parking policies adopted in employment services. Contracting arrangements have locked commissioners into contractual arrangements with one provider, reducing expertise in areas where work practices may change quickly (Grimshaw et al, 2002). When there are market failings in outsourcing and government is forced to intervene, the cost has been shown to be significant. For example, Sandford (2016) refers to insourcing – when services have to be brought back in–house by local government – as was the case with Islington Borough Council having to insource house repairs in 2013 at a cost of £2 million in setting up in–house services from scratch.

Even strong proponents of welfare markets acknowledge that markets in public services are different to conventional private markets. In private markets, considerable power rests with the individual purchasing the product or service. Taylor Gooby et al (2004, p 589) referred to the Labour government 'experiment' in developing the welfare state within a market-oriented public policy as having made real progress towards welfare ends but facing limitations in 'stimulating and regulating private market provision in areas such as childcare, the care of older people and pensions'. In the period since 1997, it is possible to identify a stronger focus on provision by private sector organisations as new 'markets' created difficult competitive environments for voluntary sector organisations. This, in turn, has presented challenges to some of the rhetoric about the building of collaborative relationships and community involvement, which became somewhat subservient to achieving cost savings.

NINE

Involving users and the public in the governance and delivery of welfare

Introduction

Public and user involvement as a concept is now firmly embedded in welfare policy and legislation across the UK. This chapter examines key developments with regard to user and public participation. It begins by looking at terms and definitions and at the rationale for user and public participation from the perspective of government, users and the public. It identifies key policy and legislative developments and some of the structures and initiatives put in place to encourage participation. Much of the debate has focused on degrees of involvement and on the effectiveness of the models of engagement being used, as well as at whether these can result in user and public participation being transformative in service delivery.

Terms and definitions

The complexity of terminology and definition in this area has been recognised (Beresford, 2010; Conklin et al, 2012). Although user involvement is distinct from public involvement in that it can be about individuals having a say over their own care as well as broader issues, the distinction between public and user is often not made. The term 'citizen' is sometimes used rather than 'public', and 'involvement' is often used interchangeably with 'participation'. Participation has been defined as:

> everything that enables people to influence the decisions and get involved in the actions that affect their lives.... It includes but goes beyond public policy decisions by including initiatives from outside that arena, such as community-led initiatives. It includes action as well as political influence. It also encompasses the need for governance systems and organizational structures to change to allow for effective participation. (Involve, 2005, p 19)

Coulter's (2002) reference to the 21st-century health service user as a decision-maker, a care manager, a co-producer of health, an evaluator, a potential change agent, a taxpayer and an active citizen whose voice must be heard by decision-makers usefully encapsulates the way in which ideas about participation have broadened.

Rationale for user and public participation

Across a range of social policy areas, public and user participation is seen as an important aspect of enhancing democracy and building accountability, and as a solution to some of the problems associated with the planning and delivery of welfare services. In part, this has been seen as a response to discontent with traditional paternalistic models of welfare ill suited to the needs of users. The principles of participation are often associated with greater accountability and the opening up of knowledge previously seen as the domain of experts.

In the growth of participation and involvement the emerging service user movements were central. The work of the disability movement, in particular, in trying to achieve representation and empowerment was pivotal to putting user participation on the political agenda. To those involved in the disability and service user movements in areas such as mental health and HIV/AIDS, for example, fundamental to the desire for greater participation was the idea that the involvement of users could alter the structure of power relations (Oliver, 1996; Barnes and Bowl, 2001). Motivation for collective action was based around what Barnes (2008) describes as 'shared identities' on issues such as stigma, discrimination and injustice.

Politicians have long been concerned about the decline in voting levels and reduced levels of trust in politicians and political institutions, seeing this as a threat to representative democracy and institutions. Dalton (2004) referred to two general trends across developed nations that posed a challenge to representative democracy: the rising expectations of government among citizens; and the growing complexity of contemporary political agendas, which makes it increasingly difficult for governments to satisfy most of the people most of the time. Also underpinning political disaffection is the argument that democratic politics has become too captured by the interests of powerful elites (Runciman, 2013), with the interplay between political and economic power ensuring that these elites assert their interests in the democratic process at the expense of ordinary citizens. Others have identified how lack of confidence in representative democracy has contributed to weak policies, poor accountability and low standards in service delivery (Leadbeater and Mulgan, 1994; Mahendran and Cook, 2007). This perspective has been challenged by writers pointing to the number of people active through citizen-led campaigns and the success of online activist networks such as 38 degrees and AVAAZ, which are not single-issue-based, but work across a range of national and international issues (Purcell, 2014). Political parties have increasingly adopted the methods of the early collective-based initiatives, although not yet in the UK in the way that has happened in countries such as the US or France (Williamson et al, 2010).

These challenges have resulted in governments recognising the need to find different ways of engaging with citizens, both in terms of reviving democracy and in terms of a recognition that government and providers alone cannot address many of the challenges confronting welfare services (Simmons and

Birchall, 2005). The Labour government's modernisation agenda for local government and public services was couched in discussion of reviving local democracy, and as 'conceiving public participation as part of a fundamental remodelling of the public sector requiring a ... shift in emphasis from the individual to communities' (Purcell, 2014, p 149). This emphasis was continued by the Conservative–Liberal Democrat Coalition government through its pursuit of the development of a 'Big Society' in which there would be mass engagement, more civic responsibility, more power to communities and the reform of public services (Cabinet Office, 2010a).

A strong influence on the policy direction of public and user involvement since the 1980s has been ideas and practices relating to managerialism and new public management (Newman, 2000). A key element of this approach to public services was strengthening the accountability and responsiveness of institutions through giving people a greater say and more choice and representation in governance structures. This more empowered consumer was to be a part of ensuring that providers were more accountable (Connolly, 2011); in England, a key element of consumerism was user choice. This thinking shaped social welfare governance and delivery in the UK, with a greater role for the private and voluntary sectors in service provision and through the establishment of cross-sectoral partnerships as discussed in Chapter Seven. The thrust towards using user choice and involvement as a way of driving up quality in public services and greater accountability continues to be a key driver of participation policies and initiatives in England. The emphasis on user choice is less apparent in other parts of the UK, and for that reason, there is a stronger focus in this chapter on initiatives in England with regard to user choice. However, user involvement and greater personalisation of services are common themes across the jurisdictions and this is reflected in the discussion.

An increasingly significant factor in the move to more openness and transparency in welfare services and the participation of users and lay people in the governance of services has been the revelations about poor standards and abuse in health and social care provision. The BBC *Panorama* exposé and subsequent inquiries into Winterbourne View residential home and the inquiries into serious failings at Mid Staffordshire NHS Foundation Trust highlighted the need for whole-system cultural change. The Transforming Care Programme set out in the wake of the Winterbourne View inquiries stressed that cultural change would require meaningful engagement with users and families, the empowerment of users, and much greater openness (DoH, 2015). The King's Fund (2013, p 25), commenting on what would be necessary to achieve the outcomes set out in the Francis Inquiry into the failings at Mid Staffordshire, refers to how much previous patient and public engagement had been taken over by institutional interests and used as a buffer against change. It advocates the idea of 'patients as leaders', seeing them as playing two key roles: as a community channel, keeping in touch with local communities; and as acting as a critical friend.

Definition and types of participation

Definition may depend to some extent on the rationale for participation, intended outcomes and type of participation (Rowe and Frewer, 2005). Arnstein's (1969) ladder of participation set out several levels and degrees of participation, reflecting a progression from non- or limited participation to citizen control. How meaningful participation is in practice may be related to the rationale for participation and the actual form of involvement. Table 9.1 sets out some examples of the types of involvement, the related methods or processes often adopted, and the likely outcome for participants. Information, consultation and involvement are associated with hierarchical structures of government and empowerment, and co-production is associated with non-hierarchical structures of self-governance and co-governance (Bochel et al, 2008).

Table 9.1: Public participation, processes and outcomes

Type of involvement	Example of form/process of involvement	Likely outcome for participants
Provision of information	Newsletters; websites; posters	Receive information but no direct input
Consultation	Public or user surveys; user feedback; suggestion schemes; focus groups; public meetings; opportunity to respond to policy consultations with pre-defined issues set by government	Ability to input views or concerns but may or may not be provided with feedback on how input influenced decisions
Participation/ involvement	Focus groups; citizens' juries; user involvement in research; deliberative democracy techniques	May be able to make direct recommendations and be more directly involved in identifying solutions and alternatives; may find out how participation has impacted on decisions made
Collaboration	Citizen advisory committees; involvement in scrutiny/ inspection processes; participatory decision-making; participatory budgets	Views and advice will be actively sought; involved in formulating solutions; input incorporated into decisions to a significant extent – potentially transformative
Empowerment	Delegated decisions; ballots; co-production; personal budgets	Citizen/user control with potentially transformative outcomes for individuals and communities
Co-production	Equality of users and providers. Focus on service as product.	Services reflect more strongly user perspectives

The provision of information and traditional consultation processes, associated with non-control, are still a major focus of participation arrangements in the UK, and the limitations of these have been frequently discussed (see, eg, Beresford and Croft, 1993, 1996; Attree et al, 2011; Campbell, 2014). Deliberative structures, such as focus groups and citizens' juries, and parliaments, such as youth parliaments and older people's parliaments, have become a common method of engagement and participation. While such processes do provide opportunities for people to express views and share experiences, studies show that it is often not clear to participants if and how their views have been considered or used. The term 'consultation fatigue' has been used to describe both how frequently people's views are sought and the frustration of users at the lack of feedback on their input. User-led organisations, often in the field of disability but other examples include organisations of older people, young care leavers and people living with HIV/AIDS, can be seen to operate on a rather different basis. They are generally not established by the state and their focus and activities often extend beyond service provision to broader citizenship and civil rights issues.

Policies, initiatives and structures for user and public participation

User participation is now in the mainstream. Durose et al (2013, p 328) refer to how:

> In council chambers, hospital board rooms, patient forums, day care centres and community groups, people express contrasting but equally strong felt views on whether citizens, service users and communities should be involved in decision making, why, how and to what extent.

The marketisation of public services from the 1980s has meant that public and user participation developments have largely been situated within a neo-liberal policy and delivery framework, which has influenced the discourse around participation (Newman et al, 2004; Carey, 2009). The neo-liberal welfare agenda views the market as the quintessential participative device, where rationality, individuality and self-interest guide all actions (Peters, 2001), and that participation, through choice and diversity within a state-funded system, would bring considerable benefits. The 1997 Labour government, with its agenda to modernise welfare services, also identified the involvement of the public and users as an important element of its reform plans. A range of initiatives were introduced to enhance participation, including multi-agency partnership working with public and user representation, the setting up of new mechanisms for public and patient involvement in the National Health Service (NHS), and the involvement of local stakeholders in area-based initiatives such as Sure Start and education and health action zones. These developments were linked to Labour's broader social inclusion agenda and were underpinned by a rationale about strengthening democratic legitimacy, improving civic life and community cohesion, enhancing the legitimacy of decisions, and contributing to the provision of more effective and efficient services (Barnes et al, 2003). The Blair/Brown administrations' official policy was strongly focused on a new 'localism', within which there was to be a stronger role for community governance (Stoker, 2006) and the 'active citizen', with mandated participation in local government. Localism was also a theme of the 2010–15 Coalition government, ideologically centred around the creation of a 'Big Society', where social issues and problems would be addressed in and by local communities (Purcell, 2014). The Conservative government elected in 2015 has continued to produce a strong rhetoric on involvement and civic responsibility.

Newman and Clarke (2009, p 219) refer to a 'dispersal of power', where the process of modernisation provided for a new organisational environment with traditional forms of participation increasingly challenged, on the grounds that they achieved no real shift in power to individuals or communities. While there are examples of more innovative and radical approaches to participation, this continues to be a highly contested area, with consensus on the need for meaningful user and public involvement but less certainty about government motivation and actual outcomes. This section looks at key developments in public and user participation, providing examples of initiatives and structures in several areas of welfare. Beresford (2016, p 199) drew attention to the developing interest in policies and practices that are supportive and empowering rather than restrictive and patronising.

Public and user participation in health and social care

Of the main welfare services, it is perhaps on health and social care that governments and, indeed, user movements and campaigners have focused, with policies and initiatives spanning many years. By the 21st century, user and public involvement in health and social care had become a duty and the majority of health policy narratives produced by governments and health bodies now address the issue. A wide range of mechanisms have been used, including lay management boards, user representation on national boards, user panels, the production of information by users and contribution to education and to research (Duffy, 2006; Mockford et al, 2012; Boxall and Beresford, 2013). Developments have included the involvement of users in regulation and inspection processes, such as the Care Quality Commission's 'experts by experience' – people with experience of care services who take part in inspections and visits to monitor the use of the Mental Health Act. The introduction of personal budgets, while controversial, has been argued to given greater control to some users (Waters and Hatton, 2014; Larsen et al, 2015), although there has been recognition of political and practical challenges (Glasby, 2014b; Slasberg et al, 2014). There is also a tradition of user-led campaigning organisations in health and social care around issues such as disability and rights, stigma and discrimination, cuts to funding services, human rights, training and employment issues, and recovery and enablement (Barret et al, 2014).

The timeline in Table 9.2 highlights key policy and legislative developments in England with regard to user and public participation in health and social care.

Table 9.2: Key policy and legislative developments in England relating to public and user participation in health and social care

1989 Working for Patients	Introduces the idea of the health-care consumer participating in a quasi-market in health care
1991 Patients Charter	Entitlements
2001 Health and Social Care Act	Imposed a duty on all NHS organisations to involve patients and the public
2002 Wanless Review	Talked about people being 'fully engaged' in their own health and focused on a public health agenda, with public and user involvement ranging from taking preventative measures to secure their own heath to involvement in decision-making
2002 National Commission for Patient and Public Involvement established	The establishment of this national body was accompanied by the setting up of local public and patient involvement forums (although their remit was defined by the National Commission)
2006 National Health Service Act	Imposed a legal duty on NHS bodies to involve people in planning and decisions regarding services
2007 Local Government and Public Involvement in Health Act	Abolished public and patient involvement forums but imposed a duty on local authorities to involve local representatives when conducting any of their functions. It established local involvement networks (abolished in 2010)
2007 Putting People First	Set out a new vision of adult social care with a strong focus on personalisation
2008 Health and Social Care Act	Established the Care Quality Commission and placed a duty on it to show how it would promote user engagement
2009 The NHS Constitution (revised 2013)	Public and user engagement prioritised but the shift in power was accompanied by a shift of responsibility to users
2010 *Equity and Excellence: Liberating the NHS* (White Paper)	Underpinned by the principle 'No decision about me without me'
2012 Health and Social Care Act	New health and well-being boards with a statutory duty to involve people living and working in their local areas
2013 Healthwatch England and 150 local Healthwatch organisations established	Set up in local authority areas in England to champion the rights of users, and to hold the system to account for how they engage the public
2014 NHS England published *The NHS Five Year Forward View*	People having more control of their care was one of the top priorities

There is continuing evidence of a consumerist approach in policies and initiatives, evidenced by a continuing focus on user and public involvement as a way of driving up quality in services. Increasingly, participation is located in an outcomes-based approach, where involvement is linked to achieving designated outcomes, which includes economic sustainability through individual and community action to reduce ill-health. Underpinning participation initiatives is the thinking that the more people are involved in the design, development and implementation of services, the more likely it is that they will become more 'responsible' citizens in terms of their own health and the way that they use services. The narrative of, and provisions in, the NHS England (2014) *Five Year Forward View* with regard to user and public involvement provide an insight into the different perspectives on involvement (Foot et al, 2014): a person-centred approach is promoted through objectives linked to independence and the holistic needs of individual users; a shift in power is accompanied by a shift in responsibility to manage your own health; a democratic approach is evident, with the recognition that those affected by services should be involved in how they are run; and it is recognised that shared decision-making needs to acknowledge the experience of users – their experience of illness, their social circumstances and their values.

As shown in Table 9.2, developments have seen health bodies and local authorities increasingly subject to statutory duties to involve the public and users. NHS England has a legal duty under the NHS Act 2006 (as amended by the Health and Social Care Act 2012) to properly involve patients and the public in commissioning processes and decisions, and all health-care trusts have a duty to involve. NHS England's (2013) policy paper, 'The NHS belongs to the people: a call to action', sets out a programme of engagement aimed at achieving wide input, using forms of participation including online platforms and 'Future of the NHS' surgeries with staff, patients and the public. Developments, including the establishment of health and well-being boards in 2012 in each top-tier and unitary local authority in England, have seen more responsibility for local involvement and scrutiny being placed with local authorities. With a remit to promote the integration of services and produce joint strategic needs assessment and health and well-being strategies, the boards are to develop close local links. A new national body, Healthwatch, was set up as an independent consumer champion for health and social care, with a statutory role to:

- provide information about services and how to access them;
- promote the involvement of people in the commissioning, design, delivery and scrutiny of services;
- obtain the views of people about their needs;
- provide access to independent complaints advocacy; and
- recommend how services could be improved.

About 150 local Healthwatch organisations were also established to signpost people to local health and social care services, collect and analyse the experiences that people have of local care to help shape local services, and feed views and any recommendations to Healthwatch England to act on at a national level. Each of the health and well-being boards has one representative from a local Healthwatch on them.

There is also some involvement of public and user participation at the level of national bodies. The National Institute for Health and Clinical Excellence, which has a remit to provide evidence-based guidance to government (including on the licensing of drugs) and develop quality standards, has user and public representation on a number of its committees. All advisory groups and working groups have at least two members and it has a Citizens' Council – a panel of 30 members reflecting the demographic characteristics of the UK. The aim of the Council is to provide the Institute with a public perspective on overarching moral and ethical issues that it has to take into account when publishing guidance. The Care Quality Commission, the national regulator for health and social care in England, works with 500 'Experts by Experience', who are recruited, supported and managed by support organisations funded by the Commission.

NHS England has declared a future commitment to citizen participation and empowerment through: putting patients in control and promoting self-management; public participation through active citizen involvement in the design of every part of the health and social care system; and supporting citizen participation (NHS England, 2016b). While similar themes emerge in policies and initiatives on participation in other jurisdictions of the UK, there is somewhat of a lesser emphasis on user choice. Scotland moved from putting emphasis on patient choice or using choice as a mechanism for change, partly based on doubts about the capacity of patients to make rational choices concerning the place of treatment (Kaehne, 2014), and partly based on a belief that standards and quality of health care may be more significant. Scotland has, however, treated public involvement and user participation as a priority. This was put on a statutory basis in the Patient Rights (Scotland) Act 2011, leading to the creation of the Patient Advice and Support Service. Healthcare Improvement Scotland has a role in strengthening voice through developing public input, supporting and encouraging public involvement, and ensuring that people's views are expressed and used in health improvement activities. The Scottish Health Council has a role in monitoring and improving engagement through monitoring the NHS health boards and also supports some 100 public participation groups. There has also been a shift away from a paternalistic approach to service planning and delivery in Scotland for older people's services. *Reshaping Care for Older People: A Programme for Change 2011–2021* (Scottish Government, 2011) is a major reform programme designed to achieve a greater degree of personalisation. The Social Care (Self-directed Support) (Scotland) Act (Scottish Government, 2013) established a legal framework for entitlement to care. The principles underpinning the legislation include users having as much involvement as they wish.

Public and user participation structures in Northern Ireland lack the localism that is a strong feature of approaches elsewhere in the UK. Although the framework document for health and social care in Northern Ireland (DHSSPS, 2011) refers to the involvement of patients, clients, carers and communities, and engagement with other partners, as having a central role in the commissioning process, direct participation by users or user organisations in the commissioning process has not developed extensively in Northern Ireland. The main mechanism for public/user participation is a centralised quasi-autonomous non-governmental organisation (quango), the Patient and Client Council (PCC), covering the whole of Northern Ireland and adult and children's social care, as well as all health services. Some attempt has been made to achieve a more localised approach through the establishment of a local advisory committee in each of the five health and social trust areas, but, again, using an appointed quango model. The local committees also have very limited powers and responsibilities and their remit is restricted to advising the PCC on issues in the local area. The five trusts in Northern Ireland have also developed user-involvement schemes, but these are largely consultative and are often focused on trying to link public involvement to the different, though related, concept of community development (Gray and Birrell, 2012). While there is a strong emphasis on formal strategic policy and planning consultation, the size and complexity of health and social care bodies in Northern Ireland and the difficulty in establishing where some decisions originate may have a bearing on accountability. The high degree of centralisation and the widespread use of quangos in the Northern Ireland health and social care structures have contributed to an absence of localism, most obviously, in the lack of any role for local government in the delivery of health or social care or in scrutiny or monitoring. This contrasts with the major responsibilities of local councils for public and user involvement in Britain and with the health-care overseeing and scrutiny role of local councils in England.

Wales, like Scotland, places less emphasis on choice to drive improvement and change (Kaehne, 2014). The Welsh government has a strong commitment to public participation and citizen engagement in the design of public services (Welsh Local Government Association and NHS Confederation, 2013). It has retained a system of eight community health councils to represent the views of local people on health services and health organisations. The health councils have statutory powers to be consulted and also powers to inspect NHS premises. A national survey has been used to help measure patient satisfaction. In Wales, the 2015 Green Paper *Our Health, Our Health Services* includes discussion on how patient and public representation and participation can be strengthened (NHS Wales, 2015). In recent years, the personalisation agenda and the growing interest in and use of co-production (discussed later in the chapter) has been a dominant influence on user participation debates, especially in adult social care.

Assessment of approaches in health and social care

Evidence suggests a mixed picture with regard to impact on users. Benefits of user participation and engagement have been identified as: improving information to users and enhancing accessibility to services; better integration and coordination of care; improved confidence in dealing with professionals and policymakers; new and innovative solutions to policy issues; and greater cost efficiency (Crawford et al, 2002; Coulter and Ellins, 2007; Mockford et al, 2012). A key vehicle for promoting user involvement in the area has been the growth in user-led organisations in promoting knowledge and capacity. However, it is clear that significant challenges remain, including progressing beyond tokenistic approaches to involvement. Despite the policy focus and the introduction of new legislation and initiatives, there is some consensus on the lack of systematic progress and the lack of strong evidence on impact (Conklin et al, 2012; Coulter et al, 2014; Foot et al, 2014; Ridley et al, 2014). Allen et al (2012, p 252), in their study of public and patient involvement in the governance of foundation trusts, concluded that:

> despite new opportunities for patient members and governors to be informed about developments and consulted about their views and experiences, the extent to which Foundation Trusts provided ways for public and patients to become involved in decisions about health care delivery … was variable and limited.

Carers continue to report difficulty accessing information, with a gap between what policy suggests and the reality of what happens (Ridley et al, 2014). While the Care Act 2014 (DoH, 2014a) set out a series of measures under which users and carers were to have a right to choice and control, a survey by the Independent Living Strategy Group (2015) found that 45% of respondents said that their quality of life had reduced and 30% said that they had experienced a reduction in choice and control in the previous 12 months. A degree of dissatisfaction with existing models of participation and empowerment has prompted advocacy as a supporting mechanism.

There has been some concern that initiatives may be compromised by complexity and by the potential for conflict and overlap. Baggott (2013), for example, has suggested that tensions could arise as the Healthwatch organisations carry out their different and potentially conflicting roles. They participate in the health and well-being boards through representation and work alongside the local authority overview and scrutiny committees. The Healthwatch organisations participate in decisions made by the health and well-being boards but also have the right to refer controversial commissioning issues to local authority overview and scrutiny committees and to support the committees to scrutinise the decisions. The ability of single representatives to have significant influence on a board made up mainly of professionals and local representatives, as is the case with the Healthwatch representatives on the health and well-being boards, could also be questioned.

Local government, localism and user and public participation

The Labour government modernising local government agenda included plans to renew local democracy and ultimately to renew local authority legitimacy by embedding participation into the culture of local government (DETR, 1998), and this has been a continuing focus for successive Westminster governments. Since the 1990s, increasing obligations have been placed on local government to give local citizens a say, including a statutory duty to involve and to ensure provision for engagement across all their activities (DCLG, 2006, 2008), although with some lack of clarity on how the transfer of power from central to local government and from local government to communities was to take place (Connolly, 2011). The drive for localism continued with the Coalition government's Localism Act 2011 (DCLG, 2011a), which devolved more decision-making powers from central government to individuals, communities and councils. A Department for Communities and Local Government (DCLG, 2013b) document, *You've Got the Power: A Quick and Simple Guide to Community Rights*, set out a number of rights introduced to give people more control over their neighbourhood, specifically around neighbourhood planning, community right to build and the setting up of town and parish councils (DCLG, 2013b). The 2015 Conservative government's *The New Burdens Community Governance Review Fund 2015–2016* (DCLG, 2015b) is intended to support this devolution and is to be used by local authorities to facilitate communities wanting to set up town and parish councils.

In Britain, local government has been seen as an important forum for taking forward participatory approaches. In Scotland, the Local Government in Scotland Act 2003 (Scottish Government, 2003) required that communities be engaged in community planning. A *Scottish Community Empowerment Action Plan* (Scottish Government, 2009b) aimed to bring community voices into policy and service debates, with focus being placed on the need for Community Planning Partnerships to play a lead role. In 2015, further legislation, the Community Empowerment (Scotland) Act (Scottish Government, 2015b), placed community planning partnerships on a statutory footing and imposing duties on them around the planning and delivery of local outcomes. The legislation contains a new regulation to enable ministers to require Scottish authorities to promote and facilitate the participation of members of the public, including in the allocation of resources. There is also a mechanism for community bodies to bid for taking on the delivery of services. In Wales, policies have developed around what has been termed a 'citizen model', stated to be in line with Welsh values and the sense of ownership of public services. This was reinforced in 2012 when the Welsh government's *Shared Purpose, Shared Delivery* policy statement discussed the need for processes to support democratic governance rather than a consumer-based model of involvement (Welsh Government, 2012b). However, a 2013 evaluation of local government policies in Wales (Martin et al, 2013) concluded that the Welsh government had not done enough to convey what the 'citizen model' meant in political terms.

It did find evidence of improvement in citizen engagement but argued that co-production (discussed later) was not embedded in public services in Wales. Local government in Northern Ireland has no responsibility for the main areas of welfare provision, so there is less scope for a major role for local government in developing localised approaches to participation. The Local Government Act (Northern Ireland) 2014 gave Northern Ireland's 11 local councils power of community planning. There is little information on how the principles of community planning will be applied or the extent to which user and public participation will be markedly strengthened.

User and public participation in the governance of welfare services

It is accepted that meaningful user participation requires a say at the heart of where decisions about services are made: in the design of services, the monitoring of services and the governance of services and evaluation. Earlier sections identified how national health and social care bodies have sought to involve users in policy, inspection and governance. At the local government level, there are examples of how public and user participation has been built into the design of projects around Sure Start, children's centres and housing provision and management. The Sure Start programme, established in 1999 as part of the Labour government's wider social exclusion and anti-poverty agenda, did include the involvement of parents in the design and delivery of local programmes. In fact, the embeddedness of the programmes in local communities was seen as central to the success of the project, and local programmes were required to involve parents in the governance structures of local Sure Start partnerships (Gustafsson and Driver, 2005). Commenting on the outcomes of this, Gustafsson and Driver, (2005, p 17) conclude that if the role of parents was assessed in relation to traditional models of participative democracy, then outcomes would have to be judged as limited. However, parents did participate in informal ways, which could be equally important indicators of engagement. Positive outcomes were stated as the development of new relationships between professionals and parents and some evidence that parents were prepared to and could use their influence to shape or oppose local plans. For example, in one setting, the proposal for greater social work involvement in the development of Sure Start family services was successfully opposed by parents. There was also some evidence that the involvement of parents helped keep the programme focused. Parents themselves described the important aspect of their participation as influencing decision-making.

Subsequent developments to the funding and structure of Sure Start children's centres, including locating the decision to fund centres through children's services departments in local authorities rather than Sure Start local partnerships, and allowing greater local authority oversight, led the House of Commons Education and Skills Committee (2005) to question whether this would dilute parental involvement. Concern about the nature and extent of parental involvement has continued. In 2013, the All Party Parliamentary Sure Start Group (2013) identified differences in the approach taken by centres, with variance in the extent and comprehensiveness of the approach to community engagement. A later initiative saw the Department for Education fund the Sure Start Children's Centres Community Management Programme to support 10 groups of parents and community members to help them bid to run their local children's centre. This was part of the Open Public Services Agenda, which aimed to improve public services by opening up their provision and giving citizens more choice and control to shape services.

Involving tenants in the running of their homes is an accepted principle in social housing, and local authorities have to demonstrate good tenant engagement. Developments since 2010 have seen a shift towards more individualised and consumerist forms of involvement (Pawson et al, 2012). The Localism Act 2011 extended the right of local council tenants to take over the management of local housing services and provided for the introduction of co-regulation, with tenants adopting a governance role and scrutinising the performance of social housing landlords. This was to happen through, for example, the setting up of tenant panels and gave these panels new powers to solve disputes at the local level. Housing in Northern Ireland is not a local government responsibility; a central quango – the Northern Ireland Housing Executive (NIHE) – has overall responsibility. While there has been less policy reference to tenant empowerment, recent policy consultation documents on a *Community Involvement Strategy* (NIHE, 2014) and a *Tenant Participation Strategy* (NIHE, 2015) have proposed enhancing the scrutiny role of social housing tenants. The former proposes that each of the 12 NIHE areas will develop scrutiny panels, which would be resident and inter-agency partnerships nominating one representative to a central housing community forum. This forum would be consulted about all major policy and procedural changes. The draft *Tenant Participation Strategy* focuses on participation rather than empowerment. While the stated ambition is tenant empowerment, this is seen as something for the long term.

Personalisation

Personalisation has become a dominant narrative in public services and has been a major factor in a fundamental shift in the commissioning and delivery of adult social care in England, with the philosophy and practice of personalisation extending to other areas, including health care, housing and employment advice. A discretionary power to make direct payments for working-age disabled adults had been introduced in 1997 under the Community Care (Direct Payments) Act. *Putting People First* (HM Government, 2007) set out a new vision and a commitment to personalisation in adult social care, which would see people having choice, control and power over the support services they needed. The subsequent Coalition government endorsed these principles (DoH, 2010, 2012b) and the Conservative government elected in 2015 is committed to the personalisation agenda.

In England, personalisation in social care was largely to be achieved by users being given greater freedom through access to personal budgets, which they then manage themselves or can be managed by a third party or local authority to be spent on agreed outcomes. Those individual users holding a personal budget would then act as commissioners of their own care. In 2013/14, £1.4 billion of expenditure was on direct payments (Health and Social Care Information Centre, 2015). Much of the justification for personal budgets, and especially those taken as direct payments, is that control over money is an important factor in users achieving greater control of service provision. In Control, which played a central role in promoting the philosophy and practices of personalisation in social care, saw the transformative aspect of personal budgets as their upfront allocation on the basis of outcomes agreed by service users rather than the way money was used by recipients (Duffy, 2010).

Leadbeater (2004), whose work influenced the wider personalising public services agenda, saw individuals engaged in meaningful participation to devise their own bottom–up solutions. Thus, social care was tailored to each individual's needs and preferences. Personalisation has been seen as shifting the emphasis in service delivery directly to those requiring assistance. Without this, the personalisation agenda would represent an essentially top–down consumerist approach. He saw personalisation only making sense in services that are face-to-face – social care, education, housing and non-emergency health care – and viewed personalisation through participation as involving a number of steps, as set out in Box 9.1.

Box 9.1: Dimensions of participation

- Intimate consultation – through which the individual's needs, preferences and aspirations can be expressed.
- Expanded choice – over how needs might be met and to ensure that solutions centre around the needs of the individual rather than the institution.
- Enhanced voice – it is argued that expanded voice should help to enhance the voice of users and ensure that they can articulate their preferences.
- Partnership provision – it is argued that institutions need to be gateways to networks of public provision.
- Advocacy – professionals should act as advocates for users and this can only be achieved through continuing relationships.
- Co-production – more involved users should be expected to become more active and responsible users.
- Funding – should follow the choices users make.

The Care Act 2014 (DoH, 2014a) placed personalisation on a statutory footing in England, with those who are eligible having a legal entitlement to a personal budget, although it has been argued that the Act has made no change to the basic process whereby it is local authorities that will decide what a person's needs are and which of these will be met. Budgetary cuts have been seen to have a negative impact on good support planning and to have led to a re-colonisation by social services (Williams, 2014). The Act does perceive adult social care as having a broader care and support function, which could include the potential for housing-related support, including for homeless people to be eligible for a personal budget (Cornes et al, 2015). From 2014 in England, patients requiring continuing health care also have the right to ask for a personal health budget. Personal health-care budgets do not seem to have attracted even the initial optimism expressed about personal budgets in social care. Williams and Dickinson (2015), for example, claim that the suggestion that government tax revenues can be subdivided into individual service user entitlements is highly problematic in institutions such as the NHS.

As personal budgets have been rolled out, reservations have been expressed about their centrality to achieving more autonomy for users and more person-centred care. There is a view that they have not grown as rapidly as hoped and that their impact on the care system as a whole has been less profound than envisaged (Glasby, 2014b). There continues to be less uptake of personal budgets among some groups, including older people and people with mental health problems (ADASS, 2012; Royal College of Psychiatrists and the Association of Directors of Adult Social Services, 2013). The early evaluations of personal budgets (Glendinning et al, 2008) showed that most users still spent their budgets on mainstream services and subsequent research has questioned the adequacy of personal budgets for achieving genuinely personalised and quality care (Waters and Hatten, 2014). Ultimately, it is argued, what matters most is not so much who provides care and support, but what is available and the quality of that provision (Blackender and Prestidge, 2014). Questions have also been raised about the ability of individual commissioners of services to navigate care markets in which, relative to other stakeholders, they may be relatively weak players. A number of variances of personalised delivery have developed through self-directed care services and managed personal budgets by social services (Baxter et al, 2013). In Scotland, legislation has put self-directed care on a statutory basis.

Co-production

The New Economics Foundation (2008, p 9) explains that:

> the term 'co-production' was coined originally at the University of Indiana in the 1970s when Professor Elinor Ostrom was asked to explain to the Chicago police why the crime rate went up when the police came off the beat and into patrol cars. She used the term as a way of explaining why the police need the community as much as the community need the police.

Co-production is often presented as a response to the widespread failure to effectively address social needs because the skills and assets that users have are not recognised or rewarded and users are viewed as passive recipients of consumer services. It emphasises the role that service users play in the production of services, not just their consumption (Needham, 2012), and has a major emphasis on the service delivery process. In this analysis, co-production is seen as addressing the dominant role of the professional. Boyle and Harris (2009) define co-production as the delivery of public services in an equal and reciprocal relationship between professionals, people using services, their families and their neighbours. It is seen as a values-led approach that, while offering the potential for genuine transformation, is only really happening when a shift in power occurs between the professional and individuals or groups (Brown, 2014). There is a growing body of work exploring the theoretical concept and the application and practice of co-production. Much of this draws on case studies and practice examples, with a focus on the processes of participation. There are few longitudinal studies and there is little evidence on the costs and benefits of co-production.

Co-production can occur at different stages in the governance and delivery of welfare. The component parts of co-production could be described as:

- Co-creation.
- Co-design.
- Co-commissioning.
- Co-management.
- Co-assessment.

Co-production has been used by people using a range of different services. For example, the development of a Co-operative Councils Network was a response to a rising demand for public services in a context of austerity, aiming to do 'differently with less'. There was a recognition among the councils involved that substantive structural change was required, which involved giving residents more power, including through cooperative commissioning (Durose et al, 2013, p 17). Sunderland City Council's Community Leadership Programme was seen as successfully transforming the governance and delivery of services in a number of areas: environmental services, youth services and local and highways maintenance. Factors cited as underpinning this success included the way in which the Community Leadership Programme engaged councillors more effectively as community leaders and the creation of new governance and engagement mechanisms (Bovaird and Loeffler, 2014). Dorset Age Partnership is a network of older people drawn from forums and groups across the country, strategic leads from a range of services, and voluntary and community organisations. Established as a partnership body where older people are the majority, it has resulted in 4,000 older people being directly involved in the development of strategies impacting on them and in defining and using outcomes measures that reflect their priorities (Brown, 2014).

Box 9.2: Benefits of successful co-production

- More tailored support and services sensitive to user preferences.
- Innovation in the design and provision of services.
- Increasing the economic efficiency of services.
- Users more involved and satisfied with services.
- Building the capacity of local communities.
- Empowering citizens and communities.

It is clear that there are successful and innovative approaches to co-production. Some of these could be argued to be 'bottom-up' initiatives developed to present a challenge to existing public services or a commitment to the values of sharing, accessibility and reciprocity (SCIE, 2013). Others have been supported by policy developments such as the introduction of community planning in Scotland and the setting up of the Older People's Assembly (Brown, 2014). However, there is perhaps a question mark over the extent to which co-production has been taken up at the centre of organisations. Although co-production may have emerged as a counter to criticisms of service delivery as unresponsive to users, undemocratic and impersonal, the concept has not gained much traction in local service implementation (Scourfield, 2015). Bovaird and Loeffler (2014), in a review of co-production, found that few local authorities had adopted a corporate vision that explicitly incorporated co-production. They describe the barriers to co-production as cultural and systemic. The challenges to co-production are set out in Box 9.3.

Box 9.3: Challenges to co-production

- Embedding co-production within commissioning activity.
- Generating evidence as to the value of co-production.
- Scaling up successful approaches to co-production.
- Gaps in public sector professionals' understanding of the factors relevant to the success of co-production.
- Professional reluctance to lose status.
- Political reluctance to lose control.

Source: Boyle et al (2010)

A study of co-production by citizens in five countries (France, Germany, Denmark, the UK, the Czech Republic), focusing on three different subsectors of public services – health, community safety and care of the local environment – found the UK to have the highest level of co-production. Denmark has the lowest. The authors suggest that this may be linked to further findings which demonstrate that those most satisfied with public services are the least likely to get involved in co-production (Bovaird et al, 2015).

As noted earlier, there is not a strong evidence base about the economic value of co-production. Despite this, in the area of health care in particular, co-production is seen as having future economic benefit. This is largely based on a public health perspective that the involvement of communities and individuals will support the development and uptake of early interventions and preventative work, which will reduce the need for more expensive intervention and result in a more informed and responsible 'consumer' of health care. It has been argued that some programmes, such as the People Powered Health Programme (NESTA), can deliver savings of about 7%, with more economic benefit accruing in future.

There is some contention over whether co-production can be seen as individual action or if it needs to be collectively provided, co-production requiring a long-term relationship between state agencies and collective groups of citizens (Joshi and Moore, 2004; Bovaird et al, 2015). Bovaird et al have questioned the collective value in user co-production and state that if public sectors want to achieve benefits from collective production, they need to find ways to persuade and convince people to shift production activities towards more collective action.

How effective are policies and mechanisms for public and user participation?

There are not well-established, evidence-based or large-scale studies about the effectiveness of user and public participation. Research suggests that there continue to be challenges around changing the culture of organisations and traditional approaches to welfare service delivery. Some organisations may accept involvement at the periphery but not to the extent where participants have real influence. A diverse range of structures has been put in place around user and public involvement in welfare services. This is particularly the case in health and social care, leading some to caution that initiatives may end up having such complex organisational structures that participation is actually limited.

Methods of participation have been shown to be not always conducive to meaningful involvement. A critical literature has emerged around the notion that 'participation has become a new tyranny' and is often little more than tokenistic (Pollock and Sharp, 2012; Omeni et al, 2014). Slasberg and Beresford (2015), referring specifically to personalisation in social care, have argued that contrary to the rhetoric about participation in policy documents, service user organisations have felt that they have had little say in shaping developments. With regard to how policymakers/providers view participation, Newman and Clarke (2009) found that local authorities tended to view the public as consumers clamouring for more or better services. There was a sense that the public had to be 'skilled up' to participate effectively, with little acknowledgement of the value of their experience. This is interesting in the context of Barnes' (2008) analysis of the role of emotion in engagement between users and officials. Reporting on qualitative research with user groups, she reflects on how officials found angry and emotional input from users difficult, suggesting that there are limitations as to how they perceive the role of the user in bringing real-life experience and expertise.

There has been some suspicion about the motivation of a participation agenda developed, as it has been in recent decades, in a neo-liberal political context, with a strong policy emphasis on personalisation and co-production. The way in which the application of these policies has resulted in primarily individual engagement has led some to question what can be achieved for users in the long term. One of the most consistent issues raised in assessments of co-production is the difficulty of scaling up – taking it into the mainstream. Durose et al (2013) ask whether a better way of looking at this would be to think of scaling out rather than scaling up. Scaling out, they argue, occurs because 'ideas are spread through horizontal connections and geographical proximity, political similarity and socio-economic equivalence rather than vertical connections' (Durose et al, 2013, p 327).

With many forms of participation, including co-production, questions about representation arise: 'Who participates?' and 'Participation on whose terms?'. Some groups continue to be under-represented, including minority ethnic groups and those marginalised as a result of poverty. Those who are already linked into networks are more likely to be involved in initiatives. Webb's (2008) study showed how service user groups can be self-selecting and asks whether accountability to a wider public is uncertain in such circumstances. Critical questions also surround who defines the terms of participation. If user and public involvement is about challenging existing norms and practices, this will be more challenging if policymakers or providers do so and existing power relations remain unaddressed, meaning that participation is little more than the inclusion of individuals into pre-existing institutional forms of decision-making (Newman et al, 2004), or, as De-Freitas and Martin (2015) describe them, 'invited spaces' that some are chosen to occupy.

Durose et al (2013, p 328), in guidance on involving citizens in the design and delivery of services, suggest that for some of the difficulties of participation to be avoided and opportunities realised, some 'dos and don'ts' of involvement should be applied (see Box 9.4).

Box 9.4: 'Dos and don'ts' of involvement

- The agenda and rules of the game cannot be set by government; nor should decisions be made prior to 'consultation'.
- Assumptions should not be made about the level of interest from citizens and users. In some studies, community apathy was assumed rather than demonstrated.
- People need to have the opportunity for generating alternatives for redesigning services.
- Assumptions should not be made about what the public will be able or not able to understand. This fails to recognise the limits of the expertise of decision-makers and the equally valuable expertise of citizens.

- People should be trusted and valued; too often they are treated as the 'usual suspects' – the well-organised but unrepresentative. While representativeness can be a concern, it can also be used as a way to limit or avoid involving citizens.
- Do be clear about what you are asking; ideas should be tempered with reality – be clear where there are situations where involvement is not possible or will be limited (Durose et al (2013) talk of how commissioners, service planners and so on are themselves subject to central direction and need to be honest when engagement exercises will not have an impact on policy. When there is an honest conversation, communities have scope for making decisions about engagement.)

Conclusion

There is much consensus around the need to achieve greater user and public participation and it will continue to be an important aspect of the design, delivery and governance of welfare services. Governments see public and user participation as a way of reducing costs and increasing efficiency. The Local Government Association (2014c, p 11) *Adult Social Care Efficiency Report* notes that 'In order to manage the funding challenge … and to ensure the sustainable delivery of personalised care, many councils see they need a new contract with the citizen and the local community'. There has been a shift in rhetoric about participation, with more explicit reference to rights to involvement being accompanied by responsibilities. The 2020 Public Services Trust (2010) final report calls for a new 'social citizenship' approach, with citizens having a duty to contribute, as well as a right to receive support. This has been seen by some as a way of shifting responsibility for difficult decisions (TUC, 2013) but there is a need for more change to attain personal and political empowerment.

Critics of the lack of progress claim that there has been no radical transformation for the public. They may have been given some new voice, but there are new challenges arising from the weakening of local government and public expenditure cuts. Ultimately, the concern is that the focus on and increase in public participation can be used to depoliticise policy and to support a changing relationship between the state, the public and the private sector (Connolly, 2011), moving participation away from collective action to a kind of individual participation where the individual participant is a consumer – a purchaser of their own services.

TEN

Regulating welfare delivery and performance

Measuring the effectiveness of delivery and making comparisons between the performance of delivery bodies have become a major aspect of social welfare provision. Developments in the the different models and forms of performance management have involved a range of institutions which differ across service areas and take different forms throughout the UK. The institutional models are subject to change, disputes about their appropriateness and value and criticisms of various methodologies. The area of performance management has also been marked by new initiatives and priorities. This chapter identifies the main aspects of regulating welfare delivery and performance and covers: the use of performance indictors; league tables; user based outcomes and other outcome based approaches; audits; parliamentary scrutiny; inspection and review; public inquiries and ombudsmen.

Performance indicators

The increase in the scale and significance of the measurement of performance in service delivery using performance indicators has been dramatic over the last 25 years, described as blossoming into 'a performance movement' (Pollitt and Bouckaert, 2011, p 106). One of the consequences of major changes to the delivery of services was greater concern about the quality and consistency of performance, leading to the establishment of new standards and new regulatory bodies (Bochel, 2016, p 72). The basic underlying assumption has been that performance and quality can be measured and assessed, usually closely related to targets that have been pre-set. Performance indicators are variables that are designed to measure the closeness of the service to achieving set objectives. This potentially involves quite a complex process of establishing performance objectives and tariffs, calculating measurable indicators or standards, monitoring activities and outputs, and assessing the results and outcomes. It became the norm for indicators to be clearly articulated in the form of numerical calculations, for example, length of hospital waiting lists or the number of children obtaining a level of GCSEs, although targets and indicators could also be expressed in broader definitions.

Overall, the language of performance indicators was to become prevalent in the evaluation of service delivery, raising the importance of statistical monitoring and analysis, and comparative analysis between delivery bodies. Performance indicators became a key factor in the development of strategies by government and other bodies to embed performance management as an aspect of delivery.

One of the most developed strategies based on performance indicators was the introduction of public service agreements (PSAs). This framework followed the 1998 comprehensive spending review and was intended to galvanise public service delivery and drive major improvements in outcomes. Every government department had to produce PSAs detailing aims and objectives, and setting out key priority outputs and outcomes and how they would be achieved. Each PSA would be underpinned by a single delivery agreement, later a delivery plan, and some 600 were agreed with the Treasury. Each PSA had four sections, comprising a vision, measurement, delivery strategy and data sources, but the wording of the PSAs often appeared too broad to relate clearly to service delivery. Their implementation appeared to lead to enhanced control by the Treasury, using performance criteria (Lee and Woodward, 2002). Other critics called for more focus on local delivery, greater local autonomy and wider participation in constructing more meaningful targets, and independent assessment of whether targets had been met (Gay, 2005). In 2007, all but 30 of the top-down targets were abolished, with more delegation in setting performance targets. What was interpreted as a strategy for micromanagement was ended by the Coalition government but departments continued to use performance indicators.

Emerging with performance indicators was the use in some government bodies of rankings or league tables, which facilitated comparison between similar organisations and comparisons over time. League tables achieved popularity in the case of hospitals, schools, health trusts, local authorities and universities. Such exercises required composite performance measures, bringing together an aggregate of performance statistics into a single score. NHS trust ratings for 180 acute trusts from 2001 to 2005 covered around 40 performance indicators, and comprehensive performance assessment ratings for around 150 local authorities from 2001 to 2005 covered around 110 Best Value performance indicators (Jacobs and Goddard, 2007). League tables have been seen as having wide appeal as they, in effect, summarise a wealth of underlying performance data and are simple to understand. The advantages have been noted as offering a rounded assessment of performance, offering a summary of complex issues, indicating which organisations achieve best performance, indicating the nature of a performance gap and presenting the big picture in a way the public can understand (Jacobs et al, 2007). The use of league tables has, however, come under strong criticism over: the selection of performance measures; variations in the quality of data; the focus on aggregate scores or league positions, which masks failings in parts of the system; and controversy over the weighting of certain measures, for example, adjustments for environmental influences. Composite performance measures presented methodological challenges (Jacobs, 2007, p 2). League tables have continued to be used and regarded as important for establishing benchmarks and standards, as well as rewarding or penalising public bodies (Flynn, 2012, p 140), despite the view that the complexity and opacity of such exercises and the anxiety caused may outweigh the advantages (Hood, 2007, p 100).

A related development from league tables was the adoption of star rating systems. Star ratings could be applied to public bodies or areas of activity and service provision, and generally covered a one- to four-star rating, indicating an idea linked to long-standing hotel ratings. Star ratings became popular in health, education, social care and other local government provision. Up until 2005, NHS trusts were given an annual star rating from no stars up to three stars on the basis of some 40 indicators. Star ratings were a somewhat rough-and-ready measure but did spark much attention as to whether hospital trusts were moving up or down. There was less discussion concerning the indicators or aspects of provision not covered by the selected indicators. It was suggested that distinctions between stars assumed greater significance than the data justified and were prone to errors (Davies, 2003, p 44). A variation of star ratings was 'Beacon status', a scheme to award Beacon council status to local councils that was launched in 2000 in England Each year, a group of councils was selected to act as models of excellence for chosen service areas, using performance indicators, and they were required to disseminate best practice. Beacon themes were chosen each year, for example, the delivery of quality services through better procurement, schemes to deliver services to hard-to-reach groups, tenant involvement and improving rural services. Plans to extend the Beacon principle to the NHS, schools and central government were not implemented. In 2006, star ratings in the NHS were replaced by an annual health check, which looked at a broader range of indicators in assessing performance and used two rankings on two scales – for the quality of services and the use of resources (McConway, 2006).

League tables have continued to be produced, whether officially or unofficially constructed by the media, justified by a desire for transparency by users and regulators, to promote competition or to incentivise the improvement of performance. Education has remained as a major area for the use of league tables. At the level of schools, the Department for Education in England has gone back to publishing tables. School league tables were abolished in Northern Ireland in 2001, and were abolished for Scotland in 2003, but examination data are still published online. Wales has moved to publishing tables of school performance in five bands. In England, fewer indicators have been used and one indicator became very much a key one: the percentage of pupils getting five or more GSCEs at grades A to C, published in league tables. The criteria were later amended to include maths and English. The claim that schools' rating at the top of leagues proved that they were the best schools was contentious. Account was later taken of added value factors achieved by students since their performance at age 10 and 11 and contextual value added, taking account of area social deprivation (McConway, 2006). School league tables have continued to play an important role in influencing assessments and comparisons between different categories of schools, between state and private, between grammar and comprehensive, and between local authority, academies and free schools, and have also been introduced for A Levels. The 2015 Conservative government has expanded and amended the nature and consequently the role of school performance tables. A standard of achievement can be set to identify underperforming schools. Primary school performance tables provide school-level information on the achievement and progress of pupils, and can be used to compare a school's performance nationally, within a local authority area and with similar schools (DfE, 2015). Changes to the secondary school performance tables in 2015 brought much criticism. Some qualifications, such as international GCSEs, were removed, as were resits; consequently, there were claims that the new indicators and calculations made the tables meaningless. The latest league table provided by government in England is for multi-academy trusts. The other aspect of education subjected to performance tables has been higher education, with routine assessment of research performance and, at times, teaching performance. The official component of the research performance exercise conducted by the Higher Education Funding Council does lead directly to influencing the funding allocation to universities. The media uses these data, combined with other performance-related data on admissions criteria, student satisfaction, drop-out rates and employment destination, to produce composite rankings of the 'best' universities. In 2016 the UK government announced its intention to create new league tables based on teaching quality.

The use of key performance indicators has continued to diversify and been expanded through government policies, public demand and technological advances. Standards have been set for the development of indicators. The UK Performance Indicators Steering Group produced guiding principles for higher education, requiring that they should be evidence-based, robust and have longevity. Among the guiding principles was: the measurement of what matters, reflecting the core mission of institutions; providing an aggregate picture of provision; and also putting information into the public domain that would not otherwise be available (Department for Culture, Media and Sport, 2014). A major expansion in the collection and publication of data on performance took place in health in England. Performance indicators are now commonly used to examine and compare performance across the NHS.

The Health and Social Care Information Centre has brought together hundreds of health indicators into one place. These data are intended for use in service planning and performance management, but also for the information of users and the public, and are published on a special MyNHS website. In 2014, a new development saw performance data on 5,000 hospital consultants gathered, measuring performance against a set of professional standards, such as survival rates, repeat operations and length of stay in hospital. This innovation proved controversial and some 2,500 consultants did not provide information. While the declared objective was to drive up standards, there were criticisms that the calculation was crude and omitted important information (National Health Executive, 2014).

Performance indicators have been used most clearly in the setting of targets and in checking on the effectiveness of the organisations, procedures, structures and activities in meeting the objective. The scope of uses to which performance indicators can be put are outlined in Box 10.1.

> **Box 10.1: Use of performance indicators**
>
> - To highlight the successful achievement of a target or the failure to achieve a target, or to indicate progress and the direction of travel;
> - to improve performance, efficiency, productivity and effectiveness;
> - to indicate areas of weakness in performance, including speed of delivery;
> - to compare the performance of different delivery options;
> - may be linked to resource allocation and a system of rewards or sanctions;
> - may be linked to staff management, motivation, appraisal, performance-related pay;
> - to provide politicians with evidence of what is happening with service provision;
> - linked to accountability as a means of holding organisational bodies to account and identifying responsibility;
> - to provide transparency to the public, service users, the media and other stakeholders, including professional bodies; and
> - linked to the development of standards and benchmarks.

Performance indicators have become strongly established. Burnham and Horton (2013) draw attention to the assumption that performance indicators assume a product that can be measured and also targets that can be easily identified or quantified. Flynn (2012, p 117) makes the criticism that performance indicators, targets and standards all cascaded from those on high to those delivering services, and discuss this as the 'principal–agent' problem, arguing that the process is an attempt to control the behaviour and performance of the agent by the principal (Flynn, 2012, p 121). Also raised is the existence of gaming, in which the agents or providers may manipulate the system and focus on ways to score highly on measurement, while neglecting other aspects of their functions. It is a general criticism that the selection of performance indicators may isolate aspects of performance and allow these to dominate while not measuring other important elements. Davies (2003, p 38) argues that performance indicators are not helpful when there are no clear measures or when they are not appropriate to evaluating service delivery goals in some areas, or when they may be so vague as to cause ambiguity. Evidence that there can be dysfunctional consequences let to innovations through balanced scorecards with more emphasis on key performance indicators, or public value indicators or use of more specific matrices (Pidd, 2005).

Outcomes and performance

There has been a refocusing of performance measurement, with a rejection of a target-driven approach and an emphasis on the importance of outcome indicators. Outcomes are more broadly defined than performance indicators, that is, broader than using specific and concrete action, detailed components of a policy or service, or a numerical target. Outcomes also have an emphasis on qualitative data rather than quantitative data, in particular, being based more on the views and evaluations of users of services. At the same time, the definition of an outcome is flexible and can verge towards the specification of broader societal outcomes. The main developments in outcomes has occurred within health and social care, where there is an acceptance of the significance of the views of patients and social care users in helping to manage performance. This meant a switch from a focus on output indicators to the ultimate outcomes of care, as measured by health–related quality of care and lifestyle changes (Appleby and Devlin, 2005). In England, three key outcomes frameworks for the NHS, adult social care and public health and have been placed at the heart of the health and social care system. The NHS outcomes framework has developed since 2010 and is updated annually. The framework is designed to be a set of indicators that together form an overarching picture of the current state of health services but is not meant to be an exhaustive list (DoH, 2015). Five domains are created for the NHS outcome indicators, as listed in Box 10.2.

Box 10.2: Domains for high-level NHS outcomes

1. Preventing people from dying prematurely.
2. Enhancing the quality of life for people with long-term conditions.
3. Helping people to recover from episodes of ill-health or following injury.
4. Ensuring that people have a positive experience of care.
5. Treating and caring for people in a safe environment and protecting them from avoidable harm.

For each domain, there are a small number of overarching indicators, followed by a number of improvement area indicators, which focus on improving health and reducing health inequalities. The number of changes to the indicators each year has been kept to a minimum. The NHS outcomes framework also plays a key role in assessing the progress of NHS England against the objectives set by the Department of Health. The assessment in 2015 found that the majority of the 68 indicators of the outcomes framework had shown improvements in the past year. Some failures were noted in the challenges of mental health, winter pressures and access to GPs (DoH, 2015). The other two frameworks, for public health and adult social care, reflect the different delivery systems and accountability models but have the same overarching aim of improving the outcomes for people (DoH, 2015, p 4). The public health outcomes framework is based on an overarching vision and outcomes: increased healthy life expectancy and reduced differences in life expectancy and healthy life expectancy between communities (DoH, 2012a). Four domains for grouping indicators are listed (see Box 10.3).

Box 10.3: Domains for public health framework

1. Improving the wider determinants of health.
2. Health improvement.
3. Health protection.
4. Health care, public health and preventing premature mortality.

In adult social care, the focus had been on monitoring efficiency, unit costs and more simple analysis of performance data, used to produce star ratings for social service departments in local authorities (Clarkson and Challis, 2006). A change in direction came with the introduction of the Adult Social Care Outcomes Framework (ASCOF) in 2011. The Framework was linked to the NHS and public health frameworks and its key roles were described as: demonstrating the performance of the adult social care system as a whole, its success in delivering high-quality, personalised care and support; strengthening accountability to local people; and supporting local councils to improve the quality of the care and support services they provide (DoH, 2013). Four domains were described, as listed in Box 10.4.

Box 10.4: Domains for adult social care outcomes

1. Enhancing quality of life for people with care and support needs.
2. Delaying and reducing the need for care and support.
3. Ensuring that people have a positive experience of care and support.
4. Safeguarding adults whose circumstances make them vulnerable and protecting them from avoidable harm.

While one domains uses mainly quantitative data, the others use mainly qualitative data on users' opinions and satisfaction. The Framework facilitates the comparison of the experiences of care and the support for different groups of users and carers. Findings for 2013 (DoH, 2013) noted increases in social care-related quality of life and satisfaction of people with the quality of their care and support but found that most councils missed their target for the provision of personal budgets and that there were large variations in the number of people with a learning disability who live independently. A key role of the ASCOF is to promote more joined-up working at the local level, underlined by a number of shared and complementary measures in the three frameworks. A methodology named 'Outcomes Based Accountability' has been adapted by some local authorities in England (Friedman, 2009). This is based on desired outcome measures and activities but the validity of such frameworks for social policy interventions has been questioned (Bovaird, 2014).

Performance outcomes are also used by unofficial bodies, that is, voluntary, research and professional bodies, to support judgements on delivery and performance. A quality and outcomes framework for GP practices operates on a voluntary basis, with data collected over three domains (Health and Social Care Information Centre, 2015). The clinical domain originally covered 69 indicators over 19 clinical areas, the public health domain covered seven indicators and the public health and additional services domain covered five further indicators. This exercise does give an overall indication of the achievement of a surgery through a points system. The list of indicators has been adjusted and reduced in number and it is recommended that the data should not be used to create league tables. QualityWatch is a major research programme by non-statutory bodies, the Nuffield Trust and the Health Foundation Trust, which scrutinises and monitors the quality of health and social care in England. The programme tracks an extensive range of quality indicators and uses the general domains of access, capacity, effectiveness, equity, safety and person-centred care and experience. Topics have included access to emergency care, social care, depression, emergency attendance and hospital admissions from care homes, and an annual quality report is produced (QualityWatch, 2015). Between 2010 and 2015, UK departments moved to performance criteria of 'impact indicators'. There were 207 impact indicators, with the largest number in the Department for Education (28). An evaluation report (Freeguard et al, 2015 found that half the indicators had improved. However, the whole exercise was criticised as focusing on the actions of departments and not public views of end results.

Outcomes and devolved administrations

The devolved administrations have established a significant use of outcomes-based performance measurement for the performance of their whole administration. This is most developed in Scotland, with Wales following a similar pathway and Northern Ireland adopting some aspects of the approach. Scotland's National Performance Framework set out a framework for all public services in Scotland based on delivering outcomes that improve the quality of life rather than on inputs and outputs (Scottish Government, 2015d). Scotland Performs reports on progress of the government in achieving strategic objectives and seven purpose targets, supported by 16 national outcomes and 50 national indicators covering health, social care, education, poverty, the economy, justice, housing and the environment. Examples of the 16 national outcomes are listed in Box 10.5 and indicate a strong social service commitment, but also a marked degree of generality.

Box 10.5: Examples of Scotland's national outcomes

- Our children have the best start in life and are ready to succeed.
- We live longer, healthier lives.
- We have tackled the significant inequalities in Scottish society.
- We are better educated, more skilled and more successful.
- We have improved the life chances for children, young people and families at risk.

The 60 national indicators are designed to track progress towards the achievement of the national outcomes, and focus on current priorities. Again, many of the national indicators read like general aspirations for improvement, while others are expressed in more specific language, and some may appear vague, as illustrated in Box 10.6.

Box 10.6: Examples of Scotland's national indicators

- Improve levels of educational attainment.
- Improve children's services.
- Improve mental well-being.
- Reduce children's deprivation.
- Improve support for people with care needs.
- Improve access to suitable housing options for those in housing need.
- Increase the proportion of healthy-weight children.
- Reduce emergency admissions to hospital.
- Reduce the percentage of adults who smoke.
- Increase the number of new homes.
- Increase the proportion of graduates in positive destinations.
- Improve people's perception of their neighbourhood.

Scotland Performs provides an online tool for reporting on progress on the overall delivery of the outcomes, indicating whether performance is improving, worsening or being maintained. Discursive updates are published that are usually centred around a quantitative measure for each indicator. Thus, the measure for 'Improve support for people with care needs' is 'the number of adults receiving personal care at home or direct payments for personal care, as a percentage of the total number of adults needing care'. The procedure adopted for updating each indicator involves a discussion on: why the indicator is important; what influences the indicator; what the government's role is; and how Scotland is performing. Other public bodies in Scotland may use a similar approach in relation to more targeted services, for example, the outcomes framework for older people.

In Wales a list of national indicators has been drawn up to track progress in the achievement of objectives set by Welsh ministers and, since 2015, supported by legislation. There are 46 indicators and some examples are provided in Box 10.7 (Welsh Government, 2016b).

Box 10.7: Welsh Government National Indicators for Wales examples

- Percentage of live single births with a birth weight of under 2,500g.
- Healthy life expectancy at birth including the gap between the least and most deprived.
- Measurement of development of young children.
- Percentage of pupils who have achieved the 'Level 2 threshold' including English or Welsh first language and Mathematics, including the gap between those who are eligible or are not eligible for free school meals. (To be replaced from 2017 by the average capped points score of pupils.)
- Percentage of adults with qualifications at the different levels of the National Qualifications Framework.
- Percentage of people in employment, who are on permanent contracts (or on temporary contracts, and not seeking permanent employment) and who earn more than 2/3 of the UK median wage.
- Number of households successfully prevented from becoming homeless per 10,000 households.
- Gender pay difference.
- Percentage of people in education, employment or training, measured for different age groups.

It can be argued that the list is mainly performance indicators both qualitative and quantitative. A process has been introduced to identify key actions needed to deliver improvements under each indicator and update the actions required. A study of outcomes based approaches to local service delivery in Wales found limited and mixed evidence of benefits in complex environments (Law, 2013). An annual report discusses the performance in wider and more outcome-focused terms, for example, the impact on the most deprived areas of Wales (Welsh Government, 2015c).

Assessing performance in relation to the Northern Ireland programme for government was originally focused more on targets. These were drawn from the 2008–11 programme for governments list of 23 PSAs. The following programme for government used the language of priorities and objectives, really targets rather than outcomes, and progress was judged against annual milestones. Most targets were expressed numerically, for example, 'Deliver 8,000 social and affordable homes' and 'Improve literacy and numeracy levels', but others were more statement of general policy.

A feature of the use of outcomes and measuring progress towards their achievement in all the devolved administrations has been the use of visual performance management or traffic light images. This is seen as a method of reviewing and communicating performance against evaluative judgements and indicates that it is not just a matter of financial results (Manville et al, 2016). Scotland has adopted a visual 'Performance at a Glance' system based on the direction of travel arrows, which indicate whether performance is improving, worsening or being maintained. Wales has used a similar direction marker for indicators. In the case of targets drawn from PSAs in Northern Ireland, the traffic light system was used, the red, amber and green framework, with red indicating those at risk of not being completed. The framework was amended to a five-item scale of red, amber, amber/green, green and completed, with green indicating progress to completion was on target (Gillen, 2012).

Equality impact

As well as efficiency and effectiveness, the value of equality has also emerged as an aspect of assessing performance. A set of legal public sector equality duties impose obligations on public authorities throughout the UK to ensure that in making policy decisions and delivering services, they must not unfairly discriminate. The statutory equality duty covers the grounds of age, disability, gender, race, religion or belief, or sexual orientation. Public authorities, including government departments, are required to carry out equality impact assessments on new policies or reviews of policies. Equality impact assessments are mainly directed at an analysis of the content and implications of policy proposals on users and employees but are expected to embrace the full range of functions and activities and may cover aspects of service delivery. The process includes not just the collection of data, evidence and analysis, but consultation with stakeholders. The formal assessments will check that there is no discernible adverse discrimination against people based on the characteristics of age, ethnicity, disability, gender, sexual orientation or religion or beliefs. Equality impact assessments are carried out by individual bodies and some of the outcomes have related to access to buildings for disabled people, access to services, information on services given in an alternative format, the attainment of disabled pupils and issues for carers. The commission responsible for equality has produced numerous reports on equality issues, some closely related to service delivery, for example, social housing allocation, early years, inequality in education, work and care, and flexible working policies (Equality and Human Rights Commission, 2016).

Audit processes by government

Audit offices in the UK perform an official role in assessing the performance of government departments. The purpose of the National Audit Office (NAO) in England was to assist Parliament through a value-for-money report on whether government bodies used public money efficiently, effectively and with economy. In doing this, there is a focus on: how bodies can improve services; the effective delivery of major programmes; and improving outcomes for a diverse range of providers. In 2011, the NAO was established as a corporate public body including the Comptroller and Auditor-General (National Audit Office, 2016b). The scrutiny by the NAO does not question government policies, but uses value-for-money criteria to assess government activities. It often reports on what enables and inhibits good performance in departments and gives advice on improving performance (Bundred, 2007). The NAO addresses a range of components of performance, including: operation and programme delivery; use of data and information; contract management; oversight of service delivery; financial management; fraud, error and debt management; and consumer protection. The most impact has been through detailed analysis of the implementation of new government programmes. It has been critical of various aspects of the implementation of welfare reform from the value-for-money perspective, for example, delays in the digital delivery of universal credit, including references to management and leadership failures (National Audit Office, 2015b). The introduction of the new personal independence payments was criticised for long delays in the benefit decisions of outsourced providers, and the NAO found that the Department for Work and Pensions (DWP) did not achieve the savings it expected (National Audit Office, 2015b). Box 10.8 sets out some examples of the recommendations of the NAO for improving services and making savings.

Box 10.8: Improvements proposed by the National Audit Office

- Better carers' advice for young people by aiming at specialist information.
- Driving a customer focus for education funding agencies by improved use of data and business processes.
- Improved procurement of consumables by NHS trusts, ending wide variation in payments for the same product.
- Driving improvements in stroke care by better use of clinical and support processes to improve outcomes and reduce costs.
- Making clearer the division of responsibilities for tracking fraud and error in housing benefit between the department and local councils.
- Dealing with delays in providers getting contracts to provide accommodation for asylum seekers.
- Improving Social Fund debt management.
- Inadequate recording of money raised and houses built through disposal of public land for house building.

Source: National Audit Office (2015b)

In England, the audit of local public bodies, local councils, and local NHS and policing bodies had been the responsibility of a separate Audit Commission, but in 2010, the Coalition government abolished the Audit Commission and the performance of local public bodies was outsourced. The Local Audit and Accountability Act 2014 introduced new arrangements for local public bodies to appoint their own auditors, giving rise to criticisms of lower-quality audits, less independent audits and higher-cost audits (Ellwood, 2014). The NAO has, however, been given the role for the preparation, publication and maintenance of a code of audit practice, which sets out what local auditors are required to do under the new Act. It may examine the efficiency, effectiveness and economy with which the local authority sector uses resources. The NAO has produced some six such reports a year and has focused on a series on local adult social care and local health issues. The overview of adult social care noted the reductions in spend and packages of care, and proposed that all local authorities need to set outcomes that care services aim to achieve (National Audit Office, 2014b). A study of planning for the introduction of the Better Care Fund to promote more integrated health and social care found that the early planning did not match the scale of ambition (National Audit Office, 2014c). A report on out-of-hours GP services in England called for more understanding of variations in cost and performance, and improved oversight and integration with the urgent care service. NHS England was also criticised for the allocation process of funding to local clinical commissioning groups and it was asked to address the risk that changes in local populations may jeopardise financial stability (National Audit Office, 2014d). These reports are cross-sectoral and do not assess individual local bodies. The disappearance of the local Audit Commission in England has meant the end of the detailed performance monitoring of local councils and no expert assessment of the impact of funding cuts on council service outputs (Ferry and Eckersley, 2015). In Scotland, Wales and Northern Ireland, the role of the national audit bodies continues to cover all public bodies, including individual local councils.

Audit Scotland, the Welsh Audit Office and the Northern Ireland Audit Office (NIAO) have drawn on their combined knowledge and experience to develop a good practice checklist, setting out key principles for improvement that apply to bodies in all the devolved administrations. The checklist is structured around three elements (see Box 10.9).

Box 10.9: Devolved audit checklist

- Adopting a priority-based approach to budgeting and spending.
- Improving information on productivity, service quality and performance.
- Improving collaboration and joint working to deliver efficient and user-focused services.

Source: Welsh Audit Office (2016)

Parliamentary scrutiny of performance

One of the main functions of the Westminster Parliament and the devolved Parliament and Assemblies is the scrutiny of government activities, which involves the assessment of policy, expenditure and administration. The most important mechanism for scrutiny lies with select and subject committees, and within the extensive structures of scrutiny committees, the most significant in relation to performance are the Westminster Public Accounts Committee (PAC) and the equivalent committees in the devolved systems. The PAC is the oldest committee in Westminster, has high status and has a reputation for carrying out robust inquiries. The remit of the PAC is to scrutinise value for money, economy, efficiency and effectiveness, and to hold government and civil servants to account for the delivery of public services. It looks at how money is spent, not directly at the merits of government policy. As delivery models have changed, the scope of the PAC has extended to examine the work of quasi-autonomous non-governmental organisations (quangos) and private providers responsible for delivering services on the government's behalf. The PAC consists of 15 MPs and is always chaired by a member of the opposition. Some 50–60 inquiries are conducted by the PAC each year and their work is based on the value-for-money reports of the NAO. The majority of the NAO reports go for scrutiny and the NAO provides briefings to indicate key questions to ask witnesses (Dunleavy et al, 2009). During the 2010–15 Parliament, the PAC published 244 reports, almost all unanimous (Public Accounts Committee, 2016). An indication of the topics of the inquiries relating to social service delivery is given in Box 10.10. The inquiries can mainly be categorised as relating to: value and efficiency issues; service delivery; the performance of organisations; and the implementation of new policies.

Box 10.10: Topics of Westminster Public Accounts Committee inquiries, 2015

Value and efficiency issues
- Government funding of Kids Company.
- Funding for disadvantaged pupils.
- Overseeing financial sustainability in the further education sector.
- Disposal of public land for new houses.
- Hospital consultants and temporary staff.

Service delivery
- Management of adult diabetes services in the NHS.
- Services to people with neurological conditions.
- Fraud and error in housing benefit.
- Care leavers' transition to adulthood.

- Access to general practice in England.
- Quality of services for care leavers.
- How the pupil premium is improving disadvantaged pupils' attainment.

Performance of organisations
- Care Quality Commission.
- HM Revenue and Customs performance.
- Sustainable and financial performance of acute hospital trusts.

Implementation of new policies
- Care Act first-phase reforms and local government new burdens.
- Contracted-out health and disability assessments.
- Universal credit – progress update.
- Role of Jobcentre Plus in welfare reform.
- Devolving responsibilities to cities in England: Wave 1 city deals.

Source: Public Accounts Committee (2016)

The UK government departments subject to the most PAC inquiries were found to be the Department of Health, DWP, the Department of Defence and the Home Office (Dunleavy et al, 2009, p 28), and the major topics were procurement, efficiency, resource use and EU financial, but use of information technology (IT) has moved up in frequency. Following the publication of each report with its recommendations, the department has to reply within two months through a process administered by the Treasury. The acceptance rate of the recommendations and of the criticisms on which they are based is very high, around 85–90%. Thus, overall, the PAC's scrutiny does have an influence on improvements in service quality and efficiency, encourages savings, and impacts on policies.

With the new Conservative government in power, the proportion of acceptances has dropped to around 78% but an examination of some examples of recommendations shows an impact on improving effectiveness and improvement in service delivery in many cases. An inquiry into the financial sustainability of NHS bodies resulted in major recommendations being accepted: on assessing whether changes to service provision are achieving measurable and sustainable savings; that all local health boards should submit integrated operational plans; and that the department should require NHS bodies to use acute care within a national framework. Almost all the recommendations from an inquiry into the Planning for Better Care Funding in relation to integrated health and social care provision were accepted by the government, including that all 150 Better Care Funds should demonstrate how they will protect social care, and that there should be a scorecard to demonstrate reductions in emergency admissions and saving money. An inquiry into Improving Cancer Services had recommendations accepted relating to: the reversal of the loss of momentum in the drive to improve cancer services; the variation in services across the country; their failure to meet waiting time standards; and the need for better understanding of the impact of age on cancer services. There was evidence of the status of the PAC when criticisms made of the implementation of universal credit were accepted by the government; these were that the department had not set out clearly what had been achieved, set out milestones or examined more realistic options for delivering universal credit. In the case of an inquiry into children in care, several recommendations were not accepted by the government, relating to criticisms: that the department was not using data from local authorities to drive improvements in foster care and residential care; that the department was not holding local authorities to account for their performance; that insufficient inspections of children's care were taking place; and that good practice was not being disseminated (HM Treasury, 2015b).

It has been noted that a positive government statement in its response to a select committee report will not necessarily translate into immediate action and committees may not check (White, 2015). If not satisfied with the government response or if there is possible concern at the nature of government action, the PAC can return to the topic with further inquiries. The delays with the implementation of universal credit are producing annual inquiries, and a further report in 2016 recommended that the department: set out how the business case has changed; state how it was tracking the costs of continuing delays; and set out clear and specific milestones. Cancer services have had repeat examinations and an inquiry into the Cancer Drugs Fund was very critical, finding that NHS England and the department: had not managed the Fund effectively; had not used their buying power efficiently to pay a fair price for cancer drugs; did not have data to evaluate the outcomes for patients; and had not made it clear whether variations in access had reduced. The Scottish Parliament, and the Assemblies in Wales and Northern Ireland, all have a similar committee to the PAC.

Departmental and subject select committees at Westminster have developed as a major mechanism of scrutiny since 2002, with core tasks related to policy, expenditure and administration. The task of examining the administration of departments can cover the implementation and delivery work of departments. Although influential, the scrutiny performance of committees across the spectrum has been described as uneven (Brazier and Fox, 2011). Some subjects have a stronger emphasis on service delivery, for example, the Education Department inquiring into mental health and looked-after children, and foundation years and life chances strategies, while other subjects are more related to policy and structures, for example, the work of the Office for Standards in Education (Ofsted) and the role of regional schools commissioners. Again, most recommendations are accepted by departments, and even on core controversial government strategies, criticisms may be accepted, for example, in relation to academies and free schools and criticisms of the transparency of the Education Funding Agency and parental involvement. In the health field, important recommendations have been made on public health, end-of-life care and NHS Improvement. The implementation of welfare reform has produced a series of reports on benefit delivery, the new state pension, welfare to work and benefit sanctions. A report on the local welfare safety net (House of Commons Work and Pensions Committee, 2016) had made recommendations on mitigating the impacts of reductions in entitlements but also on delivery, advocating better joint working in the administration of the local welfare safety net. Recommendations on improving access to work for disabled people produced a guarded response from the DWP. The relatively new Public Administration Committee in the House of Commons has added to the parliamentary scrutiny of the quality of administration and service delivery, and has heard inquiries into: funding the voluntary sector, the Putting People First strategy and the Big Society (Dorey, 2014). The work of these committees has been supplemented by House of Lords committees, whether ad hoc inquiries, for example, on affordable childcare, or permanent investigative committees on economic and EU matters. There is not so much evidence on the actual outcomes of the reports and the acceptance of recommendations. Subject/departmental committees in Scotland, Wales and Northern Ireland may also evaluate the performance of departments or public bodies. Major reports by the committees in all three countries relating to policies, strategies or bodies are, however, limited in number, at the rate of only two or three per committee in Scotland and Wales and even less in Northern Ireland.

The formal proceedings of the House of Commons, debates and Question Time can give MPs the opportunity to raise issues or make information available to the public on aspects of service delivery, policy implementation and departmental performance, which can impact upon change in certain circumstances. Overall, the scrutiny landscape has been described as a web of interconnected activity that produces and builds on a wealth of information and evaluation, which has the potential to improve the performance and delivery of services (White, 2015, p 9), if not always used in practice.

Inspection

Inspection and regulation have become part of the processes for measuring performance in social service provision. Inspection has a focus on the quality of services but has some distinctive characteristics. Clarke and Ozga (2011) describe these as threefold: inspection is directly observational of sites and practices; is a form of qualitative evaluation; and is embodied evaluation, that is, is carried out by trained inspectors, although also involving standards, benchmarks and the collection of data. Regulation has an emphasis on fitness to practice, staffing, training and work procedures, and may link closely with inspection. The main social service areas for inspection and regulation are education and social care but there has been much change caused by the restructuring of services, changes in the principles of inspection and standards, and the exercise of national control. The landscape of inspection and regulation is also marked by different structures between England, Scotland, Wales and Northern Ireland.

In England, education has developed with a single uniform structure of inspection while health and social care has a wider range of bodies involved. Government inspection of schools by an inspectorate is long-standing and was eventually, in part, taken over by local education authorities in the 20th century. Resulting inconsistencies and government concern about standards led to the establishment of a national scheme in 1992 through Ofsted. Ofsted was established as a non-ministerial government department reporting directly to Parliament and led by a chief inspector and a board. The scope of Ofsted was to regularly inspect all primary and secondary schools, with a policy of improvement through inspection. The remit of Ofsted was extended in 2000 to cover further education colleges and nursery education, including a regulatory role of maintaining a register of approved childminders. A further major expansion took place in 2007 to include children's social care work, bringing together parts of the work of four existing inspectorates. This change was part of the Every Child Matters agenda and the integration of children's social care services with education in local government. The very wide range of the main inspection responsibilities are listed in Box 10.11.

Box 10.11: Bodies and provision inspected by Ofsted

Education
- Maintained primary and secondary schools.
- Non-association independent schools.
- Further education and skills providers.
- Initial teacher training education providers.
- Early years providers.
- Boarding and residential schools.
- Local authority arrangements for supporting school improvement.

Children's services
- Local authority children's services.
- Children's homes.
- Children's centres.
- Adoption support agencies and voluntary adoption agencies.
- Independent fostering agencies.
- Registered childcare providers.
- Secure training centres.
- Children and Family Court Advisory and Support Service.

Ofsted operated within a framework for collecting evidence from school records but with a focus on observing lessons. The framework was amended in 2009 to improve consistency and quality in what was called a 'tougher' approach, but it removed much of the 'tick box' element from inspection (Baxter and Clarke, 2013). It has been claimed that this represented a narrowing of inspection from that existing under the Labour government, which used a wider set of outcomes, including cultural, moral and social development (Bailey and Ball, 2016). The new model of inspection had a focus on: achievement and results; the quality of teaching; leadership; and pupil behaviour. The number of judgements was also reduced to four and the number of contracted companies to carry out inspections was reduced to three. Following a widespread consultation on further reforms, in 2015, a new Common Inspection Framework was introduced. This brings together the inspection of different education settings for greater consistency. Schools are given an overall rating on a four-point scale: outstanding; good; requires improvement; and inadequate. The inspection outcomes between 2009/10 and 2014/15 are listed in Table 10.1.

The statistics show a significant movement from 'requires improvement' to 'good'. It can be noted that the percentage judged good or outstanding (73%) is far higher for primary than for secondary schools (51%). There was only a 4% gap between the proportion of good or outstanding primary academies and local authority schools. The inspection outcome for further education colleges was as follows: 13% were rated 'outstanding'; 68% were rated 'good'; 15% were rated as 'requiring improvement' and 3% as 'inadequate'. The activities of Ofsted have been very controversial, with often tensions involving schools, teachers, unions, educational interests and the government. There has been much discussion about the nature of the dependence on the professional judgements of inspectors (Cullingford, 2015) and ideological divisions over the nature of teaching and aims of schooling.

Ofsted's credibility and judgement was called into question after the re-inspection of five schools involved in the Birmingham 'Trojan Horse' affair saw them downgraded from good or outstanding to inadequate, in some cases, in less than a year. The difficult question concerning Ofsted has been to ask if school inspections have improved the quality of provision. Evidence has been produced suggesting that school visits and inspections had an adverse effect on exam results (Rosenthal, 2004), and the precise impact of inspections on performance is difficult to untangle. The House of Commons Education Committee has called for fundamental change and, in particular, proposed that Ofsted should split into two organisations: an Inspectorate for Education and an Inspectorate for Children's Care. It was suggested that very different approaches were needed and Ofsted had concentrated too much on its schools remit. It appears likely that Ofsted

Table 10.1: Ofsted inspection outcomes (%)

	Outstanding	Good	Requires improvement	Inadequate
2014/15	12	59	24	5
2009/10	13	43	37	8

Source: Ofsted (2015)

inspections have driven up the quality of early years provision and standards but there is an unawareness of Ofsted's role and the priority given to early childhood education and care (Daycare Trust, 2011). The trend for inadequate childcare providers to leave the sector suggests that inspection has contributed to an overall increase in quality.

Inspections of children's services since 2006 in England are based on judging the effectiveness of local authority services to help and protect children. The single inspection framework focused on leadership, management and governance arrangements, the impact on children, and the quality of professional practice. A major review of child protection work (Munro, 2011) had criticised the excessive burden of inspection on child protection departments, and argued that a focus on compliance with performance management could lead to standardised services that do not respond to the variety of need arising. The view was expressed that if services were measured by inputs and bureaucratic processes, too little is learnt about when children are being helped and what impact services have (Munro, 2011). The Munro review did not change Ofsted's responsibility and a revised single inspection framework has still been criticised by local authorities as more concerned with compliance than outcomes. There has been support for a new alternative model, especially when services were becoming more integrated. Of the first 43 local authorities inspected in 2013 under the new framework, not one was judged outstanding and seven were inadequate. Ofsted holds to the view that the new framework has played a powerful role in driving cultural change in local authorities (Wilshaw, 2014).

Local authorities in England had themselves launched a Children's Improvement Board as a response to the performance of child protection becoming a high-risk and high-profile issue. It had the aim of promoting greater self-improvement and self-regulation, disseminating excellent practice, tackling service delivery failure, being a channel for innovation, and acting as a peer challenge process. Funding originally came from the Department for Education but this was controversially withdrawn by the minister in 2013/14. Controversy over inspection continued when a new Education Bill in 2015 proposed that as soon as Ofsted reports that a school is inadequate, the school will be removed from local authority control and forced to become a sponsored academy, while inadequate children's services could also be removed from local councils.

The inspection of educational provision is a devolved responsibility. All three administrations have broadly similar structures and procedures and all cover education, but not child protection as in England. The process appears more low-profile and less robust, unlike in England, despite some concern at attainment in all three countries. The process of inspection is carried out by a single dedicated body in each country and is broadly similar, with the collection of data, visits and the observation of teaching. There are, however, a number of differences, including the categories for measuring performance.

The Scottish system is also based on school self-evaluation, which emphasises support and development rather than a totally judgemental approach or a focus on performance indicators (Arnott and Ozga, 2012). Education Scotland uses three reference quality indicators, covering improvement in performance, children's experience and meeting learning needs, and engaging in a professional dialogue. Schools are assessed in each indicator as very good, good or satisfactory, or positive criteria not met. In 2014, 24% of schools were judged good or better in the three categories, while 10% did not meet the positive criteria. The performance aim set down in the National Performance Framework is to increase the proportion of schools satisfactory or better in all three reference quality indicators.

The Inspectorate of Education and Training in Wales (Estyn) describes its role as inspection plus giving advice and guidance and identifying best practice. Three aspects are judged – the outcomes, the provision and the leadership – and schools are rated as excellent, good, adequate or unsatisfactory. In 2014, one sixth of schools were rated excellent and one sixth unsatisfactory (Estyn, 2015). The Northern Ireland Education and Training Inspectorate also reports on three aspects: leadership and management; provision; and achievement and standards. A six-point scale is used and the percentage breakdown in 2014 was: 15% were rated 'outstanding'; 27% as 'very good'; 24% as 'good'; 27% as 'satisfactory' and 7% were rated 'inadequate' with no 'unsatisfactory' ratings. A major attainment issue in Northern Ireland is described as 'it is unacceptable that 60 per cent of pupils in non-grammar schools are still not achieving five or more GCSEs at A to C including English and mathematics' (Education and Training Inspectorate, 2014).

The organisation of the main aspects of the inspection of health and social care again differ across the UK and also differ in their configuration of health with social care, as set out in Table 10.2.

The Care Quality Commission is a non-departmental public body with wide-ranging functions but with the key function of monitoring, inspecting and rating health and adult social care services. It carries out in-depth investigations into care across the system and reports on the quality of care services, making performance ratings. The main sectors regulated are hospitals, GPs and primary health services, mental health, adult social care, including care homes, dental mental health services and community services. In carrying out inspections and ratings, the Care Quality Commission has five key questions – 'Are they safe?';

Table 10.2: Health and social care inspection in UK

Country	Organisation	Services covered
England	Care Quality Commission	Health, and adult social care
Scotland	Healthcare Improvement Scotland	Health
	Social Care and Social Work Improvement Scotland	Adult and children's social care
Wales	Healthcare Inspectorate Wales	Health
	Care and Social Services Inspectorate Wales	Adult and children's social care
Northern Ireland	Northern Ireland Regulation and Quality Improvement Authority	Health and adult and children's social care

'Are they effective?'; 'Are they caring?'; 'Are they responsive to people's needs?'; and 'Are they well-led?' – and uses standard key lines of enquiry (Care Quality Commission, 2016). Inspections use pre-inspection information, onsite inspection and interviews with users, carers and staff. The four ratings are: outstanding, that is, performing exceptionally; good, that is, performing well and meeting expectations; requires improvement, that is, not performing well and told how it must improve; and inadequate, that is, performing badly and action taken. Normally, a rating is given for each of the five key questions and also an overall rating for the service. By law, service providers must display their ratings. Table 10.3 shows the outcomes relating to services inspected in 2015/16 by the Care Quality Commission.

The Care Quality Commission has also developed special measures for GP practices and for adult social care. Although not all services have been rated, more than 80% of the GP practices and 60% of adult social care were good or outstanding. However, 65% of hospitals were rated as requiring improvement or inadequate. The main concerns discussed by the Commission have related to: the continuing level of variation in the quality of care; concern with safety at one in 10 hospitals, with a similar proportion of adult social care homes being judged inadequate for safety; and the importance of good leadership (Care Quality Commission, 2015). The Care Quality Commission has also come under criticism for not taking into account the context of funding cuts, for example, in relation to putting Addenbrooke's hospital into special measures (Mann, 2015) and more general criticism of the adverse impact of inspections (British Medical Association, 2016.

Inspection processes exist in other areas of social service provision or related areas. A Social Security Advisory Committee (SSAC) covers the whole UK and provides advice on social security and legislative regulations. The SSAC reports

Table 10.3: Inspection rating by Care Quality Commission (2015/16)

Sector	Rating	Number of providers
Adult Social Care	Outstanding	90
	Good	9,039
	Requires Improvement	3,983
	Inadequate	506
Hospitals (NHS and Independent)	Outstanding	5
	Good	151
	Requires Improvement	170
	Inadequate	20
Primary Medical Services	Outstanding	130
	Good	2,678
	Requires Improvement	233
	Inadequate	126

Source: Care Quality Commission, 2016

on issues relating to the operation and delivery of the benefits system. The SSAC (2015) reported on the localisation of aspects of social services and recommended that the DWP give leadership on the implementation of localised benefits. In higher education, an inspection process has been in place to assess and compare the research performance of universities, the Research Excellence Framework. A teaching inspection process in higher education had existed for a period and a new version, a teaching excellence framework, is planned. A Housing Inspectorate had functioned but was closed in 2011, although housing services by social landlords improved over that period. The Inspectorate of Probation covers England and Wales and, like other inspection bodies, aims to assure the public that the service delivers effective practice, while challenging poor practice and identifying barriers to good practice and making recommendations to improve quality. There is a focus on youth offending work. For England and Wales, there is also a Prison Inspectorate that, as well as making visits to prisons, produces a substantial number of thematic studies, for example, on substance abuse in adult prisons.

Regulatory functions

Inspection and regulatory functions are often closely aligned and sometimes performed by the same body. The definition of a regulatory function can be quite open but tends to cover four perspectives: the registration of providers of services; the assessment of compliance with statutory standards; the registration and oversight of the professional workforce; and regulating practices on behalf of the user. The registration of providers can be exercised by inspection bodies. In England, the Care Quality Commission must register care providers, who have to satisfy statutory requirements, and Ofsted registers early years and childcare providers. The social care inspectorates in Scotland and Wales register childcare providers, including childminding, day care and crèches. Health Improvement Scotland has the specific responsibility of regulating independent providers, and residential care facilities can be seen as regulated to ensure their services meet statutory obligations.

The regulation of professional staff involved in delivering key services has usually been the responsibility of specialist bodies. Thus, looking at the social work and social care workforce, special councils exist in each of the devolved countries to: register social workers; set standards for practice; oversee conduct; impose sanctions; promote training and education; promote professional development; and investigate staff falling below set standards. In England, the Health and Care Professions Council registers both allied health professionals and social work and care staff, suggesting some downgrading of the professional development of social care professionals. A General Medical Council registers all practising medical doctors.

Regulatory bodies for health and other professions have been given wider and more standardised powers, designed to guarantee a standard of excellence in practice and there has been a growth of regulatory bodies tasked with representing the user or consumer. In England, Monitor was set up to regulate NHS foundation trusts in 2004 but its remit was broadened into a role as sector regulator for health services in England and the body issuing NHS provider licences. In this role, it was also given a responsibility, akin to utility regulators, to protect and promote the interests of NHS patients and improve services. To do this, Monitor is required to promote the provision of health-care services that maintain the required standards, are efficient and effective, and improve quality. With the status of sector regulator, Monitor was to make sure that patients do not lose out through poor purchasing or restrictions on their right to choice. It was also given a duty to enable the better integration of health and social care services. Monitor was absorbed with other bodies into NHS Improvement in 2016.

Another area of growth in regulation has been housing associations, where all the jurisdictions have developed structures and processes to regulate the activity of housing associations. Social housing, as provided by housing associations and local authorities, is subject to special regulatory regimes. The regulatory requirements are more important than the governance arrangement and the arrangements again differ across the UK. In England, the providers of social housing must meet the requirements of a regulatory framework. The Homes and Communities Agency, an executive agency, is responsible for this task and provides must-follow guidance, submits information to the regulator and obtains consent for activities such as any disposals of social housing. The Scottish Housing Regulator is also an executive agency and has a focus on driving improvement in services, governance, finance and efficiency. The Welsh regulatory framework has the overall aim of putting the tenant at the heart and ensuring good-quality housing, and details 10 delivery outcomes on provision, governance and financial management. Northern Ireland is proposing to move to a copy of the system in England.

Public inquiries

Public inquiries are relatively rare but have been used by the UK government in recent years in the case of apparent serious failures in service delivery. This is usually a response to concerns expressed by either users, whistleblowers, the media, MPs or ministers. There have been a number of high-profile inquiries in the area of health, social care and children's services. What is significant is that such inquiries have resulted in both changes in delivery structures and practices, and criticisms of inspection processes and performance management. The Victoria Climbié inquiry into the death of a child from abuse and neglect identified failures across the system. The report proposed that there should be better inter-organisational cooperation and this led to the 'Every Child Matters' strategy and integrated children's departments in local councils in England, led by a director of children's services (Laming Inquiry, 2003). Following another case of the death of a child, 'Baby P', in 2007, the secretary of state ordered a review of child protection headed by Lord Laming. This report directly commented on the inspection process as Haringey council social services had recently been given 'good' ratings. A series of recommendations were made, including new standardised targets and the transformation of social work training. Not all the recommendations were implemented, but action was taken to strengthen local safeguarding children's boards (HM Government, 2010).

Following a death at Stafford Hospital, controlled by the Mid Staffordshire NHS Foundation Trust, and an investigation of high mortality rates, services were transferred to another trust. A number of inquiries took place, leading to the Francis Report (The Stationery Office, 2013). Overall, Francis found that managers lacked insight and awareness into the reality of the care being provided and went on to make 230 recommendations. The report was critical of poor clinical management, poor oversight by the trust board and poor local council scrutiny. A review of the impact of the inquiry on other trusts (Thorlby et al, 2014) found problems with how regulatory and inspection bodies still interacted. Following the report of the Francis Inquiry, a stronger focus on quality and safety emerged.

A BBC *Panorama* programme in 2012 had revealed abuse by staff at Winterbourne View Hospital for people with learning disabilities. This led to 11 criminal convictions and emergency responses, including 150 inspections by the Care Quality Commission of learning disability facilities. An inquiry by the Department of Health (DoH, 2012c) found quality and management failures by multiple agencies, a closed and punitive culture, and high rates of restraint. While recommendations were made for more appropriate training and placements, there were also recommendations for the tighter regulation and inspection of procedures and new performance indicators. General concern over child protection had led to a review of child protection (Munro, 2011), which proposed a change from bureaucratic procedures to a focus on how children were being helped. This report did not deal with children's sexual exploitation and this was to become an issue of major concern. Revelations about lengthy and widespread sexual exploitation in Rotherham produced criminal convictions and a series of reviews of children's care by several agencies. An independent inquiry was set up (Jay, 2014) and its report was critical of management, council governance, understaffing, inter-agency cooperation and also Ofsted. Recommendations for improvements by the local council and police were made in 15 priority areas.

The Keogh Report (Keogh, 2013) on the quality of treatment and care provided by hospitals that had high mortality rates, which resulted in a number of trusts being investigated and placed under special measures, also illustrated a greater focus on service quality. A major component of the public inquiries discussed and the recommendations made has been performance management, inspection and regulation, along with other factors, and this does indicate how these processes have become an integral part of the whole service delivery system. Following the report on Winterbourne View and the Francis Report, the Care Quality Commission vowed to make a new start, with clear standards of care, and to always be on the side of people who use services (Care Quality Commission, 2013).

Ombudsmen and service improvement

The influential inquiries discussed earlier had originated in complaints made by or on behalf of individuals and the whole area of the handling of complaints by users of services raises questions of how this has affected delivery practices. Every delivery agency dealing with social services has an internal complaints procedure. Dissatisfied complainants can pursue grievances to a higher level, particularly through ombudsman offices. While the main powers of the various ombudsman offices address individual complaints, they have a role in making more general reports arising from their investigations and can make recommendations for the improvement of service delivery. The configuration of ombudsmen is set out in Box 10.12 and has been undergoing change in recent years.

Box 10.12: Ombudsmen in the UK for social services

- Parliamentary and Health Services Ombudsman.
- Scottish Public Services Ombudsman.
- Local Government Ombudsman.
- Public Services Ombudsman for Wales.
- Housing Ombudsman.
- Northern Ireland Ombudsman.
- Prisons and Probation Ombudsman.

In 2015, the UK government announced plans to introduce a Bill to amalgamate offices into a new Public Services Ombudsman following recommendations of the House of Commons Public Administration Committee. This would not affect the devolved ombudsmen. The Parliamentary and Health Services Ombudsman (PHSO) covers all UK departments, agencies the NHS and other public bodies. It has operated with a filter system in that complainants must have used organisations' internal procedures and then must submit complaints through an MP, although this restriction does not apply to NHS or local government complaints. The scope of ombudsmen investigations is restricted to findings of maladministration where injustice or hardship has been caused and covers failure to follow procedures, delays, misinformation and unfair treatment, but can include failures in the quality of a service or care. The PHSO can make a finding of a complaint upheld or partly upheld and ask the delivery body to apologise or pay compensation. The Housing Ombudsman could order a particular action. There are few cases of a department not accepting the ombudsman's conclusions.

The PHSO mainly adjudicates on individual complaints, with findings, for example, that a man was not fully assessed to be a kidney donor, an ambulance delay and a jobcentre failure to explain benefits. The final decision may have more general consequences beyond an individual complaint, for example, a finding on the eligibility of people for NHS continuing care when people go to live in a nursing home and for retrospective compensation. Significantly, the PHSO has made more wider-ranging reports that recommend improvements to the way services are provided or to procedures and communication (PHSO, 2015). The main reasons for findings of maladministration in the NHS were; poor communication; errors in diagnosis, poor treatment and staff attitudes (PHSO, 2015). Departments to have been the main subject of complaints are the Department of Justice, DWP, HM Revenue and Customs and the Home Office, related mainly to immigration cases.

The operation of the PHSO has come under much criticism and there have been calls for reform. A report by a House of Commons committee has recommended the abolition of the restriction on citizens' direct and open access, own-initiative powers to investigate areas of concern without having to receive a complaint, and more freedom to engage the public (Public Administration Select Committee, 2015). A report in 2014 had seen the structures of ombudsman services as unnecessarily complex and a barrier to the potential of the sector, and called for harmonisation plans (Kirkham and Martin, 2014). The Public Administration Committee was to go on to recommend the creation of a single public services ombudsman for England to bring together the PHSO, the Local Government Ombudsman (LGO) and the Housing Ombudsman, and possibly education. This would, it was argued, promote learning and good practice. The LGO looks at complaints about councils and includes education admission appeals. There is direct access for complaints. In 2015/16 there were approximately 65,000 individual contacts leading to 22,102 new complaints. Table 10.4 gives a breakdown of the subject of complaints received for 2014/15.

Some 46% of all complaints were upheld and 99.9% of findings were complied with. The LGO does look at recommendations that may help others in the same situation and can publish special interest reports, for example, on changes to commissioning services. The LGO has also adopted a practice of publishing focus reports to highlight particular subjects or systematic issues coming from

Table 10.4: Local Government Ombudsman complaints by subject

Subject	2014 (%)	2015 (%)
Education/children	17	18
Tax/benefits	15	13
Adult social care	14	16
Housing	14	9
Planning	13	16
Road/transport	11	13
Environment/regulation	9	9
Other	7	8

Source: Local Government Ombudsman (2016)

casework and draws on lessons to make recommendations on good practice, as recorded in Box 10.13.

Box 10.13: Focus of Local Government Ombudsman reports

- Councils' role in allocating social housing.
- Councils' role in informing public choices about care homes.
- Are we getting the best from children's social care complaints?
- Local people and the planning process.
- Schools admission appeals.
- Special educational needs.
- Council services to family and friends who care for others' children.
- Councils' use of unsuitable bed and breakfast accommodation for homeless families and young people.
- Adult social care: LGO the single point of contact for complaints.

Source: Local Government Ombudsman (2016)

While there has been a trend to bring together specialist ombudsman offices, the number of specialist ombudsman offices has grown, as has the total configuration of complaints machinery, appeal bodies, tribunals, equality commissioners and special courts. In Scotland, an attempt was made to review the whole scrutiny landscape and streamline the number of bodies. The Crerar Report's recommendation for the creation of a single national scrutiny body in the longer term was not pursued, but some amalgamations did happen and an outcome was a set of principles for public service complaints and a statutory user focus (Scottish Government, 2011). Greater joining up of citizens' redress has also been suggested for central government in England but this is a difficult task (Dunleavy et al, 2009). The offices of ombudsman has shown that it can develop in the direction of conducting detailed investigation of failings in delivery, undertaking systematic investigations and proposing remedies (Kirkham et al, 2009).

Conclusions

The scope of this chapter indicates the extensive nature of the various mechanisms and specialist bodies covering performance management: performance indicators; value for money; audit; inspection; regulation; outcome frameworks; inquiries; parliamentary scrutiny; ombudsmen; and complaints procedures. A number of other statutory bodies with a different major focus may also produce reports relevant to service delivery, for example, the Equality and Human Rights Commission, children's commissioners and Commissioners for Older People. Other statutory bodies, such as the Financial Services Ombudsman, Pensions Ombudsman or the Energy Ombudsman, may also produce reports relevant to delivering policies and services of relevance to dealing with aspects of poverty, ill-health and poor housing. A wider input to the assessment of service delivery also exists in the form of research reports and evaluation carried out by charitable research trusts, research institutes, think tanks, universities and professional bodies. Research and policy reports from The King's Fund, the Nuffield Trust and the Social Care Institute for Excellence have been particularly influential on health and social care delivery.

Improving services through performance measurement has moved to a significant place and role within the operation of provider organisations, as well as in the view of government and political leaders, and in media attention. There is more scepticism about reliance on competition or choice to automatically drive up standards, even though performance measurement is based on retrospective analysis (Brooke, 2009). The prominence of performance management also carries dangers in that the main focus may become the actual processes of performance measurement, targets and inspection rather than the content and impact of services. The complexity of the landscape of assessing service delivery is demonstrated in the overlapping and sometimes conflicting views on the best means of taking forward this task. There has been a trend away from performance indicators and target setting to outcomes and outcome frameworks, which reflects the growing centrality of user perceptions. In some contexts, outcomes have appeared little different from traditional objectives or targets but outcomes suggest a focus on the wider consequences of services and the more personalised impact.

The complexity of performance management arrangements has been augmented by two developments. First, the growth of providers from the non-statutory sector, the private sector, the voluntary sector, from partnerships and international organisations have raised issues concerning the role and scope of statutory inspection, regulatory and ombudsmen bodies. Issues of market confidentiality have been used by private providers to refuse the disclosure of information. The second development has been devolution, bringing the replication of many bodies but also new forms of performance management and new approaches. In Scotland, there has been a major initiative in the use of national performance indicators and attempts to streamline the number of investigatory and regulatory bodies. In Wales, the four main inspection, audit and regulation bodies, the Care and Social Services Inspectorate Wales, Estyn, Healthcare Inspectorate Wales and the Wales Audit Office, launched a joint paper (Care and Social Services Inspectorate Wales et al, 2011), 'Developing our work together in a climate of change', outlining how the four organisations were collaborating to deliver improvements, develop joint working and share information and knowledge.

A number of problems still exist in finding a consensus on the best and most effective approach to assessing delivery performance. The scale of the processes, the bureaucracy and the time consumed is not always acceptable to providers, managers and professional staff. One local NHS foundation trust in England calculated that 19 bodies were involved in the monitoring and inspection of their services. The whole process has also been seen as challenging the role of Parliament as some bodies have appeared to become quite powerful, and also as challenging locally elected politicians and their authority, and in relation to local education in England has raised issues of democratic legitimacy. There have been concerns about too much standardisation, tick boxes and centralisation, with arguments for more localist approaches. Overall, the developments in outcome indicators, inspection and audit have assisted in improving checks on the quality of services and their delivery. There remains the difficulty that it is not always easy to demonstrate the exact impact of performance management in all its forms in discriminating among the multiplicity of factors that may determine the characteristics of services.

ELEVEN

Conclusion

Changes to the governance and delivery of welfare throughout the UK have been such as to suggest that there has been a fundamental shift in thinking about the role of the state in welfare provision. This has been described as a 'restructuring of the role of government in social provision so far reaching as to be systemic, rather than programmatic' (Bochel and Powell, 2016, p 17). Here, we identify: the principles underpinning changes and trends; the impact of the modernisation agenda; changes in the main delivery sectors; and, finally, the main influences on what we describe as the reformulation of the delivery of welfare services.

Principles underpinning changes in the delivery and governance of welfare services

A number of principles have emerged as influences on changes in delivery and governance, and the degree of their importance has been demonstrated in this analysis. These principles can be set out as follows:

- *Outsourcing to private and voluntary sector providers* – the outsourcing of provision, formerly directly provided by statutory bodies, has become extensive. Funding still remains the responsibility of government bodies. The principle of commissioner–provider can also be invoked but a defining element is the involvement of private and voluntary sector providers.

- *Privatisation* – in its narrowest definition, privatisation as a principle describes a good or service moving from a statutory responsibility to a non-statutory responsibility, with the implication that it becomes a private good. In practice, there are some variations in the use of the term and it has been used to refer to: any involvement of the private sector; the imposition of charges; or elements of privatisation but not total privatisation. There are relatively few examples of a service having its status changed to becoming totally provided by the private sector.

- *Devolution* – the principle of devolution to Scotland, Wales and Northern Ireland has developed into a major factor in changing the delivery and governance pattern of the UK as a whole and has key importance for all areas of social welfare services. The three devolved administrations have also introduced innovations in delivery, raising the possibility of devolved principles of governance and service delivery.

- *Localism* – in the UK, there has been a long-standing commitment to the value or principle of localism but it has been given different interpretations and emphasis by successive governments. It is, in part, closely related to the activities of local government and increasing the role of local authorities but localisation of services can involve other forms of statutory governance and the involvement of local populations.

- *Centralisation* – a principle in contrast to localism but both principles can be identified as having influence within the same government. Centralisation is associated with a transfer of functions to central government departments from local government, quasi-autonomous non-governmental organisations (quangos) or public bodies. This may directly impact upon the delivery of welfare services or may relate to other extensions of central government powers and regulation or exercising greater usage of financial powers. While central administration has in the past referred to Whitehall departments, since 1999, there are also devolved central administrations.

- *Fragmentation* – changes in service delivery have led to a range of different actors and providers, resulting in a 'less coherent and more fragmented process of policy making' (Bochel, 2016, p 54). In practice, transformation in delivery has involved shifts in responsibilities between central government, quangos, local government and other agencies. This has led to greater developments in relation to multi-level governance and confusion for users, has produced a need for greater regulation and inspection, and has increased complexity with regard to inspection.

The modernisation agenda and the delivery of welfare

The modernisation agenda has led to the adoption of a number of principles in the delivery of services:

- *User involvement and coproduction* – although strategies to encourage user and public participation have a long tradition, the user involvement moment has developed as a more focused dimension, with strong underpinning values. User involvement can be seen as developing along a spectrum to forms of direct control over service provision, especially in adult social care. It is also possible to discern influence across other services, including a strong focus on public participation and engagement in health care.

- *Personalisation* – this principle has come to the fore as a desirable characteristic of service design and delivery. There has been a shift from a low-key principle of person-centred services to personalised control and direction over financing, the nature of services and methods of delivery.

- *Regulation* – in most service areas, there has been a growth of initiatives and experimentation in regulation, audit, inspection and assessments of performance in the delivery of services. Demands for more public accountability and transparency have led to a range of measures to augment more traditional functions of audit and parliamentary scrutiny.

Changes to the delivery sectors in social welfare

Consideration of the delivery sectors includes how the impact of policy developments and the principles noted earlier have resulted in changes to the configuration and balance of the main sectors of delivery. It is possible to make an assessment of the scale and scope of each sector, the degree of change in functions, and likely future trends, as follows:

- *Government departments* – responsibility for direct delivery of services has been limited and mainly concentrated in education. The degree of influence, direction and guidance over a range of services has increased, as has the related scale of new policies and changes in funding arrangements. This is particularly marked in social security, housing, health and social care.

- *Local government* – in England, there have been contrasting processes, as exemplified by a loss of direct delivery responsibilities in the area of schools, social housing, social care and probation, but the acquisition of new functions in relation to public health, health scrutiny and well-being, council tax relief, aspects of social security, and control over the audit process. City devolution has been a new development relating mainly to health and social care functions.

- *Quangos and public bodies* – there has been a concentrated attempt throughout the UK to reduce the area of delegated governance and the role of executive quangos closely involved in the delivery of services. The actual transfer of functions from quangos to central government or local government has been limited but there are some examples. Again, this has to be measured against the creation of some new quangos. While, overall, there has been a reduction in the number of quangos, this has been more focused on advisory quangos rather than bodies with delivery functions, or has been based on mergers of existing quangos.

- *Partnerships* – governance and delivery through the mechanisms of partnerships have become extensive and take a number of formats. Partnerships between statutory bodies or the different statutory sectors can be identified as promoting joined-up governance. In the area of health and social care, partnerships are largely associated with the goal of integrated working. The main format for partnerships involves collaborative partnerships between statutory, private and voluntary bodies. In this context, a distinction exists with the contracted provision of services or outsourcing in a business relationship.

- *Private sector* – the importance of private providers has continued to grow, contributing to not only welfare pluralism, but also the complexity of provision. Throughout the UK, private sector provision has increased in scale and importance, particularly in adult social care, social security assessments and employment training provision. In England, private provision in education, health, housing, probation and prisons has expanded, but to a lesser extent in the devolved administrations.

- *Devolved administrations* – since 1999, devolution for Scotland, Wales and Northern Ireland has introduced major changes to the overall system of welfare service delivery within the UK, with responsibility for the major welfare services becoming fully devolved. Devolution has contributed to a more complex landscape of service delivery.

- *Voluntary/third sector* – historically, the voluntary sector has played a significant but increasingly specialist role in the delivery of welfare services. The original idea of the Big Society heralded a shift from state provision to responsibility shifting to the voluntary sector, civil society, communities and families. The possibility of a developing role through the Big Society strategy has faded and the voluntary sector has struggled to compete with large private companies to win government service contracts. Cuts in public expenditure for government departments, quangos and local authorities have also had a negative effect on the growth of the voluntary sector.

The main characteristics of service delivery by country of the UK with regard to major social welfare services are summarised in Boxes 11.1, 11.2, 11.3 and 11.4.

Box 11.1: Service delivery in England

Service	Delivery structures
Social security	Main delivery still by government department. Involvement of private providers in assessments, limited trend to involve local councils.
Health	Main delivery by quangos, national and local, increase in involvement of private providers and limited involvement of local councils in scrutiny and partnership working.
Adult social care	Main responsibility lies with local councils but delivery by the private and voluntary sector.
Children's social services	Main delivery by local councils, some involvement by voluntary bodies.
Education	Still mainly delivered by local councils but increasingly replaced with delivery by 'independent' providers, such as academy chains, with strong oversight by the government department.
Social housing	Main delivery by housing associations (voluntary), local councils and some quango involvement.
Probation	By government department, through an executive agency – with contracting to private companies, sometimes working in collaboration with voluntary organisations.

Service	Delivery structures
Youth services	Local councils have responsibility but increasingly delivered by contracting with voluntary agencies.
Employment and training services	Mainly by private and voluntary sector providers on the basis of contracts.

Box 11.2: Service delivery in Scotland

Service	Delivery structure
Social security	Mainly by UK department, some private providers with subcontracting to the voluntary sector and limited devolved functions with plans for further devolution.
Health	Mainly by quangos with partnerships on integrated care.
Adult social care	Mainly by local councils with private and voluntary providers and partnerships on integrated care.
Children's social services	Mainly by local councils, some voluntary providers.
Education	Mainly by local councils.
Social housing	Mainly by local councils with housing associations, and quangos.
Probation	Mainly by local councils.
Youth services	Mainly by local councils and voluntary bodies.

Box 11.3: Service delivery in Wales

Service	Delivery structure
Social security	Mainly by UK department, with some private providers and limited devolved function.
Health	Mainly by quangos with some integration with social care.
Adult social care	Mainly by local councils with private and voluntary sector providers and some integration with health.
Children's social services	Mainly by local councils with some voluntary providers.
Education	Mainly by local councils.
Social housing	Mainly by local councils with housing associations.
Probation	By UK government department, through an executive agency – with contracting to private companies, sometimes working in collaboration with voluntary organisations.
Youth services	Mainly by local councils.
Employment and training services	Mainly by private and voluntary sector providers on the basis of contracts.

Box 11.4: Service delivery in Northern Ireland

Social security	Mainly by devolved department with some private providers.
Health	Mainly by quangos.
Adult social care	Mainly by quangos but involving contracts to private and voluntary sector providers.
Children's social services	Mainly by quangos but some delivery by voluntary sector providers.
Education	Mainly by quangos.
Social housing	Quangos and voluntary providers.
Youth services	Mainly by quangos with some voluntary delivery.
Employment and training services	Mainly by private and voluntary sector providers on the basis of contracts.

The reformulation of the delivery of social welfare services

The main characteristics and trends in the delivery and governance of social welfare services in the UK can be identified from this analysis. These trends can be looked at under four main headings:

1. A reformulation of social welfare services towards a less comprehensive role under neo–liberal influences. This is the most significant overall trend, which can be described as an adjustment of the balance in welfare pluralism that has developed over the last 35 years. Policy changes are closely identified with the scale and functions of the major governance sectors, modes of delivery and the restructuring of welfare delivery.

2. Reformulation and restructuring is also associated with the austerity drive: to reduce the fiscal deficit by introducing expenditure cuts, efficiencies and savings, steamlining structures and reducing staff while not increasing taxation.

3. Fundamental to reformulation and restructuring has been the establishment and development of devolution, especially as most social welfare services are devolved to Scotland, Wales and Northern Ireland. Divergence with policies and structures exist and there is a continuing emphasis in the balance of welfare pluralism, statutory provision and innovations in delivery and governance.

4. Reformulation and restructuring has occurred in response to modernisation influences that impact on delivery, especially through partnerships, user participation, co–production, personalisation and greater regulation.

The combination of influences resulting in the reduced role for the state in welfare delivery has different implications for each set of welfare services, even for parts of each service and also for the four different countries of the UK. There is no universal convergence or a single mode of divergence.

There is evidence of a strong element of continuity in delivery and governance, which means that caution should be adopted in using terms such as 'radical change' or 'transformation'. It has been possible to identify some common themes and approaches over several different governments. The use of markets, consumer choice, personal budgets, managerialism, performance management and residualisation of local government provision all illustrate change. However, as Bochel and Powell (2016) note, the reasons for change may be varied and change may be slow given doubts about direction and implementation difficulties. There can also be unintended consequences. The responsibility for driving change in policy delivery and in the structures and governance of welfare continues to rest with government strategies; the configuration of welfare pluralism is the result of government decisions, not the decisions of the constituent sectors.

A final context that cannot be ignored is the disputed discourses in the narratives surrounding this issue. A wide range of institutions contribute to these divisions based on political parties, including the House of Commons, the House of Lords, parliamentary committees, devolved bodies and many public bodies. But particularly divisive have been disputes between central and local government in England. Key contributions to the debate have also come from professional bodies, research institutes, think tanks and research foundations, organisations representing public bodies, and lobbying groups, although the impact of such contributions is ultimately determined by the government itself. Looking ahead, the indications are that public expenditure is likely to remain flat, some aspects of the modernisation agenda may continue where it is not so politically divisive and experiments such as city devolution may have further impact. Greater emphasis may also be placed on the prevention agenda. Devolution, especially in Wales and Scotland, is likely to result in more divergence, and in Britain, there is likely to be further reduction in the powers of local government, either directly or through partnerships and as a result of financial uncertainty. Looking across the range and scale of changes to the governance and delivery of welfare covered in the book, it could be argued that these have contributed to establishing a different relationship between the state and users of welfare as the state increasingly withdraws from the direct provision of services and the co-production agenda expands. It could be anticipated that the UK government will pursue further contracting out pursuing greater diversity in delivery of services.

References

Adam, S. and Browne, J. (2012) *Reforming Council Tax Benefit*, York: Joseph Rowntree Foundation.

ADASS (Association of Directors of Social Services) (2012) *The Case for Tomorrow*, London: ADASS.

ADASS (2014) *Future Funding Outlook 2014: Funding Outlook for Councils to 2019/2020*, London: ADASS.

ADASS (2015) *Distinctive, Valued, Personal – Why Social Care Matters: The Next Five Years*, London: ASASS.

Addicot, R. (2014) *Commissioning and Contracting for Integrated Care*, London: Kings Fund.

Alcock, P. (2003) *Social Policy in Britain* (2nd edn). London: Palgrave.

Allen, C. (2003) 'Desperately seeking fusion: on "joined up thinking", "holistic practice" and the new economy of welfare professional power', *British Journal of Sociology*, vol 54, no 2, pp 287–306.

Allen, G. (2015) *Civil Service Statistics*, Briefing Paper No 2224, London: House of Commons Library.

Allen, P., Townsend, J., Dempster, P., Wright, J., Hutchings, A. and Keen, J. (2012) 'Organizational form as a mechanism to involve staff, public and users in public services: a study of the governance of NHS Foundation Trusts', *Social Policy and Administration*, vol 46, no 3, pp 239–57.

All Party Parliamentary Sure Start Group (2013) *Best Practice for Sure Start: The Way Forward for Children's Centres*, London: House of Commons.

Allsop, J. (1984) *Health Policy and the National Health Service*, London: Longman.

Andrews, R. and Boyne, G. (2012) 'Structural change and public service performance: the impact of the reorganisation process in English local government', *Public Administration*, vol 90, no 2, pp 297–312.

Andrews, R. and Entwistle, T. (2015) 'Public–private partnerships, management capacity and public service efficiency', *Policy and Politics*, vol 43, no 2, pp 273–90.

Appleby, J. (2005) *Independent Review of Health and Social Care Services in Northern Ireland*, Belfast: Department of Health and Social Services and Public Safety.

Appleby, J. and Devlin, N. (2005) *Measuring NHS Success*, London: The King's Fund.

Armstrong, P. (2015) *Effective School Partnerships and Collaboration for School Improvement: A Review of the Evidence*, London: Department for Education.

Arnott, M. and Ozga, J. (2012) 'Education policy and social justice', in G. Mooney and G. Scott (eds) *Social Justice and Social Policy in Scotland*, Bristol: The Policy Press.

Arnstein, S. (1969) 'A ladder of citizen participation', *Journal of American Institute of Planners*, vol 35, no 4, pp 216–24.

Attree, P., French, B., Milton, B., Povall, S., Whitehead, M. and Popay, J. (2011) 'The experience of community engagement for individuals: a rapid review of evidence', *Health and Social Care in the Community*, vol 19, no 3, pp 250–60.

Audit Commission (1998) *A Fruitful Partnership: Effective Partnership Working*, London: The Audit Commission.

Audit Scotland (2011) *Review of Community Health Partnerships*, Edinburgh: Audit Scotland.

Audit Scotland (2012) *Commissioning Social Care*, Edinburgh: Audit Scotland.

Audit Scotland (2014a) *Turning Ambition into Action*, Edinburgh: Audit Scotland.

Audit Scotland (2014b) *School Education*, Edinburgh: Audit Scotland.

Audit Scotland (2014c) *Self-Directed Support*, Edinburgh: Audit Scotland.

Audit Scotland (2015a) *NHS in Scotland 2015*, Edinburgh: Audit Scotland.

Audit Scotland (2015b) *Health and Social Care Integration*, Edinburgh: Audit Scotland.

Audit Scotland (2016) *Community Planning: An Update*, Edinburgh: Audit Scotland.

Bache, I. and Flinders, M. (2004) *Multi-Level Governance*, Oxford: Oxford University Press.

Baekkeskov, E. (2011) 'Issue framing and sector character as critical parameters for government contracting-out in the United Kingdom', *Public Administration*, vol 89, no 4, pp 1489–508.

Baggott, R. (2004) *Health and Healthcare in Britain*, Basingstoke: Palgrave MacMillan.

Baggott, R. (2013) *Partnerships for Public Health and Well-being*, Basingstoke, Palgrave MacMillan.

Baggott, R. (2015) *Understanding Health Policy*, Bristol: The Policy Press.

Baggott, R. (2016) 'Health policy and the Coalition government', in H. Bochel and M. Powell (eds) *The Coalition Government and Social Policy*, Bristol: The Policy Press.

Bailey, N., Bramley, G. and Hastings, A. (2015) 'Symposium introduction: local responses to "austerity"', *Local Government Studies*, vol 41, no 4, pp 571–81.

Bailey, P.L.J. and Ball, S.J. (2016) 'The Coalition government, the general election and the policy ratchet in education: a reflection on the "ghosts" of policy past, present and yet to come', in H. Bochel and M. Powell (eds) *The Coalition Government and Social Policy*, Bristol: The Policy Press.

Baines, D. and Cunningham, I. (2015) 'Care work in the context of austerity', *Competition and Change*, vol 19, no 3, pp 183–93.

Ball, S.J. (2007) *Education Plc: Understanding Private Sector Participation in Public Sector Education*, London: Routledge.

Balloch, S. and Taylor, M. (2007) *Partnership Working: Policy and Practice*, Bristol: The Policy Press.

Barlow, J. and Köberle-Gaiser, M. (2009) 'Delivering innovation in hospital construction: contracts and collaboration in the UK's private finance initiative hospitals program', *California Management Review*, vol 51, pp 126–43.

Barnes, M. (2008) 'Passionate participation: emotional experiences and expressions in deliberative forums', *Critical Social Policy*, vol 29, no 3, pp 374–97.

Barnes, M. and Bowl, R. (2001) *Taking Over the Asylum: Empowerment and Mental Health*, Basingstoke: Palgrave.

Barnes, M., Newman, J., Knops, A. and Sullivan, H. (2003) 'Constituting "the public" in public participation', *Public Administration*, vol 81, no 2, pp 379–99.

Barret, D., Benson, J., Foster, R. and Leader, A. (2014) 'Prosper: a social movement approach to mental health', *Mental Health and Social Inclusion*, vol 18, no 4, pp 188–97.

Bates, A. and Foster, D. (2015) *Surestart (England) Briefing Paper No 7257*, London: House of Commons Library.

Baxter, J. and Clarke, J. (2013) 'Farewell to the tick box inspection? Ofsted and the changing regime of school inspection in England', *Oxford Review of Education*, vol 39, no 5, pp 702–18.

Baxter, K., Rablee, P. and Glendinning, C. (2013) 'Managed personal budgets for older people: what are English local authorities doing to facilitate personalised and flexible care', *Public Money and Management*, vol 33, no 6, pp 399–406.

BBC (2016a) 'G4S Medway Centre: government to take over young offenders centre'. Available at: http://www.bbc.co.uk/news/uk–england-36210923

BBC (2016b) 'Government climbdown over forced academies plan in England'. Available at: http://www.bbc.co.uk/news/education-36227570

Beecham, J. (2006) *Beyond Boundaries. Citizen-Centred Local Services for Wales*, Cardiff: Welsh Assembly Government.

Bell, D. and Christie, A. (2007) 'Funding devolution: the power of money', in A. Trench (ed) *Devolution and Power in the United Kingdom*, Manchester: Manchester University Press.

Bennett, L. and Humphries, R. (2014) *Making Use of the Better Care Fund*, London: Kings Fund.

Beresford, P. (2010) 'Public partnerships, governance and user involvement: a service user perspective', *International Journal of Consumer Studies*, vol 34, pp 495–502.

Beresford, P. (2016) *All Our Welfare: Towards Participatory Social Policy*, Bristol: The Policy Press.

Beresford, P. and Croft, S. (1993) *Citizen Involvement: A Practical Guide for Change*, Basingstoke: Macmillan.

Beresford, P. and Croft, S. (1996) 'The politics of participation', in D. Taylor (ed) *Critical Social Policy: A Reader*, London: Sage.

Beresford, P., Fleming, J., Glynn, M., Bewley, C., Croft, S., Branfield, F. and Postle, K. (2011) *Supporting People: Towards a Person-Centred Approach*, London: Policy Press.

Berry, K. (2014) *Housing (Scotland) Bill – Parliamentary Consideration Prior to Stage 3*, Spice Briefing, Edinburgh: Scottish Parliament.

Bevir, M. and Rhodes, R. (2013) 'The stateless state', in M. Bevir (ed) *The Sage Handbook of Governance*, London: Sage.

Birrell, D. (2006) 'The disintegration of local authority social services', *Local Government Studies*, vol 32, no 2, pp 139–51.

Birrell, D. (2007) 'Divergence in policy between Great Britain and Northern Ireland: the case of local taxation', *Public Money & Management*, vol 27, no 5, pp 323–30.

Birrell, D. (2008) 'Devolution and quangos in the United Kingdom: the implementation of principles and policies for rationalisation and democratisation', *Policy Studies*, vol 29, no 1, pp 35–49.

Birrell, D. (2009) *Direct Rule and the Governance of Northern Ireland*, Manchester: Manchester University Press.

Birrell, D. (2010) 'Public sector reform in Northern Ireland: policy copying or a distinctive model of public sector modernization?', *Public Money & Management*, vol 30, no 2, pp 109–16.

Birrell, D. (2012) *Comparing Devolved Governance*, Basingstoke: Palgrave MacMillan.

Birrell, D. and Gormley-Heenan, C. (2015) *Multi-level Governance and Northern Ireland*, Basingstoke: Palgrave Macmillan.

Birrell, D. and Heenan, D. (2014) 'Integrated care partnerships in Northern Ireland: added value or added bureaucracy?', *Journal of Integrated Care*, vol 22, nos 5/6, pp 197–207.

Birrell, D. and Gray, A. (2014) 'Welfare reform and devolution: issues of parity, discretion and divergence for the United Kingdom government and the devolved administrations', *Public Money and Management*, vol 34, no 3, pp 205–12.

Birrell, D. and Gray A.M. (2016) 'Social policy, devolution and the UK Coalition government', in H. Bochel and M. Powell (eds) *The Coalition Government and Social Policy*, Bristol: The Policy Press.

Blackender, L. and Prestidge J. (2014) 'Pan London personalised budgets for rough sleepers', *Journal of Integrated Care*, vol 22, no 1, pp 23–6.

Bochel, C. (2011) 'The Conservatives and the governance of social policy', in H. Bochel (ed) *The Conservative Party and Social Policy*, Bristol: The Policy Press.

Bochel, C. (2016) 'The changing governance of social policy', in H. Bochel and M. Powell (eds) *The Coalition Government and Social Policy*, Bristol: The Policy Press.

Bochel, C. and Bochel, M. (2004) *The UK Social Policy Process*, Basingstoke: Palgrave MacMillan.

Bochel, C., Bochel, H., Somerville, P. and Worley, C. (2008) 'Marginalised or enabled voices? User participation in policy and practice', *Social Policy and Society*, vol 7, no 2, pp 201–10.

Bochel, H., Bochel, C., Page, R. and Sykes, R. (2009) *Social Policy: Themes, Issues and Debates*, London: Pearson Longman.

Bochel, H. and Powell, M. (2016) *The Coalition Government and Social Policy*, Bristol: The Policy Press.

Boddy, J., Stratham, J., Warwick, I., Hollingworth, K. and Spencer, G. (2016) 'What kind of trouble? Meeting the health needs of troubled families through intensive family support', *Social Policy and Society*, vol 15, no 2, pp 275–88.

Bode, I. (2006) 'New mixed economies of welfare: the case of domiciliary elderly care in Germany, France and Britain', *European Society*, vol 8, no 4, pp 527–44.

Bode, I. and Brandsen, T. (2014) 'State–third sector partnerships: a short overview of key issues in the debate', *Public Management Review*, vol 16, no 8, pp 1055–66.

Bojke, C. and Goddard, M. (2010) *Foundation Trusts: Retrospective Review*, The Centre for Health Economics Research Paper 58, York: University of York.

Booth, L. and Starodubtseva, V. (2015) *PFI: Costs and Benefits*, London: House of Commons Library.

Bovaird, T. (2012) 'Community empowerment', in J. Raine and C. Staite (eds) *The World Will be Your Oyster? Reflections on the Localism Act 2011*, Birmingham: Institute of Local Government Studies.

Bovaird, T. (2014) 'Attributing outcomes to social policy interventions', *Social Policy and Administration*, vol 48, no 1, pp 1–23.

Bovaird, T. and Loeffler, E. (2014) *Bringing the Power of the Citizen into Local Public Services – An Evidence Review*, Birmingham: University of Birmingham Institute for Local Government Studies.

Bovaird, T., Van Ryzin, G.G., Loeffler, E. and Parrado, S. (2015) 'Activating citizens to participate in collective co-production of public services', *Journal of Social Policy*, vol 44, no 1, pp 1–23.

Boxall, C. and Beresford, P. (2013) 'Service user research in social work and disability studies in the United Kingdom', *Disability and Society*, vol 28, no 5, pp 587–600.

Boydell, L. (2015) *A Review of the Effectiveness of Inter-agency Collaboration at the Early Intervention Stage*, Dublin: Centre for Effective Services.

Boyle, D. and Harris, M. (2009) *The Challenge of Co-production: How Equal Partnerships between Professionals and the Public Are Crucial to Improving Public Services*, London: National Endowment for Science, Technology and the Arts.

Boyle, D., Slay, J. and Stephens, L. (2010) *Public Services Inside Out: Putting Co-Production into Practice*, London: NESTA.

Brazier, A. and Fox, R. (2011) 'Reviewing select committee tasks and modes of operation', *Parliamentary Affairs*, vol 64, no 2, pp 354–69.

British Medical Association (2016) Care Quality Commission GP Survey Results, Press release (https://www.bma.org.uk/collective-voice/committees/general-practitioners-committee/gpc-surveys/cqc-survey).

Brooke, R. (2009) 'New development: the future of public services regulation – the professional's perspective', *Public Money and Management*, vol 29. no 5, pp 268–72.

Brown, H. (2014) *National Development Team for Inclusion: Co-Production Involving and Led by Older People: An Evidence and Practice Review*, Bath: National Development Team for Inclusion.

Buckingham, H. (2012) 'Capturing diversity: a typology of third sector organisations' responses to contracting based on empirical evidence from homelessness services', *Journal of Social Policy*, vol 41, no 3, pp 569–89.

Bundred, S. (2007) 'New roles for auditors in government performance and accountability', in M. Lavender (ed.) *Watchdogs Straining at the Leash*, London: Public Management and Policy Association.

Burchardt, T. (1997) *Boundaries between Public and Private Welfare: A Typology and Map of Services*, CASE paper 2, London: LSE Centre for Analysis of Social Exclusion.

Burchardt, T. (2013) *Re-Visiting the Conceptual Framework for Public/Private Boundaries in Welfare: Social Policy in a Cold Climate*, Research Note Series RN2002, London: LSE Centre for Analysis of Social Exclusion.

Burgess, P., Hall, S., Mawson, J. and Pearce, G. (2001) *Evolved Approaches to Local Governance: Policy and Practice in Neighbourhood Management*, York: Joseph Rowntree Foundation.

Burnham, J. and Horton, S. (2013) *Public Management in the United Kingdom*, Basingstoke: Palgrave MacMillan.

Burt, P. (2006) *A Fairer Way: Report by the Local Government Finance Review Committee*, Edinburgh: Scottish Executive.

Burton, M. (2013) *The Politics of Public Sector Reform*, Basingstoke: Palgrave Macmillan.

Burton, P., Croft, J., Hastings, A., Slater, T., Goodlad, R., Abbott, J. and Macdonald, A. (2004) *What Works in Community Involvement in Area-based Initiatives? A Systematic Review of the Literature*, London: The Home Office.

Butcher, T. (1995) *Delivering Welfare*, Buckingham: Open University Press.

Cabinet Office (1998) *Opening the Doors to Quangos*, London: The Cabinet Office.

Cabinet Office (1999) *Modernising government*, Cm 4310, London: The Stationery Office.

Cabinet Office (2004) *Civil Service Reform: Delivery and Values*, London: The Stationery Office.

Cabinet Office (2006) *Executive Agencies: A Guide for Departments*, London: The Cabinet Office.

Cabinet Office (2008) *Excellence and Fairness: Achieving World Class Public Services*, London: The Stationery Office.

Cabinet Office (2010a) *Building the Big Society*, London: Cabinet Office.

Cabinet Office (2010b) *Public Bodies Reform – Proposals for Change*, London: The Cabinet Office.

Cabinet Office (2011) *Government Response to the Public Administration Select Committee Report 'Smaller Government: Shrinking the Quango State'*, Cm8044, London: The Stationery Office.

Cabinet Office (2012) *Categories of Public Bodies: A Guide for Departments*, London: The Cabinet Office.

Cabinet Office (2013) *Civil Service Reform Plan: One Year On Report*. London: The Cabinet Office.

Cabinet Office (2014) 'Public bodies reform programme update'. Available at: www.gov.uk/government/speeches/public-bodies-reform-programme-update

Cabinet Office (2015) *Public Bodies*, London: The Cabinet Office.

Cabinet Office (2016) *Cabinet Office Single Departmental Plan: 2015 to 2020*, London: The Cabinet Office.

Cabinet Office and Efficiency and Reform Group (2014) 'Guidance: public bodies reform'. Available at: www.gov.uk/public-bodies-reform

Cairney, P. (2011) *The Scottish Political System Since Devolution*, Exeter: Imprint Academic.

Cairney, P. (2012) *The Scottish Political System Since Devolution*, Exeter: Imprint Academic.

Campbell, C. (2014) 'Community mobilisation in the 21st century: updating our theory of social change?', *Journal of Health Psychology*, vol 19, no 1, pp 46–59.

Care and Social Services Inspectorate Wales, Estyn, Healthcare Inspection Wales and Wales Audit Office (2011) *Developing Our Work Together in a Climate of Change*, Cardiff: Wales Audit Office.

Care Quality Commission (2013) *A New Start, Consultation on Changes to the Way CQC Regulates, Inspects and Monitors Care*, London: Care Quality Commission.

Care Quality Commission (2015) *Hitchingbrooke Health Care Quality Report*, London: Care Quality Commission.

Care Quality Commission (2016) *Annual Accounts and Report 2015–2016* HC 467, London: Care Quality Commission.

Carey, M. (2009) 'Happy shopper? The problem with service user and carer participation', *British Journal of Social Work*, vol 39, pp 179–88.

Carmel, E. and Papadopoulos, T. (2003) 'The new governance of social services in Britain' in J. Millar (ed.) *Understanding Social Security: Issues for Policy and Practice*, Bristol: The Policy Press.

Carr, S. (2010) *Personalisation: A Rough Guide*, London: SCIE.

Carr-West, J. and Diamond, P. (2015) *Devolution: A Road Map*, London: Local Government Information Unit.

Carter, E. and Whitworth, A. (2015) 'Creaming and parking in quasi-marketised welfare-to-work schemes: designed out of or designed in to the UK Work Programme?', *Journal of Social Policy*, vol 44, no 2, pp 277–96.

Challis, L., Fuller, S., Henwood, M., Klein, R., Plowden, W., Webb, A., Whittingham, P. and Wistow, G. (1988) *Joint Approaches to Social Policy: Rationality and Practice*, Cambridge: Cambridge University Press.

Chandler, J. (2001) *Local Government Today*, Manchester: Manchester University Press.

Chaney, P. and Drakeford, M. (2004) 'The primacy of ideology: social policy and the first term of the National Assembly for Wales', *Social Policy Review*, vol 16, pp 121–42.

Chaney, P. and Wincott, D. (2014) 'Envisioning the third sector's welfare role: critical discourse analysis of "post-devolution" public policy in the UK 1998–2012', *Social Policy and Administration*, vol 48, no 7, pp 757–81.

Chapman, C. and Muijs, D. (2014) 'Does school-to-school collaboration promote school improvement? A study of the impact of school federations on student outcomes', *School Effectiveness and School Improvement*, vol 25, no 3, pp 351–93.

Chapman, C., Lowden, K., Chestnutt, H., Hall, S., McKinney, S., Hulme, M. and Watters, N. (2014) *The School Improvement Partnership Programme: Using Collaboration and Enquiry to Tackle Educational Inequity*, Livingstone: Education Scotland.

Charity Commission (2007) *Stand and Deliver: The Future for Charities Delivering Public Services*, RS15, London: Charity Commission.

Checkland, K., Harrison, S., Snow, S., McDermott, I. and Coleman, A. (2012) 'Commissioning in an English National Health Service: what is the problem?', *Journal of Social Policy*, vol 41, no 3, pp 533–50.

Children, Schools and Families Select Committee (2008) *Testing and Assessment*, HC 169-1, London: House of Commons Library.

Chisholm, M. (2010) 'Emerging realities of local government reorganisation', *Public Money and Management*, vol 30, no 3, pp 143–50.

Christie, C. (2011) *Commission of the Future Delivery of Public Services*, Cardiff: Welsh Assembly Government.

Civil Service (2014) *Introduction to Sponsorship: An Induction Pack for Non-Sponsors of Arm's Length Bodies*, London: The Stationery Office.

Clarke, J. and Glendinning, C. (2002) 'Partnership and the remaking of welfare governance', in C. Glendinning, M. Powell and K. Rummery (eds) *Partnerships, New Labour and the Governance of Welfare*, Bristol: The Policy Press.

Clarke, J. and Ozga, J. (2011) 'Governing by inspection? Comparing school inspection in Scotland and England', a paper for the Social Policy Association Conference, July 2011, University of Lincoln.

Clarkson, P. and Challis, D. (2006) 'Performance management in social care: a comparison of efficiency measurement methods', *Social Policy and Society*, vol 5, no 4, pp 461–78.

Cohen,S. and Eimicke, W.B. (2003) *The Effective Public Manager*, Oxford: Wiley.

Cole, A., Jones, B. and Storer, A. (2003) 'Inside the National assembly for Wales: the welsh civil service under devolution', *Political Quarterly*, vol 74, no 2, pp 223–32.

Collins, F. and McCray, J. (2012) 'Partnership working in services for children: use of the common assessment framework', *Journal of Interprofessional Care*, vol 26, pp 134–40.

Commission on 2020 Public Services (2009) *A Brief History of Public Service Reform*, London: 2020 Public Services Trust.

Commission on Devolution in Wales (2014) *Empowerment and Responsibility: Legislative Powers to Strengthen Wales*, Cardiff: Commission on Devolution in Wales.

Commission on Scottish Devolution (2009) *Service Scotland Better: Scotland and the United Kingdom in the 21st Century*, Calman Report, Edinburgh: The Scottish Government.

Commissioner for Public Appointments (2014) *Annual Report 2014-15*, London: Commissioner for Public Appointments.

Communities and Local Government Committee (2016) *Devolution: The Next Five Years and Beyond*, HC369, London: The Stationery Office.

Conklin, A., Morris, Z. and Nolte, E. (2012) 'What is the evidence base for public involvement in health-care policy? Results of a systematic scoping review', *Health Expectations*, vol 18, pp 153–65.

Connolly, M. (2011) 'Constructing legitimacy in the new urban governance', *Urban Studies*, vol 48, no 5, pp 929–46.

Conservative Party (2010) *Invitation to Join the Government of Britain*, London: UK Conservative Party.

Copus, C. (2004) *Party Policies and Local Government*, Oxford: Oxford University Press.

Corbett, S. and Walker, A. (2012) 'The Big Society: back to the future', *The Political Quarterly*, vol 83, no 3, pp 487–93.

Cornes, M., Mathie, H., Whiteford, M., Manthrope, J. and Clarke, M. (2015) 'The Care Act, personalisation and the new eligibility regulations'. Available at: http://eprints.lse.ac.uk/61135/1/Clark_%20discussion_paper_about_the_future_of_care_author.pdf

Coston, J. (1998) 'A model and typology of government–NGO relationships', *Nonprofit and Voluntary Sector Quarterly*, vol 27, no 3, pp 358–82.

Coulter, A. (2002) The Autonomous Patient: Ending Paternalism in Medical Care, London: The Nuffield Trust.

Coulter, A. and Ellins, J. (2007) 'Effectiveness of strategies for informing, educating and involving patients', *British Medical Journal*, vol 335, no 24, pp 24–7.

Coulter, A., Locock, I., Ziebland, S. and Calabrese, J. (2014) 'Collecting data on patient experience is not enough: they must be used to improve care', *British Medical Journal*, vol 348, p 2225.

Cousins, C. (1988) 'The restructuring of welfare work: the introduction of general management and the contracting out of ancillary services in the NHS', *Work Employment and Society*, vol 2, pp 210–28.

Craig, G. and Manthorpe, J. (1999) *The Impact of Local Government Reorganisation on Social Services Work*, York: Joseph Rowntree Foundation.

Crawford, M.J., Rutter, D., Manley, C., Weaver, T., Blui, K., Fulop, N. and Tyrer, P. (2002) 'Systematic review of involving patients in the planning and development of health care', *British Medical Journal*, vol 325, p 1263.

Crouch, C. (2003) *Commercialisation or Citizenship*, London: Fabian Society.

Crouch, C. (2011) *The Strange Non-death of Neoliberalism*, Cambridge: Polity Press.

Cullingford, C. (2015) *An Inspector Calls: Ofsted and its Effect on School Standards*, London: Taylor and Francis.

Cunningham, I. and James, P. (2014) 'Public service outsourcing and its employment implications in an era of austerity: the case of British social care', *Competition and Change*, vol 18, no 1, pp 1–19.

Cutler, T. and Waine, B. (1997) *Managing the Welfare State*, Oxford: Oxford University Press.

Dalton, D. (2014) *Examining New Options and Opportunities for Providers of NHS Care: The Dalton Review*, London: DoH.

Dalton, R.J. (2004) *Democratic Challenges, Democratic Choices: The Erosion of Political Support in Advanced Industrial Democracies*, Oxford: Oxford University Press.

Daly, M. (2003) 'Governance and social policy', *Journal of Social Policy*, vol 22, no 1, pp 113–28.

Damm, C. (2012) 'The third sector delivering employment services: an evidence review', TSRC Working Paper 70.

Davies, M. (2003) 'Performance measurement in the UK public sector: understanding performance indicators', *Journal of Finance and Management in Public Services*, vol 3, no 7, pp 31–47.

Daycare Trust (2011) *The Role and Performance of Ofsted, Evidence to Education Select Committee*, London: The Daycare Trust.

DCLG (Department for Communities and Local Government) (2006) *Strong and Prosperous Communities*, London: DCLG.

DCLG (2008) *Communities in Control: Real People, Real Power*, London: DCLG.

DCLG (2011a) *Laying the Foundations: A Housing Strategy for England*, London: DCLG.

DCLG (2011b) *The Localism Act*, London: DCLG.

DCLG (2012) *Local Authority Housing Statistics 2011–12*, London: DCLG.

DCLG (2013a) *Annual Report and Accounts 2012–13*, HC 17, London: The Stationery Office.

DCLG (2013b) *You've Got the Power: A Quick and Simple Guide to Community Rights*, London: DCLG.

DCLG (2014) *Annual Report and Accounts*, London: DCLG.

DCLG (2015a) *Local Government Financial Statistics England. No. 25*, London: DCLG.

DCLG (2015b) *The New Burdens Community Governance Review Fund 2015–2016*, London: DCLG.

DCLG and HM Treasury (2015) *Bolder, Braver and Better: Why We Need Local Deals to Save Public Services: The Government's Response to the Service Transformation Challenge Panel Report*, London: DCLG.

De-Freitas, C. and Martin, G. (2015) 'Inclusive public participation in health: policy, practice and theoretical contributions to promote the involvement of marginalised groups in healthcare', *Social Science and Medicine*, vol 135, pp 31–9.

Defty, A. (2016) 'The Coalition, social policy and public opinion', in H. Bochel and M. Powell (eds) *The Coalition Government and Social Policy*, Bristol: The Policy Press.

Denton, M. and Flinders, M. (2006) 'Democracy, devolution and delegated governance in Scotland', *Regional and Federal Studies*, vol 16, no 1, pp 63–82.

Department for Culture, Media and Sport (DCMS) (2014) *Annual Report and Accounts*, London: DCMS.

Department for Education and Skills (2003) *Every Child Matters Green Paper*, London: Stationery Office.

Department for Education and Skills (2004) *Every Child Matters: Change for Children*, London: Stationery Office.

Department for Employment and Learning (2013) *Steps 2 Success (NI) Consultation*, Belfast: DEL NI.

Department of Justice (2016) 'Contracted out prisons'. Available at: https://www.justice.gov.uk/about/hmps/contracted-out

Department of the Environment (NI) (2013) *Community Planning Forum: Guidance to Councils – Community Planning Foundation Framework, Circular No LG 25/2013*, Belfast: Department of the Environment.

DETR (Department of the Environment, Transport and the Regions) (1998) *Modern Local Government: In Touch with the People*, London: DETR.

DETR (2000) *Quality and Choice: A Decent Home for All*, London: DETR.

DETR (2001) *Local Strategic Partnerships: Government Guidance*, London: DETR.

Devine, L. and Parker, S. (2015) *Rethinking Child Protection Strategy: Learning from Trends*. Working Paper. Bristol: Centre for Legal Research, University of the West of England.

DfE (Department for Education) (2011) *Munro Review of Child Protection: Final Report – a Child-Centred System*, London: Department for Education.

DfE (2014) *Consolidated Annual Report and Accounts 2012–13*, HC 49, London: The Stationery Office.

DfE (2015) *School and College Performance Tables*, London: Department for Education.

DfE (2016a) *Education Excellence Everywhere*, London: Department for Education.

DfE (2016b) *Schools that Work for Everyone*, London: Department for Education.

DHSS (Department of Health and Social Services) (1983) *Circular HS (83) 18*, London: HMSO.

DHSSPS (Department of Health, Social Services and Public Safety) (2011) *Transforming Your Care: A Review of Health and Social Care in Northern Ireland*, Belfast: Department of Health and Social Services and Public Safety.

DHSSPS (2015) *The Right Time, the Right Place* (Donaldson Report), Belfast: Department of Health and Social Services and Public Safety.

Dickinson, H. and Glasby, J. (2013) 'How effective is joint commissioning? A study of five English localities', *Journal of Integrated Care*, vol 21, no 4, pp 221–3.

Diffley, M. (2013) *Public Services Reform and Public Opinion*, Edinburgh: IPSOS MORI.

DoH (Department of Health) (1990) *NHS and Community Care Act*, London: DoH.

DoH (2006) *Our Health, Our Say*, London: DoH.

DoH (2007) *Putting People First*, London: DoH.

DoH (2010) *Equality and Excellence: Liberating the NHS*, London: DoH.

DoH (2011a) *Modernising the NHS: The Health and Social Care Bill*, London: DoH.

DoH (2011b) *Equity and Excellence: Liberating the NHS*, London: DoH.

DoH (2012a) *Public Health in Local Government*, London: DoH.

DoH (2012b) *Health and Social Care Act*, London: DoH.

DoH (2012c) *Transforming Care: A National Response to Winterbourne View Hospital*, London: Department of Health.

DoH (2013) *The Adult Social Care Outcomes Framework 2014/15*, London: Department of Health.

DoH (2014a) *The Care Act*, London: DoH.

DoH (2014b) 'Department of Health improvement plan'. Available at: www. gov.uk/government/publications/department-of-health-improvement-plan-april-2014

DoH (2015) *Culture Change in the NHS: Applying the Lessons of the Francis Inquiries*, CM9009, London: DoH.

DoH (2016) *Shared Delivery Plan 2015–2020*, London: DoH.

Doheny, S. (2015) *The Organisation of the NHS in the UK: Comparing Structures in the Four Countries*, Research Paper 15/020, Cardiff: National Assembly for Wales.

Dommett, K., Flinders, M., Skelcher, C. and Tonkiss, K. (2014) 'Did they "read before burning"? The Coalition and quangos', *Political Quarterly*, vol 85, no 2, pp 133–42.

Donnelly, C. (2011) 'Privatization and welfare: a comparative perspective', *Law and Ethics of Human Rights*, vol 5, no 2, pp 336–93.

Donnelly, C. and Osborne, R. (2005) 'Devolution, social policy and education: some observations for Northern Ireland', *Social Policy and Society*, vol 4, no 2, pp 147–56.

Dorey, P. (2014) *Policy Making in Britain*, London: Sage.

Dowling, B. and Glendinning, C. (2003) *The New Primary Care*, Maidenhead: Open University Press.

Dowling, H., Powell, M. and Glendinning, C. (2004) 'Conceptualising successful partnerships', *Health and Social Care in the Community*, vol 12, no 4, pp 309–17.

Downe, J. and Martin, S. (2006) 'Joined up policy in practice? The coherence and impacts of the local government modernisation agenda', *Local Government Studies*, vol 32, no 4, pp 465–88.

Doyle, J. (2013) 'Local enterprise partnerships to deliver progressive social outcomes', *Local Economy*, vol 28, no 7, pp 921–6.

Driver, S. and Martell, L. (2002) *Blair's Britain*, Oxford: Polity Press.

Duffy, J. (2006) *Participating and Learning – Citizen Involvement in Social Work Education in a Northern Ireland Context*, London: Social Care Institute for Excellence.

Duffy, S. (2010) 'The citizenship theory of social justice: exploring the meaning of personalisation for social workers', *Journal of Social Work Practice*, vol 24, no 3, pp 253–67.

Duffy, G. and Gallagher, T. (2015) 'Collaborative evolution: the context surrounding the formation and the effectiveness of a school partnership in a divided community in Northern Ireland', *Research Papers in Education*, vol 30, no 1, pp 1–24.

Dumbleton, S. and McPhail, M. (2012) 'The coming of age of Scottish social service?', in G. Mooney and G. Scott (eds) *Social Justice and Social Policy in Scotland*, Bristol: The Policy Press.

Dunleavy, P. (1986) 'Explaining the privatisation boom', *Public Administration*, vol 64, pp 13–34.

Dunleavy, P. (2010) *The Future of Joined-Up Public Services*, London: 2020 Public Services Trust and ESRC.

Dunleavy, P., Gilson, C., Bastow, S. and Tinkler, J. (2009) *The National Audit Office, the Public Accounts Committee and the Risk Landscape in UK Public Policy*, London: The Risk and Regulation Advisory Council.

Dunleavy, P. and White, A. (2010) *Making and Breaking Whitehall Departments*, London: Institute for Government.

Durose, C., Richardson, L., Dickinson, H. and Williams, I. (2013) 'Do's and don'ts for involving citizens in the design and delivery of health and social care', *Journal of Integrated Care*, vol 21, no 6, pp 326–35.

DWP (Department for Work and Pensions) (2010) *Concordat between the Department for Work and Pensions and the Scottish Government*, London: DWP.

DWP (2012) *Concordat between the Department for Work and Pensions and the Welsh Government*, London: DWP.

DWP (2013) *Annual Report and Accounts 2012–13*, HC 20, London: The Stationery Office.

DWP (2014) *Departmental Improvements Plan 2014*, London: Department for Work and Pensions.

Edmonds, T., Parry, K., Woodhouse, J. and Webb, D. (2010) *Public Services (Social Enterprise and Social Value) Bill*, Research Paper 10/77, London: House of Commons Library.

Education and Training Inspectorate (NI) (2014) *Summary Inspection Outcomes for Schools from the 2012–2014 Chief Inspector's Reporting Period*, Belfast: Education and Training Inspectorate.

Education Funding Agency (2014) *Annual Report and Financial Statement for 2012–13*, HC 920, London: The Stationery Office.

Edwards, M. (2009) *Civil Society*, Bristol: The Policy Press.

Efficiency Unit (1988) *Improving Management in Government: The Next Steps*, London: The Stationery Office.

Ellison, N. and Ellison, S. (2006) 'Creating opportunity for all? New Labour, new localism and opportunity society', *Social Policy and Society*, vol 5, no 3, pp 337–48.

Ellwood, S. (2014) 'Debate: autonomy, governance, accountability and a new audit regime', *Public Money and Management*, vol 34, no 2, pp 139–41.

Elston, T. (2013) 'Developments in UK executive agencies: re-examining the disaggregation–reaggregation thesis', *Public Policy and Administration*, vol 28, no 1, pp 66–89.

Elvidge, J. (2011) *Northern Exposure: Lessons from the First Twelve Years of Devolved Government in Scotland*, London: Institute for Government.

Equality and Human Rights Commission (2016) List of research reports. Available at: https://www.equalityhumanrights.com/en/our-research/list-all-our-research-reports

Escobar, O. (2015) *Re-Imagining Community Planning in Scotland: A Vision from the Third Sector*, Edinburgh: What Works Scotland.

Estyn (2015) *School to School Support and Collaboration*, Cardiff: Estyn.

Evans, A. and Forbes, T. (2009) 'Partnerships in health and social care: England and Scotland compared', *Public Policy and Administration*, vol 24, no 1, pp 67–83.

Farnsworth, K. and Holden, C. (2006) 'The business–social policy nexus: corporate power and corporate inputs into social policy', *Journal of Social Policy*, vol 35, no 3, pp 473–94.

Fenwick, J. (2014) 'The problem of sub-national government in England', *Public Money and Management*, vol 35, no 1, pp 7–14.

Fenwick, J. and Elcock, H. (2004) 'The new political management in local government: public engagement or public indifference?', *Local Government Studies*, vol 30, no 4, pp 519–37.

Ferguson, H. (2003) 'Welfare, social exclusion and reflexivity: the case of child and woman protection', *Journal of Social Policy*, vol 32, no 2, pp 199–216.

Ferguson, I. (2007) 'Increasing user control or privatising risk?', *British Journal of Social Work*, vol 37, no 3, pp 387–403.

Ferguson, I. and Lavalette, M. (2013) 'Crisis, austerity and the future(s) social work in the United Kingdom', *Critical and Radical Social Work*, vol 1, no 1, pp 95–110.

Ferry, L. and Eckersley, P. (2015) 'Budgeting and governing for deficit reduction in the UK public sector: act three "accountability and audit arrangements"', *Public Money and Management*, vol 35, no 3, pp 203–10.

Field, J.E. and Peck, E. (2004) 'Concordat or contract', *Public Management Review*, vol 6, no 2, pp 253–72.

Finn, D. (2012) 'Sub-contracting in public employment services: the design and delivery of outcome based and black box contracts', DG Employment, Social Affairs and Inclusion, European Commission.

Fitzgerald, A. and Lupton, R. (2015) 'Limits to resilience? The impact of local government spending cuts in London', *Local Government Studies*, vol 41, no 4, pp 582–600.

Fleming, S. (2015) 'New development: a game of responsibility? The regulation of health and social care professionals', *Public Money and Management*, vol 35, no 2, pp 169–71.

Flinders, M. (2006) 'Controlling modern government: variety, commonality and change', *Public Administration*, vol 84, no 1, pp 241–2.

Flinders, M. (2008) *Delegated Governance and the British State*, Oxford: Oxford University Press.

Flinders, M. (2011) 'Devolution, delegation and the Westminster model: a comparative analysis of developments within the UK, 1998–2004', *Commonwealth and Comparative Politics*, vol 44, no 1, pp 1–28.

References

Flinders, M. and Skelcher, C. (2011) 'Shrinking the quango state: five challenges in reforming quangos', *Public Money and Management*, vol 32, no 5, pp 327–334.

Flynn, N. (2012) *Public Sector Management*, London: Sage.

Foot, C., Gilburt, H., Dunn, P., Jabbal, J., Seale, B., Goodrich, J., Buck, D. and Taylor, J. (2014) *People in Control of their Own Health and Care: The State of Involvement*, London: The King's Fund.

Freeguard, G. Munro, R. and Andrew, E. (2015) *Whitehall Monitor: Deep Impact?*, London: Institute for Government.

Freud, D. (2007) *Reducing Dependency, Increasing Opportunity: Options for the Future of Welfare to Work*, London: Department for Work and Pensions.

Friedman, M. (2009) *Trying Hard is Not Good Enough*, North Charlston: Booksurge Publishing.

Fuertes, V., Jantz, B., Klenk, T. and McQuaid, R. (2014) 'Between cooperation and competition: the organisation of employment service delivery in the UK and Germany', *International Journal of Social Welfare*, vol 23, pp 71–S86.

G4S (2016) 'G4S to sell its UK children's services business', 26 February. Available at: http://www.g4s.com/en/Media%20Centre/News/2016/02/26/G4S%20Sale%20of%20UK%20Childrens%20Services%20business/

Gallagher, J., Gibb, K. and Mills, C. (2007) *Rethinking Central–Local Government Relations in Scotland: Back to the Future?*, Edinburgh: The David Hume Institute.

Gash, T. and Rutter, J. (2011) 'The quango conundrum', *The Political Quarterly*, vol 82, no 1, pp 95–101.

Gash, T., Magee, I., Rutter, J. and Smith, N. (2010) *Read Before Burning: Arm's Length Government for a New Administration*, London: Institute for Government.

Gash, T., Panchamia, N., Sims, S. and Hotson, C. (2012) *Making Public Services Work*, London: Institute for Government.

Gash, T., Randall, J. and Sims, S. (2014) *Achieving Political Decentralisation*, London: Institute for Government.

Gay, O. (2005) *Public Service Agreements*, Briefing Paper, London: House of Commons Library.

Gillen, B. (2012) *Programme for Government Northern Ireland 2008–11 – Departmental Performance Research and Information Service*, Briefing Paper, Belfast: Northern Ireland Assembly.

Gingrich, J.R. (2011) *Making Markets in the Welfare State: The Politics of Varying Market Reforms*, Cambridge: Cambridge University Press.

Glasby, J. (2003) 'Bringing down the "Berlin Wall": the health and social care divide', *British Journal of Social Work*, vol 33, pp 969–75.

Glasby, J. (2014a) 'The end of local government as we know it – what next for adult social care?', in Z. Irving, M. Fenger and J. Hudson (eds) *Analysis and Debate in Social Policy 2015, Social Policy Review 27*, Bristol: The Policy Press.

Glasby, J. (2014b) 'The controversies of choice and control: why some people might be hostile to English social care reforms', *British Journal of Social Work*, vol 44, no 2, pp 252–66.

Glasby, J. and Dickinson, H. (eds) (2009) International Perspectives on Health and Social Care: Partnership Working in Action, Oxford: Blackwell-Wiley.

Glendinning, C., Powell, M. and Rummery, K. (2002) Partnerships, New Labour and the Governance of Welfare, Bristol: The Policy Press.

Glendinning, C., Challis, D., Fernandez, J., Jacobs, S., Jones, K., Knapp, M., Manthorpe, J., Moran, N., Netten, A., Stevens, M. and Wilberforce, M. (2008) Evaluation of the Individual Budgets Pilot Programme: Final Report, York: IBSEN.

Goodwin, M. (2015) 'Schools policy, governance and politics under New Labour', Political Studies Review, vol 13, no 4, pp 534–45.

Gove, M. (2011) 'Michael Gove's speech to the Policy Exchange on free schools'. Available at: https://www.gov.uk/government/speeches/michael-goves-speech-to-the-policy-exchange-on-free-schools

Gray, A.M. and Birrell, D. (2012) 'The structures of the NHS in Northern Ireland: divergence, policy copying and policy deficiency', Public Policy and Administration, vol 28, no 3, pp 274–89.

Greany, T. and Allen, T. (2014) School Improvement Network and System Leadership in Coventry, London: Institute of Education.

Greener, I. (2008) 'Markets in the public sector: when they work, and what do we do when they don't?', Policy and Politics, vol 36, no 1, pp 93–108.

Greener, I. (2015) 'Wolves and big yellow taxis: how would we know if the NHS is at death's door? Comment on "Who killed the English National Health Service?"', International Journal Health Policy Management, vol 4, no 10, pp 687–9.

Greer, I., Greenwood, I. and Stuart, M. (2011) 'Beyond national "varieties": public-service contracting in comparative perspective', in I. Cunningham and P. James (eds) Voluntary Organisations and Public Service Delivery, Abingdon: Routledge, pp 153–67.

Grimshaw, D., Vincent, S. and Willmott, H. (2002) 'Going privately: partnership and outsourcing in UK public services', Public Administration, vol 80, no 3, pp 475–502.

Grimstone, G. (2016) Better Public Appointments: Review of the Public Appointments Process, London: The Cabinet Office.

Grimwood, G. (2014) Prisons: The Role of the Private Sector, London: House of Commons Library.

Gunter, H.M. (2012) 'New Labour and the governance of educational reform in England'. Paper presented at the conference proceedings of the American Educational Research Association, San Francisco, 1 January.

Gustafsson, U. and Driver, S. (2005) 'Parents, power and public participation: Sure Start, an experiment in New Labour governance', Social Policy and Administration, vol 39, no 5, pp 528–43.

Haase, T. and McKeown, K. (2003) Developing Disadvantaged Areas through Area-Based Initiatives: Reflections on Over a Decade of Local Development Strategies, Dublin: Area Development Management Limited.

Hadfield, M. and Jopling, M. (2006) *The Potential of Collaboratives to Support Schools in Complex and Challenging Circumstances*, Wolverhampton: University of Wolverhampton.

Ham, C., Heenan, D., Longley, M. and Steel, D. (2013) *Integrated Care in Northern Ireland, Scotland and Wales*, London: Kings Fund.

Hart, E. (2009) 'Health in Wales: written statement: NHS reforms'. Available at: www.wales.gov.uk/news/13330

Harvey, B. (2003) *Review of the Peace II Programme*, York: Joseph Rowntree Trust.

Hastings, A., Bailey, N., Besemer, K., Bramley, G., Gannon, G. and Watkins, D. (2013) *Coping with the Cuts? Local Government and Poorer Communities*, York: Joseph Rowntree Foundation.

Hastings, A., Bailey, N., Bramley, G., Gannon, M. and Watkins, D. (2015a) *The Cost of the Cuts? The Impact on Local Government and Poorer Communities*, York: Joseph Rowntree Foundation.

Hastings, A., Bailey, N., Gannon, M., Besemer, K. and Bramley, G. (2015b) 'Coping with the cuts? The management of the worst financial settlement in living memory', *Local Government Studies*, vol 41, no 4, pp 601–21.

Hay, C. and Wincott, D. (2012) *The Political Economy of European Welfare Capitalism*, Basingstoke: Palgrave Macmillan.

Hayes, B., Moskalenko, E. and Bailey, D. (2015) *Wider Measures of Public Sector Debt*, London: Office for National Statistics.

Health and Social Care Board, NI (2015) *A Managed Change Briefing Paper: An Agenda for Creating a Sustainable Basis for Domiciliary Care in Northern Ireland*, Belfast: HSCB.

Health and Social Care Information Centre (2015) *Personal Social Services: Expenditure and Unit Costs, England – 2013–14*, London: Health and Social Care Information Centre.

Heath, S. (2014) *Local Authorities of Public Health Responsibilities (England)*, SN 06844, London: House of Commons Library.

Heenan, D. and Birrell, W.D. (2009) 'Organisational integration in health and social care: some reflections on the Northern Ireland experience', *Journal of Integrated Care*, vol 17, no 5, pp 3–5.

Heins, E. and Bennett, H. (2016) 'Best of both worlds'? A comparison of third sector providers in health care and welfare-to-work markets in Britain', *Social Policy and Administration*, vol 50, no 1, pp 39–58.

Higham, R. (2014) 'Free schools in the Big Society: the motivations, aims and demography of free school proposers', *Journal of Education Policy*, vol 29, no 1, pp 122–39.

Hills, J. (1998) *Thatcherism, New Labour and the Welfare State*, London: LSE Centre for Analysis of Social Exclusion.

Hill, M. (2000) *Local Authority Social Services*, Oxford: Blackwell.

Hill, M. (2005) *The Public Policy Process*, Harlow: Pearson Longman.

Hill, M. (2013) *The Public Policy Process*, Harlow: Pearson.

Hill, M. and Irving, Z. (2009) *Understanding Social Policy*, Oxford: Wiley Blackwell.

HM Government (2007) *Putting People First: A Shared Vision and Commitment to the Transformation of Adult Social Care*, London: HM Government.

HM Government (2009) *Working Together: Public Services on Your Side*, London: Cabinet Office.

HM Government (2010) *Decentralisation and the Localism Bill: An Essential Guide*, London: Department for Communities & Local Government.

HM Government (2011) *Open Public Services White Paper*, CM 8145, London: The Stationery Office.

HM Government (2012) *The Civil Service Reform Plan*, London: Cabinet Office.

HM Government (2015a) *Powers for a Purpose: Towards a Lasting Devolution Settlement for Wales*, CM9020, London: Cabinet Office.

HM Government (2015b) *Scotland in the United Kingdom: An Enduring Settlement*, Cm 8990, London: Her Majesty's Stationery Office.

HM Government (2015c) *Working Together to Safeguard Children: A Guide to Inter-Agency Working to Safeguard Children and Promote the Welfare of Children*, London: Department of Education.

HM Government and The Scottish Government (2016) *The Agreement Between the Scottish Government and the UK Government on the Scottish Government's Fiscal Framework*, London: HM Government.

HM Treasury (1998) *Partnerships for Prosperity: The Private Finance Initiative*, London: HM Treasury.

HM Treasury (2009) *Putting the Frontline First: Smarter Government*, CM 7753, London: The Stationery Office.

HM Treasury (2010) *Funding the Scottish Parliament, the National Assembly for Wales and the Northern Ireland Assembly: Statement of Funding Policy*, London: HM Treasury.

HM Treasury (2011) *Rebalancing the Northern Ireland Economy*, London: HM Treasury.

HM Treasury (2012) *A New Approach to Public Private Partnerships*, London: HM Treasury.

HM Treasury (2014) *Public Expenditure Statistical Analyses*, Cm 8902, London: The Stationery Office.

HM Treasury (2015a) *Efficiency Drive by Government on Public Private Partnerships Net £2.1bn*, London: HM Treasury.

HM Treasury (2015b) *Government Responses on the Thirtieth, the Thirty Fifth, the Thirty Seventh and the Forty First to the Fifty Third Reports from the Committee of Public Accounts: 2014–15*, CM9091, London: HM Treasury.

HM Treasury (2016) *Public Expenditure Statistical Analysis, 2016*, London: HM Treasury.

Hodge, G. and Greve, C. (2010) 'Public–private partnerships: governance scheme or language game?', *The Australian Journal of Public Administration*, vol 69, no 1, pp 8–22.

Hodkinson, S. (2012) 'The return of the housing question', *Ephemera: Theory and Politics in Organization*, vol 12, no 4, pp 423–44.

References

Holtham, G. (2010) *Final Report: Fairness and Accountability: A New Funding Settlement for Wales*, Cardiff: Independent Commission on Funding and Finance for Wales.

Homes and Communities Agency (2014) *Annual Report 2013–14*, London: Homes and Communities Agency.

Hood, C. (2007) 'Public service management by numbers: why does it vary? Where has it come from? What are the gaps and the puzzles?', *Public Money and Management*, vol 27, no 2, pp 95–102.

Hood, C. (2011) *The Blame Game: Spin, Bureaucracy, and Self-Preservation in Government*, New Jersey, NJ: Princeton University Press.

House of Commons Committee of Public Accounts (2014) *Forty-Seventh Report Contracting Out Public Services to the Private Sector*, London: House of Commons

House of Commons Committee of Public Accounts (2015) *An update on Hinchingbrooke Health Care NHS Trust*, Forty-Sixth Report of Session 2014–15, HC971, London: House of Commons.

House of Commons Communities and Local Government Committee (2009) *The Balance of Power: Central and Local Government*, HC 33-1, London: The Stationery Office.

House of Commons Communities and Local Government Committee (2012) *Taking Forward Community Budgets*, Ninth Report of Session, 2011/12, London: House of Commons.

House of Commons Communities and Local Government Committee (2013) *Community Budgets*, Third Report of Session 2013/14, HC163, London: House of Commons.

House of Commons Education and Skills Committee (2005) *Every Child Matters*, Ninth Report of Session 2004–05, HC40-1, London: House of Commons.

House of Commons Health Committee (2009) *Third Report, Health Inequalities*, London: House of Commons.

House of Commons Treasury Committee (2011) *Private Finance Initiative*, HC 1146, London: House of Commons.

House of Commons Work and Pensions Committee (2014a) *The Role of Jobcentre Plus in the Reformed Welfare System*, HC 479, London: The Stationery Office.

House of Commons Work and Pensions Committee (2014b) *Employment and Support Allowance and Work Capability Assessments*, London: House of Commons .

House of Commons Work and Pensions Committee (2016) *Contracting Out Health and Disability Assessments*, London: House of Commons.

House of Lords (2009) *The Barnett Formula*, HL Paper 139, London: The Stationery Office.

Humphries, R. and Wenzel, L. (2015) *Options for Integrated Commissioning*, London: The Kings Fund.

Humphries, R., Hall, P., Charles, A., Thorlby, R. and Holder, H. (2016) *Social Care for Older People: Home Truths*, London: The Kings Fund and the Nuffield Trust.

Hunter, D. (2013) 'Point–counterpoint. A response to Rudolf Klein: a battle may have been won but perhaps not the war', *Journal of Health Politics, Policy and Law*, vol 38, no 4, pp 871–7.

Hutchinson, F. and Ward, C. (2010) 'Corporate government and social housing – adopting a market model?', *Journal of Finance and Management in Public Services*, vol 10, no 2, pp 14–25.

Hutchings, M., Greenwood, C., Hollingworth, S., Mansaray, A., Rose, A. and Glass, K. (2012) *Evaluation of the City Challenge Programme* (Research Report DFE-RR215). London: Department for Education.

Independent Commission on Social Services in Wales (2010) *From Vision to Action Report*, Cardiff: Independent Commission on Social Services in Wales.

Independent Living Strategy Group (2015) *Promoting People's Right to Choice and Control under the Care Act 2014: How Are Local Authorities Performing?*, London: In Control.

Institute for Government (2013) *The Strange Case of Non-ministerial Departments*, London: Institute for Government.

Involve (2005) *People and Participation: How to Put Citizens at the Heart of Decision-Making*, London: Involve.

Jacobs, R. and Goddard, M. (2007) 'How do performance indicators add up? An examination of composite indicators in public services', *Public Money and Management*, vol 27, no 2, pp 103–10.

Jacobs, R., Goddard, M. and Smith, P. (2007) *Composite Performance Measures in the Public Sector*, York: Centre for Health Economics.

James, O. (2001) 'Evaluating executive agencies in UK government', *Public Policy and Administration*, vol 16, no 3, pp 24–52.

James, O. (2003) *The Executive Agency Revolution in Whitehall*, Basingstoke: Palgrave Macmillan.

James, O., Moseley, A., Petrovsky, N. and Boyne, G. (2011) 'Agencification in the UK', in K. Verhoest, S. van Thiel, G. Bouckaert and P. Laegreid (eds) *Government Agencies in Europe and Beyond: Practices and Lessons from 30 Countries*, Basingstoke: Palgrave Macmillan.

James, O., Jilke, S., Peterson, C. and Van de Walle, S. (2015) 'Citizens' blame of politicians for public service failure: experimental evidence about blame reduction through delegation and contracting', *Public Administration Review*, vol 76, no 1, pp 83–93.

Jay, A. (2014) *Independent Inquiry into Child Sexual Exploitation in Rotherham 1997–2013*, Rotherham: Rotherham Metropolitan Borough Council.

Jessop, B. (1999) 'The changing governance of welfare: recent trends in its primary functions, scale and modes of coordination', *Social Policy and Administration*, vol 33, no 4, pp 348–59.

Johnston, K. (2015) 'Public governance: the government of non-state actors in "partnerships"', *Public Money and Management*, vol 55, no 1, pp 15–22.

Jones, C. and Murie, A. (2006) *The Right to Buy: Analysis and Evaluation of a Housing Policy*, Oxford: Blackwell Publishing.

Jones, G. and Stewart, J. (2012) 'Local government: the past, the present and the future', *Public Policy and Administration*, vol 27, no 4, pp 346–67.

Jones, J. and Barry, M. (2011) 'Developing a scale to measure synergy in health promotion partnerships', *Global Health Promotion*, vol 18, no 2, pp 36–44.

Jones, M. and Gray, A. (2001) 'Social capital or local workfarism? Reflections on employment zones', *Local Economy*, vol 16, no 1, pp 2–10.

Jordan, B. and Drakeford, M. (2012) *Social Work and Social Policy under Austerity*, Basingstone: Palgrave Macmillan.

Joshi, A. and Moore, M. (2004) 'Institutionalised co-production: unorthodox public service delivery in challenging environments', *The Journal of Development Studies*, vol 40, no 4, p 31.

Kaehne, A. (2014) 'One NHS or many? The National Health Service under devolution', in *Political Insights*, London: Political Studies Association.

Kara, H. (2014) *Third Sector Partnerships and Capability Building: What the Evidence Tells Us*, Third Sector Research Paper, Working Paper 126, Birmingham: University of Birmingham Third Sector Research Centre.

Keating, M. (2005) *The Government of Scotland*, Edinburgh: Edinburgh University Press.

Kennedy, S. (2015) *Further Devolution of Powers to Scotland: Devolved Benefits and Additional Discretionary Payments*, SN07107, London: House of Commons Library.

Keogh, B. (2013) *Review into the Quality of Care and Treatment Provided by 14 Hospital Trusts in England: Overview Report*, London: NHS England.

Kingsnorth, R. (2013) 'Partnerships for health & wellbeing: transferring public health responsibilities to local authorities', *Journal of Integrated Care*, vol 21, no 2, pp 64–76.

Kirkham, R., Thompson, B. and Buck, T. (2009) 'Putting the ombudsman into constitutional context', *Parliamentary Affairs*, vol 62, no 4, pp 600–17.

Klein, R. (2015) 'Rhetoric and reality in the English National Health Service: comment on "Who killed the English National Health Service?"', *International Journal of Health Policy Management*, vol 4, no 9, pp 621–3.

Klijn, E.H. and Skelcher, C. (2007) 'Democracy and governance networks: compatible or not?', *Public Administration*, vol 85, no 3, pp 587–608.

Knox, C. (2010) *Devolution and the Governance of Northern Ireland*, Manchester: Manchester University Press.

Laffin, M. (2008) 'Local government modernisation in England: a critical review of the LGMA evaluation studies', *Local Government Studies*, vol 34, no 1, pp 109–25.

Laming Inquiry (2003) *The Victoria Climbié Inquiry*, London: The Stationery Office.

Larsen, J., Tew, J., Hamilton, S., Manthorpe, J., Pinfold, V., Szymczynska, P. and Clewett, N. (2015) 'Outcomes from personal budgets in mental health: service users' experiences in three English local authorities', *Journal of Mental Health*, vol 24, no 4, pp 219–24.

Law, J. (2013) *Do Outcomes Based Approaches to Service Delivery Work?*, University of South Wales: Centre for Public Policy.

Leach, S. (2010) 'The Labour government's local government agenda 1997–2009: the impact on member–officer relationships', *Local Government Studies*, vol 36, no 3, pp 323–39.

Leadbeater, C. (2004) *Personalisation through Participation: A New Script for Public Services*, London: DEMOS.

Leadbetter, C. and Mulgan, G. (1994) 'Lean democracy and the leadership vacuum', *Demos Quarterly*, vol 3, pp 45–82.

Lee, S. and Woodward, R. (2002) 'Implementing the Third Way: the delivery of services under the Blair Government', *Public Money and Management*, vol 22, no 4, pp 50-51

Le Grand, J. (1991) 'Quasi-markets and social policy', *The Economic Journal*, vol 101, no 408, pp 1256–67.

Le Grand, J. and Robinson, R. (eds) (1984) *Privatisation and the Welfare State*, London: Allen and Unwin.

Levitas, R. (2012) 'The just's umbrella: austerity and the Big Society in Coalition policy and beyond', *Critical Social Policy*, vol 32, no 3, pp 320–42.

Lindsay, C., Osborne, S. and Bond, S. (2014) 'The "new public governance" and employability services in an era of crisis: challenges for third sector organisations in Scotland', *Public Administration*, vol 92, no 1, pp 192–207.

Lindsay, G., Muijs, D., Harris, A., Chapman, C., Arweck, E. and Goodall, J. (2007) *School Federations Pilot Study: 2003–2007*, Nottingham: Department for Children, Schools and Families (DCSF).

Lister, J. (2008) *The NHS After 60. For Patients or Profits?*, London: Middlesex University Press.

Local Government Association (2013a) *Rewiring Public Services – Rejuvenating Democracy*, London: Local Government Association.

Local Government Association (2013c) *Lessons from Outsourcing Adult Social Care: The Workforce Issues*, London: Improvement and Development Agency.

Local Government Association (2014a) *Under Pressure – How Councils are Planning for Future Cuts*, London: Local Government Association.

Local Government Association (2014b) *Making an Impact through Good Governance*, London: Local Government Association.

Local Government Association (2014c) *Adult Social Care Efficiency Report*, London: Local Government Association.

Local Government Association (2015a) *The LGA's Budget 2015 Submission*, London: Local Government Association.

Local Government Association (2015b) *Making Sure Every Child has a Place at a Good Local School*, London: Local Government Association.

Local Government Association (2015c) *Children's Public Health Transfer*, London: Local Government Association.

Local Government Association (2015d) *Local Solutions, Healthy Lives: Council's Role in Drug and Alcohol Services*, London: Local Government Association.

Local Government Association (2015e) *Spending Smarter: A Shared Commitment*, London: Local Government Association.

Local Government Association (2015f) *Council Tax Support: The Story Continues*, London: Local Government Association.

Local Government Association and ADASS (Association of Directors of Adult Social Services) (2014) *Adult Social Care Funding*, London: Local Government Association.

Local Government Association and Solace (2013) *The Council Role in School Improvement*, London: Local Government Association.

Local Government Information Unit (2015) *Local Government Facts and Figures*, London: Local Government Information Unit.

Local Government Information Unit (2016) *Local Government Finance Survey*, London: Local Government Information Unit.

Local Government Ombudsman (2016) *Annual Review of Local Government Complaints*, London: Local Government Ombudsman.

Lodge, G., Henderson, G. and Davies, B. (2015) *Poverty and Devolution*, London: Institute for Public Policy Research.

Long, R. (2015) *Special Educational Needs: Support in England*, Briefing Paper SN07020, London: House of Commons Library.

Long, R. and Bolton, P. (2016) *Every School an Academy: The White Paper Proposals*, House of Commons Library Briefing Paper, no 07549, London: House of Commons.

Longley, M., Riley, N., Davies, P. and Hernández-Quevedo, C. (2012) 'United Kingdom, (Wales) health system review', *Health System in Transition*, vol 14, no 11, pp 1–84.

Lowndes, V. and McCaughie, V. (2013) 'Weathering the perfect storm? Austerity and institutional resilience in local government', *Policy and Politics*, vol 41, no 4, pp 533–49.

Lowndes, V. and Pratchett, L. (2012) 'Local governance under the Coalition government: austerity, localism and the "Big Society"', *Local Government Studies*, vol 38, no 1, pp 21–40.

Lund, B. (2008) 'Major, Blair and the Third Way in social policy', *Social Policy and Administration*, vol 42, no 1, pp 43–58.

Lynch, P. (2001) *Scottish Government and Politics*, Edinburgh: Edinburgh University Press.

Lyons, M. (2007) *Lyons Inquiry into Local Government*, London: The Stationery Office.

Mackle, P. (2015) 'Homelessness prevention and the Welsh legal duty: lessons for international policies', *Housing Studies*, vol 30, no 1, pp 40–59.

Macleavy, J. and Gay, O. (2005) *The Quango Debate*, Research Paper 05/30, London: House of Commons Library.

Maer, C. (2011) *Public Bodies Bill (HL)*, Research Paper 11/50, London: House of Commons Library.

Mahendran, K. and Cook, D. (2007) *Participation and Engagement in Politics and Policymaking. Building a Bridge between Europe and Its Citizens. Evidence Review Paper One*, Edinburgh: Scottish Executive.

Mann, N. (2015) 'Care, Quality Commission's Unfair Treatment of Addenbrooke's Hospital', *British Medical Journal*, vol 351, no 10, p h5711.

Manville, G., Greatbanks, R., Wainwright, T. and Broad, M. (2016) 'Visual performance management in housing associations: a crisis of legitimation or the shape of things to come?', *Public Money and Management*, vol 36, no 2, pp 105–12.

Martin, S., Downe, J., Entwistle, T. and Guarneros- Meza, V. (2013) *Learning to Improve: An Independent Assessment of the Welsh Government's Policies for Local Government 2007–2011*, Cardiff: Welsh Assembly Government.

Matthews, P. (2012) 'From area-based initiatives to strategic partnerships: have we lost the meaning of regeneration?', *Government and Policy*, vol 30, pp 147–61.

McAnulla, S. (2006) *British Politics: A Critical Introduction*, London: Continuum.

McLean, I., Gallagher, J. and Lodge, G. (2013) *Scotland's Choices: The Referendum and What Happens Afterwards*, Edinburgh: Edinburgh University Press.

McConway, K. (2006) 'Performance indicators, targets and league tables'. Available at: www.open.edu/openlearn/science-maths-technology

McCormick, J. (2013) *Welfare in Working Order: Points and Principles for the Scottish Debate*, Edinburgh: Scottish Council for Voluntary Organisations.

McCormick, J. and Harrop, A. (2010) *Devolution's Impact on Low-Income People and Places*, York: Joseph Rowntree Foundation.

McCrae, J., Harris, J. and Andrews, E. (2015) *All in it Together. Cross-departmental responsibilities for improving Whitehall*, London: Institute for Government.

McGarvey, N. and Cairney, P. (2008) *Scottish Politics: An Introduction*, Basingstoke: Palgrave MacMillan.

McKee, K. and Phillips, D. (2012) 'Social housing and homelessness policies: reconciling social justice and social mix', in G. Mooney and G. Scott (eds) *Social Justice and Social Policy in Scotland* (2nd edn), Bristol: The Policy Press, pp 227–42.

McKee, M., Edwards, N. and Atun, R. (2006) 'Public–private partnerships for hospitals', *Bulletin of the World Health Organisation*, vol 84, no 11, pp 890–6.

McKenna, H. and Dunn, P (2015) *Devolution: What it Means for Social Care in England*, London: The Kings Fund

McPhail, M. (2006) 'Children and young people social work and Scotland', in G. Mooney, T. Sweeney and A. Law (eds) *Social Care, Health and Welfare in Contemporary Scotland*, Paisley: Kynoch and Blaney.

McQuaid, R. (2010) 'Theory of organisational partnerships: partnership advantages, disadvantages and success factors', in S. Osborne (ed) *The New Public Governance*, London: Routledge.

Mills, H., Silvestri, A. and Grimshaw, R. (2010) *Prison and Probation Expenditure, 1999–2009*, London: Centre for Crime and Justice Studies.

Ministry of Justice (2013) *Transforming Rehabilitation: A Revolution in the Way We Manage Offenders. Consultation Paper CP1/2013*, CM8517, London: Ministry of Justice.

Minogue, M., Polidano, C. and Hume, D. (1998) *Beyond the New Public Management*, Cheltenham: Edward Elgar.

Mitchell, J. (2009) *Devolution in the UK*, Manchester: Manchester University Press.

Mockford, C., Staniszewska, S., Griffiths, F. and Herron-Merx, S. (2012) 'The impact of patient and public involvement on UK NHS health care: a systematic review', *International Journal for Quality in Health Care*, vol 24, no 1, pp 28–38.

Monitor (2014) *Annual Report and Accounts 2013–14*, HC 340, London: Monitor.

Mooney, G., Scott, G. and Williams, C. (2006) 'Rethinking social policy through devolution', *Critical Social Policy*, vol 26, no 3, pp 483–497

Mullins, D. and Murie, A. (2006) *Housing Policy in the United Kingdom*, Basingstoke: Palgrave Macmillan.

Munro, E. (2011) *The Munro Review of Child Protection: Final Report*, London: Department for Education.

Murray, J. (2014) *The Role of Government in a Modern State*, London: Centre for Labour and Social Studies.

Muscat, R. (2010) *Area Based Initiatives – Do They Deliver?*, London: Centre for Local Economic Strategies.

National Assembly for Wales (2013) *Further Education Structures in Wales* (Research Paper), Cardiff: National Assembly for Wales

National Audit Office (2003) *The Operational Performance of PFI Prisons, HC700, 2002-2003*, London: NAO.

National Audit Office (2009) *Private Finance Projects*, London: NAO.

National Audit Office (2011) *The Care Quality Commission: Regulating the Quality and Safety of Health and Adult Social Care*, London: The Stationery Office.

National Audit Office (2012) *Delivering Public Services through Markets: Principles for Achieving Value for Money*, London: National Audit Office.

National Audit Office (2013a) *The Performance of the Department for Community and Local Government 2012–13*, London: National Audit Office.

National Audit Office (2013b) *Review of the VFM Assessment Process for PFI*, London: National Audit Office.

National Audit Office (2014a) *Progress on Public Bodies Reform*, HC 1048, London: National Audit Office.

National Audit Office (2014b) *The Performance of the Department of Health 2012–13*, London: National Audit Office.

National Audit Office (2014c) *The Performance of the Department for Business, Innovation and Skills 2012–13*, London: National Audit Office.

National Audit Office (2014d) *The Impact of Funding Reductions on Local Authorities*, London: National Audit Office.

National Audit Office (2014e) *Adult Social Care in England: Overview*, HC 1102, London: National Audit Office.

National Audit Office (2014f) *Transforming Government's Contract Management*, HC269, London: National Audit Office.

National Audit Office (2015a) Local Government New Burdens, HC 83, London: National Audit Office.

National Audit Office (2015b) Good Practice Guides, London: National Audit Office.

National Audit Office (2016a) *Transforming Rehabilitation*, HC 951, London: National Audit Office.

National Audit Office (2016b) *History of the NAO*, London: National Audit Office.

National Coalition for Independent Action (2012) *Localism: Threat or Opportunity? Perspectives on the Localism Act for Union and Community Organisers and Activists*, London: TUC.

National Evaluation of Sure Start (2008) *The Impact of Sure Start Local Programmes on Three Year Olds and Their Families*, London: University of London Institute for the Study of Children, Families and Social Issues.

National Federation of ALMOS (2015) 'Annual review 2014–15'. Available at: www.almos.org.uk

National Health Executive (2014) 'Paying for Performance in the NHS: the latest evidence', London: National Health Executive. Available at http://www.nationalhealthexecutive.com/Comment/paying-for-performance-in-the-nhs-what-can-we-learn-from-the-latest-evidence

National Outsourcing Association (2016) *The Outsourcing Yearbook*, London: The National Outsourcing Association.

Naylor, C., Curry, N., Holder, H., Ross, S., Marshall, L. and Tait, E. (2013) *Clinical Commissioning Groups*, London: The King's Fund/Nuffield Trust.

Needham, C. (2010) 'Debate: personalized public services – a new state/citizen contract?', *Public Money Management*, vol 30, no 3, pp 136–8.

Needham, C. (2011) 'Personalisation: from story-line to practice', *Social Policy and Administration*, vol 45, no 1, pp 54–68.

Needham, C. (2012) *Co-Production: An Emerging Evidence Base for Adult Social Care Transformation*, Research Bulletin 31, London: Social Care Institute for Excellence.

New Economics Foundation (2008) *Co-Production: A Manifesto for Growing the Core Economy*, London: NEF.

New Economics Foundation (2015) *Outsourcing Public Services*, London: TUC.

New Local Government Network (2016) *Get Well Soon: Reimaging Place Based Health*, London: NLGN.

Newman, J. (2000) 'Beyond the new public management? Modernizing public services', in J. Clarke, S. Gewirtz and E. McLaughlin (eds) *New Managerialism, New Welfare*, London: Sage, pp 45–61.

Newman, J. (2001) *Modernising Governance: New Labour, Policy and Society*, London: Sage.

Newman, J. (2006) 'Modernisation and the dynamics of welfare governance', *Journal of Social Policy Research*, vol 52, no 2, pp 165–79.

Newman, J. (2013) 'Performing new worlds? Policy, politics and creative labour in hard times', *Policy and Politics*, vol 41, no 4, pp 515–32.

Newman, J. and Clarke, J. (2009) *Publics, Politics and Power: Remaking the Public in Public Services*, London: Sage.

Newman, J., Barnes, M., Sullivan, H. and Knops, A. (2004) 'Public participation and collaborative governance', *Journal of Social Policy*, vol 33, no 2, pp 203–23.

Newton, B., Meager, N., Bertram, C., Corden, A., George, A., Lalani, M. and Weston, K. (2012) *Work Programme Evaluation: Findings from the First Phase of Qualitative Research on Programme Delivery* (No 821), London: Department for Work and Pensions.

NHS Clinical Commissioners (2014) *Commissioning Primary Care: Transforming Healthcare in the Community*, London: NHS Clinical Commissioners.

NHS Commissioning Board (2012) *Clinical Commissioning Group Governing Body Members: Role Outlines, Attributes and Skills*, London: NHS England.

NHS Development Authority (2014) *Annual Report and Accounts*, London: NHS Development Authority.

NHS England (2013) *The NHS Belong to the People: A Call to Action*, London: NHS England.

NHS England (2014) *The NHS Five Year Forward View*, London: NHS England.

NHS England (2015) *Annual Reports and Accounts 2014–15*, HC109, London: NHS England.

NHS England (2016a) *NHS England Review of Uniting Care Contract: The Key Facts and Root Causes Behind the Termination of the Uniting Care Partnership Contract, NHS Publications Gateway Ref 05072*, London: NHS England.

NHS England (2016b) *Putting Patients First, Business Plan 2014/15–2016/17*, London: NHS England.

NHS Improving Quality (2013) *Our Strategic Intent*, London: NHS Improving Quality.

NHS Wales (2015) *Our Health, Our Health Services*, Cardiff: Welsh Assembly Government.

NIHE (Northern Ireland Housing Executive) (2014) *Draft Community Involvement Strategy 2014–2017*, Belfast: NIHE.

NIHE (2015) *Draft Tenant Participation Strategy for Northern Ireland*, Belfast: NIHE.

Northern Ireland Executive (2015) *A Fresh Start. The Stormont Agreement and Implementation Plan*, Belfast: Northern Ireland Executive.

Northern Ireland Office (2014) *The Stormont House Agreement*, Belfast: Northern Ireland Office.

OECD (Organisation for Economic Co-operation and Development) (2014) *Improving Schools in Wales: An OECD Perspective*, Paris: OECD.

OECD (2016) *Northern Ireland (UK): Implementing Joined Up Governance for a Common Purpose*, Paris: OECD.

Office of the Deputy Prime Minister (2005) *Evaluation of Local Strategic Partnerships: Interim Report*, London: Office of the Deputy Prime Minister.

Office for National Statistics (2014) *Statistical Bulletin: Civil Service Statistics*, London: Office for National Statistics

Ofsted (Office for Standards in Education) (2003) *Excellence in Cities and Education Action Zones: Management and Impact*, HMI 1399, London: OFSTED.

Ofsted (2015) *Report on Rainsbrook Secure Training Centre*, London: OFSTED.

Oliver, M. (1996) *Understanding Disability: From Theory to Practice*, Basingstoke: MacMillan.

Omeni, E., Barnes, M., MacDonald, D., Crawford, M. and Rose, D. (2014) 'Service user involvement: impact and participation: a survey of service user and staff perspectives', *BMC Health Services Research*, vol 14, p 491.

O'Neill, C., McGregor, P. and Merkur, S. (2012) 'United Kingdom (Northern Ireland) health system review', *Health System in Transition*, vol 14, no 10, pp 1–91.

Ormston, R. and Reid, S. (2012) *Scottish Social Attitudes Survey 2011: Core Module – Attitudes to Government, the Economy and Public Services in Scotland*, Research Findings No 18, Edinburgh: The Scottish Government.

Osborne, S. (ed) (2010) *The New Public Governance?*, Oxon: Routledge.

Osborne, S. and Strokosch, K. (2013) 'It takes two to tango? Understanding the co-production of public services by integrating the services management and public administration perspectives', *British Journal of Management*, vol 1, pp 31–47.

Osmond, J. (2004) *Cull of the Quangos, Monitoring the National Assembly for Wales*, Cardiff: Institute of Welsh Affairs.

Owen, J. (2015) 'Crippling Loan Deals Leave Britain £222bn in Debt'. Available at: http://www.independent.co.uk/money/loans-credit/crippling-pfi-deals-leave-britain-222bn-in-debt-10170214.html

Padley, M. (2013) 'Delivering localism. The critical role of trust and collaboration', *Social Policy and Society*, vol 12, no 3, pp 343–54.

Page, E. (2009) 'Joined-up government and the civil service', in V. Bogdanor (ed) *Joined-Up Government*, Oxford: Oxford University Press.

Page, J., Pearson, J., Jurgeit, B. and Kidson, M. (2012) *Transforming Whitehall Departments*, London: Institute for Government.

Parker, S. and Mansfield, C. (2014) *As Ties Go By: Collaboration for Counties and Districts*, London: New Local Government Network.

Parry, R. (2012) 'What can UK public administration learn from the devolved nations?', *Public Policy and Administration*, vol 27, no 3, pp 248–64.

Paun, A. and Munro, R. (2015) *Governance in an Ever Looser Union*, London: Institute for Government.

Pawson, H., Bright, J., Engberg, L. and Van Bortel, G. (2012) *Resident Involvement in Social Housing in the UK and Europe*, Edinburgh: Hyde Housing and Heriot Watt University.

Payler, J. and Georgeson, J. (2013) 'Multiagency working in the early years: confidence, competence and context', *Early Years, an International Research Journal*, vol 33, no 4, pp 380–97.

Pearson, J., Gash, T. and Rutter, J. (2015) *Out of the Ashes. Priorities for Reforming Arms-Length Government*, London: Institute for Government.

Pemberton, H., Thane, P. and Whiteside, N. (2006) *Britain's Pensions Crisis: History and Policy*, Buckingham: Open University Press and British Academy.

Penning, M. (2014) 'Hansard', House of Commons, 27 March, Column 57WS.

Perkins, N. and Hunter, D. (2014) 'Health and wellbeing boards: a new dawn for public health partnerships', *Journal of Integrated Care*, vol 22, no 5, pp 189–96.

Perkins, N., Smith, K., Hunter, D.J., Bambra, C. and Joyce, K. (2010) 'What counts is what works? New Labour and partnerships in public health', *Policy & Politics*, vol 38, no 1, pp 101–17.

Perri, 6 and Peck, E. (2004) 'New Labour's modernization agenda in the public sector: a neo Durkheimian approach and the case of mental health services', *Public Administration*, vol 82, no 1, pp 83-108.

Pestoff, V., Bransden, T. and Verschuerre, B. (2012) *New Public Governance, the Third Sector and Co-production,* London: Routledge.

Petch, A. (2011) *An Evidence Base for the Delivery of Adult Social Services*, Glasgow: Institute for Research and Innovation in Social Services.

Petch, A., Cook, A. and Miller, E. (2013) 'Partnership working and outcomes: do health and social care partnerships deliver for users and carers?', *Health and Social Care in the Community*, vol 21, no 6, pp 623–33.

Peters, B. and Pierre, J. (2006) *Handbook of Public Policy*, London: Sage.

Peters, M. (2001) *Poststructuralism, Marxism and Neoliberalism: Between Theory and Politics*, New York, NY: Rowman and Littlefield.

Phillips, D. (2013) *Government Spending on Benefits and State Pensions in Scotland: Current Patterns and Future Issues*, London: Institute for Fiscal Studies.

PHSO (Parliamentary and Health Service Ombudsman) (2015) *A Review into the Quality of NHS Complaints Investigations*, London: Parliamentary and Health Service Ombudsman.

Pidd, M. (2005) 'Perversity in public service performance measurement', *International Journal of Productivity and Performance Management*, vol 54, no 5/6, pp 483–93.

Player, S. and Pollock, A. (2001) 'Long term care: from public responsibility to private good', *Critical Social Policy*, vol 21, no 2, pp 231–55.

Pliatzky, L. (1980) *Report on Non-Departmental Public Bodies*, Cmnd 7797, London: HMSO.

Political and Constitutional Reform Committee (2015) *The Future of Devolution after the Scottish Referendum*, HC 700, London: Political and Constitutional Reform Committee.

Pollitt, C. and Bouckaert, G. (2011) *Public Management Reform* (3rd edn), New York, NY: Oxford University Press.

Pollitt, C., Van Thiel, S. and Homburg, V. (eds) (2007) *New Public Management in Europe: Adaptations and Alternatives*, Basingstoke: Palgrave/Macmillan.

Pollock, A.M. (2005) *NHS Plc: The Privatisation of Our Health Care*, London: Verso.

Pollock, A.M. (2015) 'Morality and values in support of universal healthcare must be enshrined in law; comment on "Morality and markets in the NHS"', *International Journal of Health Policy Management*, vol 4, no 6, pp 399–402.

Pollock, A.M. and Sharp, R. (2012) 'Real participation or the tyranny of participatory practice? Public art and community involvement in the regeneration of the Raploch, Scotland', *Urban Studies*, vol 49, no 14, pp 3063–79.

Pollock, A.M., Hellowell, M., Price, D. and Liebe, M. (2009) *Submission to the House of Lords Economic Affairs Committee Inquiry in to Private Finance Projects and Off- Balance Sheet Debt*, Edinburgh: CIPHP.

Pollock, R. (2014) 'The Public Service Transformation Network', *Public Services Executive*, February/March.

Postle, K. and Beresford, P. (2007) 'Capacity building and the reconception of political participation: a role for social care workers?', *British Journal of Social Work*, vol 37, pp 143–58.

Powell, M. (2012) 'Horizontal subsidiarity in Lombardy and the UK: decentralization, partnership and governance of welfare', in A. Brugnoli and A. Colombo (eds) *Government, Governance and Welfare Reform*, Cheltenham: Edward Elgar.

Powell, M. (2015) 'Who killed the English National Health Service?', *International Journal of Health Policy and Management*, vol 4, no 9, pp 621–3.

Powell, M. and Hewitt, M. (2002) *Welfare State and Welfare Change*, Maidenhead: Open University Press.

Powell, M. and Miller, R. (2014) 'Framing privatisation in the English National Health Service', *Journal of Social Policy*, vol 43, no 3, pp 575–94.

Powell, M. and Miller, R. (2016) 'Making markets in the English National Health Service', *Social Policy and Administration*, vol 49, no 1, pp 109–27.

Powell, T. and Heath, S. (2013) *The Reformed Health Service and Commissioning Arrangements in England*, Commons Library Standard Note SN06749, London: The Stationery Office.

Power, A. (2014) 'Personalisation and austerity in the crosshairs: government perspectives on the remaking of adult social care', *Journal of Social Policy*, vol 43, no 4, pp 829-846.

Prosser, S., Connolly, M., Hough, R. and Potter, K. (2006) *Making it Happen in Public Services: Devolution in Wales as a Case Study*, Exeter: Imprint Academic.

Public Accounts Committee (2013a) *Restructuring the National Offender Management Service*, London: House of Commons.

Public Accounts Committee (2013b) *Civil Service Reform*, London: House of Commons.

Public Accounts Committee (2014) *Monitor: Regulation NHS Foundation Trusts*, HC 407, London: House of Commons Library.

Public Accounts Committee (2015) *Schools Insight and Intervention Report*, London: House of Commons.

Public Accounts Committee (2016) *Public Accounts Committee History*, London: House of Commons.

Public Administration Select Committee (2001) *Mapping the Quango State*, HC 367, London: House of Commons Library

Public Administration Select Committee (2011) *Smaller Government: Shrinking the Quango State*, HC 537, London: House of Commons Library.

Public Administration Select Committee (2014) *Who's Accountable? Relationships Between Government and Arm's-Length Bodies*, HC 110, London: House of Commons Library.

Public Administration Select Committee (2015) '*More Complaints Please!' and 'Time for a People's Ombudsman Service'*, Third Special Report of Session 2014–15, London: House of Commons Library.

Purcell, L. and Chow, D. (2011) 'The reorganisation of children's social services in England', *Public Money and Management*, vol 31, no 6, pp 403–10.

Purcell, M. (2014) 'Public participation in new local governance spaces: the case for community development in local strategic partnerships', European Conference on Politics, Economics and Law 2014: Official Conference Proceedings, pp 143–59.

Pyper, R. (2013) 'The UK Coalition and the civil service: a half-term report', *Public Policy and Administration*, vol 28, no 4, pp 364-82.

QualityWatch (2015) 'Independent scrutiny into the quality of health and social care'. Available at: www.qualitywatch.org.uk

Racioppi, L. and O'Sullivan, K. (2007) 'Grassroots peace-building and third-party intervention: the European Union's special support programme for peace and reconciliation in Northern Ireland', *Peace and Change*, vol 32, no 3, pp 361–90.

Randall, J. and Casebourne, J. (2016) *Making Devolution Deals Work*, London: Institute for Government.

Rawlings, R. (2005) 'Law making in a virtual parliament: the Welsh experience' in R. Hazell and R. Rawlings (eds) *Devolution, Law Making and the Constitution*, Exeter: Imprint Academic.

Rees, J., Mullins, D. and Bovaird, T. (2012) *Third Sector Partnerships for Public Services Delivery: An Evidence Review*, Working Paper 60, Birmingham: Third Sector Research Centre.

Reeves, P. (2014) *Affordable and Social Housing Policy and Practice*, Abingdon: Routledge.

Rhodes, R.A.W. (1996) 'The new governance: governing without government', *Political Studies*, vol 44, no 4, pp 652–67.

Rhodes, R.A.W. (1997) *Understanding Governance: Policy Networks, Governance, Reflexivity and Accountability*, Buckingham: Open University Press.

Rhodes, R.A.W. (2007) 'Understanding governance: ten years on', *Organization Studies*, vol 28, no 8, pp 1243–64.

Ridley, J., McKeown, M., Mackin, K., Rosengard, A., Little, S., Briggs, S. and Jones, F. (2014) *Exploring Family Carer's Involvement in Forensic Mental Health Services*, Edinburgh: Support in Mind, Scotland.

Roberts, A. and Charlesworth, A. (2014) *A Decade of Austerity in Wales?*, London: Nuffield Trust.

Roberts, N. and Jarrett, T. (2015) *Analysis of the Education and Adoption Bill 2015–16*, Briefing Paper 07232, London: House of Commons Library.

Robinson, G., Burke, L. and Millings, W. (2015) 'Criminal justice identities in transition: the case of devolved probation services in England and Wales', *British Journal of Criminology*, first published online 19 May, DOI:10.1093/bjc/azv036.

Robson, K. (2011) *The National Health Service in Scotland: Subject Profile*, SPICe Briefing 11/49, Edinburgh: The Scottish Parliament.

Robson, K. (2013) *Public Bodies (Joint Working) (Scotland) Bill*, SPICe Briefing 13/50, Edinburgh: The Scottish Parliament.

Roehich, R.J., Lewis, M. and George, G. (2014) 'Are public private partnerships a healthy option? A systematic literature review', *Social Science and Medicine*, vol 113, pp 110–19.

Rogowski, S. (2015) 'From child welfare to child protection/safeguarding: a critical practitioner's view of changing conceptions', *Policies and Practice*, vol 27, no 2, pp 97–112.

Rosenthal, L. (2004) 'Do school inspections improve school quality? Ofsted inspections and school examination results in the UK', *Economics of Education Review*, vol 23, pp 143–51.

Rowe, G. and Frewer, L.J. (2005) 'A typology of public engagement mechanisms', *Science, Technology & Human Values*, vol 30, no 2, pp 251–90.

Royal College of Psychiatrists and the Association of Directors of Adult Social Services (2013) 'The integration of personal budgets in social care and personal budgets in the NHS', Position Statement ps01/2013.

Rubery, J. and Urwin, P. (2011) 'Bringing the employer back in: why social care needs a standard employment relationship', *Human Resource Management Journal*, vol 21, no 2, pp 122–37.

Rummery, K. (2002) 'Towards a theory of welfare partnerships', in C. Glendinning, M. Powell and K. Rummery (eds) *Partnerships, New Labour and the Governance of Welfare*, Bristol: The Policy Press.

Rummery, K. and McAngus, C. (2015) 'The future of social policy in Scotland: will further devolved powers lead to better social policies for disabled people?', *Political Quarterly*, vol 86, no 2, pp 234–9.

Runciman, D. (2013) 'The crisis of British democracy: back to the '70s or stuck in the present?', *Juncture*, vol 20, no 3, pp 167–77.

Rutter, J. (2014) 'The quango conundrum revisited – why the government still needs a more coherent approach to arms-length bodies', *Political Quarterly*, vol 85, no 2, pp 148–52.

Rutter, J., Malley, R., Noonan, A. and Knighton, W. (2012) *It Takes Two: How to Create Effective Relationships between Government and Arm's-Length Bodies*, London: Institute for Government.

Sabry, M. (2015) 'Good governance institutions and performance of public private partnerships', *International Journal of Public Sector Management*, vol 28, no 7, pp 566–82.

Sandford, M. (2015a) *Devolution to Local Government in England*, Briefing Paper No 07029, London: House of Commons Library.

Sandford, M. (2015b) *Local Government: New Models of Service Delivery*, Briefing Paper No CBP05950, London: House of Commons Library.

Sandford, M. (2015c) *Local Government in England*, Briefing Paper No SN 07104, London: House of Commons Library.

Sandford, M. (2015d) *Whole Place Budgets*, House of Commons Library Briefing Paper Number 05955, London: House of Commons Library.

Sandford, M. (2016) *Local Government: Alternative Models of Service Delivery*, Briefing Paper, London: House of Commons.

Saunders, G. (2007) 'Reflections on the development and work of the Social Security Advisory Committee', *Benefits*, vol 15, no 3, pp 313–20.

Schuppert, G. (2013) 'Partnerships' in M.M. Bevir (ed.) *The Handbook of Governance*, London: Sage.

SCIE (Social Care Institute for Excellence) (2013) *Co-production in Social Care: What it is and how to do it*, London: SCIE.

Scotland Office (2010) *Scotland's Future in the United Kingdom*, Cm 7738, Norwich: The Stationery Office.

Scottish Affairs Committee (2015) *The Implementation of the Smith Agreement*, HC 835, London: House of Commons.

Scottish Executive (2007) *Choosing Scotland's Future: A National Conversation – Independence and Responsibility in the Modern World*, Edinburgh: Scottish Executive.

Scottish Government (2003) *The Local Government in Scotland Act*, Edinburgh: Scottish Government.

Scottish Government (2008) *Simplifying Public Services*, Edinburgh: Scottish Government.

Scottish Government (2009a) *The Scottish Government Response to the Recommendations of the Commission on Scottish Devolution*, Edinburgh: Scottish Government.

Scottish Government (2009b) *Scottish Community Empowerment Action Plan*, Edinburgh: Scottish Government.

Scottish Government (2011) *Reshaping Care for Older People: A Programme for Change 2011–2021*, Edinburgh: Scottish Government.

Scottish Government (2013) *Single Outcome Agreements*, Edinburgh: Scottish Government.

Scottish Government (2015a) *Social Security for Scotland: Benefits Being Devolved to the Scottish Parliament*, Edinburgh: Scottish Government.

Scottish Government (2015b) *Social Services in Scotland: A Shared Vision and Strategy 2015–2020*, Edinburgh: Scottish Government.

Scottish Government (2015c) *Community Empowerment (Scotland) Act*, Edinburgh: Scottish Government.

Scottish Government (2015d) *An Introduction to Scotland's National Performance Framework*, Edinburgh: Scottish Government.

Scottish Government (2016) *The Agreement between the Scottish Government and the United Kingdom Government on the Scottish Government's Fiscal Framework*, Edinburgh: The Scottish Government.

Scottish National Party (2015) SNP comment on the Smith Commission Report, www.snp.org/media-centre/news/2015

Scottish Parliament (2014) *Public Bodies (Joint Working) (Scotland) Bill*, Edinburgh: Scottish Parliament.

Scottish Social Services Council (2015) 'Scottish social service sector report on 2014 workforce data'. Available at: http://data.sssc.uk.com/data-publications/22-workforce-data-report/99-scottish-social-service-sector-report-on-2014-workforce-data

Scourfield, J., Holland, S. and Young, G. (2008) 'Social work in Wales since democratic devolution', *Australian Social Work*, vol 61, no 1, pp 42–56.

Scourfield, P. (2015) 'Implementing co-production in adult social care: an example of meta-governance failure', *Social Policy and Society*, vol 14, no 4, pp 541–54.

Seely, A. (2014) *The Scotland Act 2012: Devolution of Tax Powers to the Scottish Parliament*, Standard Note SN/BT 5984, London: House of Commons Library.

Seely, A. and Keep, M. (2015) *Devolution of Financial Powers to the Scottish Parliament: Recent Developments*, SN7077, London: House of Commons Library.

Shaw, N. (2012) 'The rise of the resilient local authority', *Local Government Studies*, vol 38, no 3, pp 281–300.

Shortridge, J. (2010) 'The evolution of Welsh devolution', *Public Money and Management*, vol 32, no 2, pp 87-90.

Shutes, I. and Taylor, R. (2014) 'Conditionality and the financing of employment services – implications for the social divisions of work and welfare', *Social Policy and Administration*, vol 48, no 2, pp 204–20.

Simmonds, D. (2011) *Work Programme Results: Perform or Bust*, Working Brief, May 2010. London: Centre for Social and Economic Inclusion.

Simmons, R. and Birchall, J. (2005) 'A joined up approach to user participation in public services: strengthening the participation chain', *Social Policy and Administration*, vol 39, no 3, pp 260–83.

Skelcher, C. (1998) *The Appointed State*, Buckingham: Open University Press.

Skelcher, C., Flinders, M., Tonkiss, K. and Dommett, K. (2013) *Public Bodies Reform by the UK Government 2010–2013: Initial Findings*, Shrinking the State Research Paper 1, Birmingham: Institute of Local Government Studies/ Economic and Social Research Council.

Slasberg, C. and Beresford, P. (2015) 'Building on the original strengths of direct payments to create a better future for social care', *Disability and Society*, vol 30, no 3, pp 479–83.

Slasberg, C., Watson, N., Beresford, P. and Schofield, P. (2014) 'Personalization of health care in England: have the wrong lessons been drawn from the personal health budget pilots?', *Journal of Health Services Research and Policy*, vol 19, no 3, pp 183–8.

Smith Commission (2014) 'Report of the Smith Commission for further devolution of powers to the Scottish Parliament'. Available at: www.smith-commission.scot

References

Smith, D. and Wistrich, E. (2014) *Devolution and Localism in England*, Farham: Ashgate.

Smith Institute (2013) *Does Council Housing Have a Future?*, London: The Smith Institute.

Smith Institute (2014) *Outsourcing the Cuts: Pay and Employment Effects of Contracting Out*, London: The Smith Institute.

Smith, K. and Hellowell, M. (2012) 'Beyond rhetorical differences: a cohesive account of post-devolution developments in health policy', *Social Policy and Administration*, vol 46, no 2, pp 178–98.

Somerville, P. (2016) 'Coalition housing policy in England', in H. Bochel and M. Powell (eds) *The Coalition Government and Social Policy*, Bristol: The Policy Press.

SSAC (Social Security Advisory Committee) (2013a) *Communications in the Benefits System*, Occasional Paper No 11, London: House of Commons.

SSAC (2013b) *The Implementation of Universal Credit and the Support Needs of Claimants*, London: House of Commons.

SSAC (2014a) *DWP/SSAC Framework*, London: House of Commons.

SSAC (2014b) *The Cumulative Impact of Welfare Reform: A Commentary*, Occasional Paper No 12, London: House of Commons.

SSAC (2015) *Localisation and Social Security: A Review*, London: House of Commons.

Starr, P. (1988) 'The meaning of privatisation', *Yale Law and Policy Review*, vol, 6, pp 6–41.

Steel, D. and Cylus, J. (2012) 'United Kingdom (Scotland): health system review', *Health Systems in Transition*, vol 14, no 9, pp 1–150.

Stephen, J., Bouchal, P. and Bull, D. (2013) *Annual Commentary and Analysis on the Size, Shape and Performance of Whitehall*, Whitehall Monitor 2013, London: Institute for Government.

Stevenson, L. (2015) '"Landmark" reforms to tackle "inadequate" children's services', *Community Care*, December. Available at: www.communitycare.co.uk/2015/12/14/david-cameron-announce-landmark-reforms-tackle-inadequate-childrens-services/

Stevenson, L. and Schraer, R. (2015) 'Councils not outsourcing child protection despite legal change', *Community Care*, 13 October.

Stoker, G. (2006) 'Public value management: a new narrative for networked governance?', *American Review of Public Administration*, vol 36, pp 41–57.

Struyven, L. and Steurs, G. (2005) 'Design and redesign of a quasi-market for the reintegration of jobseekers: empirical evidence from Australia and the Netherlands', *Journal of European Social Policy*, vol 15, no 3, pp 211–29.

Sullivan, H. (2005) 'Is enabling enough? Tensions and dilemmas in New Labour's strategies for joining-up local governance', *Public Policy and Administration*, vol 20, no 4, pp 10–24.

Sullivan, H. and Sketcher, C. (2002) *Working across Boundaries: Collaboration in Public Services*, Basingstoke: Palgrave.

Taylor Gooby, P., Larsen, T. and Kananen, J. (2004) 'Market means and welfare ends: the UK welfare state experiment', *Journal of Social Policy*, vol 33, no 4, pp 573–92.

Taylor Gooby, P. (2013) *The Double Crisis of the Welfare State and What to do About It*, Basingstoke: Palgrave Macmillan.

Teague, M. (2013) 'Rehabilitation, punishment and profit: the dismantling of public-sector probation', *British Society of Criminology Newsletter*, No 72, Summer.

The 2020 Public Services Trust (2010) *From Social Security to Social Productivity: A Vision for 2020 Public Services*, London: The 2020 Public Services Trust.

The King's Fund (2013) *Patient-Centred Leadership: Rediscovering Our Purpose*, London: The King's Fund.

The King's Fund (2015) *Is the NHS Being Privatised?*, London: The King's Fund.

The Stationery Office (2013) *Report of the Mid-Staffordshire NHS Foundation Trust Public Inquiry*, HC 947, London: The Stationery Office.

Thorlby, R., Smith, J. Williams, S. and Dayan, M. (2014) *The Francis Report: One Year On*, London: The Nuffield Trust.

Thraves, L. (2012) *A Dose of Localism: The Role of Councils in Public Health*, London: Local Government Information Unit.

Thraves, L., Sillett, J., Carr-West, J. and Sawford, A. (2012) *Care Now and for the Future: An Inquiry into Adult Social Care*, London: Local Government Information Unit.

Timmins, N. (2013) *The Four UK Health Systems: Learning from Each Other*, London: The King's Fund.

Tonkiss, K. and Noonan, A. (2013) 'Debate: arm's length bodies and alternative models of service delivery', *Public Money and Management*, vol 33, no 6, pp 345–97.

Torchia, M., Caabro, A. and Morner, M. (2015) 'Public–private partnerships in the health care sector: a systematic review of the literature', *Public Management Review*, vol 17, no 2, pp 236–61.

Tovey, A. (2016) 'Care UK debt downgrade reveals pressure on care home sector', *The Telegraph*, 20 April.

TUC (Trades Union Congress) (2013) *Making Co-Production Work – Lessons from Local Government*, London: TUC.

UK Statistics Authority (2014) *About the Authority*, London: Statistics Authority.

Wait, S. and Nolte, E. (2006) 'Public involvement politics in health: exploring their conceptual basis', *Health Economics Policy and Law*, vol 1, pp 149-62.

Wales Audit Office (2015) *Achieving Improvement in Support to Schools through Regional Education Consortia – An Early View*, Cardiff: Audit Wales.

Wales Office (2015) *Powers for a Purpose: Towards a Lasting Devolution Settlement for Wales*, CM9020, London: The Wales Office.

Walker, D. (2014) 'Quangos – why bother counting them when Whitehall can't?', *Political Quarterly*, vol 85, no 2, pp 153–8.

Waters, J. and Hatton, C. (2014) *Third National Personal Budget Survey: Think Local Act Personal*, London: In Control.

Weatherly, H., Mason, A., Goddard, M. and Wright, K. (2010) *Financial Integration across Health and Social Care: Evidence Review*, Edinburgh: Scottish Government Social Research.

Webb, S. (2008) 'Modelling service user participation in social care', *Journal of Social Work*, vol 8, pp 269–87.

Welsh Government (2011) *Sustainable Social Services for Wales*, Cardiff: Welsh Assembly Government.

Welsh Government (2012a) *Achieving Excellence: The Quality Delivery Plan for the NHS in Wales*, Cardiff: Welsh Assembly Government.

Welsh Government (2012b) *Shared Purpose, Shared Delivery*, Cardiff: Welsh Assembly Government.

Welsh Government (2013a) *Delivering Local Health Care: Accelerating the Pace of Change*, Cardiff: Welsh Assembly Government.

Welsh Government (2013b) *Social Services and Well-Being (Wales) Bill Explanatory Memorandum*, Cardiff: Welsh Assembly Government.

Welsh Government (2014a) *Improving Public Services for People in Wales*, Cardiff: Welsh Assembly Government.

Welsh Government (2014b) *Commission on Public Services Governance and Delivery*, Cardiff: Welsh Assembly Government.

Welsh Government (2015a) *Devolution, Democracy and Delivery White Paper: Reforming Local Government, Power to Local People*, Cardiff: Welsh Assembly Government.

Welsh Government (2015b) *Programme for Government Data*, Cardiff: Welsh Assembly Government.

Welsh Government (2015c) Programme Government Summary Report 2015, Cardiff: Welsh Assembly Government.

Welsh Government (2016a) *The Regulation and Inspection of Social Care Wales Act, 2016*, Cardiff: Welsh Government.

Welsh Government (2016b) *How to Measure a Nation's Progress? National Indicators for Wales*, Cardiff: Welsh Government.

Welsh Local Government Association and NHS Confederation (2013) *Transitional and Longer-Term Implications of the Social Services and Well-Being (Wales) Bill 2013*, Cardiff: Welsh Local Government Association.

Westminster Health Forum (2016) *Next Steps for Health and Social Care in Greater Manchester*, Bracknell: Westminster Health Forum.

White, H. (2015) *Parliamentary Scrutiny of Government*, London: Institute for Government.

Whitfield, D. (2006) *New Labour's Attack on Public Services*, Nottingham: Spokesman Books.

Whitty, G. and Power, S. (2000) 'Marketisation and privatisation in mass education systems', *International Journal of Education Development*, vol 20, pp 93–107.

Wiggan, J. (2007) 'Reforming the United Kingdom's public employment and social security agencies', *International Review of Administrative Sciences*, vol 73, no 3, pp 409–24.

Wiggan, J. (2015) 'Varieties of marketisation in the UK: examining divergence in activation markets between Great Britain and Northern Ireland 2008–2014', *Policy Studies*, vol 36, no 2, pp 115–32.

Wilcox, S., Fitzpatrick, S., Stephens, M., Pleace, N., Wallace, A. and Rhodes, D. (2010) *The Impact of Devolution: Housing and Homelessness*, York: Joseph Rowntree Foundation.

Wilkes, C. (2014) *A Design for Life: How Councils and Housing Associations can Collaborate for Impact*, London: New Local Government Network.

Williams, I., Dickinson, H. and Robinson, S. (2010) 'Joined up Rationing? An analysis of priority setting in health and social care commissioning', *Journal of Integrated Care*, vol 18, no 1, pp 3–11.

Williams, I. and Dickinson, H. (2015) 'Going it alone or playing to the crowd? A critique of individual budgets and the personalisation of health care in the English National Health Service', *Australian Journal of Public Administration*, DOI: 10.1111/1467-8500.12155.

Williams, P. (2014) *The Report of the Commission of Public Services Governance and Delivery*, Cardiff: Welsh Government.

Williamson, A., Miller, L. and Fallon, F. (2010) *Behind the Digital Campaign: An Exploration of the Use, Impact and Regulation of Digital Campaigning*, London: Hansard Society.

Wilshaw, M. (2014) Speech to the Association of Directors of Children's Services Annual Conference, 11 July 2014. Available at: www.gov.uk/government/speeches

Wilson, D. and Game, C. (2006) *Local Government in the United Kingdom*, Basingstoke: Palgrave Macmillan.

Wilson, S., Davidson, N., Clarke, M. and Casebourne, J. (2015) *Joining Up Public Services around Local Citizen Needs*, London: Institute for Government.

Wilson, W. and Bates, A. (2016) *Extending the 'Voluntary' Right to Buy (England)*, House of Commons Briefing Paper, no 07224, London: House of Commons.

Wincott, D. (2005) 'Reshaping public space? Devolution and policy change in British early childhood education and care', *Regional and Federal Studies*, vol 15, no 5, pp 453–70.

Woodman, J. and Gilbert, R. (2013) 'Child maltreatment: moving towards a public health approach', in *Growing Up in the UK: Ensuring a Healthy Future for our Children*, London: BMA Board of Science.

Woods, P.A. and Simkins, T. (2014) 'Understanding the local: themes and issues in the experience of structural reform in England', *Educational Management and Leadership*, vol 42, no 3, pp 324–40.

Worth, S. (2012) Do the Public Back More Reform of Public Services? An Overview of the Latest Opinion Research, London: Policy Exchange.

Zayed, Y. and Harker, R. (2015) *Children in Care in England: Statistics Briefing Paper*, 04470, London: House of Commons Library.

Index

References to tables and boxes are in *italics*